# Media Effects Research

FIFTH EDITION

# Media Effects Research

## A Basic Overview

### FIFTH EDITION

**GLENN G. SPARKS**
Purdue University

CENGAGE
Learning®

Australia • Brazil • Mexico • Singapore • United Kingdom • United States

# CENGAGE
## Learning®

**Media Effects Research:**
**A Basic Overview,**
**Fifth Edition**
**Glenn G. Sparks**

Product Director: Monica Eckman

Product Manager: Kelli Strieby

Associate Content Developer: Rachel Schowalter

Product Assistant: Alexis Mackintosh-Zebrowski

Marketing Manager: Jillian Borden

Content Project Manager: Cenveo Publisher Services

Art Director: Cenveo Publisher Services

Manufacturing Planner: Doug Bertke

IP Analyst: Ann Hoffman

IP Project Manager: Farah Fard

Production Service and Compositor: Cenveo Publisher Services

Text and Cover Designer: Cenveo Publisher Services

Cover Image: Getty Images

Library of Congress Control Number: 2014953686
ISBN: 9781305077478

**Cengage Learning**
20 Channel Center Street
Boston, MA 02210
USA

Cengage Learning is a leading provider of customized learning solutions with office locations around the globe, including Singapore, the United Kingdom, Australia, Mexico, Brazil, and Japan. Locate your local office at **www.cengage.com/global**.

Cengage Learning products are represented in Canada by Nelson Education, Ltd.

To learn more about Cengage Learning Solutions, visit **www.cengage.com**.

Purchase any of our products at your local college store or at our preferred online store **www.cengagebrain.com**.

Printed in the United States of America
Print Number: 01   Print Year: 2014

*Dedicated to Cheri Wilcox Sparks*
*The love of my life*

# Contents

# Preface

M any would say that since the first edition of this text, the media landscape has completely transformed. Nevertheless, I still find that much of what I wrote in the preface to the first edition is true today. I never intended to write a textbook. I have always identified myself as a researcher and teacher of mass-communication effects—not a textbook writer. My intentions changed after teaching university undergraduates for more than two decades. In my course at Purdue University on mass-communication theory, I watched semester after semester as my students gradually sank into the dry-sand prose of most texts that attempt to present theories of mass media. Once the sinking started, I was almost never able to rescue them. I finally grew tired of this routine.

Since my approach to teaching media theory involves teaching the theoretical concepts in the context of research findings, I decided to try my hand at writing a text that reflected this perspective. Theory is fully realized when it meets the soil of observation. I have found that students can digest incredible doses of theory in the context of discovering what research says about media impact. So, this book attempts to introduce an array of theoretical ideas—but in the context of asking about the effects of media. If you teach a more conventional media theories course, I am betting that you will find plenty of theory to keep your students occupied. You'll find an updated list of theories and theoretical concepts that are covered in this edition on page 326. If you check out the list, you'll see that the book provides a good deal of contact with the major theoretical ideas in media effects research.

I became convinced that I should write a book for undergraduate students when I realized that it *was* possible to write a text that was not dry and boring. My two primary exemplars are Robert Cialdini's classic text on persuasion, *Influence*, and Em Griffin's best-selling introduction to communication theory, *A First Look at Communication Theory*—a book that I've now signed on to as a coauthor. Years ago, when Em asked me to advise him about the mass-communication section of his book, I began thinking more seriously of trying to write a text of my own. Reactions to the prior editions indicate that I've succeeded beyond my hopes. Those who have used the book seem to be genuinely excited about how it connects with undergraduate students. Before you dive in, let me outline just a bit the guiding philosophy of the book and how I think the text can be used.

Above all else, I have tried to write plainly and in a style that will engage the typical undergraduate student. This means that I often share personal anecdotes and refer to myself in the first person. I am committed to this style. I think students respond better if they can sense that there is a living, breathing human being behind the words. The reactions of my own students have helped to convince me that this is truly the case. Recently, I've also published a personal memoir that was designed, in part, to give students a chance to *really* know that their textbook's author is a real person. The memoir (*Rolling in Dough: Lessons I Learned in a Doughnut Shop*, White River Press) is a collection of stories from my adolescence, when my parents owned a franchise doughnut shop. I believe that learning to write in the style of the personal memoir makes it much easier to connect to today's students when writing a more conventional textbook.

As you evaluate the text, keep in mind that I have attempted to only *introduce* the topic of media effects—not to write everything known by the research community. I believe that textbook writers make a tragic mistake when they try to cover the whole terrain of their topic. This might satisfy textbook reviewers and serve as a valuable reference for scholars, but I don't think it does much good at generating genuine interest among the students who ultimately have to pay for and read the text. Because of my commitment to limiting this textbook to an introduction to media effects, I know that some professors will examine this text and spot crucial omissions that simply *must* be included. I am well aware that the book fails to cover everything. I planned it that way. One of my goals is to keep the material manageable so that students will actually read the chapters. I also want students to finish the book and still be interested in finding out more about media effects. I have decided to sacrifice a little breadth on the altar of student interest. I think it is a sacrifice well worth making. Of course, I realize that this places an additional burden upon me to make difficult choices about what to include and exclude. I'm grateful to those who have reviewed the material and given me expert advice. I know I won't please everyone with the choices I've made, but I've tried to respond as best I can to various suggestions.

How can this book be used? I think the text can fit into two different kinds of courses. First, it can obviously be used in a mass-communication theory course or a mass media research course. Second, the book can be used as a secondary text in a basic introduction to mass communication course. Most of the texts for the basic course have little or no coverage of media effects research. For professors who want their students to develop a deeper understanding of the effects literature, this book should not be too overwhelming as an accompanying volume in the basic introductory course. I have deliberately held the presentation of material to 12 chapters in order for the book to fit comfortably into different course formats. In the fifteen-week semester, I have found that students would rather ease in and ease out. For years, I attempted to fight that attitude; now I find myself subscribing to it. Once again, my philosophy here is to meet the needs of the audience. If I don't assign a chapter of reading in either the first or last week, I can still assign a chapter per week for the rest of the semester and have one week for some additional reading that I might select. If there is a topic that a professor believes must be in the course that I don't cover, the flexible week fills the need. The chapters are also short enough and easy enough to read that more than one chapter *could* be assigned in a single week for schools that are on a shorter semester. In the end, my primary goal is to have students understand more about media research and still be interested in the topic when they finish reading. I am eager to discover if you think the goal has been achieved.

If you used any of the other editions, I hope you'll discover that this edition looks familiar. I haven't made changes just for the sake of making changes. Instead, I've tried to take the main comments from the reviewers on each chapter and attempt to respond in a reasonable way to their suggestions. Essentially, I've tried to update examples and, wherever appropriate, include some of the latest research in a given area. While every chapter has updated examples and other material, below is a summary of the most major changes you'll find. In total, there are nearly 90 new research citations, 19 new Study Boxes, and 36 new questions to focus attention.

## Chapter 1

- Integration of new examples into the same discussions of the fourth edition (e.g., the shootings in Newtown, CT)
- More nuanced discussion of the goals of science—particularly "prediction" and "control"
- New Study Box on evaluating the claims of a consumer product about improving your brain
- New "Questions to Focus Your Attention"
- Five new research citations

## Chapter 2

- New example to illustrate content analysis—a study of popular novel content
- New example to illustrate the experimental method—a study on whether playing a video game can repair a bad mood
- New "Questions to Focus Your Attention"
- New Study Box on evaluating the validity of any experiment
- Three new research citations

## Chapter 3

- New Study Box on media use and sleep
- New Study Box on the colorful personalities involved in the Decatur Study
- New "Questions to Focus Your Attention"
- Five new research citations

## Chapter 4

- New discussion of uses and gratifications and new media
- New section on electronic media and sleep displacement
- Updated research on TV viewing and obesity
- New Study Box on binge viewing
- New Study Box on the nature of the parasocial relationship
- New "Questions to Focus Your Attention"
- Seven new research citations

## Chapter 5

- New material on media cultivation theory that pertains to media violence
- New discussion of violence in YouTube videos
- New discussion on research about an anti-drug campaign in the context of making assumptions about media effects
- New discussion of the "law of emotional desensitization"
- New discussion on research on effects of violent video games
- New section on why people doubt the effects of media violence on aggression
- New Study Box on prolonged exposure to media violence
- New Study Box on why violent crime is decreasing
- New Study Box on reasons why people doubt the effects of media violence on aggression
- New "Questions to Focus Your Attention"
- Eleven new research citations

## Chapter 6

- New research on effects of rape pornography
- New discussion of the Annenberg Sex and Media Study
- New Study Box on the effects of MTV's program, "16 and Pregnant"
- New "Questions to Focus Your Attention"
- Nine new research citations

## Chapter 7

- New discussion of research on emotions in cooperative video game play
- New Study Box on symptoms of lingering fright reactions to media
- New "Questions to Focus Your Attention"
- Three new research citations

## Chapter 8

- New material on first- vs. second-order cultivation
- Discussion of research on an anti-smoking campaign
- New Study Box featuring an experiment about children's advertising
- New Study Box on impact of removing cigarette ads from radio and TV
- New "Questions to Focus Your Attention"
- Six new research citations

## Chapter 9

- New introductory material including discussion of the Malaysian jumbo jet that went missing
- New research integrated on agenda-setting theory
- New section on whether attractive news anchors increase memory for news
- New section on whether news on Twitter is more emotional than in other media

- New research on new media and imitative suicides
- New Study Box on the measurement of "Need for Cognition"
- New Study Box on the move to online news consumption
- Eleven new research citations
- New "Questions to Focus Your Attention"

## Chapter 10

- New discussion of George Gerbner's comments on sex stereotypes
- New discussion of research from Annenberg Public Policy Center on racial stereotypes in advertising
- New Study Box on Females and Careers in Computer Science
- New "Questions to Focus Your Attention"
- Twelve new research citations

## Chapter 11

- Updated statistics on Internet use
- New section on screen time and face-to-face interaction
- New section on new technology, cognitive and physical health
- New discussion of multitasking
- New Study Box on the role of eye-contact in virtual interactions
- New Study Box on using Facebook to connect with old friends
- New "Questions to Focus Your Attention"
- Fifteen new research citations

## Chapter 12

- New Study Box on provocative ideas in McLuhan's thinking
- New "Questions to Focus Your Attention"
- One new research citation

## RESOURCES FOR STUDENTS

This text is accompanied by a student companion Web site, which includes web links that provide students with additional online resources relevant to the concepts in each chapter. The Web site can be accessed by going to www.cengagebrain.com.

## RESOURCES FOR INSTRUCTORS

This text is also accompanied by an instructor companion Web site, which includes web links, video links, and test banks for every chapter. The Web site can be accessed with an instructor account at www.login.cengage.com.

# ACKNOWLEDGMENTS

Writing a book of this type is not easy. Very simply, I could never have done it without help from lots of people. My students over the years helped to shape my thinking about a book of this type. To the extent that the book is successful at communicating well about media effects, I am indebted to my students' willingness to share their reactions and insights. Before I ever started my work at Purdue, I was fortunate enough to be mentored in graduate school by Joanne Cantor. Her integrity and dedication to my training as a scholar were unparalleled. I could never have written this text without the kind of education that Joanne provided.

The book would never have been completed if I hadn't been blessed with a working environment that was conducive to productive labor. I have been in what is now the Brian Lamb School of Communication at Purdue University for 28 years. It is a fabulous place to teach, conduct research, write, and generally enjoy life. Until last year, I had served for 12 years as the Associate Head of Communication—11 of those under Howard Sypher, who served as the Head during that time. Without Howard's complete support in helping to set up a climate conducive for this project, I could never have completed the task. For all of these things, I am thankful.

The people at Cengage have been fantastic to work with from the beginning. My editor for the first edition, Karen Austin, was particularly helpful. For this fifth edition, I appreciate the work of Danielle Warchol and Rachel Schowalter, the Associate Content Developers; as well as Kelli Strieby, the Product Manager; Jillian Borden, the Marketing Manager; and Raghavi Khullar, the Project Manager. I also owe a debt of gratitude to the many reviewers of the text, including: Andy O. Alali, California State University, Bakersfield; Julie Andsanger, University of Iowa; Lisa R. Barry, Albion College; Robert M. Brady, University of Arkansas; Travis Dixon, University of Illinois; William P. Eveland Jr., The Ohio State University; Olan Farnall, California State University, Fullerton; Anita Fleming-Rife, Pennsylvania State University; Linda C. Godbold, East Carolina University; Bradley S. Greenberg, Michigan State University; Gerald Kosicki, The Ohio State University; Annie Lang, Indiana University; Eric Langstedt, University of Connecticut; Kate Madden, State University of New York, Brockport; Miriam J. Metzger, University of California, Santa Barbara; Stacy L. Smith, University of Southern California; Keith R. Stamm, University of Washington; John Sumser, California State University, Stanislaus; Nicholas A. Valentino, University of Michigan; and Wayne Wanta, University of Oregon.

I especially appreciate the feedback from reviewers of this new edition: Christopher Beaudoin, Texas A&M University; Jeffrey Bolt, Cleveland State University; Monica Brasted, State University of New York, Brockport; Sumana Chattopadhyay, Marquette University; Rachel Kovacs, The College of Staten Island; Jennifer McCullough, Kent State University; Beth Olson, University of Houston; Youngrak Park, Columbus State University; Mary Pitts, Arkansas State University; Rita Rahoi-Gilchrest, Winona State University; Sarah Rosaen, University of Michigan-Flint; Ewart Skinner, Bowling Green State University; Mark Steensland, Pennsylvania State University; and Christine Stover, Oakland University.

I also owe thanks to my late colleague, George Stevens, who provided a sounding board for my writing ideas and a willingness to read anything that I wrote—especially after his retirement from a long and distinguished career as an expert in the law of mass communication. We miss him at Purdue and remember him fondly.

If you're like me, you find it difficult to sustain work on a project over many months unless you have close friends who bear your burdens, share your joys, and offer words of encouragement. I have a few choice friends who do all of these things. I could write several pages about each of them, but that would undoubtedly embarrass them. So, I will just extend a heartfelt thanks to Em Griffin, Will Miller, Bob Ogles, Dave Horner, John Greene, and Michael Bergmann. These are the friends who nourish my soul. I also am incalculably indebted to my parents, Calvin and Betty Sparks (who have both passed on), and to my in-laws, Conrad and Laurel Wilcox (who are both still here). Their constant love and devotion to me and my family have been nothing short of inspirational.

Finally, I owe everything to my wife, Cheri Sparks. A Ph.D. in her own right, she has contributed to this project in ways too numerous to count. Most importantly, she offered her daily encouragement and support. It was Cheri who convinced me that I ought to try my hand at this project. She is also the mother of my three incredible children, David, Erin, and Jordan. To my family, both immediate and extended, I offer my deepest thanks for helping me in all of the little ways (and big ones too) to achieve whatever I manage to achieve.

1
_____

# A Scientific Approach to the Study of Media Effects

On December 14, 2012, less than five years after the worst school shooting in America's history at Virginia Tech University, another horrible assault gripped the nation. At Virginia Tech, 33 were killed. This time, the victims were 20 young elementary school children and six of their teachers who were shot at Sandy Hook Elementary School in Newtown, Connecticut. This sort of event has become all too regular in American culture. In prior editions of this text, I referred to the shocking shootings at Columbine High School in 1999. Since the last edition was published, not only has the nation endured the Newtown tragedy, it was also traumatized by a shooting in Aurora, Colorado in which 12 people died and 70 were injured as theater patrons watched a special midnight showing of *The Dark Knight Rises*—the last film in a trilogy about the superhero Batman.

The national discussion that followed each of the incidents at Columbine, Virginia Tech, Aurora, and Newtown had some striking similarities. After Columbine, a persistent theme was sounded over and over again: The mass media must share a significant part of the blame for this incident and others like it. President Clinton called on the producers of mass media messages to reduce gratuitous violence. The clear implication of Clinton's rhetoric was that exposure to violent entertainment images increased the probability of this type of violent behavior. Similarly, after Virginia Tech, it took only hours before the media devoted intense coverage to the possibility that the perpetrator of the shootings had been influenced by playing a violent video game. The prominent TV psychologist Dr. Phil McGraw appeared on CNN's *Larry King Live* and said: "We're going to have to start … recognizing that the mass murderers of tomorrow are the children of today that are being programmed with this massive [media] violence overdose."[1]

The concern that media violence was somehow responsible for the Aurora movie theater shootings was fueled by photographs of the man arrested in the aftermath. He was shown with his hair dyed orange—suggesting that he may have been attempting to imitate the Joker character in the *Batman* series. After the Newtown shootings, CNN carried a story that quoted someone who knew the shooter and described him as a person who "… stayed at home mostly … playing video games such as 'Call of Duty'."[2] Following those shootings, members of one town in Connecticut organized an event at which citizens could turn in their violent video games to be burned. To encourage people to donate their games for incineration, gift certificates were distributed to all donors. Clearly, those who organized this event believed that there was a solid connection between exposure to violent video games and the horrible crime committed.[3] The startling prevalence of school shootings in American life has certainly fueled concerns that consumption of media violence might be playing some role in the shooting epidemic. In February 2014, *The Washington Post* reported that since the Newtown shootings, "… there have been at least 44 school shootings in K-12 or college campuses in 24 states—an average of more than three a month … 28 people have died and 37 have been injured."[4] If past behavior predicts future behavior, by the time you read this chapter those numbers will almost certainly be higher.

Related to the concern about exposure to media violence is the potential effect of the massive amounts of news coverage that events like those at Columbine, Virginia Tech, Aurora, and Newtown inevitably spawn. After U.S. congresswoman Gabrielle Giffords was shot on January 8, 2011, in Tucson, Arizona while meeting publicly with her constituents, commentators wondered aloud whether the intense news coverage of the shooting, which killed six people and injured 13 others, might trigger "copycat" crimes. Vern Ehlers, a retired congressman, was quoted as saying, "When an event like this happens and it hits the news, very frequently it gives others the idea they should do that too."[5] In contrast to the congressman's view, others preferred to dismiss the Tucson shootings as the acts of a deranged person that would do little to inspire similar acts of violence.

In the days and weeks that followed all of these violent episodes, the media discussions mirrored similar themes. Some thought that media violence in the form of movies, video games, or news coverage may have played a direct role in causing the violent attacks. Others thought that the media were being used as scapegoats in an effort to identify a simple cause instead of recognizing a much more complex set of circumstances. If you listened carefully to any of these national discussions, you may have heard viewpoints that seemed consistent with your own values or political positions. It may have seemed tempting to embrace one or more of the ideas that you heard about how to prevent similar events in the future.

In the end, *opinions* about the events at Columbine, Virginia Tech, Aurora, Newtown, and Tucson were easy to come by. But if you were thinking carefully about the variety of opinions that were expressed about the causes of these shootings, you probably realized that opinions had limited ability to bring you to an understanding of the truth. Despite the fact that President Clinton, Dr. Phil, and Congressman Ehlers were nationally recognized by many as credible leaders, their opinions about the role of the mass media in these shootings were still only opinions. To see whether their views have any scientific merit, you can read more about the actual effects of media violence in Chapter 5. In this chapter, you will learn about how science is different from casual opinion.

## WAYS OF KNOWING

### Experience

There are many ways that we try to know things about the world around us. One way is through direct **experience**. This approach is sometimes called **empiricism**. Experience is often a reliable path to knowledge. One morning many years ago when I was just a youngster, I left my home in the Chicago area without a map and found myself a few hours later in Milwaukee, Wisconsin. The only problem was that I was trying to get to Muskegon, Michigan. If you consult a map, you will discover that I had gone up the wrong side of a rather large lake (Lake Michigan). I have now learned from my experience to consult a map before I travel long distances. My family eventually complied with my request for a GPS navigation unit, and I'm confident that it has saved me from additional navigating disasters. But learning by experience can also be filled with many trials and errors. Progress can be painfully slow and can lead down blind alleys. For nearly 300 years, the people of Europe were afraid to eat tomatoes, which had been introduced from Central America in the 1500s. Personal experience told them that any fruit from the nightshade family was unsafe.[6] Legend has it that someone may have eaten a tomato and died shortly thereafter. In this case, experience proved to be very misleading.

When it comes to our knowledge of media effects, many of us tend to rely on our own personal experience to reach a conclusion. In class discussions about the media violence controversy, it is not uncommon for me to hear students expressing the following viewpoint:

> Well, I don't really think that media violence makes us more violent. After all, look at me. On Saturday mornings, I watched every violent cartoon that the networks put on. Today, I love violent movies—the more blood and guts, the better. My parents love violent movies, too. I grew up on them. I also enjoy playing a good violent video game like *Call of Duty*. But am I a violent person? Of course not! I have never even gotten into a fight. I don't own a gun. I've never been arrested for anything. I'm a peaceful and law-abiding citizen. In fact, my whole life is a personal testimony to the fact that media violence has no negative effect at all. Kids can tell the difference between real violence and fantasy violence. So, I'm sorry, I just don't buy it. Media violence is just fun entertainment. I don't see the harmful effects.

It shouldn't be difficult to recognize that this viewpoint is a great example of knowledge gained through personal experience. It might be more difficult to recognize that a person's individual experience may be a poor guide to the best *general* knowledge on a given topic. Just as people thought that tomatoes were poisonous for everyone, people might also think that media violence poses no risks for anyone. In both cases, personal experience might seem to point to a solid conclusion. But a more careful look might show such a conclusion to be solidly wrong. One possibility is that the conclusion from personal experience is valid for oneself but not for others. The fact that violent media might not trigger aggressive behavior for one individual does not necessarily imply that media violence functions the same way for everyone. Another possibility is that one's impression about being invulnerable to media impact is simply incorrect. Perhaps the effects of media violence are difficult for people to detect in themselves—even though the effects are definitely present.

## Authority

Another way of knowing is to rely on **authority**. Obviously, we can't know everything there is to know. When we get sick, we usually consult a doctor and follow whatever advice he or she gives. We recognize that long years of study and practice tend to have qualified the doctor as an authority on medical diagnosis. Often the trust we place in medical authorities is rewarded with a cure. But, as some have learned, medical authorities are only human. They make mistakes. Some doctors are better than others. Medical horror stories of incompetent physicians who ruin the lives of their patients are not difficult to find. Blind allegiance to authority can often have debilitating effects on our search for reliable knowledge. Our awareness that doctors generally know more than we do about medical cures can lead to a shortcut in our thinking that results in the conclusion that *any* doctor can be trusted as an authority. That kind of mental shortcut can lead to an undesirable and even dangerous result. Another risky mental shortcut that often occurs with authority figures is to transfer their authority to an area that is unrelated to their area of expertise. My doctor might be an authority in prescribing medication, but there may be little reason to trust the doctor's advice when it comes to finding a good auto mechanic or trying to figure out the best way to motivate my children to do well in school.

Hundreds of years ago, religious authority figures were adamant that the earth was the center of the universe and that every celestial body revolved around it. However, astronomical discoveries by Copernicus indicated that the earth actually revolved around the sun. Copernicus feared the actions of the church leaders so much that he kept his discoveries secret for over a decade before publishing them. Nearly 100 years later, Galileo was still confronting resistance from the Roman Catholic Church with regard to the Copernican model of the solar system.[7] Many people continued to reject the truth about the movement of the celestial bodies, because they relied on religious authorities for all knowledge. In this case, reliance on authority resulted in incorrect beliefs.

Over the years, television network executives have made various statements about the effects of media violence that tend to minimize the possibility of negative impact. Shouldn't these network executives be regarded as authorities on the topic?

After all, they are in the day-to-day programming business. They sell advertising time on the basis of their understanding of the effects of commercials. If network executives say that media violence isn't a problem, shouldn't we listen? As we shall see later, one of the problems with arriving at knowledge by appeal to authority is that the supposed authority figures often have interests to protect. Just as religious authorities rejected new views of the solar system to protect what they believed to be their religious interests, so the TV networks can probably be blamed for issuing statements downplaying the importance of media violence out of their concern for maintaining economic profits.[8]

## Science

In the chapters that follow, I have attempted to summarize the key scientific theories and scientific evidence on the question of media effects. **Science** is a particular way of knowing. One of the hallmarks of the scientific method is **systematic observation**, as opposed to casual observation. Science combines empiricism with logical thought and is always pressing onward toward greater precision of observation.[9] One of the best arguments in favor of the power of the scientific way of knowing is the observation that *science works*. A commitment to science has brought us powerful antibiotics to cure our diseases. It has also put human beings on the moon and enables you to browse the Internet and send text messages to your friends. Although science is a human activity that suffers from the multitude of human shortcomings, it is still the most powerful way of knowing that humans have at their disposal. One of the best ways to understand the scientific method of arriving at new knowledge is to under-stand the **goals of science**.[10] Whether one is doing natural science or social science, the goals are the same. Natural scientists attempt to achieve the goals of science in their study of biology, chemistry, physics, astronomy, and the like. Social scientists attempt to achieve the goals of science in their study of social and psychological phenomena that involve human beings.

## GOALS OF SCIENCE

### Prediction

Accurate prediction is one of the coveted goals of science. If you turn on the weather forecast tonight on your local TV news, you will discover that the meteorol-ogist has employed a wide array of instruments, maps, and satellite photos in an attempt to provide an accurate prediction of tomorrow's weather. **Prediction** can be defined simply as **foretelling the future**. Over the years, the science of meteorology has produced increasingly accurate forecasts. Forecasts for a day in advance are usu-ally reliable enough that people can trust them in planning their picnics. That doesn't mean people always exercise that trust. When meteorologists predicted a rare three-inch snowfall for Atlanta, Georgia in late January 2014, few people heeded the prediction. In the storm's aftermath that left at least 13 people dead and thousands of motorists stranded in their cars for hours, many blamed the meteorologists. But the record showed clearly that the public had been warned about the storm. Weather forecasters believe that making accurate predictions can save lives—if their predictions are heeded. Nevertheless, *perfect* prediction is rarely attainable. The state of meteorology is not advanced enough yet to make accurate, long-range forecasts. Science is in continual pursuit of better prediction.

In the area of media effects, accurate prediction is also one of the chief goals. For example, if researchers can predict ahead of time which children are most likely to imitate violent behavior seen in films, parents might be able to intervene to prevent exposure to films. Likewise, if scholars can predict that certain types of characters will facilitate learning on programs like *Sesame Street* or *Sid the Science Kid*, then young children might have a better start upon entering elementary school.

## Explanation

Science certainly has no monopoly on prediction. Insurance companies are also in the prediction business. When each of my children, David, Erin, and Jordan, celebrated their 21st birthdays, I received notice that my auto insurance rates would be going down. Data collected by the insurance industry led to the prediction that unmarried drivers who have reached their 21st birthdays will be much less likely to have accidents than those who are younger. The next price break based on accident rates for females comes at the 25th birthday. For males, it comes when they reach 30. The data also indicate that females who marry after their 17th birthdays enjoy the same reduced risk as an unmarried 25-year-old. These statistics are so dramatic that the insurance companies can pass on premium savings to the customer. The insurance companies don't really care much about *why* accidents drop off after female drivers turn 21 or male drivers turn 30. You can probably identify several possible reasons without thinking too long (more years of driving experience, increased social maturity, and so on). The insurance companies care mainly about the fact that they can predict that the decrease will happen. It is on this point that the scientist and the insurance company may begin to part ways. They are both interested in prediction. But the scientist is also interested in **explanation**—knowing *why* something occurs the way it does.

If prediction means foretelling the future, then what does it mean to say that something has been explained? Think about something simple, like flicking a light switch. If someone asked you to explain why the lights go on and off each time you flick the switch, what would you say? You would probably say something about the electric circuitry behind the switch, including wires, light-bulb filaments, and the flow of electricity. All of these ingredients provide a broader framework or pattern that you invoke to help uncover the "why" behind the phenomenon of flicking the light switch to affect whether a room is dark or illuminated. And this is usually what it means to explain something. **Explanations place the phenomenon to be**

**explained into a broader framework or pattern that doesn't really require much additional elaboration.**

Scientists are always searching for the best explanation of why something happens the way it does. You can probably appreciate the fact that arguments will often erupt about the adequacy of specific explanations. A parent might answer a three-year-old child's question about why the leaves turn colors in autumn by saying something like "That's the way God made trees." In this case, "God" becomes the broader framework or pattern that requires no additional elaboration. Such an answer might satisfy the three-year-old but will seem increasingly inadequate as the child gets older. On occasion, you've probably witnessed a child responding to an adult's explanations by repeatedly asking, "Why?" While the adult who has to endure this steady line of questioning may not appreciate it, the child has actually discovered something very important about explanations. Explanations can continually be scrutinized and pressed until more detail emerges that seems more satisfying.

It isn't necessarily the case that an explanation with less detail is wrong. It just might not provide the desired level of intellectual satisfaction. The esteemed geneticist Francis Collins, former director of the National Human Genome Institute and current director of the National Institutes of Health, has made landmark discoveries about the genetic contributions to certain diseases and also led the stunningly successful Human Genome Project. In his book, *The Language of God*, Collins readily acknowledges his own personal belief that God is the master designer behind the complexity of life.[11] But in his explanations for why a given individual inherits a particular disease, Collins finds a simple appeal to God to be an unsatisfactory *scientific* explanation. Instead, he wants to delve into the particular complexities of human DNA. One of the characteristics of science is that it always encourages additional scrutiny. Sometimes, deeper levels of explanation are perfectly compatible with simpler levels. In other cases, the push for deeper explanations might completely challenge the simpler explanations that seek to account for a given phenomenon.

In media effects research, as in other sciences, scholars argue about how adequate certain explanations are for given research findings. For example, some researchers have located the primary explanation for people's increased tendency toward aggression after seeing media violence in the aggressive images shown in programs or films.[12] Other researchers have argued that these images are not the most important factor. Instead, they have identified the increased physiological arousal caused by exposure to violent images as the critical explanatory ingredient in the increase in aggressive behavior.[13] You will read more about these explanations in Chapter 5 on media violence.

## Understanding

Good explanations provide a sense of **understanding**. What does it mean to say that we understand how something works? Usually, **understanding relates to knowing the particular sequence of causal events** that unfold in a given phenomenon of interest. An explanation that yields a high level of understanding of how the light switch turns on the light would be one that ordered the causal chain of events beginning with the flick of the switch and ending with the illumination of the bulb. Because good explanations provide understanding, these two goals of science are closely related and tend to go hand in hand.

In the case of explanations of how watching media violence might increase aggressive behavior, our understanding would not be very deep if the explanation simply amounted to the statement that children watch the shows and then copy what they see. If this were the extent of the explanation, we might ask what really happens between the viewing and the copying. In other words, what is the exact causal sequence of events? Another hallmark of science is the constant quest for deeper levels of understanding.

## Control

When scientists can accurately predict, explain, and understand a phenomenon, they are afforded greater **control** over that phenomenon. My oldest brother, Dale, is one of over five million Americans who suffer from Alzheimer's disease. Although scientists have made progress in understanding this devastating condition, there are still more questions than answers. Ultimately, scientists would like to know if the condition could ever be cured once it developed and, if so, how that could be done. The quest to understand and explain every facet of Alzheimer's disease is done with the hope of discovering a sure-fire cure. But even if a cure remains elusive, researchers would still love to be able to predict who will get the disease. Am I more likely to get it because my brother has it? While discovering a cure would provide us with ultimate control in managing the disease, being able to determine in advance who will get it would also provide an important measure of control. If I could know today that I would get the disease, I could do some advance planning that might make things much easier for my family. According to a recent discovery announced in March 2014, there could be a simple blood test available in a few years that would predict with uncanny accuracy who will get Alzheimer's disease.[14] If the test proves effective, it could dramatically increase the control we have over the ravages of this killer. Not only would people be able to plan more effectively to deal with the disease's consequences, but physicians and researchers would be able to target new drugs and therapies to the people who are most at risk. Some of those treatments could slow down the progress of the disease or reduce its impact. Even though the control implications of some scientific investigations seem unclear, there's almost always potential for some increased measure of control lurking behind any scientific quest. Advances in prediction, explanation, and understanding of Alzheimer's disease inevitably provide a greater measure of control over the disease itself.

Much like the scientific investigation of diseases, the investigation of media effects also holds ramifications for controlling events. A good example of the control implications of media effects research is easily seen in a study conducted by researchers Brad Bushman (Ohio State University) and Joanne Cantor (University of Wisconsin-Madison) in 2003. Bushman and Cantor discovered that over the years, there had been a total of 18 research reports on how different media ratings systems affected attraction to media content. For example, if a movie is rated R, will people be more attracted to it than if it carried a rating of PG-13? The total number of people involved in these 18 studies exceeded 5,000, so there was a reasonable basis for drawing some firm conclusions. What did Bushman and Cantor discover? In fact, just as they suspected, they found that "media ratings do more to attract than to repel viewers." The research in this area makes a distinction between "descriptive" ratings, which simply provide information about the nature of the content, and "evaluative" ratings, which make recommendations about who should be restricted from media exposure. The rating system used by the Motion Picture Association of America (MPAA) is an evaluative rating system (G, PG, PG-13, R, and NC-17). Both descriptive and evaluative ratings made programming more attractive—particularly for male viewers. The authors believe that viewers use the ratings as a general clue to how much violence, sexual content, or other themes of a mature nature might be present in a movie. Being curious about these themes, children and adolescents are more attracted to films that carry ratings suggesting the presence of this sort of content. One implication of this research is that the ratings system used by the MPAA may actually tend to attract older children to the very film material that is theoretically not intended for their consumption. As a result of their study, Bushman and Cantor have several different recommendations about how the entertainment industry ought to use rating systems (see Study Box 1-1).[15] Just as in prediction about who will get Alzheimer's disease, an increase in the ability to predict and understand a given media effect results in increased control.

Sometimes the implications for control that may arise out of scientific research are controversial. The MPAA has resisted the policy suggestions that spring from Bushman and Cantor's research. This is not the first time that research has ultimately led to controversy about media policy. Back in 1974, researchers discovered that a short commercial message ("The Swing") that was designed to promote sharing and turn-taking behavior in young children was effective in modifying children's behavior. But the commercial caused great controversy among some people who were concerned about its potential to "brainwash" children. According to these critics, the message about sharing a swing on the playground might promote passive compliance among children who need to learn to stand up for their rights.[16]

Although lawmakers, organizations, and other policymakers might debate the pros and cons of particular strategies for controlling a phenomenon, scientists usually hesitate to become identified too closely with a particular policy. Instead, they are more comfortable pointing out the range of control strategies that are available as a result of the increased ability to predict, explain, and understand a given phenomenon. Although the goal of science is not necessarily to push any particular remedy for controlling an event, scientific progress is generally oriented toward providing greater measures of control over the things that are studied.

---

### STUDY BOX 1-1 Policy Recommendations from Research on the Effects of Media Rating Systems

1. Rating systems need to provide guidance by using a system that people can easily understand without having to memorize definitions or decode letters and icons. Current ratings systems tend to be vague and confusing, and they provide insufficient guidance for parents.
2. Rating systems need to provide information about the content of the media. Parents are less interested in what the MPAA recommends for their children and more interested in what specific material is present in movies.
3. The criteria used for assigning ratings need to be explicated clearly. In general, there is a need for the ratings committees to include psychologists, who can explain exactly why certain movies should be rated in a particular way.
4. Many ratings of media material are self-assigned by the distributor or producer of the material. Consumers need to have a procedure for appealing a rating or putting the rating through some sort of public review.
5. The media industries need to devote significant efforts toward educating parents about their rating systems and attempting to make it easier for parents to find ratings information and apply it without confusion.
6. In the American media environment, censorship is not a practical solution. Parents assume the burden for controlling their children's viewing. But if this system is to work effectively, parents must have clear, reliable information about media content.

**SOURCE:** Summarized and paraphrased from Bushman, B. J., & Cantor, J. (2003). Media ratings for violence and sex: Implications for policymakers and parents. *American Psychologist,* 58(2), 130–141.

---

## HOW ARE THE GOALS OF SCIENCE ACHIEVED?

### Theory

When I teach the fundamentals of science to students, and I ask them how they think the goals of science are usually achieved, I typically get a variety of answers. Students often identify experiments, testing, observation, data analysis, surveys, and so on. While these are all tools of the scientist that certainly help, the most powerful single way to achieve the goals of prediction, explanation, understanding, and control does not appear on that list. The most important factor in generating experiments, testing, data analysis, and the like is **theory**. It is also true that theories often arise *after* making observations from data, so some would say that we have a classic example of the "chicken and egg" problem—which comes first? The answer is that it can work both ways. But ultimately, having a strong theory to guide observation probably places the scientist in the most advantageous position to best achieve the goals of science.

Scientific theory is a bit different from the kind of theory that we might refer to in everyday conversation. When my wife and I were driving home from campus one evening, we noticed that there was much more traffic than usual, and we wondered about the reason for the increase. I announced that I had a theory about the change, and I proceeded to speculate that road construction in another part of town had caused traffic to divert to our usual route home. Thus, we were in a traffic jam— even though the road construction was nowhere near our location. In this case, my casual use of the term *theory* was really just a synonym for the word *idea*. I could just as easily have said that I had an *idea* about the traffic change. The meaning would have been the same. But in science, the word *theory* cannot easily be replaced with the word *idea*.

There are several parts to the notion of scientific theory. First, a scientific theory **consists of more than one statement**. My notion of why traffic had increased on our route home was easily stated in a single sentence. But scientific theories take much more than a sentence to state completely. Often, they involve an entire manuscript that might even be as long as a book. Darwin explicated his theory of evolution in a book called *The Origin of Species*.[17] Albert Bandura took an entire book chapter to present his "social cognitive theory of mass communication."[18] You will read more about that theory in Chapter 5. The point here is that scientific theories consist of a *set* of statements—not just a single statement.

One thing that this set of statements does is to **identify the key concepts of the theory and specify how they are related**. In meteorology, a theory about tornado formation might include the concepts of warm air, cold air, and updrafts. The theory might describe how these concepts relate to one another to produce conditions that are favorable for tornadoes. A theory about how media violence affects viewers might describe how the concepts of attention, role models, identification, rewards, and punishments relate to one another to lead to the anticipation of viewers' aggressive behavior.

Perhaps the most important characteristic of scientific theories is that **they yield hypotheses that are testable by observation. A hypothesis is a specific prediction about what will happen under a certain set of well-specified conditions.** Hypotheses are not theories. They are produced by theories. Copernicus presented his heliocentric theory of celestial motion in the 1500s. The theory yielded a hypothesis that the earth rotates around the sun. One way to test this hypothesis was to look at the stars. As one scientist put it, "If Copernicus's theory were true … then stars nearer the Earth should seem to change their position relative to more distant stars as the Earth moved around the sun."[19] This change in position is called *parallax*. Once powerful telescopes were invented, parallax was actually observed, thus lending credence to Copernicus's theory. If parallax had never been observed, the heliocentric theory would have eventually been discredited and replaced by a theory that gave a better account of the data.

In the research about media ratings, before they actually looked at the data, Bushman and Cantor thought that there might be evidence for the hypothesis known as the **forbidden fruit effect**. This hypothesis actually comes from a theory in psychology that was formulated years ago by the psychologist Jack Brehm in a theory that he called **psychological reactance theory**.[20] According to this theory, whenever a person's behavioral freedom is threatened or restricted, the person will feel psychological reactance, which is a very unpleasant feeling. In an effort to get rid of this feeling, the person will attempt to restore his or her freedom. One way to accomplish this is to engage in the behavior that is threatened or restricted. Bushman and Cantor thought that perhaps evaluative movie ratings, which suggest restriction of exposure to people of particular ages, might induce psychological reactance. If this were the case, people might be more attracted to movies that carry a restrictive rating. However, the data from their study didn't offer strong evidence for the forbidden fruit effect. As it turned out, although evaluative ratings *did* tend to attract viewers, so did the descriptive ratings, which, theoretically, should not have created any psychological reactance. Descriptive ratings, after all, simply provide a description of the content. They don't make any recommendations about who should be restricted from exposure. Bushman and Cantor concluded, then, that the forbidden fruit effect was not the best way to explain their data. Instead, they thought that both types of ratings were being used as a guide to content that people were curious about.

This example from the research on media ratings illustrates an important point about how the goals of science are actually achieved. Even though theory is a crucial element in the process, there is a constant interplay between theory and data. New theories are often inspired by certain observations. Existing theories are often modified, qualified, or discarded on the basis of data. Ultimately, theory without data is not very useful in contributing to the goals of science. In media effects research, just as in research on physical theory, hypotheses are often proposed from theories and then tested by observing the data.

## Falsifiability

What does it mean to say that a theoretical hypothesis must be testable by observing the data? A key aspect of the meaning of testability is that the hypothesis must be **falsifiable**. This does not mean that the hypothesis has to turn out to be false. Instead, it means that it **should be possible to specify ahead of time what sort of data, if observed, would make the hypothesis false**. If one is able to clearly specify in advance the data that would falsify the hypothesis, and those data are never observed in systematic tests, the hypothesis has to be taken seriously. But if one is unable to specify in advance the data that would falsify the hypothesis, then one will not be able to determine whether the hypothesis has any merit. Em Griffin uses an analogy involving a trick basketball shot to illustrate this concept in his book about communication theory.[21] His description reminded me of an experience from my own childhood that makes essentially the same point.

During the summer, I used to play a series of Wiffle-ball games with one of my friends. During that series, my friend boasted that he had found a way to throw a secret pitch that was impossible to hit. The first time he threw me the pitch, I swung and missed. "See," boasted my friend, "the pitch just can't be hit." When I swung and missed a second time, I started to wonder if he might be right. But the third time he gave me the secret pitch, I hit it down the left-field line. Before I could say a word, my friend announced, "That wasn't my secret pitch. I didn't have my fingers lined up right." For several more innings, my friend tried to protect his thesis that the secret pitch could not be hit. Each time I swung and missed, he declared that he had thrown the secret pitch. But each time I managed to hit a double or a home run, I would inevitably discover afterward that it hadn't been the secret pitch after all.

What was wrong with my friend's claim? As he eventually discovered, I couldn't take his thesis about the secret pitch very seriously. If he had really wanted to convince me that the thesis was true, he needed to announce *ahead of time* what would have to happen to disconfirm his claim. He needed to say something like, "This is the secret pitch—and if you hit it, then I can no longer say that my secret pitch is impossible to hit." The fact that he couldn't make his claim a falsifiable one undermined his ability to demonstrate that the claim was valid.

This is exactly the case with scientific theory. If a theory yields a hypothesis that can never be falsified, the theory will not ultimately enjoy acceptance in the scientific community, because there is no way to determine if the theory's claims are valid. Sometimes theories, including theories of mass communication that may sound provocative, are not able to contribute very much to the goals of prediction, explanation, understanding, and control because there is no way to falsify them. If you make it all the way to Chapter 12, you'll read about some theoretical ideas that media scholars who take a scientific approach have great difficulty accepting. A good part of their difficulty has to do with the fact that there isn't any clear way to collect evidence that disconfirms the ideas. Just like my friend's trick pitch, if there isn't any way to disconfirm the theoretical idea, there's no way to gather much confidence about it either.

## Creativity

Where do theories come from? As obvious as it may seem, the answer to that question is worth noting. Theories are created by human beings. They're made up in the heads of people. They don't just drop down from the sky as some sort of revealed truth. This is an important point to realize—especially for students of communication who are studying theory. There's a tendency to treat theory as some sort of sacred text that is beyond the ability of any mere mortal to invent. Nothing could be farther from the truth. Virtually every theoretical idea that you'll read about in this text was *made up* by a person who was once a student just like you. The notion that theories are "made up" might suggest that building a theory is similar to painting a picture or writing a poem. In fact, that's not such an outlandish thought.

Albert Einstein's theory of relativity is considered by many to be one of the most "beautiful" theories ever created. It might surprise you to learn that Einstein actually believed that if a theory wasn't pleasing to the aesthetic sensibilities in much the same way as a beautiful painting, then the theory wasn't very good. For Einstein, "we can use our aesthetic judgment to ascertain how close a scientific theory is to the truth."[22]

If a theory seems appealing, it's probably closer to the truth than some uglier alternative. Just as artists may disagree about the elements of a painting that contribute to its beauty, scientists may also disagree about the elements of a theory that make it aesthetically appealing. Nevertheless, there are at least two points to take away from this discussion: 1) If you judge a theory to be "messy" or "ugly," some scientists would argue that those are perfectly legitimate criteria to invoke in judging a theory's value, and 2) the fact that theories are created by human beings means that you shouldn't count yourself out when it comes to making up theory. Perhaps as you study some of the media phenomena mentioned later in the book, you'll invent your own theory to provide an explanation of what's going on.

## The Nature of Science

Theories that are simultaneously beautiful and falsifiable certainly form an important foundation for the achievement of the goals of science. Without research generated by such theories, there would be little progress toward those goals. A great deal of scientific activity is devoted to the actual details of the research process: What methods can be used to actually test a hypothesis? Chapter 2 will introduce you to some of the methods used to investigate mass media effects from a scientific perspective. But before we move along to a consideration of these methods, it is important to understand some of the underlying commitments of the scientific enterprise. Although we live in a culture that enjoys the numerous benefits of these commitments, the commitments themselves are not often articulated clearly—even by scientists.

At this moment, I am witnessing an event that people who lived 100 years ago would find unbelievable. My fingers are tapping on lettered keys, and words are instantly appearing on an illuminated screen. If, during this process, I get a headache, I know that I can take two aspirin tablets and my headache likely will disappear in less than an hour. The application of science is responsible for these benefits—for my opportunity to use the computer and for the relief of my headache. It is easy to take the benefits of science for granted while simultaneously remaining ignorant of how these benefits were derived. To the extent that we can understand the underlying nature of science, we will be in a better position to actually implement the scientific method, understand the outcomes of science, and make additional advances. In Study Box 1-2, you will find a brief list of qualities that sociologist Earl Babbie identified as describing the nature of social science.[23] Following this list, I expand on one of the dimensions noted by Babbie, and I also add a few other aspects of science that are important to grasp.

## Science Is General

One of the important aspects of science that is often misunderstood is the quest for generality. Think back to the opening discussion about the shootings at Columbine High School, Virginia Tech University, Aurora, Colorado, and Newtown, Connecticut. Much of the public discussion that followed these incidents focused on uncovering the particular reasons a person would turn guns on other people. Social commentators cited a wide range of possible explanations, including mental illness, parental neglect, social isolation from some larger community, the influence of violent video games such as *Counter-Strike* and *Call of Duty*, the impact of a particular scene from a movie, like *Basketball Diaries*, and the impact of mood-altering drugs. You may have noticed that on the various news and talk shows that proliferated in the aftermath of these shootings, few scientists went before the cameras claiming that the cause of the shootings was easy to identify. Their reluctance to identify the specific causes may not have been very satisfying to the news media, but it made sense from the standpoint of what constitutes good science.

## STUDY BOX 1-2 Characteristics of Social Science

**Social science is:**

**Logical:** Scientists use inductive and deductive logic to achieve their goals. Theories must not contain logical inconsistencies.

**Deterministic:** Scientists assume that events happen for reasons. Things do not "just happen."

**General:** The aim is to understand overall patterns of events. The larger the scope that is explained, the more useful the explanation is.

**Parsimonious:** The aim is to gain the greatest amount of understanding from the smallest number of variables.

**Specific:** Scientists must be specific about the methods of measurement used to investigate a given phenomenon.

**Empirically verifiable:** Propositions and theories must be testable in the real world.

**Intersubjective:** Descriptions of observations must be sufficiently detailed that other scientists will be able to replicate the observations.

**Open to modification:** As time passes, new evidence may be expected to revise existing ways of thinking about a phenomenon.

SOURCE: Babbie, E. R. (1973). *Survey research methods*. Belmont, CA: Wadsworth.

The predominant quest of the news commentators following the events of Columbine, Virginia Tech, Aurora, and Newtown was to find the particular reason or reasons for the attacks. In research, this would be analogous to a "case study" approach to knowledge. In such an approach, the investigator seeks to describe a given case with as much detail as possible—invoking as many variables as possible—so that a full and complete understanding of the event can be achieved. Once this understanding is reached, it *could* be helpful in generalizing to other cases—but the details of a given case are typically so idiosyncratic that generalizing is likely to be impossible. For example, one of the boys who did the shooting at Columbine was an avid participant in a fantasy baseball league. In the case study approach, this fact could turn out to be highly significant. Perhaps the boy had become disenchanted with his team's progress and his mood had sunk, thus contributing to his outrage. While this detail could be crucial for understanding a single case, it isn't likely that participation in fantasy baseball leagues would ever become a key variable in generalizing to other school shooting cases.

Unlike the case study approach to knowledge, science searches for **general patterns or principles**. These patterns are usually stated in terms of probability and attempt to employ as *few* variables as possible. For example, researchers might know that the probability of antisocial behavior among youth increases with parental neglect. Or media researchers might know that boys who play violent video games are more likely to exhibit aggressive behaviors. Notice that it might be difficult or nearly impossible for a scientist to connect these *general* findings with a *specific* case. In a given incident, violent video games or parental neglect may have little to do with a specific crime. And even if they were contributors, it might be difficult for any scientist to proclaim this on the basis of any compelling evidence. In dealing with specific cases, it may be quite difficult to know exactly why a person acted in a particular way. Even though scientific research on fantasy baseball leagues might reveal that such a hobby is generally healthy (I've never read any scientific research on this topic), it might turn out to be a significant culprit in a crime in any given case.

In the end, case studies do much more to inform us about idiosyncratic cases than they do to help us understand broader patterns. Scientific research does more to inform us about broad, general patterns across large groups of individuals than it does to help us understand the particulars of a given case. Scientists who did participate in the public discussions after the Columbine, Virginia Tech, Aurora, and Newtown shootings tended to take the opportunity to discuss the general patterns found in research pertaining to playing violent video games, taking mood-altering drugs, or mental illness. The fact that they stopped short of claiming that these variables had anything to do with the actual shootings may have frustrated some viewers. But the commitment of science to uncovering general patterns is viewed among scientists as more valuable to society than an emphasis on specific cases. You would probably appreciate this value if your doctor informed you that the drug you were about to take was effective in 99% of cases that had been observed in a very large scale clinical trial. The information about this general pattern of effectiveness would undoubtedly be much more pertinent to your decision about whether to take the drug than if he told you that his only knowledge of the drug was based on how his friend had reacted to it when he took it.

## Science Acknowledges the Existence of Objective Truth

It is fashionable today to proclaim that there is no objective **truth** to be uncovered. Some of my students can often be overheard saying that there is no such thing as truth—truth is relative. Something may be true for you but not true for me. When classroom discussions turn to the effects of the media, I can almost always count on at least one person saying something like the following:

> It is certainly OK for you to believe that media have bad effects on children. I mean, if that's true *for you,* then no one can really argue with you about that.

And I'm certainly not going to argue with you. But *for me,* the media don't have bad effects on children. I grew up with TV and I don't think it hurt me at all. I kind of liked cartoons and then I got into science fiction for a while. So no one will convince me that it has bad effects. But if it does *for you,* that's OK. You know—what is true for you is true *for you* and what is true for me is true *for me.* There is no such thing as something that's true for everybody.

If all of my students take this sort of perspective, it certainly produces great harmony in the classroom. It sounds very tolerant. But tolerance notwithstanding, there are certain features of the statement that make little sense when subjected to critical scrutiny. Let's start with the last statement: "There is no such thing as something that's true for everybody." The problem can be uncovered quite simply by asking this question: Is that statement true for everybody? If, on the one hand, the statement is true for everybody, then the existence of this fact stands as a complete disconfirmation of the statement itself. In other words, if the statement is true for everybody, then the claim the statement makes is false. In this case, the statement would be self-contradictory. If, on the other hand, the statement is *not* true for everybody, then we ought to reject it and consider it to be false. In either case, the statement runs into significant problems as a claim to be taken seriously as a "true" statement. Two scientists, Theodore Schick Jr. and Lewis Vaughn, have summarized the situation this way:

> Each time we assert that something is the case or we think that something is a certain way, we assume that there is objective reality. Each time a relativist denies it, he entangles himself in self-refutation and contradictions. In the very argument over the existence of objective truth, both those who accept it and those who deny it must assume it or the argument would never get off the ground. (p. 80)[24]

With respect to arguments about media effects, the assertion that the media affect children is incompatible with the assertion that they don't affect children. The two assertions cannot both be true. There is, in fact, an objective reality "out there" to be discovered by the media effects researcher. The fact that the truth is out there to be discovered is no guarantee that scientists will actually discover it. But when one takes a scientific approach, one is definitely committing oneself to the notion that objective truth exists.

Let's go back to the student's statement about media effects, just to make sure that we don't get things confused. It may well be that the media might affect two people differently. If that is the point the student is trying to make, then we surely have to grant it. But when this position gets articulated in a general way that results in the denial of the existence of an objective truth, the scientist would issue a correction. Look again at the student's statement. The actual effects of the media may, in fact, be relative. That is, the media may affect various people differently. But the *fact* that the media affect people differently is an objective truth for everyone. As Schick and Vaughn note, "Certain states-of-affairs … may be relative to individuals. *But the truth about those states-of-affairs isn't relative*" [emphasis in original].[25]

The point, then, is to recognize that **scientific activity is concerned with uncovering the truth about things**. In the area of media effects, scientists want to uncover the truth about media impact.

## Science Assumes a Skeptical Attitude

If you scan through the ads in some popular magazines and newspapers, it probably won't be long before you come to an ad that advertises psychic advice. Such ads were especially prevalent on cable TV until a 2002 decision by the Federal Trade Commission charged that ads placed by "Miss Cleo" were fraudulent because they promised "free" advice but then charged customers large telephone fees. Nevertheless, if you want advice about your future, you can still find a psychic to satisfy your desire. Many self-professed psychics will talk to you over the telephone and tell you things about your life that the psychic supposedly knows only by some psychic process. After you become convinced (if you do) that the psychic knows the details of your life, he or she will proceed to give you advice about how to conduct your future affairs. Of course, this advice usually doesn't come for free. In past years, the telephone psychic industry has done literally billions of dollars of business.[26] Obviously, many people believe the psychics and take their advice. But should they?

A person with a **scientific attitude** would approach the phenomenon of psychic advice with great skepticism. If such a psychic process did actually exist, it would violate the current understanding of natural law. That is, scientists currently would have no way to explain how such a process took place. This feature alone would not cause the scientist to rule out psychic phenomena. For years, scientists could not explain how the firefly lit up, but there was no disagreement that it did. Now, of course, scientists understand the chemistry of the firefly's light so well that they have been able to harness it. Children now carry luminescent sticks on Halloween and wear luminescent necklaces that became possible after the chemistry of the firefly was discovered and explained. However, upon examining the claims of the psychic's ability to see into the future, a scientist still has many unanswered questions. Unlike the firefly phenomenon, about which there was no disagreement, scientists are quite skeptical about the claim that psychics can know the future any better than the average person. If psychics can really see future events, why can't they purchase winning lottery tickets before a drawing for a huge jackpot? Psychics inevitably dodge such questions with a variety of explanations of how the psychic process doesn't permit them to see lottery numbers. But it is harder for the psychic to deal with the fact that certain people who have studied their craft can seem to duplicate their amazing powers—without claiming any psychic ability.

Finally, remember the acid test of science—falsifiability. If the psychic's power is real, then why not offer a specific prediction about a future event that would clearly demonstrate that power? Actually, there is a large monetary award (more than $1 million) waiting for the first psychic who can meet this challenge successfully. It is offered by the professional magician and illusionist James Randi.[27] In the final analysis, scientists are skeptical about psychic claims because no scientific evidence exists for their validity. Social scientists should likewise be skeptical about claims of media impact until clear evidence is offered in favor of those claims. As you will read in some of the later chapters, plenty of ideas have been offered about media effects that turn out not to be supported. With the rapid dissemination of digital devices and computer technology, all sorts of interesting claims are being made about new media effects that have yet to be thoroughly researched. Some of those claims may sound plausible. But plausibility is not the ultimate scientific standard that must be met before accepting a claim. See Study Box 1-3 for discussion of a plausible claim about a media effect—but one for which compelling scientific evidence may still be needed.

---

## STUDY BOX 1-3 Does Lumosity Help Your Brain?

Well-trained journalists who specialize in science reporting can sometimes shed light on the current state of scientific progress in a given area. In March 2014, a reporter for *The New York Times*, Tara Parker-Pope, wrote an article titled, "Do Brain Workouts Work? Science Isn't Sure." She reported that lots of money is being made today by companies promising that people can increase their brain function—or at least keep their brains from losing their edge—by playing specially designed digital games. Perhaps the most popular option is Lumosity, which allows users to take advantage of its brain-training games for a monthly fee of $14.95. The premise that we can improve our brain functions by playing certain kinds of video games is one that most people would like to believe. But is there convincing evidence that we ought to believe it?

Parker-Pope recognized that the only reliable place to turn for an answer to this question is to scientific research. She contacted Dr. Murali Doraiswamy, who directs the neurocognitive disorders program at Duke University's Institute for Brain Sciences. He told her that "Almost all the marketing claims made by all the companies go beyond the data." He went on to say that "We need large national studies before you can conclude that it's ready for prime time."

Parker-Pope reported on several scientific studies that actually *do* show various cognitive improvements after certain types of brain-training activities. But the overall gist of her article is that we simply don't have enough compelling scientific evidence at this point to render a clear conclusion about the exact nature and extent of any brain benefits of Lumosity and other similar products. She concluded that when they use their smartphones or computers to engage brain-improving products, "consumers should know that the scientific jury is still out" on whether a person is "boosting their brain health" or "just paying hundreds of dollars to get good at a game." Perhaps sites like Lumosity actually do deliver what they promise—cognitive improvement as a result of using their product. More research needs to be conducted.

---

SOURCE: Parker-Pope, T. (March 11, 2014). Do brain workouts work? Science isn't sure. *The New York Times* [Online: Accessed 3-11-14]. Available: http://well.blogs.nytimes.com/2014/03/10/do-brain-workouts-work-science-isnt-sure/?ref=science

## Science's Skeptical Attitude Often Leads to Controversy

The fact that some scientific claims appear initially to be promising but end up with little support is a fact that implies something that's very important to realize about the nature of science: the application of the scientific method almost guarantees that controversies will emerge. At any given time, science can be characterized as an activity that has numerous new unsupported claims touted by some and viewed with suspicion by others. It also has claims that have been around for a while and may be waning in support—but might not be completely dead.

A recent example of a running controversy in the social science literature concerns the evidence pertaining to the existence of ESP (extrasensory perception). In January 2011, Professor Daryl Bem, a widely respected social psychologist with an illustrious career, reported the results of research on over 1,000 people that he claimed supported the existence of ESP.[28] For example, when participants in one experiment were asked to click on one of two identical curtains to reveal the one that hid an erotic picture instead of a blank wall on their computer screen, there was a slight tendency (about 53% of the time) for participants to correctly click on the curtain that hid the picture. In fact, a computer randomly generated where the pictures showed up only *after* participants had indicated their choices, so Bem reasoned that the evidence indicated a slight tendency for his participants to be able to forecast a future event. The difference between 53% and 50% (50% would be expected by chance) might seem small. But the statistical tests that Bem employed showed that this difference was not likely to occur by chance alone (you will read more detail about "statistically significant differences" in the next chapter). Bem's conclusion was that some sort of precognition or ESP process seemed to be taking place—although he didn't attempt to explain that process. The results of his experiments were compelling enough to lead the editors of the flagship journal in social psychology to publish the findings. As you might imagine, his research has generated controversy. It earned him a special TV appearance on *The Colbert Report*.[29] It also generated a scholarly rebuttal written by several other scientists that was published in the same issue of the journal that carried the report of Bem's experiments.[30] If you asked scholars who have read the research, you'd probably find some who believe that ESP has now been confirmed as a real phenomenon. You'd also find some who believe nothing of the sort.

Over the years, I've noticed that beginning students often become impatient and frustrated with the controversies that characterize the scientific literature. They desire clear, unambiguous conclusions about scientific findings. Controversy seems to cloud the search for truth. Sometimes this frustration leads students to adopt a very low view of the value of scientific thinking. Preconceived notions about the precision and accuracy of scientific procedures can exacerbate the frustration. When a student begins with the assumption that science always yields definitive conclusions and then discovers uncertainty in so many areas, it's easy to become disconcerted. Some students even jettison the whole scientific enterprise as a worthless endeavor. That's unfortunate. The fact that we can't always tell with certainty whether something is happening is a poor reason for discarding science as a powerful way of knowing. It's true that the pace of scientific progress can be painstakingly slow and marked by controversy.

But over time, the application of the scientific method usually clarifies what's going on and leads to stronger and stronger consensus. Healthy skepticism might mean that it takes science much longer to come to consensus about something—but it also means that once consensus is formed around a particular conclusion, that conclusion is more likely to be correct. In the final analysis, science actually thrives on controversy. The same frustration that might lead some to form a low view of science serves as a powerful motivation for scientists to move forward in the quest for truth. Susan Haack, a professor in philosophy, understands the temptation to dismiss the scientific method as nothing special. She admits that science "is a thoroughly human enterprise, fallible and messy, its progress ragged and uneven."[31] But she also points out that this doesn't mean that science is not a very distinguished way of knowing things. In the end, she embraces science—with all of its flaws—as the most powerful way we've found to accumulate knowledge.

## Science Can't Answer Certain Kinds of Questions

Some people think that a scientist is a person who believes that all things are knowable and that scientists are "know-it-alls" who look down on others as "know-nothings." Unfortunately, there are too many scientists who don't do a lot to combat this image. One of the things that a good scientist will readily admit is that certain kinds of questions fall outside the purview of scientific investigation. Scientists may have invented the atom bomb, but science can never give a definitive answer to the question of how the bomb should be used. In the area of media effects research, science can tell us *how* viewing violent images is likely to affect children, but it can't tell us *what* the federal government should do about media violence—or whether it should do anything at all.

There are other kinds of mass communication theory and research that won't be presented in this book, because they are not really concerned with documenting the effects of the media. These other theories (e.g., critical, cultural and normative theories) address questions that scientists can't answer by applying scientific methods. Likewise, by applying their methods of criticism or interpretation, these other theories can't answer questions that science can answer about media impact. In their book *Mass Communication Theory*,[32] two media scholars, Stanley Baran and Dennis Davis, present a number of questions that don't lend themselves well to scientific methods—including these:

- Should media do something more than merely distribute whatever content will earn them the greatest profits in the shortest time?
- Should media become involved in identifying and solving social problems?

In contrast, questions such as the following are most appropriately addressed within a scientific framework:

- Does viewing media violence cause people to become desensitized to violence in real life?
- Are the outcomes of political elections affected by the news media's projections of winners prior to the closing of the polls?

Scholars who take different perspectives in their search for knowledge may be trying to answer different questions. Sometimes the tension that exists between scholars who identify with different traditions of inquiry can be alleviated a bit by recognizing the differences in the kinds of questions that are capable of being addressed from each perspective. Scientists do themselves no favor when they give the impression that their perspective can be used to answer every kind of question. It can't. But the general power of science as a mode of inquiry can hardly be denied. Without the knowledge that has been generated about media effects from a scientific perspective, we would be left with little but opinion and speculation. Science is not after opinion and speculation. It is after truth. As Ralph Estling, a writer from the United Kingdom, has recently argued in an essay,

> In science, pluralism and tolerance will imperceptibly fade into relativism where there is no such thing as external truth, objective facts, intrinsic, self-sustaining reality, where there is only "my truth" and "your truth." There is never any need to compare, contrast, question, doubt, argue, seek to learn from what the data say and what the Universe tells us. When this happens, truth—for there is such a thing—is in dire peril. And science ceases to function. (p. 55)[33]

Some of the most interesting questions to consider regarding mass media are questions that can't be answered by any sort of scientific study. For example, should journalists be permitted to ride on tanks with the soldiers on the front line? Should individual states design powerful shield laws to protect journalists from having to reveal their confidential sources? Should the Federal Communications Commission (FCC) reinstitute the "fairness doctrine" requiring broadcasters to give coverage of differing viewpoints on controversial issues? How important are media messages in determining the climate of any national culture? Should Comcast's proposed purchase of Time Warner be approved? Questions such as these are addressed best by normative, cultural, and critical theory—not scientific theory. On the other hand, questions about how media content affects people's thoughts, feelings, and actions are best addressed by scientific theory. The focus of this book is on theory and research that is properly situated within the scientific tradition of the field.

## SUMMARY

This chapter began with a discussion of the tragic events at Columbine High School, Virginia Tech University, Aurora, Colorado, and Newtown, Connecticut. Many opinions about the causes of those events were expressed in the popular press, but it is often difficult to determine the truth from sifting through a host of opinions. Personal experience and appeal to authority are different ways of knowing—but they don't apply the systematic observation and logic that is included in a scientific approach. The goals of science are prediction, explanation, understanding, and control. Scientists achieve these goals by creating theories and testing theoretical hypotheses that are falsifiable. There are a number of important ingredients that characterize a scientific approach. Science is concerned with uncovering truth. But it maintains a **skeptical attitude** and acknowledges that it can't answer every question. Although controversies abound in science, that's no reason to become disenchanted with a way of knowing that has demonstrated its power over the centuries. Ultimately, the scientific method seeks to make general statements about the way variables are related. Consequently, while scientists may have much to contribute to a general discussion about events such as the shootings at Columbine, Virginia Tech, Aurora, and Newtown, they will probably refrain from making statements about the particular causes involved in an isolated incident.

## QUESTIONS TO FOCUS YOUR ATTENTION

1.  How would you answer the critic who minimized the scientific way of knowing because scientific progress is too slow?
2.  Can you think of an important question about the media not covered in the chapter that a scientific perspective is not well equipped to address well?
3.  How do you think the controversy about the scientific evidence pertaining to the existence of ESP could best be resolved?

## KEY TERMS AND CONCEPTS

| | | |
|---|---|---|
| experience | foretelling the future | psychological reactance theory |
| empiricism | explanation | falslflablllty |
| authority | understanding | truth |
| science | control | scientific attitude |
| systematic observation | theory | skeptical attitude |
| goals of science | hypothesis | |
| prediction | forbidden fruit effect | |

## NOTES

1. Entertainment C⟨ Accessed on 3-1⟨ massacre#.UyEB
2. Candiotto, S., B⟨ documents. *CNN* shooting-docume
3. Gabbatt, A. (Jan⟨ *Guardian* [Onlin⟨ shooting-video-g⟨
4. Strauss, V. (Febr⟨ [Online: Accesse⟨ least-44-school-s⟨
5. Scott, M. (Januar⟨ ing. *Grand Rapid* index.ssf/2011/01

*⟩ames Collide* [Online: ⟩mes-for-virginia-tech-

ed in newly released 03/28/us/connecticut-

⟩returns to school. *The* /jan/03/newtown-

*The Washington Post* ⟩t/wp/2014/02/13/at-

⟩ielle Giffords shoot- ⟩ws/grand-rapids/

*Handwritten notes:*
1. Summarize
2. Make connection
3. Think critically
4. Think critically
5. Term to know
6. Reflect ... any ?s

6. Forest Preserve District of Cook County (Illinois) (1968). *The Tomato* [Online: Accessed on 3-10-14]. Available: http://www.newton.dep.anl.gov/natbltn/300-399/nb313.htm

7. Schick, T., & Vaughn, L. (1995). *How to think about weird things: Critical thinking for a new age*. Mountain View, CA: Mayfield.

8. Liebert, R. M., & Sprafkin, J. (1988). *The early window: Effects of television on children and youth*. New York: Pergamon Press.

9. Graziano, A. M., & Raulin, M. L. (1989). *Research methods: A process of inquiry*. New York: Harper & Row.

10. Although I have not consulted my notes from graduate school in writing about the goals of science, I am certainly aware that my thinking on this and other topics I discuss in this chapter was crystallized in a course that I took from Professor Joseph Cappella at the University of Wisconsin–Madison in 1981.

11. Collins, F. S. (2006). *The language of God: A scientist presents evidence for belief*. New York: Simon and Schuster.

12. Jo, E., & Berkowitz, L. (1994). A priming effect analysis of media influences: An update. In J. Bryant & D. Zillmann (Eds.), *Media effects: Advances in theory and research* (pp. 43–60). Hillsdale, NJ: Erlbaum.

13. Zillmann, D. (1991). Television viewing and physiological arousal. In J. Bryant & D. Zillmann (Eds.), *Responding to the screen: Reception and reaction processes* (pp. 103–133). Hillsdale, NJ: Erlbaum.

14. Cohen, E. (March 9, 2014). Blood test predicts Alzheimer's disease. *CNN* [Online: Accessed 3-10-14]. Available: http://www.cnn.com/2014/03/09/health/alzheimers-blood-test/

15. Bushman, B. J., & Cantor, J. (2003). Media ratings for violence and sex: Implications for policymakers and parents. *American Psychologist, 58*(2), 130–141.

16. Liebert, R. M., & Sprafkin, J. (1988). *The early window: Effects of television on children and youth*. New York: Pergamon Press.

17. Darwin, C. (1900). *The origin of species*. New York: Burt.

18. Bandura, A. (1994). Social cognitive theory of mass communication. In J. Bryant & D. Zillmann (Eds.), *Media effects: Advances in theory and research* (pp. 61–90). Hillsdale, NJ: Erlbaum.

19. Schick, T., & Vaughn, L. (1995). *How to think about weird things: Critical thinking for a new age*. Mountain View, CA: Mayfield.

20. Brehm, J. W. (1966). *A theory of psychological reactance*. New York: Academic Press.

21. Griffin, E. (2000). *A first look at communication theory*. Boston: McGraw-Hill.

22. McAllister, J. (1998). Is beauty a sign of truth in scientific theories? *American Scientist, 86*, 174–183.

23. Babbie, E. R. (1973). *Survey research methods*. Belmont, CA: Wadsworth.

24. Schick, T., & Vaughn, L. (1995). *How to think about weird things: Critical thinking for a new age*. Mountain View, CA: Mayfield.

25. *Ibid.*, p. 81.

26. Nisbet, M. (1998). Psychic telephone networks profit on yearning, gullibility. *Skeptical Inquirer, 22*, 5–6.

27. One Million Dollar Paranormal Challenge [Online: Accessed 3-12-14]. Available: http://www.randi.org/site/index.php/jref-news/1239-mdc-changes.html

28. Bem, D. J. (2011). Feeling the future: Experimental evidence for anomalous retroactive influences on cognition and affect. *Journal of Personality and Social Psychology*. 100, 407–425.

29. Schindler, M. (January 31, 2011). Professor defends ESP study on *Colbert Report*. *The Cornell Daily Sun* [Online: Accessed 3-12-14]. Available: http://cornellsun.com/blog/2011/01/31/professor-defends-esp-study-on-colbert-report/

30. Wagonmakers, E. J., Wetzels, R., Boorsboom, D., & van der Maas, H. L. J. (2011). Why psychologists must change the way they analyze their data: The case of Psi: Comment on Bem (2011). *Journal of Personality and Social Psychology, 100*(3), 426–32.

31. Haack, S. (1999). A fallibilist among the cynics. *Skeptical Inquirer, 23*, 47–50.

32. Baran, J., & Davis, D. K., (1995). *Mass communication theory: Foundations, ferment and future*. Belmont, CA: Wadsworth.

33. Estling, R. (1998, July/August). Is science concerned with truth? *Skeptical Inquirer, 22*(4), 55–56.

# 2

# Scientific Methods in Media Effects Research

When I was about 14 years old, my grandmother came to visit for the summer. She loved to watch soap operas in the middle of the afternoon. My father didn't think much of soap opera content, and he didn't hesitate to voice his opinion that soap operas affect viewers in a negative way. The gist of his complaint was that he thought soap operas encouraged viewers to see their own lives as a constant melodrama. I was never sure that I agreed with my dad about the impact of soap operas on viewers, but his strong opinions on the subject made me wonder. **How would one ever go about discovering the effects of media content?**

Having read Chapter 1, you may suspect that a good general answer to this question is to use a scientific approach. But what would such an approach entail? One of the main goals of this chapter is to introduce three specific methods that social scientists use to answer questions related to media impact. Taken together, these methods constitute the main arsenal of the media effects researcher. The three methods are: **content analysis**, the **survey**, and the **experiment**.

## ANALYZING MEDIA CONTENT

In general, the first step in scientific investigation is to *describe* the phenomenon of interest with precision. **Content analysis** allows a researcher to describe the nature of the content of communication in a systematic and rigorous fashion. Content analysis can be applied to almost any type of communication, but it is particularly appropriate for mass media messages because it permits us to describe precisely a vast diversity of message content that might otherwise prove elusive. Content analysis is a logical beginning point for the investigation of media effects because it helps us to discover what content is present that might be bringing about various effects. The controversy about the impact of media violence on children would hardly capture our attention if none of the programs or movies that were made contained any violent scenes. On the other hand, it is important to understand that **the results of a content analysis do not permit one to make inferences about the effects of that content**.

I used to carry a card in my wallet that was distributed by a group called TV Tune-In, located in Cleveland, Ohio. Over the years, the card became faded and worn so I retired it to a desk drawer for posterity. One of the "TV Awareness Facts" that appears on the card is particularly striking: "More guns are fired on TV in one evening than are fired in the course of an entire year by a metropolitan police force of 504 officers!" This "fact" was based on content analyses of prime-time TV and since the card is at least 30 years old, the statistics it reports can no longer be trusted as dependable. They'd have to be updated by doing new content analyses. The researchers who conducted the study that this old statistic is based on arrived at this figure after counting the number of guns fired during an average evening of prime-time offerings. It may seem like an easy jump to move from this "fact" to the inference that TV influences people to shoot guns. But such an inference would be unjustified. It could be the case that people become disgusted with all the guns fired on TV and consequently use guns less frequently than they would otherwise. Alternatively, it could be that people carefully separate the world of TV and the real world such that seeing guns fired on TV has no effect at all on guns fired in real life. The facts themselves that come from a content analysis don't ever permit us to answer the question about the *effects* of the content. To answer that question, other research methods must be used. Before we examine some of those other methods, let's take a closer look at the method of content analysis and examine the role that it can play in mass-communication research.

## What Is Content Analysis?

One researcher, Bernard Berelson, defined content analysis in the following way: "Content analysis is a research technique for the *objective, systematic,* and *quantitative* description of the *manifest* content of communication."[1] Essentially, content analysis is a method that allows the researcher to describe messages in quantitative terms even though those messages are essentially verbal or non-quantitative in nature.

Content analysis is *objective* in the sense that the method permits multiple researchers to examine the same content and come to identical conclusions. This is possible because the method is *systematic.* That is, it specifies an unambiguous set of rules or procedures for coding the message content. Theoretically, any **coder** (a person who examines the content and classifies it into categories) who understands the rules or procedures will arrive at the same coding of the message content as any other coder. The data that result from a content analysis are *quantitative.* That is, certain aspects of the content are coded and tallied in some quantitative way. This aspect of content analysis is important because it permits the researcher to conduct various statistical tests on the results of the coding.

Finally, content analysis is concerned with the coding of manifest content rather than latent content. **Manifest content** refers to the material that actually appears, and requires a minimum of interpretation by the coder. **Latent content** is content that might become apparent after a coder has interpreted or "read between the lines" of the message before coding. For example, a coder might classify the following statement in a TV sitcom as a compliment: "Gee, Jerry, that's a real attractive outfit you're wearing." The surface meaning of the statement suggests that it should be coded as a compliment. However, it might be apparent from other cues in the program (perhaps the vocal tone of the person who spoke) that the statement was uttered with sarcasm and was not actually intended as a compliment. It might even take special knowledge about the character's personality in order to make a clear interpretation about whether the statement was sarcastic. If the coder classified the statement as an insult instead of as a compliment, that might be an example of coding the latent content. As you can probably begin to appreciate, the issue of manifest versus latent content is controversial among content analysts. Some researchers are inclined to code only the manifest content and discuss alternative interpretations after the data have been analyzed. Other researchers may be interested in coding the latent content directly, as long as agreement among different coders can be established.

Although this overview may provide a general conceptual introduction to content analysis, chances are good that your understanding of this method is still a little vague. An example is in order.

Suppose you believe that adolescent novels can potentially influence readers by setting certain expectations, norms, or standards for using alcohol or other illegal substances. In particular, suppose you think you have noticed that many popular novels directed to adolescents contain references to smoking, alcohol consumption, and drug use. You want to study the best-selling novels in some systematic fashion to determine whether your casual observation has any merit, but you aren't sure how to proceed. Content analysis is the method that can help you to learn whether your casual observation has any merit.

## An Example: The Content of Popular Novels for Adolescents

If you were actually curious about references to substance use in adolescent novels, you wouldn't be alone. In 2011, three researchers published a study after they wondered about this same question and decided to attempt to get an answer. To do so, Sarah Coyne, Mark Callister, and James Phillips decided to design a content analysis.[2] A closer look at their study will reveal the essential steps that one goes through in designing this sort of research.

**The Sample** Every content analysis has to be done on a particular sample of messages. In this case, the researchers wanted to find out the content of popular adolescent novels. They decided to use one of the industry's most important lists for establishing the top novels at any given time: *The New York Times* Best Sellers list for children's books. They chose to examine the 40 most popular novels on the list that was published between June 22, 2008 and July 6, 2008. When the authors counted the number of pages that appeared in all of these novels, they had a total of 14,005 pages to analyze. When researchers rely on published lists such as the ones used in this study, there may be questions about how those lists were assembled. For example, in this case, the precise way in which this "best sellers" list is constructed is an inside secret that *The New York Times* refuses to reveal. Over the years, authors and publishers have criticized the list for various reasons and argued that it may not actually reflect the true "best sellers." Nevertheless, this list is highly influential in the publishing industry and the authors of this study believed the list to be useful for their purposes. Researchers must always think carefully about the way their sample of material is generated and what the conclusions drawn from the sample actually mean.

In this study, the researchers had a manageable population of 40 novels and they chose to analyze every one. Sometimes, the population that a researcher wants to draw from is so large that a smaller random sample is chosen. For example, imagine that the researchers could be interested in generalizing across a 20-year period and had thousands of novels to consider. In that case, they may have decided to select a random sample from the total. A **random sample** is one that permits every member of the population to have an equal chance of being selected in the sample. It is a crucial technique if the researcher wants to be able to generalize the results of the sample back to the larger population. In many content analysis problems, the population of interest is so large that it simply wouldn't be worth the time and expense to use all members. That would certainly be the case if the researchers of this study had several thousand novels to analyze.

**Units of Analysis** After the sample is selected, the researchers must decide what units of the content will be coded. For example, in a newspaper article, the researcher might code each paragraph for certain attributes. Thus, the paragraph would be the **unit of analysis**. If each sentence were coded, then the sentence would be the unit of analysis. Sometimes TV shows are broken into scenes and each scene is coded. In this case, although the authors don't clearly state the unit of analysis, it appears to be the entire novel and each novel could have had multiple instances of alcohol or substance use that were coded individually.

**Categories** In every content analysis, the content of the message is coded according to a **category scheme**. Coyne and her coauthors wanted to code each incident in several ways. For example, they wanted to code type of substance used (e.g., alcohol, tobacco, illegal drugs, prescription drugs, etc.) as well as the reason for its use (e.g., celebrating, relaxing, coping, addiction, etc.), the age of the user (minor or adult), and the consequences of use (no consequences, positive consequences, or negative consequences).

Sometimes, it is difficult to tell from a research report exactly how the category scheme was actually applied. For example, suppose a character is using alcohol at one point in the novel and the scene changes for the next 10 pages and then returns to the same instance of alcohol use. Does this count as two instances of alcohol use or is it just counted as a single incident? The only way to get answers to questions like this is to carefully examine the coding rules that the authors applied in the study. In some studies, the coding rules aren't completely specified. In cases where they aren't, the only way to discover the rules is to try to contact the authors directly and ask them for more detail. In this case, Coyne and her coauthors recognized that readers might have numerous questions about the coding rules and that the journal publishing their article had placed them under strict space constraints. Consequently, they invited readers to contact them with any questions.

**Coding Agreement** After more than one coder has coded the data, some statistical index of agreement among the coders is computed. Sometimes this statistic is simply calculated by dividing the number of times the coders agree by the total number of coding decisions they make. For example, consider the case of a researcher who wanted to code the biological sex of the person who consumed alcohol (Coyne and her coauthors did code for this information). Suppose that there were 10 incidents of alcohol use and that two independent coders agreed on the sex of the user in nine out of the 10. Their percentage of agreement would be 90% or .90. Although this may seem like a pretty good percentage of agreement, consider the fact that there are only two possible categories in this case: male and female. The possibility of agreeing just by chance is 50%. Because of the possibility of chance agreements, many researchers compute coding agreement (often referred to as **coding reliability**) with a special formula that makes an adjustment for the chance hits. A rule of thumb in content analysis is that coding reliability must be at least .70 (a coefficient of 1.0 indicates perfect agreement and lower levels are accepted if a formula that adjusts for chance agreements is employed). In the study of popular adolescent novels, the authors used five independent coders who had been trained for three weeks to code substance use in the novels. For purposes of demonstrating reliability, all five coders coded the content of the same four books (10% of the total sample) and their coding reliability was never lower than .66 for any of the categories that they coded. Normally, scholars would like to see the coding reliability statistic for each separate category that was coded, but this information is not always reported. Since Coyne and her coauthors didn't provide this information in the published article, a reader could always try to contact the authors directly for this information. That's what I did in preparation for writing this section. In a simple email exchange that took just a matter of hours (Coyne and I didn't know each other before our email exchange), Coyne provided the coding reliability for each of the categories that she used. As it turned out, her coders had perfect coding reliability (1.0) for all but three of the categories used in the study. The coders had less than perfect agreement when they coded whether or not there was an instance of substance use (.66), the age of the user (.71), and the consequences associated with the use (.71). Even though agreement wasn't perfect for these categories, it was high enough to trust the coders as they independently coded the remaining novels. After coding reliability is demonstrated on a subset of the entire sample, the coders usually go on to divide the labor, with each coder taking a portion of the remaining material to be coded.

**Statistical Analysis** Once the researchers have established coding reliability, the data from the study can be described in statistical terms. In Coyne's study of adolescent novels, it turned out that 73% of the novels contained substance use, and there were 357 incidents of substance use—about one for every 39 pages coded. Nearly 90% of all the incidents coded were for either alcohol use (67.2%) or tobacco use (22.1%). About 47% of the total incidents involved substance use by children and teens. In 83.2% of the incidents, there were no consequences associated with substance use. Just over 10% of the incidents were associated with some negative consequence and 6.7% were associated with some positive consequence. The size of the difference between the number of incidents depicting no consequences and the ones that depicted either a negative or positive consequence turned out to be *statistically significant*. This was also the case for the difference between the number of incidents that depicted negative consequences instead of positive ones. The concept of a statistically significant difference will be explained later in this chapter. Another finding that was statistically significant was the fact that alcohol use as opposed to tobacco or use of illegal drugs was much more likely to be used in a context of celebrating.

**Interpretation of Findings**  After the results have been summarized, the authors of a content analysis usually discuss the implications of the study. The authors of the study on popular novels discussed the fact that adolescents who read these novels are being exposed on a regular basis to messages about substance use. Specifically, they stated:

> While substance use was absent in some novels, nearly three-fourths of the books contained instances of use and nearly a third contained 10 or more instances, especially in books for ages 14+. The prevalence of substance use, though less than adolescents might find in other media such as television and film, may contribute to perceptions that consumption among adolescents is normative … When the contextual variables are considered together, the recurring message regarding substances is often that access is easy, acceptance is normative, and consumption is consequence-free and takes place in relatively positive settings. Thus, as a source for teaching youth the risks of substance use and tools for responding to peer pressures and offers, adolescent novels fall short. (pp. 514–515)

The authors went on to express concern about the possibility that substance use messages in novels may affect young readers adversely and they called on researchers to design studies that actually tested the direct effects of exposure to these messages—something that a content analysis is not designed to do.

Although the results of a content analysis cannot be used to document the effects of the media, these types of studies often have implications for claims about media effects. Suppose that a researcher wanted to investigate the possibility that the prevalence of substance use in adolescent novels causes adolescent readers to use more of these substances. The presumed media effect in this case would be based on an assumption about the lack of negative consequences from substance use in these books—an assumption that Coyne's study helps to document. This example illustrates an important relationship between content analyses of media content and research on media effects. Ideas about media effects are usually based on assumptions about the presence or absence of certain kinds of media content. Content analyses are often an excellent way to begin research on media effects because they can confirm or disconfirm these assumptions.

More recently, another team of researchers (Brian Primack, Erika Douglas, and Kevin Kraemer) have been concerned about the potential effects of popular songs that mention substance use on those who listen to the songs. In a survey of nearly 1,000 high school students in the ninth grade, they obtained individual reports of music exposure and favorite singers. Based on a content analysis of the songs of various artists and the students' reports of their listening habits, they were able to estimate the number of times each day that students were exposed to some song lyric that referred to cannabis use. They also asked students to report their own cannabis use during the last month. Their major finding is at least consistent with the idea that exposure to song lyrics can affect behavior. Students with the highest level of exposure to song lyrics that referred to cannabis use were nearly twice as likely to report that they had actually used cannabis in the last month.[3] While this finding may appear to implicate media exposure as a cause of cannabis use, you'll see from the remainder of the chapter that such a conclusion would be premature.

## THE SAMPLE SURVEY

Primack's study on cannabis use employed two different methods—content analysis and a survey. Just as Coyne used a best sellers list to document substance use in books, Primack used content analysis to document lyrics that referred to cannabis in songs listed on the top charts in *Billboard* magazine. Content analysis in mass-communication research focuses on message content. But there are hosts of interesting research questions that can't be answered with this method. Many of the most important questions require researchers to investigate *people* instead of message content. One of the best ways of investigating people is to ask them questions directly. That's what Primack did when he asked ninth-graders for reports on their music exposure and their cannabis use in the last month. The method that is designed particularly for this purpose is the survey. It is often referred to as the **sample survey** because, in most cases, it is based on a random sample of some larger population of interest.

The survey method is probably the most familiar to the average citizen. If you haven't actually participated in a survey as a respondent in the past month, you have almost certainly heard the results of at least one survey reported by the mass media. The quest by politicians and government officials for an accurate gauge of public opinion has served to refine the methods of survey research over the years. Today, sample surveys play a vital part in the governmental process. Mitt Romney and Barack Obama used sample surveys throughout their fierce battle for the presidency in 2012 to determine where they needed to concentrate their campaigning. The U.S. Census Bureau relies heavily on sample surveys to reveal information about the changing demographics in the population.

In mass-communication research, surveys are invaluable in helping us to understand people's media habits. Through survey research, scholars now have a good sense of how much TV the average person watches, what types of content are most popular, and what people report about their own reactions to that content. The survey, as it turns out, is an excellent method for getting descriptive insight into a given phenomenon.

Beyond simple descriptive data, the survey is an excellent way of exploring relationships between different variables. Suppose, for example, a researcher thought that children who tend to watch lots of television during a typical week also tend to be more obese. This relationship could be uncovered in a sample survey. Phone numbers in a given area might be selected randomly, and parents who answered the phone might be asked a number of questions about their child's weekly TV viewing. After getting estimates of the child's daily viewing, the researcher might also solicit estimates of each child's weight. After the researcher had collected these data, a statistical analysis could be applied to the data to see if the children who watch more TV during the week also tend to be the children who weigh more.

Studies similar to the one described have actually been conducted. For example, a group of researchers writing in the *Journal of the American Medical Association* reported a survey of well over 50,000 women. They found that TV viewing was especially related to a significantly higher level of obesity and type 2 diabetes.[4] These research findings are consistent with the results of the survey reported by Larry Tucker and Marilyn Bagwell. These authors surveyed nearly 5,000 adult females and found that obesity was twice as likely to occur among those who viewed four or more hours of TV per day as compared to those who viewed less than one hour of TV per day.[5] More recently, a team of medical researchers examined the possible relationship between TV viewing and hypertension in obese children. Obese children who viewed over four hours of TV per day were over three times more likely to have hypertension than were the obese children who watched less than two hours of TV per day.[6] Statistical analyses that reveal these types of findings are important tools of the mass-communication researcher. This chapter will introduce you to a few of the most important basic concepts. First, let's take a closer look at an example of an actual survey that was conducted to study media effects.

## An Example: Does Watching a Traumatic Event on TV Cause Post-Traumatic Stress Disorder?

At some point in your TV viewing experience, the chances are high that you've watched news reports of some traumatic event. As I write these words, Purdue University is in the process of communicating its annual warning to faculty, staff, and students about the appropriate procedures to take if severe weather strikes. Spring in the Midwest brings the risk of violent storms that can include tornadoes. Some of the news footage that follows from these storms can be quite upsetting. I can still remember watching news images of the monstrous tornado that slammed into Joplin, Missouri in May 2011. And who can forget the unbelievable news reports on September 11, 2001 when the world watched replay after replay of jumbo jets crashing into the twin trade towers of the World Trade Center? Even if you were back in grade school on that fateful day, you probably still remember something of that event. There's little question that events such as these are profoundly disturbing and people who experienced them first-hand went through life-changing emotional turmoil that will affect them for years to come. What about those of us who didn't experience these events first-hand in real life? Instead, we watched a steady stream of televised images. Does exposure to this type of news coverage threaten the emotional well-being of those who watch? Perhaps at some point during the coverage of one of these events, you may have heard someone give voice to the position that so much exposure to traumatic news might not be such a good thing. As a news junkie myself, I'll never forget when my youngest daughter, Jordan, who was 16 years old at the time, came over to me as I sat spellbound late into the evening watching the TV coverage of the 9-11 terrorist attacks. She gently put her hand on my shoulder and said, "Dad, why don't you turn it off now? It doesn't do any good to just keep watching it over and over." I sensed that she was right and I wondered whether any researchers would become motivated to study this question scientifically. I didn't have to wonder for very long.

Four researchers, Jennifer Ahern, Sandro Galea, Heidi Resnick, and David Vlahov wanted to investigate the possibility that people who watched the most news coverage after the attacks on 9-11 may have also been more likely to suffer from post-traumatic stress disorder. They decided to conduct a survey of people who lived closest to the disaster—citizens of New York City.[7]

**The Sample** In January and February of 2002, the researchers used a random-digit dialing technique to call the residents of New York City. If they reached a household, they requested an interview with the person at home who had most recently celebrated their birthday (an unbiased way of selecting one person from the residence). The final sample of the study included 2,011 respondents. The researchers noted that the demographic characteristics of their final sample matched closely the characteristics of residents of New York City according to the U.S. Census Bureau. The fact that their sample was selected randomly enabled the researchers to generalize their findings to the larger population of New York City. Strictly speaking, it permitted them to generalize to the population who had telephones. To their credit, the researchers recognized that because the events of 9-11 actually took place in New York City, the people in their sample might have reacted differently compared with a sample of people from some other geographical part of the country. They urged readers to be aware of this possible limitation in extrapolating the results to others.

**The Questionnaire** The questionnaire itself took about 35 minutes to complete and included a number of demographic questions (e.g., age, sex, race, marital status, education level, etc.) and questions about past experiences that were traumatic in nature. People were also asked about how many times they had seen certain specific scenes from the 9-11 events on television during the seven-day period after the attacks. They were also asked questions from a standard measure of post-traumatic stress that enabled the researchers to categorize each person according to their probable post-traumatic stress level after the 9-11 events.

**Descriptive Findings** One of the chief advantages of a sample survey is that the researcher can often generate a brief statistical summary that provides a descriptive glimpse of the phenomenon under investigation. This descriptive glimpse may reveal things that no amount of speculation could ever produce. For example, in this case the results revealed that televised images of the catastrophe were viewed very frequently in the seven days following the attacks. The most frequently viewed image was of one of the planes hitting the building. On average, the respondents reported seeing that footage about 41 times. That was followed by images of the buildings collapsing or people running from clouds of smoke (an average of about 37 times), and by people jumping from the buildings (an average of about 12 times).

**Statistical Relationships** When the researchers examined the relationship between the reports of TV viewing and the scores on the measure of post-traumatic stress, an interesting finding emerged. People who reported the lowest levels of TV exposure to the 9-11 events were the least likely to have scores indicating a high probability of post-traumatic stress. The scores that indicated the highest probability of post-traumatic stress tended to be observed for those people who reported the highest levels of TV exposure to the attacks. In fact, the researchers were able to draw the following statistical conclusion: Viewers who were in the top third of the sample on TV exposure to the attacks were almost 2.5 times more likely to suffer from post-traumatic stress than viewers who were in the bottom third of the sample on TV exposure. There seems to be little question about the fact that a relationship exists between TV exposure and post-traumatic stress for this sample of respondents.

**Interpretation of the Findings** The researchers concluded that based on their findings, it appears quite possible that people might suffer from higher stress levels as a result of heavy exposure to TV coverage of traumatic events. They recommended that more research be done on this possibility and that scholars devote more attention to this general phenomenon. As it turns out, when my daughter encouraged me to stop watching the TV coverage of the 9-11 events, her instincts about the effects of that coverage may have been correct. But notice in that last sentence, I wrote that her instincts *may* have been correct. Based on this study, can't we say for certain? There are some other possible interpretations of the study's results that the authors discussed. You will read about those later in this chapter. In the final analysis, it is difficult to be sure about whether media exposure causes people to react in some particular way when our only evidence is based on a survey study.

## Types of Surveys

The survey conducted by Ahern and her colleagues on TV exposure to the events of 9-11 is one of the most common types of survey reported in social science research. It was a survey of a single sample of a population. This kind of survey is commonly referred to as a **cross-sectional survey**. The distinguishing characteristic of a cross-sectional survey is that it occurs at a single point in time and involves a single sample. Often, researchers are not satisfied with a single sample. They have research questions that cannot be answered unless a separate questionnaire is administered at more than one point in time. When a researcher designs a survey project that includes more than one sample taken at different points in time, the survey design is referred to as longitudinal. There are three kinds of **longitudinal survey** designs.

The first type of longitudinal design is a **trend study**. About eight years ago, I became especially interested in the possible changes that were taking place among college students in their use of new technology. I decided to begin surveying a small group from each freshman class. Before the project ended, I had data from the freshman classes of 2006 through 2009. You probably won't be surprised to learn that over those four years, the data suggest that students spent more time each year engaged in text messaging and Facebook. Notice that in a trend study, the individuals who are surveyed the first time are not the same individuals who are surveyed the second time. The only similarity between the four groups I surveyed is that everyone was a member of a freshman class (but a different freshman class) at the time of the survey.

A second type of longitudinal survey is a **cohort study**. Suppose I became interested in any change in the use of new technology among students who were in the freshman class of 2006. Instead of continuing to survey freshmen from each year's entering class, I might choose another sample of individuals who were sophomores in 2007, juniors in 2008, or seniors in 2009. Samples of students from these classes would be members of the same **age cohort** as the freshmen from the entering class of 2006. But they wouldn't be the same students. Perhaps you have seen news reports on how the attitudes of the post-World War II baby boomers have changed as they have grown older. These changes are typically detected with a cohort design. If people between the ages of 40 and 50 were surveyed in 2005, then people between the ages of 50 and 60 would be surveyed in 2015. The cohort survey allows the researcher to assess changes in a general cohort group—but not in the same individuals.

The final type of longitudinal survey design is a **panel study**. If I wanted to see how use of new technology changed in exactly the same individuals, then I would use a panel design. Long-term panel designs are relatively rare because of the time and effort involved in keeping track of the same individuals over time. In Chapter 5 on media violence, you will learn about a long-term panel study that followed young children into their adult years. Although such studies are rare in mass-communication research, the results are usually very important in revealing trends that no other method is capable of detecting. Short-term panel designs are used more frequently. Researchers often design short-term panels during political campaigns to track attitudinal changes that might take place in response to media messages and other political events.

## THE SEARCH FOR CAUSAL RELATIONSHIPS

Before considering the third general method used by researchers in mass communication, it is important to understand that one of the principal goals of doing research on media effects is to explore the possibility that media messages bring about some change in people's thoughts, attitudes, emotions, behaviors, and so on. That is, the researcher is interested in documenting **causal relationships** between media and people. Documenting causal relationships is not nearly as easy as one might suspect. Three general criteria need to be met before a researcher can make the claim that one thing (the media message) is causing another (a change in attitude or behavior, for example).

## Criteria for Causal Relationships

The first thing a researcher needs to establish before making a claim that one thing causes another is that the two things in question are empirically related to each other. Recall the studies mentioned earlier that investigated the relationship between TV viewing and obesity. To document that watching TV *caused* people to become more obese, researchers first needed to establish that these two variables (TV viewing time and level of obesity) were actually related to each other. As it has turned out in several studies, the two variables are empirically related. That is, there was a tendency for the people who spent more time watching TV to also be the people with higher body weights. Researchers need a specific tool to detect an empirical relationship like this one. They can't simply eyeball the data and make a casual declaration that two variables seem to be either related or unrelated. The methods of science are more precise than that. The most common statistical tool used to determine relationships between two variables is the technique of **correlation**.

**Correlation Coefficients** When researchers want to know whether two variables are related to each other, they often apply a statistical formula to the data and compute a **correlation coefficient**. The particular formula for the correlation coefficient is commonly available in introductory statistics texts, and you don't need to be concerned with formulas here. But because of their importance in documenting empirical relationships between variables, it is helpful to know how to interpret correlation coefficients.

Correlation coefficients are computed between two variables. The data in the obesity studies conform nicely to the sort of situation where correlation can be useful. The researchers who published these studies had a measure of two different variables for each person in the sample. If increases in one of the variables tended to go along with increases in the other variable, then the two variables would have a **positive correlation**. This was actually the case in the two obesity studies mentioned earlier. People who had higher TV viewing times tended to weigh more. Sometimes, increases in one of the variables tend to go along with *decreases* in the other variable. When this situation arises, the two variables have a **negative correlation**. Some studies have documented a negative correlation between income level and TV viewing. People who make more money tend to watch less TV. Of course, it is not always the case that the two variables being correlated are related to each other in either a positive or a negative way. In some cases, the two variables might be unrelated. To get a picture of relationships between variables, check out Figure 2-1. This figure displays graphs of five different correlation coefficients.

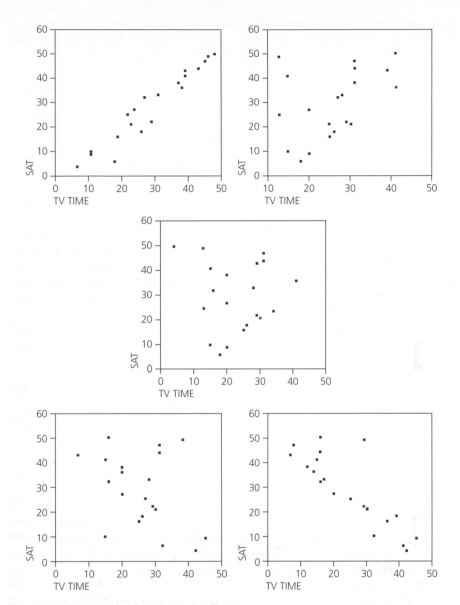

**Figure 2-1 Examples of Correlation Coefficients**
The figure consists of five different scatter plots that illustrate hypothetical relationships between the number of hours that 20 high school students spent watching TV during the week before their Scholastic Achievement Test (SAT) and their SAT scores. Moving from left to right, the two plots on the top show correlation coefficients of .97 and .48, respectively. As TV time increases, SAT scores tend to increase as well. The graph in the middle shows a correlation coefficient of .03 or nearly zero. The variables appear to be unrelated. The bottom two graphs show correlation coefficients of −.38 and −.85, respectively. As TV time increases, SAT scores tend to decrease.

**Interpreting Correlation Coefficients**  When researchers compute correlation coefficients between two variables, the result is a specific number that provides an index of how strongly the variables are related. The formula for the correlation coefficient is designed so that variables that are perfectly related have an index of $+1.0$ (if the relationship is positive) or $-1.0$ (if the relationship is negative). No correlation coefficient can exceed $+1.0$ or $-1.0$. The smallest correlation that could exist between two variables is no relationship at all—indicated by a coefficient of zero (0.0). The statistical symbol for the coefficient is $r$. Typically, then, when correlation coefficients are reported, you might read something like $r = .34$ (if the relationship between the variables is positive) or $r = -.21$ (if the relationship between the variables is negative).

Once a correlation coefficient has been computed (usually by a computer), its meaning must be interpreted. Suppose the correlation between two variables is indicated by $r = .45$. What do we know? Although we know that the two variables have some association, we still don't know how likely it is that this result occurred by chance alone. If the correlation between two variables is very likely to occur by chance, then we wouldn't want to attach too much importance to the particular coefficient that was computed. Fortunately, statisticians have determined how likely it is that correlation coefficients of given magnitudes occur by chance, given samples of various sizes. These probabilities appear in statistical tables and are built right into the computer programs that compute correlation coefficients. Scientists have agreed by consensus to adopt a particular standard for determining a chance occurrence. If a statistical result could happen by chance more than five times in 100, it is generally considered to be a chance finding. If, on the other hand, a statistical result could happen by chance five times in 100 or less, the result is considered unlikely to be due to chance. A statistical result that is unlikely to be due to chance is referred to as a **statistically significant** result. When correlation coefficients are reported in the scientific literature, they usually look something like this: $r = .32, p < .04$. The first part of this expression reports how likely it is that a correlation this large would occur by chance alone. In this case, it would be expected by chance less than four times in 100 and thus would be considered statistically significant.

Although we're talking here about correlation coefficients, the concept of statistical significance is the same regardless of what type of statistical test is being applied. Recall the results from the content analysis on adolescent novels mentioned earlier. In 83% of the substance-use incidents that were coded, no negative or positive consequences were evident. Only 17% of the incidents included any description of positive or negative consequences. The difference in these two percentages was statistically significant. This means that when Coyne and her colleagues compared the two statistics with the appropriate test, the results indicated that a difference this large would only occur by chance less than five times in 100. In this case, the concept of statistical significance was applied to a difference between two percentages—not a correlation coefficient.

Once a researcher determines that a correlation is statistically significant (i.e., unlikely to be due to chance), the first criterion for documenting a causal relationship has been met (see Study Box 2-1 for more detail on interpreting correlation coefficients). The researchers who documented that there was a significant positive correlation between TV viewing and obesity met this first criterion. But recall that there are three criteria for establishing causal relationships. Unless all three are met, the researcher is on faulty ground in declaring a causal relationship between the two variables. Determining that TV viewing and obesity are positively correlated is only the first step.

In the study that showed a relationship between exposure to TV coverage about 9-11 and the tendency to score high on a measure of post-traumatic stress, it might have been tempting to conclude that exposure to TV actually caused post-traumatic stress. But the authors of that study correctly noted that they had only met the first step in establishing a causal relationship. There were other possible interpretations for their data.

The second criterion that must be met to establish a causal relationship is the **time-order** of the two variables. One thing can't cause another thing unless it precedes it in time. A baseball soaring over the center-field fence cannot be the cause of the batter's swing that resulted in the ball's flight. To clearly establish causality, researchers must document the fact that **the variable doing the causing precedes the variable that is caused**.

This second criterion often is more challenging than it first appears. Think about the surveys that documented an empirical relationship between TV viewing and obesity. We learned that people who watch a lot of TV tend to have higher body weights. But do we know from the survey data that TV viewing preceded body weight in the sequence of time? The answer to this question is clearly no. Because all the data in these surveys were collected at the same point in time using a cross-sectional survey design, the researchers have no way of sorting out which variable came first. Could body weight cause TV viewing instead of the reverse? If you think about it, that possibility is perfectly plausible. Perhaps, for whatever reasons, some people weigh more than others. Perhaps these heavier people prefer to lead a more passive lifestyle because exercise is an extra effort that strains the body. In their passivity, they might naturally turn to TV as a form of entertainment more frequently than to physical exercise. The same sort of possibility exists in the study on TV exposure to the events of 9-11 and post-traumatic stress. Perhaps people who were already high on post-traumatic stress were especially likely to be drawn to the TV coverage of a traumatic event. Some scholars have suggested that TV coverage of disasters may actually help people cope with a stressful event by emphasizing that the disaster is being addressed or controlled. It seems plausible then that people who are already high on a measure of stress might actively seek TV coverage of disasters to seek reassurance that everything will be fine. In this case, a cross-sectional survey is simply an inadequate tool for establishing the time-order between the two variables.

One of the advantages of longitudinal surveys is that they can establish the time-order between variables. In Chapter 5 on media violence, you will read about a panel study that found that early viewing of TV violence was significantly correlated with aggressive behavior much later in life. Longitudinal surveys of this type are capable of establishing empirical relationships between two variables as well as establishing the time-order between the variables.

For the sake of our example, let's suppose that the researchers studying TV viewing and obesity had conducted a longitudinal survey and had established that reports of TV viewing in the first survey were significantly correlated with weight gains reported in the second survey. In such a case, both of the first two criteria for

---

**STUDY BOX 2-1 Interpreting Magnitudes of Correlation Coefficients**

Correlation coefficients can range in value from $-1.0$ to $+1.0$. Coefficients are treated as if they were zero (indicating no relationship between the variables), unless the statistical test for significance reveals that the magnitude of the correlation is not likely due to chance. It is important to keep in mind that even in the case of a zero correlation coefficient the variables still could be related in a non-linear fashion. That is, correlation coefficients test only for linear relationships—not for relationships that are non-linear. Imagine a situation where people who watch no TV at all are very high on knowledge of current events, perhaps from reading a lot. In the same scenario, people who watch TV for many hours are also well informed, in this case because they watch many news programs. A third group, with the lowest knowledge of current events, consists of moderate watchers of TV. Although this example is completely hypothetical, it does illustrate a non-linear relationship between TV viewing and knowledge of current events. In such a case, the correlation coefficient would be a poor test of a relationship between the two variables. Fortunately, researchers are able to apply special statistics to cases where variables are related in non-linear ways.

When a statistical test does indicate that a correlation is not likely to be the result of chance ($p < .05$), then it is important to examine the magnitude of the relationship. One statistician, J. P. Guilford,* suggested that correlation coefficients between 0.0 and .20 were very slight and should be viewed as indicating nearly no relationship at all. Coefficients between .20 and .40 should be considered as indicating small but definite relationships. Moderate relationships are indicated by coefficients between .40 and .70. Coefficients above .70 (rare in the social sciences) are considered to be substantial and large.

Another way of judging the size of the relationship between two variables is to simply square ($r^2$) the value of the correlation coefficient. This value, the **coefficient of determination**, provides a statistical indication of how much information or variance in the dependent variable is explained or accounted for by knowing the values of the **independent variable**. For example, if the correlation between TV viewing and obesity was $r = .30$, $p < .05$ you would know that the relationship was not likely due to chance. In addition, you would know that TV viewing was able to account for 9% ($.30^2 = .09$) of the variance in the measure of obesity. In this example, 91% of the variance in obesity would be unexplained by TV viewing. This is a valuable tool to apply because it tells us something about the relative **statistical importance** of the relationship between the two variables.

---

*Guilford, J. P. (1956). *Fundamental statistics in psychology and education* (3rd ed.). New York: McGraw-Hill.

establishing causal relationships would have been met. But this is still not enough evidence to establish the causal claim. There is a final criterion that also needs to be met.

After empirical relationships and time-order have been established, a researcher must also establish that the observed relationship is not due to some unmeasured variable (sometimes called a "third" variable) that is causally related to both of the others. All possible **third-variable explanations** must be eliminated. In the studies on TV viewing and obesity, one plausible third-variable explanation for the relationship might be socioeconomic status. People with low incomes may only be able to afford housing in poor, urban areas. Such areas may not provide many opportunities for recreation and physical exercise. People living in these neighborhoods may perceive that they are in danger when they go outside, so they prefer to stay indoors for their recreation, thus burning fewer calories and gaining more weight. TV viewing is the predominant type of entertainment available indoors, so these folks also watch more TV. In this scenario, low income would be causing both TV viewing and obesity. If a researcher examined TV viewing and obesity without including a measure of income, the empirical relationship might emerge and lead the researcher to think that watching TV causes obesity—but this would be a mistaken conclusion. The true cause of the relationship in this case (low income) would remain hidden.

From the preceding discussion, it might seem impossible to design a study that simultaneously meets all three criteria for establishing a causal relationship. If an unmeasured variable might be responsible for the relationship between two measured variables, then clearly a sample survey (whether cross-sectional or longitudinal) can never provide the definitive evidence needed for a causal relationship. Because no survey can measure every possible variable, there is always a chance that a variable that went unmeasured is precisely the one that explains why two measured variables are related to each other. A good survey design can anticipate some of the obvious variables that might play the role of an explanatory third variable. Once these variables are measured, they can be tested to see if they might be responsible for an observed relationship between two other variables of interest (this was done in Tucker and Bagwell's study on TV and obesity). But no matter how clever the survey design, no survey can measure everything. Consequently, the survey is, in principle, not capable of satisfying all three of the criteria needed to say that one thing causes another.

Where does this leave us? If the sample survey is capable of establishing only two of the three criteria for causal relationships (empirical relationship and time-order), is there an alternative method that might allow us to meet all three criteria simultaneously? The answer to this question leads to the last of the three fundamental methods used to study media effects: the experiment.

## THE EXPERIMENTAL METHOD

Like the survey method, experiments in mass communication gather data directly from people. But unlike the survey, the experiment seeks to gather these data under controlled conditions. If an experiment is carefully executed, a researcher is often able to make a case that all three of the criteria for documenting causal relationships have been met. What are the key ingredients that make this possible?

## Manipulation of a Key Variable

Once an experimenter has identified a variable (usually called the independent variable) that is thought to be a potential cause of another variable (usually called the **dependent variable**), the strategy is to manipulate the independent variable to create more than one experimental condition. The purpose of this manipulation is to be able to observe the impact of various levels of the independent variable on some dependent variable. My daughter has always been concerned about drinking too much diet soda. Her concern stems from reports she has heard from her friends that too much of the sugar substitute in diet soda might cause cancer. We did a little investigating and discovered that researchers have completed many experiments on this topic. In this case, the sugar substitute is the potential causal variable. Consequently, researchers manipulated this variable and created a number of experimental conditions. In one condition of a typical experiment, laboratory animals might be injected with very large doses of the substance over a period of weeks. In a second condition, moderate doses might be administered. A third group of animals might get very light doses. The animals in each of these conditions can then be compared for their incidence of cancer.

## Random Assignment to Experimental Conditions

One crucial feature in experiments is **random assignment** of people (or animals) to experimental conditions. In experiments on the impact of sugar substitutes, laboratory animals are randomly assigned to one of the doses. Why is random assignment so important? The answer to this question should be clear upon thinking about the population of the laboratory animals. Suppose that one of the cages where a group of the animals is housed resides in a corner of the building that contains cancer-causing asbestos. If all the animals in that cage were placed in the same experimental condition, the researchers might erroneously conclude that the experimental treatment was responsible for a higher incidence of cancer in this condition. Or suppose that some of the animals are already developing the early stages of cancer. If those animals are spread evenly across the experimental groups, then researchers can still detect the impact of the sugar substitute. Random assignment to experimental conditions theoretically makes the experimental groups equivalent just prior to their exposure to the experimental manipulation. Consequently, any difference that emerges after the manipulation can be confidently attributed to the manipulation itself.

## Identical Treatment Except for the Manipulation

Random assignment to experimental conditions theoretically makes the experimental groups equivalent at the beginning of the experiment. Random assignment must be followed by identical treatment in all ways except for the **manipulation of the variable**. In the sugar substitute experiment, the animals in all three conditions should have identical diets except for the difference in the dose of sugar substitute. They should be housed in identical cages with equal amounts of light and dark, equal numbers of other animals in their cages, and so on. In short, *anything* that introduces a difference in the experimental conditions, except the manipulated variable, must be avoided. Otherwise, once the experiment is over, the researchers can't be confident that differences in the manipulated variable among the experimental groups caused the dependent variable of interest (in this case, incidence of cancer).

Recall the discussion of the three criteria for establishing causal relationships. Survey designs are capable of meeting two of the three: revealing the presence of a relationship and establishing the time-order of the variables. As we saw, however, the survey design could not eliminate all third variables that might present themselves as possible alternative causes to consider in a given relationship. The experimental method, however, is able to meet all three criteria at once. Consider the experiment on sugar substitutes. If one of the conditions shows a higher incidence of cancer, then a relationship between consumption of the substitute and cancer has been found. That's the first criterion. If the experimental groups were equivalent at the beginning of the experiment, then time-order has also been established. The increased incidence of cancer in one of the groups occurred *after* consumption was manipulated. That's the second criterion. Finally, if the experimental groups were equivalent at the beginning of the experiment and were treated equally throughout the experiment except for the manipulation, then there are no third variables that can offer a rival explanation for how differences in cancer emerged in one of the groups. The experiment theoretically controls all possible third variables that might compete with the manipulation to explain the outcome of the experiment. It is this feature of the experiment that makes it such a valuable tool for investigating questions of media effects.

## Control Groups

To properly assess the impact of a manipulated variable in an experiment, some sort of **control group** is typically used. Suppose that, in the experiment on sugar substitutes, animals in the large-dose group were more likely to develop cancer than animals in the small-dose group. Such a finding might be interpreted to mean that the sugar substitute is dangerous and consumption should be avoided. Notice, however, that the experiment described earlier did not contain a control group that received *no* sugar substitutes. The inclusion of a control group in the experiment might completely change the interpretation of the results. What if, in an experiment that included a no-substitute control group, animals in the control group had the *highest* incidence of cancer? In this case, the interpretation of the results is completely changed. With the inclusion of the control group, it now appears that consumption of any level of the sugar substitute *reduces* the incidence of cancer. Heavy consumption reduces it less than light consumption, but both doses reduce it. These results are completely hypothetical, but they help to illustrate how the inclusion of a control group in an experimental design can often aid the researcher in interpreting the results of an experiment clearly. Before examining a specific example of an experiment designed to investigate a media effect, let's look briefly at some of the possible designs that a researcher might employ.

## Different Experimental Designs

Not every experiment is designed in exactly the same way. Researchers have various choices to make about how they want to set up a study and what they want to measure at which point in the experimental process. The study of experimental designs can get quite complicated; graduate students frequently take semester-long courses in experimental design. Although that sort of in-depth treatment is beyond the scope of this text, it might be useful to get at least some passing insight into the types of choices that experimenters have to make.

Consider the case of a researcher who wants to know whether playing certain types of video games causes a person's heart rate to increase. There are at least two possible ways to set up the experiment. In the first approach, the researcher could have people sit quietly before playing one of several different video games in order to get a baseline heart rate reading. Then, immediately after playing a particular game, heart rate could be measured again. By comparing the first reading with the second across groups of people who were randomly assigned to play different games, the researcher could determine which game caused the greatest increase in heart rate. In this case, because the researcher measures heart rate both *before* and *after* playing the game (the game is the experimental stimulus), the experimental design would be called a **pre-test, post-test** design. If the research added a control group condition in which people played no video game between the two heart rate measurements, it would be a **pre-test, post-test, control group** design. In studies where heart rate is measured, the pre-test, post-test design would be a common approach.

A second approach to this experiment is called the **post-test-only** design. You can probably guess what the difference in this design is just by thinking about its name. In the post-test-only design, the researcher would examine heart rate only once, after the game playing is over. What is the logic of taking this approach? Wouldn't the researcher be losing some valuable information by eliminating the first heart rate readings? Perhaps not. If you think about a carefully designed experiment, once the participants have been randomly assigned to the experimental conditions, the groups of people assigned to play different video games should have, on average, heart rates that are statistically equivalent to those of the other group. Recall that random assignment to conditions should theoretically result in groups that are equivalent on any variable of interest. If the heart rates of the different groups are theoretically equivalent at the start of the experiment, a researcher might not care very much about taking a pre-test measurement. It is true, however, that some information is lost with this type of design. In this case, the researcher wouldn't be able to describe how many average beats per minute a group either increased or decreased as a result of playing the game. But the researcher would still be able to make the crucial comparison that the experiment was intended to make. That is, the researcher would still be able to describe the differences in heart rate between the various groups right after the game playing was over.

Is there any reason that a researcher would deliberately want to pass up the pre-test measure? The answer to this question is yes. Consider the situation where the pre-test measure might be a questionnaire about your attitude toward particular video games. Now imagine that after playing a game, you are asked to complete the same attitude measure that you filled out just before the beginning of the experiment. Instead of reporting your true attitude afterward, you might think about your responses on the first attitude measure and strive to be consistent with your earlier answers. In this case, the pre-test would have sensitized you to the post-test. If that sort of sensitization happens, the whole purpose of the experiment is defeated. Instead of being able to see how the experimental manipulation affected your attitude, the researcher would really be observing how the pre-test measure of attitude affected your response on the post-test. Researchers are often willing to lose a little pre-test information to avoid the risk of ruining the whole experiment.

You can probably see from this discussion that designing good experiments requires plenty of careful thought and analysis. It usually takes several years of training before a researcher is able to consistently make good choices about experimental designs.

## An Example: Using a Video Game to Repair a Bad Mood

One topic that some media researchers have shown interest in over the years is how our media use affects our emotional moods. In fact, a researcher named Dolf Zillmann has proposed an entire theory on this topic known as **mood-management theory**.[8] The theory states that people deliberately use media to alter their moods. For example, suppose you were in a bad mood and you had the chance to play a video game. Would playing the game help to alleviate your negative mood? Recently, Nicholas Bowman and Ron Tamborini attempted to answer this question by conducting an experiment to see whether a person's negative mood could be repaired in a more positive direction as a result of playing with a flight simulator video game.[9] According to the theory, one reason people turn to media to repair a negative mood is because of the "intervention potential" of media use. Put simply, using media can distract a person from their negative mood and cause them to feel better. If this logic is correct, the more involved a person becomes with media, the more their negative mood should dissipate. A closer look at Bowman & Tamborini's experiment on mood management should help you to see how this method works to document media effects.

**Participants** For this study, the authors recruited 172 college students to participate. The participants were both male ($n = 79$) and female ($n = 93$). For their participation, all of the recruits were awarded with extra course credit and the possibility of winning a $100 cash prize in a random drawing. Upon arriving at the laboratory for the study, each participant played the flight simulator game for five minutes just to get familiar with it. Then they were randomly assigned to one of the eight experimental conditions.

**Independent Variable** To test whether playing a video game can improve a person's mood, the researchers first had to know that their participants were in a negative mood before they played the game. Consequently, mood was one of the independent variables in this study. The researchers wanted to see whether playing the video game would improve two different mood states, so they randomly assigned the participants to either a "boredom" condition or a "stress" condition. Those in the boredom condition sat for 20 minutes and did nothing but put metal washers on a string. In the stress condition, participants worked for 20 minutes to solve a series of very difficult logic puzzles under time pressure (45–90 seconds for each puzzle). An experiment provided constant reminders that poor performance or missing answers might jeopardize their ability to participate in the experiment. Following these sessions, participants completed a questionnaire on their mood states and the results showed that this procedure for manipulating moods was effective. Participants in the "boredom" condition were more bored than when they started the session and those in the "stress" condition were more stressed.

A second independent variable in the study was the level of attention that was demanded to the flight simulator. The authors called this the "task demand" variable. After boring or stressing the participants, the experimenter randomly assigned them to play the flight simulator game in one of four different conditions designed to vary the level of attention and involvement required to perform well. In a very low-demand condition, the flight simulator was on autopilot and participants simply watched the flight. In a medium-demand condition, participants actually flew the plane by controlling a joystick, throttle, and rudders. In a high-demand condition, participants flew the plane with all the controls in the medium condition—plus control over an additional five functions such as landing gear and wheel brakes. Finally, the researchers were interested in comparing the mood-repair effectiveness of the computer game with an experience that resembled watching TV. They thought that the autopilot condition might not be exactly like watching TV since there was literally no reason to pay attention to the screen. So, they added another low-demand condition in which participants also saw the autopilot display but were instructed to remember certain features of the game settings in preparation for a test after the game session concluded (the test was never actually administered). Just as with the mood variable, the researchers did an independent check to show that the four task demand conditions were really different in terms of the attention and involvement that they required. They were able to verify that their manipulation was successful. Because of the two different moods and the four different task demand conditions, there were a total of eight different experimental conditions. If you had been one of the participants in the experiment, you would have found yourself randomly assigned to one of these eight conditions.

**Dependent Variable** After playing with the flight simulator for about five minutes, the participants answered questions on a standard measure of mood that has proven to be valid in a number of previous studies. This measure was also used to check boredom and stress levels after those moods had been induced at the beginning of the experiment. The difference in mood after playing the video game was taken to be a measure of mood repair.

**Experimental Results** As the researchers suspected according to mood management theory, the greater the level of involvement of the video game, the less boredom and stress was reported after the game was over—with one exception. The results showed that at the highest level of attention or involvement, moods did not continue to get better. While they still tended to be better than they were before playing the game, they weren't as good as the moods reported by those in the condition of medium attention or involvement. So, at the highest level of attention or involvement, there was drop-off in the repair of bored and stressful moods.

The researchers also thought that, in general, playing the game would improve the moods of the bored participants more than the stressed ones. Their reasoning was that in addition to *distracting* participants from their mood, playing the game would also increase their levels of *arousal*. Since part of the experience of being bored involves feeling very low arousal levels, the researchers reasoned that both the distracting and arousing properties of the game would help the bored participants. In contrast, while the distracting properties of the game should also help the stressed participants, the researchers thought that the arousing properties of the game might tend to perpetuate stress more than reduce it. Their hypothesis was supported. Playing the game resulted in better mood repair for the bored participants than the stressed ones. The difference between the two groups was statistically significant (i.e., the probability that the difference occurred by chance was less than five in 100).

**Interpretation of Results** Research results must always be interpreted. In this case, the authors of the study concluded that the main findings supported the theory of mood management in the context of computer game play. People who were in bad moods generally benefitted from playing a game. The authors were careful to discuss the limitations of their experiment; they pointed out, for example, that they studied only two different negative moods and only used one computer game. They encouraged other researchers to build upon their study.

## CONTROVERSY ABOUT RESEARCH METHODS

This chapter has introduced you to the research methods used in media effects studies. As you read about each of the methods, you may have wondered about the extent to which we should rely on them for our understanding of the effects of the media. For example, perhaps it occurred to you that when people are asked questions on a survey, they might not respond with truthful answers. Or maybe you wondered about whether a carefully controlled laboratory experiment can really tell us very much about behavior that happens in more natural environments—are laboratory experiments too artificial? For years, researchers have debated important questions like these. A full consideration of each potential problem of a particular research method is beyond the scope of this book. If you are interested in these problems, your instructor should be able to point you to additional reading on research methods or even recommend a good course on the topic. Study Box 2-2 provides a brief overview of four types of experimental validity that you can use as an initial checklist for evaluating the validity of any reported findings from an experiment.

## STUDY BOX 2-2 Evaluating the Validity of Any Experiment

Whether an experiment is conducted to determine the effects of a media message or the effects of a drug on some disease, the criteria for evaluating its validity are the same. After reading about an experimental finding, you'd like to know to what extent you should consider the finding to be valid. Years ago, psychologists Richard Petty and Timothy Brock* pointed out that **experimental validity** must be evaluated in four different areas:

1. *Statistical Validity* – In any published experiment, there will usually be at least one comparison between experimental groups that is declared to be statistically significant. The evaluation of the statistical validity of the experiment focuses on the validity of such a declaration. Did the authors use the correct statistical test for their comparison? Did they check to see that their data conformed to all of the assumptions behind those tests? Did they make the correct conclusion about the significance of the result? Usually, if an experiment is published in a reputable journal, the reader will be able to assume the statistical validity of the findings because experts in the field reviewed the article prior to publication. Being able to make an independent judgment about statistical validity requires years of study in statistical techniques so it's fortunate that readers can usually assume safely that the statistical results for a published study are valid.

2. *Internal Validity* – A crucial issue in evaluating any experiment has to do with whether the experimental treatment actually caused the effect that was observed. The informed reader of an experiment will scrutinize the description of the experiment to determine if there were factors internal to the experiment itself—other than the treatment—that could have plausibly accounted for the results. For example, if participants aren't randomly assigned to the experimental groups before the treatment is administered, the groups may be different in some way before the experiment even begins. If that's the case, any difference at the end of the experiment might be due to those initial group differences instead of the treatment. Another source of group differences other than the experimental treatment can creep into the procedures that are carried out while conducting a study. For example, if a male experimenter administers the instructions for the experiment to one of the experimental groups while a female serves the same role for another group, this introduces another difference in the groups that could account for any experimental result. It takes very careful planning for experimenters to guard against all of the potential threats to internal validity.

3. *External Validity* – After any experimental result is reported, the reader will want to know to what extent the results generalize to other people, places, times, or settings. There's no way to know with certainty the answers to these questions without additional research. Some critics of experimentation are fond of observing that results from laboratory studies are "artificial" and can't be generalized to any meaningful situation outside the lab. While this sort of critique highlights the need to do more research to show the generalizability of the findings, it is hardly a devastating critique against experimentation in general. Experiments are not designed primarily to show the generality of findings. Instead, they are designed to show that under some set of specific conditions, one variable can cause another. Once causality has been shown in one condition, more research can be conducted to explore the limitations or generality of the finding.

4. *Construct Validity* – After considering statistical, internal and external validity, readers need to think carefully about whether the variables used in the experiment actually reflect the variables that the researchers think they do. That is to say, the experimental treatment may have caused an effect—but what was it about the treatment that caused the effect to emerge? For example, in Chapter 5, you'll read about a study in which boys who watched media violence behaved less aggressively afterward than boys who watched non-violent programs. The researcher who conducted the study concluded that viewing violence was cathartic or therapeutic, leading to a reduced need for boys to act aggressively after their viewing. But even though the treatment was necessary to cause the effect, the results may have had absolutely nothing to do with whether the programs were violent or not. As it turned out, the key variable may have actually been the extent to which boys *liked* the programs in each condition. The fact that the boys who watched violence behaved less aggressively may have been due simply to the fact that they were watching programs they liked—not because the violence in those programs helped them to drain off their aggressive impulses. The issue of what *construct* (liking vs. violence in this case) the variables in a study may represent is often one of the most interesting aspects of interpreting any experimental result.

*Petty, R. E., & Brock, T. C. (1981). Thought disruption and persuasion: Assessing the validity of attitude change experiments. In R. E. Petty, T. M. Ostrom, & T. C. Brock (Eds.), *Cognitive Responses in Persuasion* (pp. 55–79). Hillsdale, NJ: Erlbaum

In spite of the difficulties with individual research methods, media effects researchers gain confidence in the results of research studies by examining the same research problem in a number of different ways. If a particular finding seems to show up again and again in studies of different types, scientists would refer to this as replicating a research result with convergent evidence. **Replication** refers to the fact that the same result can be observed over and over again. **Convergence** refers to the fact that the use of different methods still leads to the same general conclusion. In the end, researchers are reluctant to declare that they know anything about media effects until they have results from more than one or two studies. This caution helps to protect against accepting research findings that could be the product of unseen biases that can creep into a researcher's work and affect everything from the experimental design to the statistical analyses. Recently, one researcher attempted to assess these sorts of biases and rendered the very discouraging conclusion that, "most claimed research findings are false."[10] If that's true, then replication and convergence are critical parts of the research process. If a finding can't be replicated or only emerges using one type of method, it signals that caution is warranted and it's probably premature to accept the finding as true. Although no single research method is perfect or beyond criticism, careful application of the three methods discussed in this chapter provides a powerful arsenal of tools for learning about the ways that media messages affect people.

## OTHER METHODOLOGICAL APPROACHES

Although content analyses, surveys, and experiments are the major tools of media effects research, two other useful tools are worth mentioning. The first of these is the **epidemiological approach**. This approach is useful for studying the potential impact of media in the natural world. Epidemiological research is often conducted in the medical arena because it is not ethical to do experiments that might cause severe harm. The best example of this might be research on the effects of smoking on the incidence of cancer. Although researchers would never want to set up a study in which some people were randomly assigned to smoke large numbers of cigarettes, they can still study the potential causal link between smoking and cancer by simply observing what happens to people who smoke compared to those who don't. Essentially, then, the epidemiological approach is an observational science. Unlike the experiment, it doesn't seek to manipulate variables. Instead, it seeks to find connections between variables by simply observing what is happening in the world outside the laboratory.

As you might suspect, because epidemiological researchers can't control variables the way experiments do in the laboratory, the interpretation of results must be done very carefully. There are many potential "third variables" that might account for a relationship found in an epidemiological study. For example, maybe smokers also tend to have different diets than non-smokers. Of course, researchers who take the epidemiological approach seek to make simultaneous observations on other variables so that they can rule out these types of explanations for a relationship. When some medical researchers who conduct experiments on laboratory animals discover that tobacco products cause cancer, and others who take the epidemiological approach discover that smokers are more likely to die of cancer than people who don't smoke, the combination of this converging evidence is more convincing than either type of evidence alone.

Similarly, as you will discover in Chapter 5, epidemiological studies have revealed that violence in different societies tends to increase with the introduction of television. When this evidence is combined with evidence from carefully controlled laboratory experiments on the effects of media violence on aggression, we get a much more complete and compelling picture of how media violence might actually cause aggression.

A second useful methodological tool is **meta-analysis**. Unlike the other methods discussed in this chapter, the meta-analysis is a technique that doesn't involve making observations on a sample of people. Instead, this technique relies on studies that have already been completed and uses those studies as the data for a new, overall summary. The key to meta-analysis is the way in which this summary of the existing studies is constructed. The summary is based on a very precise examination of the statistical effects reported in each individual study. The result of this examination is a statistical average over the entire set of studies that is taken to be a more reliable indication of any effect than the results of a single study alone. Of course, just as with any other methodology, certain problems and limitations arise. Some published studies don't contain the statistical details that are needed for the computations. In those cases, if the authors cannot be contacted to provide the missing information, there is no recourse but to drop the study from the overall analysis. Of course, the research community would be in deep trouble if everyone decided to simply do meta-analyses for the rest of their careers. Unless basic surveys and experiments are conducted and reported, the meta-analyst would have nothing to analyze. Still, it is important to recognize that this technique is very valuable for summarizing across a large number of studies and arriving at a conclusion that might not be evident from simply reading over the literature.

## SUMMARY

In this chapter, you have been introduced to three major research methods used by media effects scholars: content analysis, the sample survey, and the experiment. Each method yields valuable information that may be pertinent to documenting a media effect. Content analysis reveals what content the media contain. Surveys can reveal valuable descriptive information as well as important relationships between variables. Surveys are capable of meeting two of the three criteria for causal relationships: documenting the presence of a relationship and documenting time-order.

Relationships between variables are often documented using the technique of correlation. Correlation coefficients can range in value between $-1.0$ and $+1.0$. Coefficients that are unlikely to occur by chance any more than five times in 100 are declared to be statistically significant. Although correlation coefficients can be computed from survey data, and time-order between two variables can often be established, surveys always measure a finite set of variables. Consequently, they are incapable of eliminating all possible third variables that might be responsible for a relationship. The third research method, the experiment, has the advantage of being able to meet all three of the criteria for causal relationships. Taken together, these three research methods constitute an invaluable set of tools for exploring the effects of the mass media. Epidemiological approaches to the study of media effects and meta-analyses can add even further insight to the discoveries made using the other three methods.

## QUESTIONS TO FOCUS YOUR ATTENTION

1. If a researcher wanted to discover how TV networks covered the story about the Malaysian airliner (Flight #370) that went missing in March 2014, what research method should be chosen? Why?
2. If a researcher studied the effects of two different videos by randomly assigning two different classrooms of students to watch one video or the other, what sort of experimental validity might be threatened by this procedure? Why?
3. Since most experiments of media effects are conducted with college students, to what extent do you think the literature suffers from an external validity problem? How should researchers seek to address the problem?

## KEY TERMS AND CONCEPTS

| | | |
|---|---|---|
| content analysis | age cohort | random assignment |
| experiment | panel study | manipulation of the variable |
| coder | causal relationships | control group |
| manifest content | correlation | pre-test, post-test |
| latent content | correlation coefficient | pre-test, post-test, control group |
| random sample | positive correlation | |
| unit of analysis | negative correlation | post-test-only |
| category scheme | statistically significant | mood-management theory |
| coding reliability | time-order | experimental validity |
| sample survey | coefficient of determination | replication |
| cross-sectional survey | independent variable | convergence |
| longitudinal survey | statistical importance | epidemiological approach |
| trend study | third-variable explanations | meta-analysis |
| cohort study | dependent variable | |

## NOTES

1. Berelson, B. (1952). *Content analysis in communication*. Glencoe, IL: Free Press.
2. Coyne, S. M., Callister, M., & Phillips, J. C. (2011). Getting boozy in books: Substance use in adolescent literature. *Health Communication*, 26, 512–515.
3. Primack, B. A., Douglas, E. L., & Kraemer, K. L. (2010). Exposure to cannabis in popular music and cannabis use among adolescents. *Addiction,* 105(3), 515–523.
4. Hu, F. B., Li, T. Y., Colditz, G. A., Willet, W. C., & Manson, J. E. (2003). Television watching and other sedentary behaviors in relation to risk of obesity and type 2 diabetes mellitus in women. *Journal of the American Medical Association,* 289(14), 1785–1791.
5. Tucker, L. A., & Bagwell, M. (1991). Television viewing and obesity in adult females. *American Journal of Public Health,* 81, 908–911.

6. Pardee, P. E., Norman, G. J., Lustig, R. H., Preud'homme, D., & Schwimmer, J. B. (2007). Television and hypertension in obese children. *American Journal of Preventive Medicine,* 33(6), 439–443.

7. Ahern, J., Galea, S., Resnick, H., & Vlahov, D. (2004). Televisions images and probable posttraumatic stress disorder after September 11: The role of background characteristics, event exposures and perievent panic. *The Journal of Nervous and Mental Disease,* 192(3), 217–226.

8. Zillmann, D. (1988). Mood management through communication choices. *American Behavioral Scientist,* 31, 327–340.

9. Bowman, N. D., & Tamborini, R. (2012). Task demand and mood repair: The intervention potential of computer games. *New Media & Society,* 14(8), 1339–1357.

10. Ioannidis, J. P. A. (2005). Why most published research findings are false. *PLoS Medicine,* 2, 696–701.

# 3

# A Brief History of Media Effects Research

During the summer of 2003, a few months after the initial invasion of Iraq by the United States, I was asked to consider writing an essay for a new book about the media coverage of the conflict. Although most of the essays in the book focused on new journalistic techniques applied in the war or new dimensions of the media environment that had never been present in past wars, I (along with my coauthor, Dr. Will Miller) decided to emphasize aspects of the media situation and environment that hadn't changed much.[1] My decision was influenced in part by the results of public opinion polls taken during the initial months of the conflict. In one poll by the Gallup organization, respondents were asked, "Do you favor or oppose the U.S. war with Iraq?" The results of this poll revealed that the percentages of people who either favored or opposed the war remained virtually constant during the entire month of the most intense news coverage of the conflict (March 22 through April 23, 2003). At the war's beginning, 72% of the respondents favored the war and 25% opposed it. One month later, these percentages were 71% and 26%, respectively. During the entire month-long period, opposition remained between 25% and 28%, and support remained between 68% and 72%. Despite hours upon hours of news coverage, special reports, and journalistic accounts broadcast live from the battlefield, public opinion about whether the war was a good thing or a bad thing didn't change much at all.

This stability of public opinion reminded me of the research findings that you'll read about in this chapter, which come from a study conducted back in 1940.[2] When researchers studied the effects of political advertising on attitudes toward the presidential candidates during the 1940 campaign, they found very little evidence that people changed their minds after being exposed to the ads. There have been many occasions like this one when I have been reminded that current research findings often echo findings that have long since found their way into dusty corners of journal stacks in university library basements.

When I started out as a graduate student in mass communication, I never regarded the history of media effects as very interesting or important. Now, however, I recognize that it is important for us to read this past research so that we don't run the risk of "reinventing the wheel"—duplicating research that has already been done. Another reason to understand the history is because it can help us to understand and interpret the present with more clarity than we might have otherwise. The increased understanding that we have can keep us from repeating past mistakes. As you'll learn later in the chapter, at one point in the history of media research, scholars made a premature conclusion that media effects were quite limited. Being able to see how that mistake was made can teach us how to avoid making similar mistakes in the future.

It is also enlightening to see how research interests change over time—or remain remarkably similar—and interact with the technologies that are available. I am now convinced that a solid understanding of any research area must include an understanding of its development over time. As it turns out, the history of media effects research is a fascinating field of study in its own right. An understanding of that history will give you an appreciation of the scholarly tradition reflected in later chapters of this book. The questions that you will raise about the study of media effects will almost certainly be different as a result of knowing some of the history behind the topic.

With that in mind, the rest of this chapter takes you on a quick tour through the history of research on media effects. What follows is not complete in any sense. It will highlight some of the most important moments and provide a basic framework for thinking about past studies on media effects—especially those that occurred before television came into its own. It also provides you with some names and citations that could take you further along the road back into the past, if you ever decide to take that journey in a more leisurely fashion.

## SETTING THE STAGE

In the wake of the tragic shootings at Sandy Hook Elementary School in Connecticut in December 2012, a number of social and political commentators observed that the country would never be quite the same. The incident seemed to crystallize a number of issues that were already on the public agenda (e.g., debate about the easy availability of guns, parental responsibility, social isolation, the effects of violent video games, and incivility). Perhaps years from now, scholars will look back and identify this event as a significant one that helped to shape a particular research agenda in sociology or family studies. Today, in mass communication, scholars have identified a number of early events that seem to have set the stage for public and scholarly concern about the impact of mass media. Although there is no universal agreement about these precipitating events, most would acknowledge that each of the situations outlined below played a role in stirring interest in the study of media effects.

## 1898—Congress Declares War on Spain

Why did Congress declare war on Spain in April 1898? Although a complete answer to this question would require reading through several book-length manuscripts, a common myth that developed pointed to the famous newspaper publisher William Randolph Hearst as a prominent player in the decision to go to war. When Hearst's illustrator, Frederic Remington, wrote him a memo from Havana that there was no trouble and there would be no war, Hearst supposedly responded with the now infamous words, "Please remain. You furnish the pictures and I'll furnish the war."[3] The fact that Congress eventually did declare war may have had something to do with the newspaper coverage in Hearst's *New York Journal;* many believe that Hearst stirred up public opinion in favor of war and helped to provide Congress with a public mandate. In retrospect, most major treatments by historians don't identify Hearst as among the major reasons for war—but the power of the newspaper to influence events was still widely recognized.

## 1917—Propaganda in World War I

President Woodrow Wilson certainly recognized the potential of publishers like Hearst to influence public opinion. He appointed a publisher, George Creel, to lead the **Committee on Public Information**. This committee helped to advise President Wilson on how public relations could be used to influence public opinion about the war. As one scholar in mass communication noted, "It [the Committee on Public Information] engaged in public relations on a scale never before seen, using movies, public speakers, articles in newspapers and magazines, and posters."[4] The use of **wartime propaganda** sensitized the public to the fact that mass media might be used to influence public opinion on a large scale.

## The 1920s—Movies Explode as Mainstream Entertainment

If you ever try to imagine what life was like in the United States over 90 years ago, you probably think of the daily routine then as being very different from your own routine today. Certainly life is different in many respects. In one respect, however, it might be similar. If you go to the movies regularly for your entertainment, you are no different than millions of people who lived in the 1920s. Shearon Lowery and Melvin DeFleur characterize the situation with respect to movies in their book *Milestones in Mass Communication Research:*

> Going to the movies was a frequent event for most families—they were great fun. Also, there were very few alternatives for inexpensive recreation. Homes had neither radios nor television sets. Some had pianos and windup Victrolas; a few even had books. But for the majority of families with limited means, taking in a motion picture was an enjoyable and affordable evening out.... Data on

movie attendance were not systematically gathered before 1922. During that year, some 40 million tickets were sold every week in the United States. By the end of the decade, the figure had more than doubled to 90 million! Among the moviegoers in 1929 were an estimated 40 million minors, and among those were approximately 17 million children under the age of fourteen. (p. 32)[5]

With so many people visiting the cinema every week, it was inevitable that people would begin to think about the effects of movies on attitudes and behaviors. Parents undoubtedly became aware that their children were picking up certain behaviors from the movies they saw on Saturday afternoons. With movies as the primary source of public entertainment, researchers started to become interested in documenting the effects of movies toward the end of the 1920s. Fortunately, the development of social science research techniques converged with the appearance of movies, and researchers were able to launch a series of studies that focused on the effects of film.

## 1929–1932—THE PAYNE FUND STUDIES

In 1928, in response to the growing public concern about the effects of movies on children, a private foundation known as the Payne Fund agreed to fund a series of studies that were conducted by the leading researchers of the time. The purpose of the **Payne Fund studies** was to discover the real impact of movies on children and adolescents. The studies represent the first systematic attempt to discover media impact scientifically. A total of 13 studies were published in 10 volumes on various topics pertaining to the impact of movies. One interesting aspect of these studies is that they introduced many themes that persist in the media effects literature to this day.

### What Was the Content of Movies?

A researcher named Edgar Dale studied the content of 1,500 films made between 1920 and 1930.[6] Although Dale did not have the advantage of today's more sophisticated techniques of content analysis, he did attempt to categorize the films in different groups according to their major themes. Imagine that you were to do such a study on today's movies and had to use the 10 categories that Dale used in 1930. His categories were children, comedy, crime, history, love, mystery, sex, travel, social propaganda, and war. Which categories do you think would see the most use today? It might be interesting to repeat Dale's study with current films to see what changes, if any, have taken place. His results revealed that more than 75% of all the films he studied could be classified using only three of the 10 categories: crime, love, and sex. If this result were released for current films, it probably wouldn't surprise many people. These same themes often provoke controversy in today's entertainment market, yet they remain prominent and readily available to consumers.

## The Emotional Impact of Movies

Of course, the *effects* of movies cannot be gauged just by looking at content. Researchers involved with the Payne Fund studies wanted to collect information about how these themes actually affected viewers. In one line of investigation, children and adults were monitored with physiological electrodes to see how they reacted to romantic or sexy content.[7] One measure that was used in this investigation was **galvanic skin response**. When a person has an emotional reaction to an event, the reaction is often reflected in a sweat response. Perhaps you have discovered that before you are called on to give a speech or visit your professor to talk about your grade, your fingers and palms get sweaty. Because moisture conducts electricity, researchers are able to measure the intensity of the emotional reaction by shooting a small (undetectable) electric current through two electrodes that are typically attached to the inner pads of two fingers. The more moisture coming off the skin, the better the conductivity in the electric circuit. The conductivity can be measured precisely in units called **micromhos**. When the researchers involved with the Payne Fund studies employed this technique, they found that young children were not much affected by romance movies. But older adolescents showed dramatically increased physiological responses. This research foreshadowed two ideas that are clearly present in current research. First, as you will discover in Chapter 7 on media that stir emotions, today's media scholars make important theoretical distinctions between younger and older children in their attempts to predict and explain the effects of media messages. Second, measuring physiological responses to media messages, including skin conductance responses, is an integral technique employed in many current studies of media impact.

## Does Watching Movies Affect Behavior?

One of the key questions addressed in the Payne Fund studies dealt with the impact of movies on actual behavior. Again, this emphasis on the impact of movies seems just as relevant today as it was in the late 1920s when the studies were done. Public discussion about the V-chip and the possible effects of violent video games is just a contemporary version of the same concerns that were voiced 70 years ago. One study that addressed the issue was conducted by a prominent scholar named Herbert Blumer. Blumer collected responses from questionnaires and interviews with children, adolescents, and young adults. In these questionnaires and interviews, the respondents were encouraged to reflect on how exposure to media messages had affected their behavior. Many of the responses indicated that people definitely believed that they had been influenced by the media. For example, one 19-year-old male said:

> In my childhood it was common for one to imitate consciously heroes of the screen. For instance, I would climb the lone tree that was in the yard of the Catholic school near us and hang by one hand or hammer my chest shouting,

"Tarzan" and the like. Jumping over fences on a run as did the heroes of the screen was usual in my young life. Fighting with one another, and after conquering him, placing one foot on his chest and raising our arms to the sky as Tarzan did was also common. (p. 22)[8]

Responses like these were typical in Blumer's study and in retrospect, raise a number of interesting issues. First, the behavior described by the 19-year-old male fits nicely with the **theory of social learning**, which you will encounter in Chapter 5. According to Albert Bandura, the author of this theory, children are more likely to imitate characters who receive rewards for their behavior and are perceived as attractive. Certainly, Tarzan fits the bill.

Second, as appealing as it might be to embrace Blumer's results and take the autobiographical comments at face value, it is important to recognize that his technique would come under criticism today (as it did in the 1930s) as a valid technique for assessing media impact. The technique assumes that people are aware of how media affect them. Although this assumption might be valid in some instances, it turns out to be misguided in many others. There are at least two kinds of problems. One problem is that people may be mistaken about the effects on their own behavior that they attribute to the media. Perhaps the young man in Blumer's study heard some of his friends talking about the impact of the media on children and used this idea to selectively reconstruct his past experiences. Maybe he did engage in the behavior described, but he may have been imitating other friends who were playing with him more than he was copying the actual behaviors on the TV show. A person's own introspection into the causes of behavior may or may not be accurate. Another problem is that by relying on people's own reports about media impact, researchers run the risk of missing effects that occur quite unconsciously. As you will see in later chapters, most of the effects of the media that are well documented in research studies are not ones that people are capable of reporting on a conscious level. People are not necessarily aware when media messages affect their attitudes and behavior. If researchers relied exclusively on introspective reports, they would miss a rich world of significant media impact.

One example that shows the potential problems of relying on self-reports for assessments of media impact comes from the annals of criminal behavior. Ted Bundy was an infamous serial killer who raped and killed women. He was eventually brought to trial and executed. Before his death, he issued a public statement containing his own analysis of his actions. What had caused him to engage in such atrocious behavior? According to Ted, it was the mass media—specifically, exposure to volumes and volumes of pornography. As you will read in Chapter 6, pornography certainly has been studied and associated with antisocial effects. But to what extent should we rely on Ted Bundy's own assessment of what caused his behavior? According to Paul Wilson, former research director at the Australian Institute of Criminology, it probably isn't a good idea to indict pornographic media as the culprit on the basis of Bundy's own self-analysis. Wilson noted:

In Ted Bundy's case, no serious social scientist or law enforcement officer takes the explanation that "pornography made me do it" seriously. Well before Bundy turned the pages of a sexually explicit magazine or watched an adult video he was exhibiting bizarre behavior. Dr. Dorothy Lewis, who conducted multiple interviews with the killer just after his arrest, reported that Bundy was a highly disturbed child at the age of three. When Bundy was first arrested in 1978, early interviews with police and psychiatrists reveal that the killer referred to popular sexually explicit magazines as "normal healthy sexual stimuli."

It was only in the 1980s, when a court refused to certify him insane and to save him from the electric chair, that Bundy became a born-again Christian and reiterated the party line on pornography. (p. 40)[9]

The Bundy case illustrates that in addition to being unaware of media impact on themselves, people may deliberately articulate a view of media effects for personal reasons. In the final analysis, although Blumer's work on the Payne Fund studies was crucial for its time and helped to launch the formal scientific examination of media effects, scholars are reluctant to attach too much weight to the introspective self-reports that Blumer's methodology generated.

## The Aftermath of the Payne Fund Studies

The Payne Fund studies played a huge role in the development of the study of media effects. In terms of the public consciousness, Lowery and DeFleur noted that the con- clusions of the studies helped to establish a **legacy of fear**—widespread beliefs that the media were dangerous and that the effects of media messages might pervert and upset the proper social order.[10] Earlier concerns about propaganda and the role of newspapers in shaping political events helped to reinforce the attitude of public concern following the publication of the Payne Fund studies. Subsequent events in American life only tended to fuel the fire of concern about the pernicious impact of the media. In the end, one thing that inevitably impresses the student of media effects about the Payne Fund studies is how many of the themes and rhetorical tidbits from the 1930s resonate with those of the modern day. For example, Study Box 3-1 high- lights one of the Payne Fund studies about how media can influence the quality of sleep—a topic that is reflected in many current studies on media impact. As Lowery and DeFleur point out in their excellent review of the Payne Fund studies, a summary document of the major findings concluded that "the commercial movies are in an unsavory mess," and "the producers ought to have heart" over their bad influences on children.[11] The current Hollywood film industry has endured many similar attacks that call upon filmmakers to exercise a greater sense of social responsibility.

## THE INVASION FROM MARS

In the late 1930s, the dominant communication medium in America was radio. If there was any doubt about the potential of radio to influence people quickly and in large numbers, those doubts ended on the night of October 30, 1938. On that partic- ular evening, the CBS radio network broadcast a radio drama as part of its *Mercury Theatre on the Air*. A young man by the name of Orson Welles narrated a radio adaptation of *The War of the Worlds*, a science fiction novel written by H. G. Wells.

**STUDY BOX 3-1 Does Your Media Use Affect Your Sleep?**

The National Sleep Foundation reports on their website that teens need about 9-1/4 hours of sleep each night but that only 15% of teens get as much as 8-1/2 hours. Recently, scholars have grown suspicious that one of the factors affecting time spent sleeping and the overall quality of sleep is the constant use of cell phones and other digital devices. One study by psychologist Karla Murdock found a clear relationship between the number of daily texts exchanged by college students and their sleep problems. The next decade promises to see much more research on how media affects sleep. But this is hardly a new area of inquiry.

One of the Payne Fund studies conducted by Samuel Renshaw, Vernon Miller, and Dorothy Marquis, published in 1932, used a sophisticated method for determining the effects of movies on children's sleep. They studied 170 boys and girls and were able to determine that watching movies in the early evening just prior to bedtime contributed to more restless nights of sleep. How were the researchers able to discover this? After children attended movies at their neighborhood theater, the researchers were able to arrange for them to sleep in beds that were attached to a device called a hypnograph. This device recorded a mark on a paper strip each time the child moved during the night. The research team determined that normally, children between the ages of six and 18 years changed their sleep position once every 8.7 minutes. After watching movies just prior to sleep, boys increased their sleep position changes by 26% and girls increased theirs by 14%. This effect persisted for several nights after seeing the movie. The researchers warned parents that motion pictures before bedtime inhibited sleep to the same extent as drinking two cups of caffeinated coffee.

SOURCES: (1) National Sleep Foundation. (2014). [Online: Accessed 3-21-14]. Available: http://sleepfoundation.org/sleep-topics/teens-and-sleep, Charters, W.W. (1933). (2) Murdock, K. K. (2013). Texting while stressed: Implications for students' burnout, sleep and well-being. *Psychology of Popular Media Culture*, 2(4), 207–221. (3) Kellogg, A. (1933). *Minds Made by the Movies*. [Online: Accessed 3-21-14]. Available: http://web.viu.ca/davies/H322%20Between%20the%20Wars/MindsMadeByTheMovies.1933.htm (4) *Motion Pictures and Youth: A Summary*. New York: Macmillan. [Online: Accessed 3-21-14]. Available: http://archive.org/stream/motionpicturesyo00charrich/motionpicturesyo00charrich_djvu.txt

An estimated audience of about 6 million listeners tuned in. Of all the programs that the producers at CBS might have thought would have an impact on the audience, *The War of the Worlds* was not one of them. In an article written for *Harper's* by John Houseman, one of the cofounders of *The Mercury Theatre on the Air* along with Orson Welles, we learn that virtually no one thought that this production was going to be anything special. In the week preceding the broadcast, the production crew even contemplated scrapping the whole idea.[12] But they didn't. The show went on as planned—and stirred the public as nothing before it ever had.

The premise of the show was simple. Listeners would be lulled into a sense of relaxation and even boredom as the show began with classical music. Then, a radio announcer would interrupt and refer to an atmospheric disturbance that had been reported over Nova Scotia. Listeners would then be returned to the light music until the announcer interrupted again. Over the course of the one-hour program, what started as an atmospheric disturbance turned into an alien invasion by Martians who had landed their invading craft in Grover's Mill, New Jersey. In retrospect, one would think that the discerning listener would easily recognize that the reported events were nothing more than a fictional drama. But the realistic format of cutting away from the music to feature what sounded like live news reports apparently fooled about one million people in the show's audience.

In some cases, random events helped to promote the illusion of reality. In the town of Concrete, Washington, an unrelated power failure occurred while the radio announcer was informing Americans that the Martians were disrupting power and communications across the country. Needless to say, the residents of Concrete didn't need any more reason to believe the broadcast was true. But even without such events, people up and down the eastern seaboard panicked. CBS eventually apologized to the public for its miscalculation. The morning after the broadcast, a bewildered Orson Welles was shown fielding questions about the incident from a crowd of reporters that must have seemed to him like an attack mob. Welles was still trying to figure out exactly what had happened.


## The Research at Princeton

Orson Welles was not the only one who wondered what had happened on that October night. A research team at Princeton University led by Hadley Cantril did a quick postmortem of the whole affair in a study that included an analysis of newspaper accounts of the incident as well as data from surveys and personal interviews.[13] Lowery and DeFleur summarized the findings of the research.[14] As for why so many listeners found the show believable, the Princeton research team cited the fact that most Americans had tremendous confidence in radio as a news medium. They never expected that their most trusted medium would be involved with a hoax. They noted, too, that the show used the brilliant creative technique of on-the-spot reporting and sounded convincing in introducing various scientific experts to the public. Also contributing to the panic was the fact that many listeners missed the announcement at the beginning of the show that the program was a dramatic adaptation.

The Princeton research also focused on the characteristics of people who believed the program was real. According to the results, these were people who had less critical ability, less self-confidence, and less emotional security than those who recognized that the program was only a dramatization. People with strong religious beliefs were also more likely than others to believe that Earth was being invaded by Martians. These results may not be particularly surprising, and they didn't exactly startle the scholarly community. But the broadcast and the subsequent research were important in the history of media effects. The broadcast itself demonstrated that the media could trigger widespread, intense responses in the audience. The research pointed the way to future studies that would employ a variety of personality and demographic variables to predict media impact. In terms of the legacy of fear, *The War of the Worlds* broadcast did little to dispel the notion that media messages were potentially dangerous for society. As the 1940s began, this assumption was widespread.

## EARLY THEORY OF MEDIA EFFECTS: THE MAGIC BULLET MODEL

In the wake of the Payne Fund studies and Cantril's study of *The War of the Worlds* broadcast, the view among scholars was that the mass media were indeed powerful agents for change and influence. The studies that were done were typical of investigations in a new area of research. They were essentially exploratory studies that attempted to discover any new information. The studies were not characterized by well-developed theory and the testing of specific hypotheses.

Contemporary scholars often look back on this early period of media effects history and see a general theoretical view that seemed to prevail, even though it wasn't stated formally. This view has come to be known as the **magic bullet model** or the **hypodermic needle model of mass communication**. According to this view, the communication of a message in a mass medium can be compared to shooting a gun that contains a magic bullet or to injecting someone with a hypodermic needle. Once the message reaches the audience, it will exert powerful, relatively uniform effects on everyone who processes it. It would probably be difficult to find a single scholar in 1940 who articulated this particular view of media impact. It seems too extreme and simplistic. Nevertheless, it does capture something of the general outlook that many scholars held at the time regarding the media's tremendous power.

Part of the explanation for this outlook had to do with the psychology of the time, with its emphasis on the uniform physiological mechanisms common to all human beings. Little consideration was given to the possibility that people might respond differently to the same message. The theoretical framework that allowed for individual differences in responding was not yet in place. The public tended to concur with the view of great media impact. The Orson Welles affair was still fresh in their minds, and the public debate about movies in the aftermath of the Payne Fund studies had resulted in an attitude of self-censorship on the part of Hollywood that only served to highlight the power of movies.[15]

The convergence between the scholarly and public views of media impact, though, was about to change. In 1940, a team of researchers from Columbia University undertook an exhaustive study of the role of radio messages on voter behavior in the presidential election. Their results significantly impacted how scholars came to think about the theoretical underpinnings of media effects. More than any other study up to that point, *The People's Choice* advanced the study of media effects both theoretically and methodologically.

## THE PEOPLE'S CHOICE STUDY: A NEW VIEW OF MEDIA EFFECTS

The 1940 presidential election was between Wendell Willkie, the Republican, and the Democratic incumbent, Franklin D. Roosevelt. As the two candidates prepared to do battle at the polls, a team of researchers from Columbia University, Paul Lazarsfeld,

Bernard Berelson, and Hazel Gaudet, set out to study "how and why people decided to vote as they did." The study took place in Erie County, Ohio, using a sample based on visitations to every fourth house in the county. The researchers decided to employ a longitudinal panel study design (see Chapter 2). That is, they followed a main panel of 600 people throughout the campaign and interviewed them repeatedly (seven times). One of the methodological innovations of this ambitious study was the use of large **control groups** of 600 respondents each.

## Why Use Control Groups?

On reflection, it is easy to see why control groups were used. Imagine that you were one of the 600 people selected for repeated interviewing during the campaign. The fact that you knew ahead of time that you were likely to be interviewed again about your voting preferences and behavior might cause you to modify your behavior or your answers in the next round of questions. That is, the panel design itself might have an effect on the data collected—an effect quite separate from the responses that people might make if they were untarnished by the repeated interviews. To determine if this was actually happening, when the researchers went back to the main panel of 600 people to interview them for a third time, they also interviewed a separate group of 600 people for the first time. Theoretically, if interviewing the main panel three times had no impact on their responses, there would be no difference between them and the control group of 600 people that had been interviewed for the first time. The researchers selected another control group of 600 people to interview when the main panel was interviewed for the fourth time. They repeated this procedure on the sixth interview. In general, the main finding from this procedure was that the responses of the control groups did not differ significantly from the responses of the main panel. This was an important finding. It indicated that the longitudinal panel design was a viable method for studying change. Concerns that multiple interviews would alter the nature of people's responses proved to be unfounded in this case. The longitudinal survey design is still an important technique in research today.

## Media Impact in the 1940 Campaign

One of the surprising results of *The People's Choice* study was that the impact of media exposure to campaign messages was rather negligible in terms of **conversion**—changing voters from an intention to vote for one candidate to an intention to vote for the other. A more significant effect of media exposure was **reinforcement**—assuring voters that their current intention was worthwhile and correct. The data showed that half of the voters had already decided for whom they were going to vote by the time of the first survey. It was important that media messages over the coming months keep these people in the fold. Although the effect of reinforcement doesn't appear in the data as a great change, it is nonetheless an important media effect.

In today's modern age of computing technology, it is a little tough to appreciate the monumental task that faced the researchers from Columbia after they had gathered their data. They had no personal computers on their desktops. There was no large mainframe computer at Columbia that could be called on for number crunching. It is little wonder, then, that it took the researchers nearly eight years to synthesize their data and bring it to publication. Consequently, the theoretical impact of *The People's Choice* study did not appear to take hold until the end of the 1940s or the beginning of the 1950s. Combined with several other significant studies of media impact in the 1950s,[16] *The People's Choice* served to usher in a new perspective on media impact. Far from the view that media effects were powerful and comparable to a magic bullet, the newer research seemed to indicate that the media had only limited effects.

## THE DECATUR STUDY: THE TWO-STEP FLOW OF COMMUNICATION

One idea that the authors of *The People's Choice* developed and discussed in that volume was the idea that media impact might not be as direct as scholars had presumed. Perhaps the media didn't really affect most people directly at all. Instead, perhaps their impact was limited to a few key people—opinion leaders—who, in turn, influenced others through face-to-face interpersonal communication. This idea was referred to as the **two-step flow**. After developing an extensive research plan to investigate the possibility of a two-step flow, Paul Lazarsfeld, working at the new Bureau of Applied Social Research at Columbia University, began a large-scale collection of data in 1945 in Decatur, Illinois. The results of the study weren't published until 10 years later but they interpreted the findings as conclusive support for the notion that media influence often went through key individuals and involved personal communication. Their book, which included the Decatur Study, *Personal Influence: The Part Played by People in the Flow of Mass Communication,* is still considered to be a classic in the history of mass communication.[17]

The Decatur Study employed a sample of about 800 randomly selected women who were at least 16 years old.[18] Extensive interviews were conducted on each of two different occasions with each woman in an effort to determine who they talked with about various topics. The goal was to analyze the interview data to see whether or not influence could be traced from one person to the next. Opinion leaders were identified from these interviews and conclusions were drawn about how information from media sources may have found their way from the opinion leaders to others. From a methodological standpoint, the Decatur Study was certainly not a masterpiece. Some of the methodological details were fuzzy. For example, it isn't clear exactly how many women were interviewed on each of the first and second interviews. The identification of opinion leaders also seemed imprecise. One technique used was to simply ask the women if they had influenced other people. To their credit, if a woman reported that she had influenced someone else on a given topic, the researchers attempted to verify that influence by asking for that person's contact information. They attempted to follow up on those contacts to confirm that a conversation had actually taken place. Unfortunately, many of the presumed contacts that the researchers were able to reach couldn't remember talking to the self-identified "opinion leader." One researcher summarized this aspect of the Decatur Study as follows:

> The Decatur investigators reported that two-thirds of the designations (69% of those designated as influentials and 64% of those nominated as influencees) were confirmed. Raising the question of the "trustworthiness" of the confirmations, they pointed out: "There are no set standards; there are not even other studies with which the present one might be compared." (Katz and Lazarsfeld, 1955: 154)[19]

Despite the fact that the Decatur Study suffered from some ambiguities and imprecision (see Study Box 3-2), it was still noteworthy in helping to introduce the notion that media influence was more complex than the direct effect of messages on receivers. That influence could be multiplied through indirect, interpersonal channels. I received a personal reminder of this important fact just recently. As I finished up a meal at a local restaurant, I received a text message from a friend asking me to phone him. When I did, he proceeded to deliver the upsetting news that he had just

---

### STUDY BOX 3-2 The Decatur Study: Colorful Research Personalities

The book *Personal Influence* was published in 1955 but the data it reported was collected a decade earlier. Why did it take so long? As it turns out, the study might never have been published had it not been for the "task-master" personality of Paul Lazarsfeld at the Bureau of Applied Social Research at Columbia University. Lazarsfeld designed the study and brought another upstart sociologist, C. Wright Mills, from Texas to Columbia to take over the data collection and analysis. Mills and Lazarsfeld ended up clashing over how to analyze the massive data set that was collected in the summer of 1945. Mills was not exactly a statistical wizard and gradually lost interest in the project. Lazarsfeld fired him and the project languished with little progress until a graduate student, Elihu Katz, was able to make progress on the data analysis according to Lazarsfeld's wishes. Lazarsfeld's ambition wasn't the only source of pressure to publish *something* after all of the effort collecting the data. In order to fund the study, Lazarsfeld had secured money from an unlikely source—a publisher, Bernarr McFadden. McFadden was a champion of health food and body building and published *True Stories*, a woman's magazine that focused on romance and true confessions. McFadden thought that the results of the Decatur Study would be of interest to his advertisers so he helped to support Lazarsfeld's effort. It was a strange alliance. In the final analysis, *Personal Influence* may have involved more researchers, interviewers, data analysts, and colorful personalities than any study in the history of mass communication.

**SOURCE:** Balas, J., Balas, G., & Simonson, P. (2007). *The Long Road to Decatur: A History of Personal Influence.* Department of Communication, University of New Mexico. Documentary Film. [Online: Accessed 3-21-14]. Available: http://www.youtube.com/watch?v=SU3vBgvmHOk

heard on TV: One of Purdue's basketball players had just been suspended from the NCAA basketball tournament for conduct that was detrimental to the team. I immediately relayed the news to my family members who were with me (all Purdue fans) and we had a variety of emotional reactions and subsequent conversations. In this case, one might say that my friend was an opinion leader who first received the media message and relayed it on to me. But from that point, the effect of the message was multiplied through interpersonal conversation.

## Experiments on World War II Movies

During the years when the researchers were preparing their data from *The People's Choice* study for publication, the United States was involved in World War II. One of the weapons that Germany took very seriously as part of its arsenal was propaganda in the form of movies. During the war years, the Germans produced hundreds of films that were seen regularly in movie theaters and were designed to convince people that the German war machine was invincible and that Germany's occupation of the countries of Europe was a great thing for the people of those countries.

The U.S. government took notice of how effectively the Germans were using film and, in response, called on Hollywood to fight back. Specifically, they asked director Frank Capra, maker of such film classics as *It Happened One Night*, *It's a Wonderful Life*, and *Mr. Smith Goes to Washington*, to make movies that would convince audiences that the German empire was evil and that the United States needed to achieve ultimate victory in the war. At first, Capra was overwhelmed by his task. But after studying the German films, he decided that he could effectively use the film footage that the Germans had used in their movies and turn it against them. Capra actually shot very little new film footage. This allowed him to make seven films in a short period of time. These films, which are now known as the *Why We Fight* film series, were shown to thousands of people during the war years— particularly to military recruits, who saw these movies as part of their standard initiation and training.

If you have never seen any of these movies, it might be worth your while to try to obtain a copy of either *Prelude to War* or *The Battle of Britain*. Even after 65 years, you can still appreciate the masterful job of filmmaking that Frank Capra achieved in putting these movies together. One day, after I had shown *The Battle of Britain* to one of my media classes, an exchange student from England, whose grandfather had fought in the battle, approached me as I was leaving class. Tears filled her eyes as she thanked me for showing this movie. She told me that until she saw the film, her grandfather's war stories had always seemed distant and unreal. The movie images brought those stories to life for her, and she told me that she left that class feeling as though she had captured an important part of her family history. It was an emotional moment.

After Capra made these movies, the U.S. government hoped that everyone who saw them would have the sort of emotional response that my student reported. More specifically, the government hoped that these movies would improve people's understanding of the facts of the war, and would change their opinions and interpretation so that they would adopt a position favorable to the United States, improve attitudes toward the Allied forces, and motivate the soldiers to fight a tough war. How could the government find out for certain if the films were really effective in bringing about these results?

From your reading in Chapter 2, you might recognize that the experimental method would be a good way to test the effects of these movies. The government assembled a team of researchers to do the experiments, and these studies are noteworthy as the first sophisticated set of experiments in media history. The results were summarized in a book published just one year after *The People's Choice* and were called *Experiments on Mass Communication*.[20] What did these experiments find? Were the movies effective? Unfortunately for the U.S. military leaders who were hoping to see evidence of profound effects, the actual evidence was somewhat disappointing. Although the movies were definitely educational and increased people's factual knowledge about the war, there was very little evidence that they changed the essential motivation of the soldiers who were fighting the war. Of course, some argued that what these studies really showed was a **ceiling effect**. The levels of motivation of most of the soldiers who saw the movies may already have been about as high as they could go—they had "hit the ceiling." After all, prior to their military service, many of the recruits had probably seen portions of the movies in newsreels that were presented at the nation's movie theaters. Perhaps the films had already had their intended effect, and the soldiers' levels of motivation couldn't go any higher. Although this was one possibility, the relatively meager effects observed in these experiments tended to reinforce the view of limited media effects that emerged after the publication of *The People's Choice*.

Carl Hovland, the main author of the book that summarized the experiments on the *Why We Fight* movies, went on to conduct numerous communication experiments at Yale University during the 1950s that focused primarily on how messages might change attitudes and behavior. Although many of these experiments did not directly test the effects of media messages, this tradition of experimental research had a significant impact on media effects studies by encouraging researchers to use the techniques of the carefully controlled experimental approach. Despite the fact that some of these experiments showed that communication variables had a great impact on attitude change, the prevailing evidence about media effects in the early 1950s was still in favor of the limited-effects model.

## The Limited-Effects Perspective

One of the chief spokespersons for the new **limited-effects perspective** was a communication consultant who worked for the General Electric Company, Joseph Klapper. In 1958, Klapper published a book that had wide influence. It argued that the effects of the mass media ranged from small to negligible.[21] Klapper's position is captured in remarks that he made as part of a program on mass media presented in New York City by the Child Study Association of America on March 21, 1960. He said:

> I think it has been pretty well demonstrated that the mass media do not serve as the primary determinant or even as a very important determinant of any of the basic attitudes or the basic behavior patterns of either children or adults. This is not to say that they have no influence at all, but only that their influence seems to be incidental to other forces; or if it is not incidental, to pertain to rather superficial aspects of attitude or behavior rather than to basic attitudes and behavior. (p. 48f)[22]

Ironically, Klapper's comments about the minimal influence of the media came just when scholars were starting to explore the impact of the new medium that had virtually exploded on the scene in the 1950s: television. Just as the limited-effects perspective was starting to take hold in the scholarly community, a new wave of research would call this perspective into question. As it turned out, the advent of the limited-effects model of mass communication is a good example of how theories about social phenomena can change as society changes. In an era of relatively high political stability, strong party identification, and straight-ticket voting, it isn't surprising that the Columbia researchers found that radio messages didn't change many votes. Today, however, political scientists work with a concept called **voter volatility**. The political system is more unstable. There are fewer people who identify strongly with a single party, more people who call themselves independents, and more people splitting their ticket at the polls. In such a volatile climate, scholars expect that the media might have more impact on the political process than they did in the 1940s. One principle to emerge from the limited-effects perspective that remains important today is the notion of **selective exposure to communication**. According to this idea, people are motivated to expose themselves voluntarily to messages with which they already agree. Likewise, they will tend to avoid messages that they find disagreeable. Study Box 3-3 focuses on this principle and discusses some of the research over the years that supports the principle. The statistics that I mentioned at the beginning of this chapter from the Gallup poll taken shortly after the U.S. invasion of Iraq are consistent with the principle of selective exposure. If people simply watch the things with which they already agree, then we shouldn't expect many attitudes to change over time.

## THE EVILS OF COMIC BOOKS

During the 1950s, the public's view of media effects probably didn't change very much from the one reflected by the phrase "legacy of fear." One reason that public attitudes didn't change was because of the research of Frederic Wertham, a famous psychiatrist. Wertham took his case right to the people in the form of articles in popular magazines like *Collier's* and *Ladies' Home Journal*. His book *Seduction of the Innocent*[23] was a virtual diatribe against the evils of comic books. (If you are lucky

## STUDY BOX 3-3 The Principle of Selective Exposure to Communication

In an amazing interview captured on videotape (Episode 9 of *A Walk through the 20th Century with Bill Moyers*), the well-known journalist Bill Moyers interviewed Fritz Hippler, one of the men who helped produce Nazi propaganda films during World War II. As Moyers listened attentively, Hippler explained that the Germans had discovered an important principle of mass propaganda: **People only want to see things that they find to be agreeable.** The Germans capitalized on the principle by showing the mass audiences images of military might, but never focusing on the problems associated with warfare. They were busy practicing a powerful principle of communication even before that principle had been formally uncovered in the annals of communication research.

Today, the principle of selective exposure is so well known and well documented that in 1985, Dolf Zillmann and Jennings Bryant edited an entire book on the subject, *Selective Exposure to Communication.* Their volume contains overviews of how the dynamic of selective exposure enters into the mass-communication process at multiple points. People are motivated to expose themselves to messages with which they already agree or to messages that make them feel good. Similarly, they are motivated to avoid messages that they find disagreeable or messages that make them feel bad.

One interesting line of research on selective exposure reported in the volume by Zillmann and Bryant is described by Jacob Wakshlag. Wakshlag reports how the principle of selective exposure should inform the work of TV producers who work on educational TV programs. In a study with first- and second-grade children, Wakshlag and his colleagues made different versions of an educational TV program available on different channels. The children were free to watch whichever channel they wished for as long as they wished. They were also free to turn off the TV. The researchers discovered that the children strongly preferred to watch the educational programs that contained humorous content. Wakshlag summarized the implications of this research in the following way:

> [T]he findings suggest that non-entertaining educational television programs are not likely to compete very well with other educational programs, such as *Sesame Street*, which contain humor and other embellishments. Furthermore, when faced with programs whose principal function is entertainment, such as those typically available from the networks, non-entertaining educational programs would probably fare even worse. (p. 194)

In today's competitive media environment, programmers would undoubtedly do well to consider carefully the wisdom of media effects research on this point of selective exposure. In general, audiences will not voluntarily expose themselves to messages that they find to be unpleasant.

---

**SOURCES:** (1) Wakshlag, J. (1985) Selective exposure to educational television. In D. Zillmann & J. Bryant (Eds.), *Selective exposure to communication* (pp. 191–201). Hillsdale, NJ: Erlbaum. (2) World War II: The propaganda battle. *A walk through the 20th century with Bill Moyers* (Episode 9). Alexandria, VA: Public Broadcasting Service. (3) Wakshlag, J. J., Day, K. D., & Zillmann, D. (1981). Selective exposure to educational television programs as a function of differently paced humorous inserts. *Journal of Educational Psychology*, 73, 27–32.

enough to find a genuine 1954 edition of this book, it might make sense to buy it. The book is becoming somewhat rare and is highly valued among comic book enthusiasts.) Wertham's research was based on selective analyses of comic book content—not random samples. He tended to highlight the most offensive material and then to characterize the entire comic book industry on the basis of the material he examined. He also studied a variety of young people who had been referred for behavioral difficulty. Wertham was convinced on the basis of his interviews and testing that comic books played an important role in corrupting the behavior of the adolescents he studied. One of the more incredible claims that Wertham made in his analysis of comic books was that the heroes Batman and Robin were homosexual lovers. He wrote:

> Only someone ignorant of the fundamentals of psychiatry and of the psychopathology of sex can fail to realize a subtle atmosphere of homoerotism which pervades the adventures of the mature "Batman" and his young friend "Robin." (pp. 189–190)[24]

Wertham also warned the public about Superman. Apparently, he was concerned about the large "S" that Superman wears on his shirt. According to him, this symbol was uncomfortably close to the famous Nazi "SS." Wertham believed that exposure to the messages of these comic books could corrupt juvenile behavior and lead young people into a life of reckless crime and self-abuse. Many lawmakers and ordinary citizens agreed. On the basis of "research" procedures that were hardly scientific, Wertham managed to convince many people that comic books had powerful effects on young people. His content analysis procedures were not systematic and did not rely on random samples. And the youth on whom he based his conclusions were members of a population that had already been referred for problems of various sorts. They did not represent the larger population of comic readers in any sense.

## THE DAWN OF TELEVISION

As the public became worked up over comic books, a new medium was exploding on the scene. In 1950, only about 10% of American homes had a TV set. Neither the scholarly community nor the public could have imagined how the next 10 years would change the media effects landscape. By the end of the decade of the 1950s, 90% of homes had a TV. From the very beginning, it seemed that something new had started to take place on a regular basis. Reports of imitative crimes, particularly among young people, proliferated. Robert Liebert and Joyce Sprafkin documented some of these crimes in their book about the effects of television on children.[25] One example that they cite from the *New York Journal-American* was reported in the following way:

> [P]olice arrested an 11-year-old who admitted having burglarized Long Island homes for more than $1,000 in cash and valuables. His accomplice was identified as a seven-year-old friend. The boy said he learned the technique of burglary by seeing how it was done on television. (p. 8)

This type of report tended to stir public and government concern. A number of government reports in the mid-1950s and 1960s called attention to the large amount of violence on TV, but the reports also noted that scientific studies that would establish a cause-effect relationship between exposure to violence and aggressive behavior were lacking in the literature.

As the government continued to keep media violence in the spotlight, it also started to make grant money available for scientists who wanted to study the media's impact on human behavior. The 1960s and 1970s were years of new theories and research about media impact. The limited-effects perspective started to give way to a new paradigm based on more sophisticated scientific techniques. Understanding how this sort of change took place teaches us to be cautious about making conclusions too quickly about media effects. Researchers must be sensitive to the changing environment and always entertain the possibility that yesterday's conclusion may not hold up well in today's environment. As the scholarly understanding of media effects moved away from the limited-effects perspective, the laboratory experiment was a critical method that was used repeatedly to study the issues surrounding the impact of media violence. Chapter 5 provides a closer look at that research.

## MANY TYPES OF MEDIA EFFECTS

Today, media scholars understand **media effects** as being more complicated than either the magic bullet or the limited-effects view would imply. Depending on the message, the medium, the audience, and the type of effect focused on, researchers have found the effects of media to be either strong or weak. In one of the classic essays written on media effects, Jack McLeod and Byron Reeves outlined a number of ways to think about media effects.[26] Their analysis reveals that there is no simple answer to the question of whether the media affect people. It depends on what type of effect you may be talking about. According to McLeod and Reeves, media effects can be classified in many ways using some of the category schemes that follow. The appearance of their essay in 1980 signaled a major move toward conceptualizing media effects in a much more sophisticated way than had been typical only 20 years earlier. Today, research on media effects makes use of all the distinctions alluded to by McLeod and Reeves.

**Micro-Level or Macro-Level Effects Micro-level effects** involve effects on individual media consumers. Studies that rely on the experimental method are typically designed to uncover micro-level effects. Studies that monitor physiological arousal while viewers watch a horror movie are concerned with how media messages affect individual body physiology. On the other hand, research on **macro-level effects** might examine media impact on large communities. Some researchers are concerned that in an age of media mergers and large corporate ownership of media outlets, the quality of news coverage in a given area might suffer and communities might not have adequate exposure to certain issues. Researchers may want to investigate the pattern of media ownership in a given community and attempt to relate it to general community awareness by studying the kinds of social programs or political action groups that citizens have available. Notice that in this case, data are not gathered from individuals. Instead, the data are gathered on communities.

**Content-Specific or Diffuse-General Effects**  One way to think about media effects is to ask whether they might result from exposure to particular kinds of content. People who watch media violence may adopt very different attitudes or behaviors than people who watch nature programs. Researchers who study this type of effect are interested in how **specific content** affects viewers. But another possibility is that the media bring about very general effects, quite apart from the content of the messages. In Chapter 4, you will read about research that links TV viewing to obesity. The presumed effect in this case doesn't arise from exposure to any particular content; it is a much more general effect of time spent with the medium. Watching TV may replace physical exercise and give rise to more frequent eating. Such an effect would be referred to as a more **diffuse** or **general effect** than the effect of media violence on aggressive behavior.

**Attitudinal versus Behavioral versus Cognitive Changes**  In 1980, when McLeod and Reeves wrote their article, they indicated that the history of media effects research "is very nearly the history of attitude change research." Up to that point, the main focus of study was the extent to which exposure to the media produced **changes in people's attitudes**. Certainly, this is an important effect to study. However, attitude change does not always produce **behavior change**. And sometimes changes in what people think about (i.e., **cognitive changes**) might also be of great interest. Since McLeod and Reeves published their essay, the study of media effects has moved beyond the narrow focus on attitudes to include more studies on the media's impact on people's behavior and thoughts. You will encounter some of this newer research in Chapters 8 and 9.

**Alteration versus Stabilization**  Most people think of media effects in terms of change. Exposure to media messages might produce an **alteration** in public opinion or in a decision about whether to buy a particular product. In contrast to an emphasis on change, another way to think about media effects is to emphasize how media messages reinforce the status quo and exert a powerful force for **stability**. *The People's Choice* investigation discussed earlier in the chapter revealed that exposure to radio commercials tended to reinforce prior voting dispositions. People tended to listen closely to the ads for their own candidates and became even more committed in their intent to vote for those candidates. The absence of dramatic change might not indicate the lack of media impact. Instead, it might indicate that the media exert a force for maintaining things as they are. In the chapters that follow, you will learn about the results of current research in a number of important areas. This research reflects a number of different types of media impact, including some of the varieties that are mentioned by McLeod and Reeves.

# SUMMARY

Examples of media effects extend back to the nineteenth century, when the impact of newspapers on political affairs seemed obvious. With the Payne Fund studies, the research community generated the first systematic attempt to investigate the impact of media. These studies revealed that exposure to movies did have various effects on children. These results, combined with the obvious impact of the infamous *The War of the Worlds* radio broadcast, introduced the "legacy of fear"—the idea that media were extremely powerful and could bring about effects that were often harmful. The research on comic books in the 1950s tended to reinforce the legacy of fear and the magic bullet model of mass communication. A study of voting behavior, *The People's Choice,* revealed a much more limited impact of mass media and ushered in the limited-effects perspective. The Decatur Study helped to reinforce the idea that interpersonal communication also played an important role in understanding media influence. As the limited-effects perspective took hold in the 1950s, television exploded on the scene and attracted research attention in the 1960s and 1970s. This early research led to a more sophisticated view of media effects that prevails to the present day. Part of that sophistication is reflected in the number and different types of media effects that scholars now recognize.

## QUESTIONS TO FOCUS YOUR ATTENTION

1. Do you think that a media producer could fool the public today in the same way that *The War of the Worlds* radio broadcast fooled people in 1938? Why or why not?
2. To what extent do you believe the duration and quality of your sleep might be affected by media? Explain.
3. Is your own view about media effects closer to the "magic bullet model" or the "limited-effects" perspective? Explain.

## KEY TERMS AND CONCEPTS

| | | |
|---|---|---|
| Committee on Public Information | control groups | macro-level effects |
| wartime propaganda | conversion | specific content |
| Payne Fund studies | reinforcement | diffuse effects |
| galvanic skin response | two-step flow | general effects |
| micromhos | ceiling effect | changes in people's attitudes |
| theory of social learning | limited-effects perspective | behavior change |
| legacy of fear | voter volatility | cognitive changes |
| magic bullet model | selective exposure to communication | alteration |
| hypodermic needle model of mass communication | media effects | stability |
| | micro-level effects | |

# NOTES

1. Sparks, G. G., & Miller, W. (2004). News coverage of the war in Iraq: Cognitive and emotional consequences for viewers. In R. D. Berenger (Ed.), *Global media go to war: The role of news and entertainment media during the 2003 Iraq war* (pp. 305–312). Spokane, WA: Marquette Books.
2. Lazarsfeld, P. F., Berelson, B., & Gaudet, H. (1948). *The people's choice*. New York: Columbia University Press.
3. Straubhaar, J., & LaRose, R. (2000). *Media now: Communications media in the information age*. Belmont, CA: Wadsworth.
4. Baran, S. (1999). *Mass communication: Media literacy and culture*. Mountain View, CA: Mayfield.
5. Lowery, S. A., & DeFleur, M. L. (1983). *Milestones in mass communication research*. New York: Longman.
6. Dale, E. (1935). *The content of motion pictures*. New York: Macmillan.
7. Dysinger, W. S., & Ruckmick, C. A. (1933). *The emotional responses of children to the motion picture situation*. New York: Macmillan.
8. Blumer, H., & Hauser, P. M. (1933). *Movies, delinquency, and crime*. New York: Macmillan.
9. Wilson, P. (1995). *Dealing with pornography: The case against censorship*. Sydney, Australia: University of New South Wales Press.
10. Lowery, S. A., & DeFleur, M. L. (1983). *Milestones in mass communication research*. New York: Longman.
11. Charters, W. W. (1933). *Motion pictures and youth: A summary*. New York: Macmillan.
12. Houseman, J. (1948). The men from Mars. *Harper's, 168*, 16.
13. Cantril, H. (1940). *The invasion from Mars: A study in the psychology of panic*. Princeton, NJ: Princeton University Press.
14. Lowery, S. A., & DeFleur, M. L. (1983). *Milestones in mass communication research*. New York: Longman.
15. Lazarsfeld, P. F., Berelson, B., & Gaudet, H. *The people's choice*. New York: Columbia University Press.
16. See the following for some of the most important studies during this time period: (1) Katz, E., & Lazarsfeld, P. F. (1955). *Personal influence: The part played by people in the flow of mass communication*. Glencoe, IL: Free Press of Glencoe. (2) Lewin, K., & Grabbe, P. (1948). Conduct, knowledge, and acceptance of new values. *Journal of Social Issues, 1*, 53–64. (3) Stauffer, S. A. (1948). *The American soldier: Studies in social psychology in World War II* (Vols. 1 and 2). Princeton, NJ: Princeton University Press.
17. Katz, E., & Lazarsfeld, P. F. (1955). *Personal influence: The part played by people in the flow of mass communication*. Glencoe, IL: The Free Press of Glencoe.
18. Lowery and DeFleur provide an excellent overview of the Decatur Study in their *Milestones in mass communication research*, cited earlier.
19. Eulau, H. (1980). The Columbia studies of personal influence: Social network analysis. *Social Science History, 4*(2), 207–228.
20. Hovland, C. I., Lumsdaine, A. A., & Sheffield, F. D. (1949). *Experiments on mass communication*. Princeton, NJ: Princeton University Press.
21. Klapper, J. T. (1960). *The effects of the mass media*. Glencoe, IL: Free Press of Glencoe.
22. Klineberg, O., & Klapper, J. T. (1960). *The mass media: Their impact on children and family life*. Comments presented to the Study Association of America. New York: Television Information Office.
23. Wertham, F. (1954). *Seduction of the innocent*. New York: Rinehart.
24. *Ibid*.
25. Liebert, R. M., & Sprafkin, J. (1988). *The early window: Effects of television on children and youth*. New York: Pergamon Press.
26. McLeod, J. M., & Reeves, B. (1980). On the nature of media effects. In S. B. Withey & R. P. Abeles (Eds.), *Television and social behavior: Beyond violence and children* (pp. 17–54). Hillsdale, NJ: Erlbaum.

4

# Time Spent with Mass Media: Reasons and Consequences

In a documentary about the history of radio that was made for Home Box Office (HBO),[1] a young child's fascination with listening to radio drama was captured with a question that he directed to his parents: "Gee, Mom and Dad, what did people do before the days of radio?" The parents hesitated as they reflected on their past and finally answered, "Well, we *talked*." As the young child started to express his incredulity at how boring life must have been before radio, the parents ordered him to stop talking so that they could listen to the radio. In the 1970s, this same conversation might easily have taken place with respect to television. When I was a teenager, I might well have been tempted to ask my own parents, "What did you ever do before the days of TV?" For my generation, growing up without TV was simply unimaginable. Today, the question I am likely to get from my own children is "What in the world did you ever do before the days of computers, cell phones, and the Internet?"

One thing that these parent-child conversations reveal is that, quite apart from the effects of media content, the mass media have had a profound impact on the way people use their time. In the 1940s, children spent time listening to their favorite radio heroes. In the 1970s, they were glued to the TV screen watching all sorts of shows, from sporting events to sitcoms. Today, they are surfing the Internet, downloading MP3s, posting on Facebook, sending out tweets, texting and chatting online with their friends across town or across the country. They have been integrated into a more complex media environment. Indeed, the traditional definition of mass communication raises more questions today than it answers. One scholar, Joseph Dominick, defines **mass communication** as "the process by which a complex organization with the aid of one or more machines produces and transmits public messages that are directed at large, heterogeneous, and scattered audiences."[2] Radio and TV certainly continue to fit that conventional definition and still occupy significant amounts of our time. But with computers, the Internet, and smartphones, what formally counts as "mass communication" is debatable. Whatever you may want to call it, most of the chapters that follow will deal with the effects of particular kinds of media content. But this chapter deals with a different issue. Quite apart from the actual content of the media, why do we elect to spend so much of our time with media messages, and what are some of the consequences of those decisions?

Before we take a look at the research on how much time we spend with the media and how that time influences who we are as human beings, this is a good place to take a step back from the idea that the media influence people. Can we gain any insights from reversing the typical logic of media impact? Instead of thinking about the media first and their impact on people second, what happens when we start with people and move to the media? It is certainly true that media messages influence us, but this influence does not take place in some sort of static environment of one-way communication. The time that people spend with mass media is often the result of a deliberate choice. Before we study the impact of the media messages that we consume, it is important to understand what leads people to the media in the first place. Why would people choose to spend their time going to a movie, watching a TV show, reading a magazine or newspaper, watching YouTube, playing a video game, browsing the newsfeed on Facebook, catching up on Twitter traffic, or reading a favorite blog?

## THE USES AND GRATIFICATIONS PERSPECTIVE

Recall from Chapter 3 that in the 1950s and 1960s, there was a shift among scholars about how to think about media effects. The idea of limited effects became popular. This perspective emphasized that audience members are not all the same. Because individuals react to media content in very different ways, the idea that the media have uniform, powerful effects on a wide audience fell out of favor. It was only natural that the limited effects perspective, which emphasized individual differences, would spawn a new interest in why individuals use media in the first place. This new emphasis, the **uses and gratifications perspective**, was formalized in an article by Elihu Katz, Jay Blumler, and Michael Gurevitch.[3] This perspective was designed to lend insight into the ways that people use media to meet their needs. It focused heavily on individual motivations for media use. Since the time of the article by Katz, Blumler, and Gurevitch, an entire tradition of studies in uses and gratifications has grown up and matured in the mass-communication literature. We now know a great deal about people's reasons for choosing media exposure of particular kinds.

### Why Do People Watch TV?

You might want to pause before you read the following paragraphs and take out a pen and paper. Why do you think people watch TV? Jot down as many reasons as you can think of, using your own experience as an example. How many reasons were you able to come up with? How does your list compare with the one that follows? Some entries on this list of **motivations for media use** were developed by Bradley Greenberg in one study of British children[4] and were replicated along with some additions by Alan Rubin in a later study.[5]

**Learning** Not surprisingly, people turn to media in order to learn things. Occasionally, I hear a very small minority of students say that when they have children, they won't permit TV in their homes. Inevitably, the rationale for this intention is that there is simply too much objectionable material on TV today. I am somewhat sympathetic with the position of these students, but having raised three children in a home with multiple TV sets, I also usually ask about the missed opportunities to use TV for **learning**. Cable TV has expanded the number of possible programs to object to. But it has also expanded the opportunities for learning that could never have taken place years ago. The data from the uses and gratifications research suggest that children and adults do use TV in order to deliberately learn things. Of course, a good deal of learning takes place with other media as well. In Study Box 4-1, I have reprinted the text of an Internet chat that I had with my daughter Jordan (when she was 14 years old) about why she used the Internet. As you will discover, learning things was an important motivation. Remember, though, that the scientific approach does not permit one to make any generalizations from just one person. If I really wanted to introduce evidence for this point, I would have to do a formal study with a random-sample survey. Going back to the Payne Fund studies reviewed in the last chapter, there is no shortage of scientific evidence for the notion that children learn from the media. Researchers who study uses and gratifications note that some of this learning is motivated—not just an accidental by-product of media exposure. Many users of smartphones report that one of the reasons they never want to part with their device is because of its capacity to find quick answers to questions that arise during interpersonal conversations.

**Habit** Watching television may be habit-forming. The research studies reveal that consumers are conscious of the fact that they may view out of **habit**. If it's there, we like to watch. Related to the habit motive is the suggestion in the literature that TV, like a drug, encourages behavior that looks like a fullblown addiction.[6] The literature on television addiction is somewhat mixed. One early survey of adults conducted by Robin Smith failed to find much evidence of a true addiction to TV.[7] But several later studies seem to indicate that **TV addiction** is a real phenomenon. One study that appeared in the journal *Addictive Behaviors* found that whereas women tend to be more addicted to caffeine and chocolate, men are more likely to be addicted to alcohol, cigarettes, gambling, and television.[8] Research by Robert McIlwrath indicates that some college students endorse the statement "I'm addicted to television," and those who do tend to be more easily bored, more introverted, and more likely to suffer from neurosis.[9] The area of television addiction, as well as possible addictions to video games, deserves more attention from scholars, especially as it pertains to children. Clearly, the current trend is for scholars to take seriously the idea that certain people can become addicted to TV. In February 2002, the prestigious journal *Scientific American* ran a cover story entitled "Television Addiction Is

---

**STUDY BOX 4-1 Jordan's Reasons for Using the Internet**

GLENN:   Hi. I have a question for you.
JORDAN: Shoot.
GLENN:   List as many reasons as you can for why you use the Internet.
JORDAN: Okay. It's a form of communication between my family members and me.
         [COMPANIONSHIP]
JORDAN: It's a way to express some things I "hold dear" to the rest of the world, or
         views I am interested in.
JORDAN: It's a source of information for school. [LEARNING]
JORDAN: It's a source of information for other facts. [LEARNING]
JORDAN: It provides things to do, like play card games. [RELAXATION]
JORDAN: It's a hobby like, my homepage ... something to do when I'm bored. [PASS
         TIME] (Note: Jordan's homepage morphed into a Facebook page when she
         attended college.)
JORDAN: It's "vast" ... it won't get boring easily. [AROUSAL]
JORDAN: It's a way to stay informed about issues in the world. [LEARNING]
JORDAN: It's a way to stay informed about ANYTHING, I guess ... music, TV, etc.
         [LEARNING]
JORDAN: It's a way to meet people—chat, email pen pals, blah blah. [COMPANIONSHIP]

---

No Mere Metaphor." In that article, communication researchers Robert Kubey and Mihaly Csikszentmihalyi review a variety of evidence that points in the direction of TV addiction being very real. They state:

> The term "TV addiction" is imprecise and laden with value judgments, but it captures the essence of a very real phenomenon. Psychologists and psychiatrists formally define substance dependence as a disorder characterized by criteria that include spending a great deal of time using the substance; using it more often than one intends; thinking about reducing use or making repeated unsuccessful efforts to reduce use; giving up important social, family or occupational activities to use it; and reporting withdrawal symptoms when one stops using it. All these criteria can apply to people who watch a lot of television.[10] (pp. 1–2)

At present, it seems safe to say that there may be a tendency for some individuals to develop a psychological dependence on TV that resembles addictive behavior in some respects.[11] One researcher, Cary Horvath, developed a self-report instrument designed to assess whether one is suffering from TV addiction. Her measure includes items that fall into several general categories of addictive behavior including tolerance of TV viewing, withdrawal symptoms when TV is unavailable, unintended viewing, desire to reduce viewing, spending too much time viewing, feeling like TV displaces other activities, and continued viewing.[12] Researchers may not have caught up yet to one of the recent phenomena in the way people watch TV: binge viewing. With the advent of successful shows like *Homeland*, *Game of Thrones*, *Breaking Bad*, and *House of Cards*, multiple episodes are available on demand or through services like Netflix. As a result, more people find themselves in marathon viewing sessions in which they can't resist the urge to watch just one more episode. A journalist who writes for *The Washington Post* recently identified the urge to engage in binge viewing as a genuine addiction. See Study Box 4-2 for more detail on this phenomenon.

---

### STUDY BOX 4-2 Are You a "Binge Viewer"?

Petula Dvorak is a columnist for *The Washington Post*. During the summer of 2013, she was so struck by what she saw happening to her own TV viewing habits that she decided to devote one of her columns to the topic. She titled it: "Online TV addiction: Man, it's hard to shake." She opened the column with a revealing statement about herself and her husband: "We are binge watchers. The on-demand television culture—where you no longer wait a week for the next episode, it's all just one click away—has spawned a new drug and a new addiction." When I first read Dvorak's title for her column, I wondered whether she was simply using the word "addiction" to catch readers' attention. But after reading it through, I recognized that the sorts of symptoms she described about her own TV viewing also matched many of the symptoms that researchers who study addictions describe. Here are some of the main things she mentioned:

1. Neglect of important household tasks—her house was a mess.
2. Neglect of sleep that affected her physical appearance—she looked like a mess.
3. A sense of squandering her time on too much television.
4. Expressing determination to quit but not having the willpower to do so.
5. Blurring fiction with reality—she caught herself with the urge to fire off a text message to "Taystee"—a fictitious character in the Netflix series *Orange is the New Black*.

As **binge viewing** becomes more common, I'm guessing that media researchers will design studies that result in systematic descriptions of the sorts of behaviors that Dvorak described. I'm also guessing that researchers will discover that certain individuals are more susceptible to binge viewing than others. What personal characteristics do you think they might discover as the ones that lend themselves to binge viewing? Are *you* a binge viewer?

---

SOURCE: Dvorak, P. (August 29, 2013). Online TV addiction: Man, it's hard to shake. *The Washington Post*. [Online: Accessed 3-28-14]. Available: http://www.washingtonpost.com/local/online-tv-addiction-man-its-hard-to-shake/2013/08/29/0e45cf50-10ce-11e3-85b6-d27422650fd5_story.html?wprss=rss_local

---

**Companionship** Many people watch TV because it gives them a sense of connection to other people—a sense of **companionship**. Why should this be? Where the Internet is concerned, the concept of companionship is easier to understand. People can actually communicate with other people in chat rooms and use e-mail to keep in touch. But how does TV foster a sense of companionship? Researchers Byron Reeves and the late Clifford Nass may have some insight into this question. According to them, the human brain does not easily separate media images from reality.

The title of their book summarizes their thesis rather well: *The Media Equation: How People Treat Computers, Television, and New Media Like Real People and Places.*[13] If Reeves and Nass are right, when we see people on TV, some primitive part of the brain is tricked into thinking that those people are physically present. Higher-order cognitive processes may tell us that the images are not real, but the images stimulate real emotional reactions just the same. A more complete confirmation of the Reeves and Nass thesis must await further testing and more complete understanding of brain functions. But the basic theoretical idea may be useful for explaining the sense that some people have of relationships with media personalities. Media researchers Elizabeth Perse and Rebecca Rubin refer to the feelings and attachments that people have toward media characters as **parasocial relationships**.[14] There seems to be no doubt that such relationships do exist. One recent study by Robin Nabi and her research associates found that having parasocial relationships with TV characters was one of the things that predicted enjoyment of both fiction and reality shows.[15] Another communication scholar, Cynthia Hoffner, has argued that children clearly form impressions about people presented to them in the media and may become emotionally attached to some of those people in ways that resemble the attachments to people seen face-to-face in the interpersonal context.[16] In Study Box 4-2, columnist Petula Dvorak describes catching herself with the urge to fire off a text message to a completely fictitious character in a program she had been watching. Study Box 4-3 describes parasocial relationships in more detail.

**Arousal** Some viewers watch TV because it stimulates them, excites them, and increases their **arousal** level. Arousal refers to the physiological system and involves responses such as heart rate, blood pressure, sweat, and respiration rate. Back in the 1950s, Donald Hebb introduced the idea that each human being is wired with an **optimal level of arousal**. For some individuals, their natural baseline **set point** of arousal is higher than their optimum. Consequently, these people would seek out calm, boring activities. For other individuals, the natural set point of arousal is lower than their optimal level. As a result, these people would seek out stimulating and arousing activities. In support of this general notion, Marvin Zuckerman has documented the presence of a personality trait known as **sensation seeking**.[17]

Sensation seekers are individuals who tend to seek out arousing activities. Unlike individuals who are low sensation seekers, those high on sensation seeking express a much greater desire for activities such as skydiving, riding roller coasters, attending wild parties, and using drugs for recreation. Zuckerman devised a simple measure of sensation seeking that consists of a number of statements about preferred activities. Respondents simply indicate whether each statement applies to them. Several studies show that high sensation seekers prefer to watch horror films.[18] One of the reasons that some children (particularly males) seem to seek out media content that is violent or frightening may have to do with the need for arousal. For such children, reading a book is not likely to be an adequate substitute for watching a movie. Riding a roller coaster may be a better alternative.

One psychologist, Ashton Trice, recently demonstrated in an experiment that sensation-seeking children prefer different types of media.[19] In this case, Trice

## STUDY BOX 4-3 What Is a "Parasocial" Relationship?

The study of parasocial relationships originated in the 1950s with two researchers, Donald Horton and Richard Wohl, who wrote about mass communication and "parasocial interaction." Since that time, other scholars have expanded on their research in an attempt to understand this concept. Three Purdue researchers (Sara Branch, Kari Wilson, and Chris Agnew) recently summarized the key studies over the years and described parasocial relationships this way:

1. A one-sided relationship that a person establishes with a media personality.
2. The relationship feels like other relationships that have face-to-face contact.
3. People respond to a media personality in ways that are similar to face-to-face relationships. They talk to the media personality and make inferences about the personality's behavior.
4. There is a sense of connection with the media personality that a person seeks to maintain over time.
5. As more time is spent with the media personality, the relationship becomes more intimate and important.

In their research, Branch, Wilson, & Agnew wanted to explain the level of commitment that people showed in their parasocial relationships. They reasoned that if parasocial relationships were like real face-to-face relationships, perhaps the ingredients that predict commitment in the two types of relationships would be the same. Their research suggested that this was in fact the case. What are the key ingredients? According to the **Investment Model of Commitment Processes**, the key ingredients are:

- The amount of satisfaction experienced in the relationship—more satisfaction results in greater commitment.
- The quality of available alternatives to that relationship—fewer quality alternatives results in greater commitment.
- The amount of investment that a person puts into the relationship—more investment results in greater commitment.

Petula Dvorak's urge to send a text message to the fictional character, Taystee, (see Study Box 4-2), shows a high level of investment in that relationship and perhaps reflects a high level of satisfaction. Based on the Investment Model of Commitment Processes, Branch, Wilson, and Agnew might predict that Dvorak is strongly committed to her relationship with Taystee and intends for the relationship to continue in the future.

SOURCE: (1) Horton, D., & Wohl, R. R. (1956). Mass communication and para-social interaction. *Psychiatry: Journal for the Study of Interpersonal Processes, 19*, 215–229; (2) Branch, S. E., Wilson, K. M., & Agnew, C. R. (2013). Committed to Oprah, Homer, or House: Using the investment model to understand parasocial relationships. *Psychology of Popular Media Culture, 2(2)*, 96–109.

presented 123 second-grade children with a viewing choice: choose to watch a video about "scary sharks" or a video about "bunnies." The children who had scored high on sensation seeking were much more likely to choose to watch the video about scary sharks. Trice also had two versions of each video that she randomly assigned children to watch after they had made their video choice. One of the versions was highly exciting while the other was low on excitement. The exciting videos had dramatic music and the less exciting ones had no music at all. For the shark video, the highly exciting version featured great white sharks while the less exciting version showed smaller sharks. For the bunny video, the exciting version showed rabbits in the wild while the less exciting version emphasized bunnies as pets. The sensation seekers who saw the exciting videos averaged a "5" on a scale of enjoyment that went from 1–7 where "7" was the maximum level of enjoyment. In contrast, for the less exciting videos, children averaged a 3.73. For those low on sensation seeking, the trend was exactly the opposite. The low sensation seekers averaged a 3.38 on the enjoyment scale for the exciting videos and a 4.25 for the less exciting videos. These differences were statistically significant (see Chapter 2 for a review on what "statistically significant" means). This study suggests that high sensation seekers prefer more exciting media while low sensation seekers actually find less exciting media to be more enjoyable.

**Relaxation** Just as some children in Trice's experiment may have wanted to use TV to raise their arousal levels, some children and adults alike seem to prefer to use it for **relaxation**. Today, when I talk to groups of parents about using TV effectively in the home, I often take a few minutes to talk about the transitional time between afternoon and evening activities. This is often a time of chaos in the household as people shift gears and change activities. For parents, the combination of winding down from the workday and preparing the evening meal can seem like a major challenge when young children are running around at a hyper pace. A carefully selected, non-arousing TV program or video can often be the perfect remedy to ease the household tension at this time of day. In this case, the parents have control over the selection. But studies show that children do select relaxing shows themselves. Just as sensation-seeking behavior is a function of one's arousal set point, so too may be the tendency to use TV for relaxation. Of course, at any given time, any person may choose a TV program for the purpose of relaxation. But those who have high arousal set points that need to be lowered may be particularly likely to choose this kind of entertainment repeatedly.

**Escape** You have probably found yourself at one time or another using the media as an **escape** from the unpleasant duties and occupations that you have in real life. This escape behavior has been documented by uses and gratifications researchers in connection with TV. It may also be related to TV addiction, discussed under the habit motive for TV use. Just as a drug addict seeks escape from reality through drug use, so the TV addict may be seeking an escape from the stresses and strains of life through watching TV programs. Although this motive has been documented by uses and gratifications researchers, not much is known about when such behavior may be healthy or unhealthy.

**Passing Time** Another motive for TV use is simply **to pass the time**. It is not uncommon today to find TV screens in a variety of public places where people have to wait for things to happen. When people sit in a doctor's waiting room, watching TV helps to pass the time if the doctor is running behind schedule. TV is becoming more commonplace in hotel elevators, at the gas pump, and even in public restrooms. As the pace of life seems to be increasing, people are less tolerant of situations in which they are forced to wait for something (apparently even their own natural bodily functions). Waiting creates frustration. If a person can catch up on the headlines while waiting for the gas tank to fill or waiting for the elevator to make it to the 20th floor, perhaps this frustration decreases a little. Major airlines caught on to this principle years ago when they started to offer movies on longer flights. They discovered that people would pay a few dollars for the headphones and would watch a film that they might not order at home or rent at the local video store. Why? The reason is simple. On an airplane, there is little else to do. Watching a movie helps to pass the time.

**Social Interaction** A final reason that people may watch TV or expose themselves to media messages is to be prepared for various sorts of interactions with other people afterward. Several of my colleagues are fans of the TV show *The Big Bang Theory*. I often tune in to see a new episode—not only because I enjoy the bizarre humor surrounding a group of university scientists—but because I know that if I miss the episode, I'll feel left out of some of the office conversation the next day. Media messages can provide people with common experiences that help to break the conservational ice with strangers or reinforce social connections with friends and family.

## Uses and Gratifications Meets New Media

It would be a mistake to give the impression that uses and gratifications research is focused only on the reasons that people watch TV. The thought may have occurred to you as you were reading through the different reasons for watching TV that these reasons also applied to your use of other types of media. In fact, researchers are actively studying how and why people use not only television but a host of other media, including radio, books, smartphones, video game consoles, tablets, and computers. As scholars attempt to study new media technology under the uses and gratifications perspective, many have noted that the reasons for using TV are easily extended to include new media. But others aren't satisfied with that simple extension. S. Shyam Sundar, who helps direct the Media Effects Research Laboratory at Penn State University, published an essay with his coauthor, Anthony Limperos, suggesting that new media have given rise to new uses and gratifications.[20] For example, these scholars suggest that among other things, people may use new media because they're "cool" or "novel," provide a heightened sense of community with others, give one a sense of interactivity or control, satisfy a need to "browse" or satisfy a need to navigate some geographical space—things that are generally missing from the old media of TV and radio. I think Sundar and Limperos have a point. I'd be lost without Google Maps on my smartphone. I also still love to display my novel ability to take control of technology and shoot a short movie, post it to

YouTube, and whip out my phone during a conversation and play the footage. These are all new uses of media that aren't reflected in the older lists of reasons for using TV.

## Beyond Mere Descriptions of Media Use

Some of the most recent research on uses and gratifications attempts to connect people's motivations for using particular media with the effects that the media might have on them. If you don't use Twitter, perhaps you wonder what those who do use it are getting out of it. A recent survey published in *Computers in Human Behavior* found evidence that people who send "tweets" are doing so to satisfy an underlying need for camaraderie. Apparently, the respondents in the study who sent the most tweets were also those who reported the greatest sense of satisfaction when it came to feelings of connection with others.[21]

In another study, Alan Rubin, Paul Haridakis, and Keren Eyal administered a questionnaire to 354 undergraduate students who were enrolled in a communication class at a large university in the Midwest.[22] One of the main purposes of the study was to discover whether viewers of different television talk shows could be distinguished from one another in terms of their motivations for using TV, their personal attitudes, their emotions, and other traits. For example, if you know someone who loved to watch Oprah Winfrey, does this fact tell you anything about how that person is when compared to another person who loves to watch Jerry Springer? As you might suspect, the results of the research did show some differences. Compared to the Oprah Winfrey viewers, those who liked to watch Jerry Springer reported that TV shows were less realistic and said that they enjoyed watching shows where people got angry, embarrassed, and hurt by someone else. They also reported that they tended to watch TV for entertainment and excitement—not to become better informed. Oprah viewers tended to be much more likely to be motivated to form a parasocial relationship with the host than were the viewers of Jerry Springer. In addition to these findings, the researchers discovered that they could differentiate viewers on the basis of how they had responded to a questionnaire that measured levels of aggressiveness. Viewers with high levels of aggression were much more likely to enjoy watching guests being embarrassed or hurt. They also tended to report more anger and had more negative attitudes toward women.

Although the researchers did not attempt to study the effects that talk shows had on these viewers, they suggested that the effects might be determined in part by the attitudes that viewers brought with them to the viewing experience. For example, viewers who think that talk shows are not very realistic might not tend to be greatly affected by what they see. On the other hand, viewers who think that these shows are quite realistic might tend to be influenced to adopt attitudes and behaviors that they see depicted on the screen. The relationship between what viewers bring with them to the viewing experience and how viewing subsequently affects them is one of the most important areas of current research in the uses and gratifications tradition. Recently, Marika Tiggemann published a study relevant to this discussion. In her survey of nearly 1,500 adolescents, she found that total TV exposure was not related to a personal sense of body image but that soap opera viewing was positively correlated with a personal drive for thinness. This was true for both men and women. For the male respondents, she also found that soap opera viewing and music video viewing was correlated with a drive for muscularity. These findings at least seem to suggest the possibility that adolescents tune in to watch certain kinds of programs to see characters that might inspire them toward achieving certain personal goals—in this case either the desire to be thin or the desire to be muscular. She concluded that the effects of media exposure on body image needed to be examined in the context of various viewing motivations.[23] Clearly, the future of research in the uses and gratifications tradition will be more closely focused upon understanding the effects of media messages rather than just a description of how people are using those messages.

## THE PROBLEM WITH SELF-REPORTS

One common criticism of the uses and gratifications perspective is that it relies heavily on self-reports. Are people able to report accurately their reasons for using the media? Even if they are able to report accurately, are they always motivated to do so? These are important questions that researchers can never answer definitively for all time. That is, whenever a given study is undertaken, these two questions must be considered. In answer to the first question, the chances of getting accurate answers about motivations improve with the recency of the behavior in question. You might be able to report quite accurately that the reason you watched the news last night was to find out how the weather would be for the football game today. But if you were called on to report your motivations for watching the news six weeks ago, you might have to resort to a reasonable speculation about your behavior, which might or might not be accurate.

The second question concerns whether people might deliberately misrepresent their viewing motives. One of the principal reasons that people might do this is to make a good impression on the researchers. This sort of misrepresentation is sometimes called the **social desirability response**. That is, they may want to make themselves look good for the researchers. As a professor, I might consider it more desirable to report that I watched TV to become better informed, instead of simply to pass the time or escape from life's stress. Passing the time doesn't sound quite compatible with the notion that, as a professor, I should be concerned about learning things. To save face, I might be tempted to alter my response. Researchers can counter the tendency for people to respond out of motives of social desirability by assuring them that their responses are completely confidential or even anonymous. These promises, combined with an emphatic statement in the questionnaire's instructions that only honest answers are valuable to the researchers, can be effective tools to combat the effect of seeking social desirability. In the final analysis, researchers need to stay sensitive to the potential problems of self-report data. But although these reports can sometimes be flawed, our knowledge about mass communication would be significantly impoverished without them.

## THE RAW NUMBERS: MEDIA MINUTES ADD UP

When it comes to the topic of time spent with the media, it would be difficult to know much at all without relying on self-report data. You have probably read or heard about some of the statistics that are generated from surveys about media use. In fact, the data indicate that people spend large quantities of time processing media messages of one sort or another.

One recent large-scale survey of media use was reported by the Kaiser Family Foundation.[24] The focus of this report was on children and adolescents up to the age of 18. The survey contained questions about multiple media sources, including television, videotapes, movies, video games, print media, radio, CDs, and computers. What did the results show? On average, children and adolescents in this age range watch nearly 4.5 hours of TV each day. Among the key findings presented in the report was the fact that, on average, children spend over 7.5 hours each day with media of some sort. This is equivalent to the amount of time that a typical worker would devote to a full-time job. While the average amount of daily time spent with media was about 7.5 hours, children were exposed to more than 10.5 hours of media content during that 7.5-hour period! How is this possible? I think you need only to watch the behavior of any child you know to arrive at the answer. How often are they surfing the Internet at the same time they're monitoring a TV show? Children use more than one medium at the same time for nearly 30% of their total media use time each day.

One major finding to emerge from the Kaiser Family Foundation survey was that reading time pales in comparison to time spent with TV. On average, the kids in this sample reported that they spend only 25 minutes per day reading books, only nine minutes per day reading magazines, and only three minutes per day reading news-papers. Many educators who are sobered by these discouraging reading statistics have placed hope in the computer as the new educational tool for young people. But if this hope is to be realized, the findings from the survey will have to change radically in coming years. On average, children between the ages of eight and 18 used the computer for about 1.5 hours per day. The numbers for computer time will undoubtedly increase as more households acquire more computers. But the survey showed that 93% of households with children between eight and 18 already own a computer, and 84% of the households have Internet access. Despite the explosive growth of computers, television is still the medium of choice for children and adolescents. During an average year, the average child spends the equivalent of over two months of 24-hour days doing nothing but watching TV (68.4 days per year). Nearly three-fourths of the sample (71%) reported that they have a TV set in their bedrooms. The astounding thing about all of these media-use statistics is their rate of increase in just a few years. One of the things driving that increase is mobile media. In fact, the report noted that kids are using their phones to watch TV, play music, and play games for more daily minutes (49 minutes) than they spend actually using their phones to talk (33 minutes). If you visit the Kaiser Family Foundation Web site, you'll be able to access their entire report and appreciate just how much time today's youth spend with media of all kinds. Study Box 4-4 contains some key summary points from a news release that accompanied the Kaiser Family Foundation report.

---

### STUDY BOX 4-4 Some Key Facts on Media Use from the Kaiser Family Foundation

1. Mobile Media Are Driving Increased Consumption: From 2005–2010, cell phone ownership increased from 39% to 66% for 8- to 18-year-olds. If the rate of increase has remained steady, it could be over 80% by the time you read this.

2. Most 8- to 18-year-olds Report No Media Rules: Only about 30% say that their parents have any rules for their media use. Rules work for those who have them. They result in nearly three hours *less* per day of media consumption.

3. TV Sets Tend to Be Turned On: Almost two-thirds of 8- to 18-year-olds say that meals are usually eaten at home while the TV is on. Nearly half say that the TV is left on even when nobody is watching.

4. Media Use Increases in the Early Teens: In the 11–14 age group, media use jumps nearly four hours per day between TV, music, computers, and video games.

5. Texting Is Increasing But Isn't Included in the Consumption Statistics: Adolescents in grades 7–12 reported spending over an hour per day sending and receiving text messages. This time was *not counted* in overall statistics on media use.

---

**SOURCE:** Kaiser Family Foundation Web site: http://kff.org/disparities-policy/press-release/daily-media-use-among-children-and-teens-up-dramatically-from-five-years-ago/ (Accessed 4-4-14).

---

In the spring of 2006, the Kaiser Family Foundation released another report that specifically focused on children between six months and six years of age. In a survey of more than 1,000 parents, the researchers who wrote the report (Victoria Rideout and Elizabeth Hamel) revealed that 84% of all children in this age range live in a home with two or more TV sets, and more than one-third of the children have a TV in their bedrooms. You might think that children who are only one year old might not have a TV in the bedroom—but 19% of them do. The authors concluded that "the vast majority of children are growing up in homes where television is a near-constant presence."[25] They noted that for one-third of the children in this age range, the home environment is one in which the TV set is either *always* on or on most of the time. These statistics ring true. I have talked with therapists in my own community who regularly visit children's homes to help them with their speaking skills or motor development. The therapists report that, almost without exception, the homes they visit have a TV set that is turned on when they arrive. In most cases, the family members do not think of turning the set off for the duration of the therapist's visit. This is anecdotal evidence for the notion that TV has simply become part of our living environment.

Television is not the only medium with which young children are spending time. More than 40% of children *between two and three years old* watch a video or DVD during a typical day. And, during a typical day, about 12% of children in this same age group use a computer.

When these statistics are combined with those from the movie business, it all adds up to a large quantity of time spent watching moving images on a screen. The National Association of Theatre Owners recently reported that about 1.36 billion movie tickets were sold during 2013 in the United States and Canada.[26] The number of tickets sold annually in the United States has remained fairly constant over the past decade. These steady sales come even though ticket prices are spiraling upward. With all of this viewing time, it seems naïve to suggest that TV and movies are merely innocuous sources of entertainment that have little or no impact on viewers. Starting with the next chapter, you will read about some of the effects associated with particular kinds of media content. For now, let's focus on a different question: Apart from the content of TV and movies, does simply spending time watching the content have any unique effects that researchers have been able to document? The answer to this question seems to be yes. Let's look briefly at some of the effects that have been examined.

## The Displacement Hypothesis

For a number of years, researchers have been concerned about the possibility that the large quantity of time spent with media (primarily television) was serving to displace time that would ordinarily be spent in other important activities. This general idea has become known as the **displacement hypothesis**. The basic notion is that people have a limited amount of time in their daily routines that can be allocated to different activities. If, as the data seem to show, the time spent watching TV and movies has increased over the years, then it would seem logical to suspect that the time spent in some other activities must necessarily have decreased. Depending on what those other activities might be, there could be reason for concern. The symmetric version of the displacement hypothesis would suggest that if TV viewing decreased, the amount of time spent in other activities would correspondingly increase.

Relative to other areas, there are fewer studies that examine the displacement hypothesis directly. One study that was specifically designed to investigate this idea was a survey (panel design) of children in South Africa. Its authors, Diana Mutz, Donald Roberts, and D. P. van Vuuren, examined data on nearly 2,000 children over an eight-year period.[27] Each year, they questioned the children about the way they spent their time. The results of this study show that if a displacement effect exists, it isn't very large. The study began in 1974, and TV wasn't introduced to South Africa until 1976. Consequently, the authors were able to study the direct impact of TV in a way that can rarely be done today. Initially, TV seemed to displace radio listening and movie attendance, but not other important activities. In fact, the authors reported that more than 60% of children's viewing time came from activities that could be regarded as marginal in terms of their overall importance.

Another major study that employed a longitudinal design (panel study) was reported by Tannis MacBeth Williams and A. Gordon Handford.[28] These researchers took advantage of a unique situation in Canada before the advent of TV in one of the towns they studied. Over a period of several years, the researchers studied three towns. One of the towns (referred to as "Notel") had no access to television at the study's outset. Another town ("Unitel") had access to only one TV station. A third town ("Multitel") had access to four stations. Just after the initial baseline data were collected from grade school children in all three towns, Notel received access to a single TV station. Two years later, the researchers returned to each town and collected more data. At that time, Unitel had gained a second TV signal, and Multitel still had access to four stations. By studying the same children two years later as well as the kindergarten children who had subsequently moved into grade school in the interim, the researchers could see if changes had occurred in the towns that increased their access to TV (Notel and Unitel). The results of the study revealed that television definitely had impacted other activities. The authors concluded the following:

> Television apparently has little if any impact on the number of community activities available, but it has a noticeable negative effect on participation in those activities. Involvement in community activities, summing across the categories, was greatest in the absence of television and fell significantly following its arrival in Notel. Television's negative impact was greatest for sports, and the effect was stronger for youths than for adults. There was also reasonably clear evidence to implicate television in decreased attendance at dances, suppers, and parties, and again, the effect was stronger for youths than adults. (pp. 182–183)

**Displacement of Important Activities**   Of course, what constitutes a marginal activity as opposed to an important activity may be debated. Should the effects from the Canadian study be regarded as ones that implicate TV in displacing important activities, or marginal ones? You may not tend to think that attending suppers and dances is important. Sometimes, however, activities that seem trivial may not be so trivial when examined more closely. If TV viewing has a tendency to decrease opportunities for social interaction, perhaps people will lose the many benefits that come from close social ties. A psychologist, David Myers, has recently noted that in the United States, a number of disturbing social trends seem to point toward a decline in close connections between people.[29] For example, he discusses the decline in marriage, the reduction of social networks, the increase in individualism, a decline in civility, and so forth. Could these symptoms in society be related to increases in time spent with mass media? For the most part, these issues have yet to be explored by researchers. Robert Putnam, a well-known sociologist, lent some credibility to this general idea in his book, *Bowling Alone*.[30] I've always been interested in the relationship between media and interpersonal connections, so I teamed up a few years ago with the therapist Will Miller to explore this thesis in a book titled *Refrigerator Rights: Our Crucial Need for Close Connection*.[31] Undoubtedly, media researchers will launch more systematic studies in this area in the coming years.

Despite the lack of research in some areas related to the displacement hypothesis, researchers have examined certain issues. Child psychologists argue that developing children need to engage in a proper amount of fantasy play to maintain an optimum level of stimulation that encourages healthy growth. Does watching TV encourage such fantasy play or discourage it? In a major review on the research pertaining to this question, two researchers, Tom van der Voort and Patti Valkenburg, concluded that the best evidence suggests that TV viewing discourages fantasy play through a displacement effect.[32] The effect may depend on the type of content viewed. In some rare cases, educational programs may actually stimulate fantasy play. Programs with high levels of violence reduce fantasy play, while non-violent programs appear to have little impact either way.

One of the chief concerns among educators is that watching TV disrupts academic learning by displacing important educational activities such as reading. A team of researchers studied this issue by collecting diaries from preschool children over a three-year period.[33] Once completed, the diaries contained information about the amount of time spent in a variety of activities. In one sense, the results from this study show some support for the displacement hypothesis. As children spent more time watching TV, they tended to spend less time on activities related to education, talking to others, or playing video games. But the general relationship between TV viewing and these activities depended on a number of other factors, including the type of content viewed and the overall quality of the home environment. For example, watching educational TV programs did not result in any decrease in educational activities.

From these data, it appears that the displacement hypothesis may not be a simple phenomenon. In a study conducted by W. J. (James) Potter, more data emerged in support of the idea that the displacement hypothesis probably didn't operate in a simplistic fashion.[34] Although Potter did uncover a negative relationship between TV viewing and academic achievement (as viewing increased, achievement decreased), the relationship did not appear to kick in until TV viewing had reached at least 10 hours per week. This kind of relationship is referred to as a **threshold effect**. In this case, no negative impact from TV viewing was observed until the 10-hours-per-week threshold had been crossed.

Educators generally agree that one of the most important skills learned during the educational process is reading. How does television viewing affect the acquisition of reading skill? Is there a negative impact, and, if so, is that impact due to a displacement effect? Do children read less because they watch TV more? The available data on these questions do not permit a strong conclusion. The issue was examined extensively by the researchers who conducted the study of Notel, Unitel, and Multitel in Canada. They concluded that there was a small negative correlation between TV viewing and reading skill, but they argued that this relationship was probably not evidence of a direct impact of TV viewing. Instead, in the opinion of these authors, "[C]hildren who are more fluent readers tend to be more intelligent, to read more, and to watch television less." Consequently, it may be that the negative relationship between television viewing and reading skill has more to do with the fact that both of these things are related to intelligence, amount of reading, and other third-variable explanations.

In one of the most recent studies that provide clues about the displacement hypothesis, two medical doctors studied more than 4,500 middle school students (grades five through eight).[35] Their conclusion shows support for the notion that media use displaces time devoted to academic achievement goals. The authors stated that

> We found a strong detrimental relationship between measures of media use and school performance in middle school children. This relationship persisted after controlling for a number of potential confounding influences. Our study supports both the displacement and the content hypotheses, with exposure to adult content having the strongest and most consistent negative impact on school

performance. In addition, increased television weekday screen time had a detrimental impact on school performance, consistent with recent reports by others. (pp. 1065–1066)

One particularly interesting question about displacement effects has to do with the impact of computers and the Internet. In one recent longitudinal study of children in Singapore, Waipeng Lee and Eddie Kuo discovered that increased use of the Internet did tend to be associated with reductions in the amounts of time that children spent watching TV. It also tended to be associated with increases in the amounts of time spent reading newspapers, listening to the radio, and talking with friends.[36] The possibility that time spent watching television may be gradually displaced by time spent on the Internet and using other newer media technologies is also suggested in several recent surveys published in the communication literature.[37]

## Do Electronic Media Displace Sleep?

When I need to wake up early in the morning, I typically set the alarm on my smartphone and set it on the bedside table. Sometimes, as a backup, I'll set a second alarm on my tablet and place it next to the phone. This usually works well to wake me up on time. But there's a huge disadvantage. If I go to bed early, someone inevitably calls me or sends me an email or text message. Too often, I wake up during the night to the chirping of one of my electronic devices. If I remember, I can turn the sound alerts off for those functions before going to bed. But I still might stir in the middle of the night and if I do, I can't resist the temptation to check my phone status. It's easy to do. I can grab my phone or tablet without getting out of bed. The next thing I know, I'm busy typing email or text replies to messages that have arrived from my nocturnal friends. When morning arrives, I'm sleep deprived. I've conducted informal surveys with my students and discovered that there's a strong unanimous opinion that electronic media displaces sleep on a regular basis. Is there any evidence for a sleep-displacement effect? Several researchers from the University of Adelaide in Australia wanted to know the answer to this question and surveyed over 1,200 high school students.[38] Their results show that there may be reason for concern.

Students in the survey responded to questions about their media use, their sleep habits and duration, as well as to the nine items on the Sleep Activity and Media Questionnaire (SAMQ). Perhaps the most surprising statistic to emerge from the Australian study was that 71% of adolescents reported getting less sleep on weeknights than was optimal for their age group. Another 20% reported bed-time delay—their sleep was delayed because of their media use. A small group in the sample (just over 8%) reported levels of media use that were considered to be "pathologically high." The term "pathological" originates from the formal assessment of pathologies such as gambling in the clinical psychology literature. In order to be considered a pathological media user, respondents had to answer "yes" to five or more items on a 10-item media use questionnaire. As it turned out, the pathological media users were more likely to report significantly later bedtimes, longer amounts of time needed to fall asleep, and more disruptions to their sleep. Because amount and quality of sleep is critically important to human health and because of the emerging relationship between media use and sleep, the future of media research is likely to contain many more studies in this area than currently exist in the literature. Recall from Chapter 3 (see Study Box 3-1) that researchers began studying media effects on sleep back in the 1920s with the Payne Fund studies. Despite the long history of interest in this topic, there is still much more to learn.

## Television Viewing and Obesity

Before I began writing this section of the chapter, I noticed that there was an exciting football game on TV. I also noticed that it was getting late in the afternoon and that I had not yet gone out for my 30-minute jog around the neighborhood. As I became more involved in the game, I found myself thinking that I might put off my jog until the next day. Fortunately, I resisted this temptation—partly because I knew that if I jogged, I would find it easier to read through the research for this section when I came back. The notion that television viewing might lead to obesity seems like a pretty reasonable conjecture. If TV displaces other activities, then perhaps it displaces activities like jogging and other forms of physical exercise that help keep extra pounds off. TV viewing may also encourage extra eating, which could lead to additional pounds. Obesity has recently attracted public attention as a health problem. On October 27, 1999, the *Journal of the American Medical Association* devoted an entire issue to obesity, which, the editors noted, is a major risk factor for heart disease. At that time, an estimated 97 million American adults (more than half the population) were considered to be overweight. According to the Centers for Disease Control, that number has now increased to nearly 155 million. The trend is even more startling. The percentage of *overweight* Americans (defined as those with a body mass index between 25 and 30; see Study Box 4-5 for more on the body mass index) increased from 46% to over 69% over the past 30 years. During that same time period, the percentage of *obese* Americans (those with a body mass index of 30 or higher) doubled, from about 15% to nearly 36%. While some recent evidence suggests that Americans may be finally starting to reverse this trend, there's little doubt that obesity is a huge public health concern. Is it possible that the high media use documented earlier in this chapter has something to do with the national proclivity toward being overweight? Is there any evidence that watching television may be playing a negative role in this national health problem? The current evidence is pretty intriguing.

More than 30 years ago, a sample of 1,000 respondents solicited through a questionnaire in *The National Enquirer* answered questions about their weight and their TV viewing.[39] The results of the study revealed that TV viewing was indeed positively correlated with snacking behavior. When the sample was broken down into subgroups, the results showed that 52% of the people who watched more than 28 hours of TV each week were overweight, compared to only 33% of those who

## STUDY BOX 4-5 Compute the Relationship Between Body Mass Index and Daily TV Viewing for Your Class

You can calculate the correlation between body mass index (BMI) and daily TV viewing for your own class. Have your instructor coordinate the following exercise. First, have each student estimate the number of hours spent watching TV on a daily basis. Second, have each student compute his or her own BMI, using the following formula:

1. Multiply weight in pounds by 703 (e.g., 190 lbs × 703 = 133,570).
2. Divide that number by height in inches (e.g., 133,570/66 in. = 2,023.79).
3. Divide the result by height in inches again (e.g., 2,023.79/66 in. = 30.66). The resulting BMI = 30.66.

Your instructor can take the average hours of TV viewing and the BMI from each member of the class and compute a correlation coefficient using some statistical software. (If the class is relatively small, a hand calculator could be used after consulting any statistics text for the computational formula for the correlation coefficient.) What did you find? Were TV viewing and BMI related for your class? What do you think these results mean?

SOURCE: Iannelli, V. (2008). BMI formula: BMI basics. *About.com Pediatrics*. [Online: Accessed 4-7-14]. Available: http://pediatrics.about.com/od/bmi/a/06_bmi_formula.htm

watched fewer than 28 hours of TV. In another study of nearly 400 adolescent males whose average age was around 16, it turned out that those who watched less TV were not any less obese than those who watched more TV, but on average, they were in much better physical condition.[40]

Some more recent evidence on TV viewing and obesity establishes a positive relationship between these two variables. In a large-scale survey of nearly 5,000 women over the age of 19, those who watched three to four hours of TV per day were compared to those who watched less than one hour per day.[41] Those who watched three to four hours each day had twice the rate of obesity. It is important to remember that any correlation like this one could be the result of some other variable that is related, in this case, to both obesity and TV viewing. But the authors of this study considered several variables, such as age, level of education, and weekly amount of exercise, and, even controlling for the impact of these variables on the relationship, TV viewing was still positively correlated with obesity levels.

In a study that included a large number of respondents, a team of researchers studied more than 20,000 males in the health profession who were between the ages of 41 and 78.[42] The results of this study showed a clear relationship between TV viewing and obesity. Some of the men reported watching TV more than 41 hours per week. Others reported watching a maximum of only one hour per week. The men in the first group were more than four times likely to be obese than the men in the second group. The authors of the study concluded that watching TV (or videotapes on the VCR) contributed to men's obesity. Because this study was conducted in 1996, watching videotapes was the common concern. Today, researchers might measure the time spent watching DVDs or online movies.

Another study of interest in this area was conducted on nearly 2,500 Pima Indians.[43] The researchers in this study concluded that physical activity and watching TV were both related to body mass index, a standard measure of obesity (see Study Box 4-5). Finally, in another large study that involved more than 50,000 women, a team of researchers who published their findings in the *Journal of the American Medical Association* found that TV viewing was associated with greater levels of obesity and the likelihood of having type 2 diabetes.[44] The most recent pertinent evidence was reported in the May 1, 2013 issue of *Pediatrics*.[45] The authors studied 91 adolescents between 13 and 15 years old. During a single week, they were able to collect time diaries as well as activity data that the adolescents provided with a personal digital assistant whenever they received an electronic signal. When researchers sent out signals to the adolescents, they asked them to report what activity was occupying their primary attention, secondary attention, and third-ranked attention at that moment. The results of the study did *not* show a significant correlation between body mass index and the amount of time devoted to any screen media (TV, computer, phone, video game, etc.). However, there was a significant correlation between the *level of attention* devoted to TV and body mass index. Adolescents who reported their primary attention was on TV tended to have higher BMIs. In fact, those who were in the top 25% in giving their primary attention to TV had an average BMI that was 2.4 points higher than those in the lowest 25%. That difference corresponded to a weight difference of about 14 pounds. Clearly, the preponderance of the evidence on the relationship between TV viewing and obesity shows that the two variables are related. Many researchers have concluded that the relationship is causal in that TV viewing displaces physical activity and consequently leads to more obesity. Although this may well be true, recall from Chapter 2 the cautions about interpreting correlations as evidence for causality. What we really need is an experimental-type design that manipulates TV viewing and measures its impact on obesity.

One study by Thomas Robinson did attempt this type of design with third- and fourth-grade children. Some of the children who participated in the study were randomly assigned to a media intervention that included a period of 10 days during which the children were encouraged to limit TV viewing and video game playing to just one hour each day. Compared to the control group who didn't receive the intervention and who tended to spend about triple the time with TV and video games, the children assigned to the intervention treatment had significant decreases in their BMI, on average, over the term of the study. Although this experiment does tend to support the causal link between TV viewing and obesity, we still must be careful about stating the relationship in strong causal terms. Part of the intervention treatment included a variety of different types of instruction that encouraged children to modify their TV habits. In the final analysis, we can't be sure which parts of the intervention directly produced the decreases in BMI. It could be that the instructional portions of the intervention sensitized children to the importance of physical activity and played a direct role in the final results of the study. Without more carefully controlled experiments, however, we have to settle for the knowledge that TV viewing and obesity are related, and that there is good reason to suspect that the relationship is partly due to the fact that TV viewing displaces physical activity.[46] Robinson has continued to employ this type of media intervention design to study the problem. He was part of a recent research team that studied 70 children who were in the highest 25% of children in their age group (four to seven years old) on the BMI measure. Half of the children were randomly assigned to a TV- and computer-use intervention group designed to reduce TV viewing and computer use by 50%. Once again, the intervention was successful and caused the authors to conclude that a powerful weapon in reducing BMI in children is to reduce their media use.[47] A final piece of suggestive evidence emerged from a recent study that showed that television viewing was strongly associated with childhood hypertension. Children who watched two to four hours of TV per day were 2.5 times more likely to have hypertension. Children who watched more than four hours per day were 3.3 times more likely to have hypertension.[48]

If TV viewing is a cause of obesity, it's important not to make an assumption about exactly how that cause may work. In reviewing this literature, it is tempting to conclude with the impression that any causal effect has to do with the inactivity that TV viewing produces. But recently, a team of scholars uncovered another possible mechanism in a large-scale study of Chinese youth. The researchers discovered that nearly half of the 1,552 respondents to a survey reported that they "sometimes" or "often" paid attention to the TV commercials. In contrast to those who didn't pay attention to commercials, this group was two to three times more likely to request snacks and buy snacks seen on those commercials and almost twice as likely to report eating snacks during TV viewing. The researchers concluded that TV viewing may exert its causal force on increased obesity simply by attracting the attention of some viewers to commercials for snacks.[49] Far from an activity displacement effect, this sort of effect is closer to persuasion—a topic that you'll read more about in Chapter 8. It's also consistent with that 2013 study in *Pediatrics* that identified *attention* to TV as the key variable that was associated with BMI—not just time spent with TV.

## SUMMARY

This chapter started with a review of some of the reasons people have for using the media. With so many different reasons, it isn't surprising to find that daily media use is quite substantial. Some people form parasocial relationships with media characters and personalities—a trend that might increase with binge viewing. With people spending so much time with mass media, questions about the effects of all this time have occupied the attention of researchers for years. Apart from the content that people are processing, some research has focused on the impact of the time spent in and of itself. The major focus of this research is on the displacement hypothesis— the idea that time spent in media use displaces other activities. Some research does indicate that TV viewing displaces social activities, reduces children's fantasy play, and leads to obesity and hypertension by reducing physical activity. One emerging area of research explores how media use displaces sleep. In the final analysis, mass-communication researchers need to study this topic with renewed vigor. The possibility that heavy media use decreases social interaction and contributes to higher levels of social isolation is one hypothesis that deserves to be taken seriously. The consequences of such a possibility are profound. Perhaps your course instructor will want to lead a classroom discussion on this topic and provide you with an opportunity to express your views.

## QUESTIONS TO FOCUS YOUR ATTENTION

1.  How much time do you spend watching TV each week? Browsing the Internet? Processing text messages? Are you satisfied with your current level of media use? Would you change it in any way? How? Why?

2.  Do you have any parasocial relationships with media characters? If so, explain how they started and how you feel about them. If not, why do you think you've chosen not to have such relationships?

3.  As young children spend increasing amounts of time with smartphones, tablets, and video games, do you think any significant activities are being displaced that could affect later development in a negative way? Explain.

## KEY TERMS AND CONCEPTS

| | | |
|---|---|---|
| mass communication | binge viewing | relaxation |
| uses and gratifications perspective | companionship | escape |
| motivations for media use | parasocial relationships | passing the time |
| learning | arousal | social desirability response |
| habit | optimal level of arousal | displacement hypothesis |
| TV addiction | set point | threshold effect |
| | sensation seeking | |

## NOTES

1. Cohn, B. (Producer), & Barry, M. (Writer). (1981). *Remember when*. Home Box Office.
2. Dominick, J. (2011). *The dynamics of mass communication: Media in transition*. New York: McGraw-Hill.
3. Katz, E., Blumler, J. G., & Gurevitch, M. (1973). Uses and gratifications research. *Public Opinion Quarterly, 37*, 509–523.
4. Greenberg, B. S. (1974). Gratifications of television viewing and their correlates for British children. In J. G. Blunder & E. Katz (Eds.), *The uses of mass communication: Current perspectives on gratifications research* (pp. 71–92). Beverly Hills, CA: Sage.
5. Rubin, A. M. (1981). An examination of television viewing motives. *Communication Research, 8*, 141–165.
6. Winn, M. (1977). *The plug-in drug*. New York: Bantam.
7. Smith, R. (1986). Television addiction. In J. Bryant & C. D. Zillmann (Eds.), *Perspectives on media effects* (pp. 109–128). Hillsdale, NJ: Erlbaum.
8. Greenberg, J. L., Lewis, S. E., & Dodd, D. K. (1999). Overlapping addictions and self-esteem among college men and women. *Addictive Behaviors, 24*, 565–571.

9. McIlwrath, R. D. (1998). I'm addicted to television: The personality, imagination, and TV watching patterns of self-identified TV addicts. *Journal of Broadcasting & Electronic Media,* 42, 371–386.

10. Kubey, R. W., & Csikszentmihalyi, M. (2002). Television addiction is no mere metaphor. *Scientific American,* February [Online: Accessed 4-21-14]. Available: http://www.commercialalert.org/issues/culture/television/television-addiction-is-no-mere-metaphor.

11. Kubey, R. W. (1996). Television dependence, diagnosis, and prevention: With commentary on video games, pornography, and media education. In T. M. MacBeth (Ed.), *Tuning in to young viewers: Social science perspectives on television* (pp. 221–260). Thousand Oaks, CA: Sage.

12. Horvath, C. W. (2004). Measuring television addiction. *Journal of Broadcasting & Electronic Media,* 48(3), 378–398.

13. Reeves, B., & Nass, C. (1996). *The media equation: How people treat computers, television, and new media like real people and places.* Cambridge: Cambridge University Press.

14. Perse, E. M., & Rubin, R. B. (1989). Attribution in social and parasocial relationships. *Communication Research,* 16, 59–77.

15. Nabi, R. L., Stitt, C. R., Halford, J., & Finnerty, K. L. (2006). Emotional and cognitive predictors of the enjoyment of reality-based and fictional television programming: An elaboration of the uses and gratifications perspective. *Media Psychology,* 8(4), 421–447.

16. Hoffner, C. (2008). Parasocial and online social relationships. In S. J. Calvert & B. J. Wilson (Eds.), *The Handbook of children, media and development* (pp. 309–333). Boston: Malden Blackwell.

17. Zuckerman, M. (1979). *Sensation seeking: Beyond the optimal level of arousal.* Hillsdale, NJ: Erlbaum.

18. Zuckerman, M. (1996). Sensation seeking and the taste for vicarious horror. In J. B. Weaver III & R. Tamborini (Eds.), *Horror films: Current research on audience preferences and reactions* (pp. 147–160). Hillsdale, NJ: Erlbaum; Lawrence, P. A., & Palmgreen, P. C. (1996). A uses and gratifications analysis of horror film preference. In J. B. Weaver III & R. Tamborini (Eds.), *Horror films: Current research on audience preferences and reactions* (pp. 161–178). Hillsdale, NJ: Erlbaum. 17.

19. Trice, A. D. (2010). Sensation-seeking and video choice in second grade children. *Personality and Individual Differences,* 49(8), 1007–1010.

20. Sundar, S. S., & Limperos, A. M. (2013). Uses & grats 2.0: New gratifications for new media. *Journal of Broadcasting & Electronic Media,* 57(4), 504–525.

21. Chen, G. M. (2011). Tweet this: A uses and gratifications perspective on how active twitter use gratifies a need to connect with others. *Computers in Human Behavior,* 27(2), 755–762.

22. Rubin, A. M., Haridakis, P. M., & Eyal, K. (2003). Viewer aggression and attraction to television talk shows. *Media Psychology,* 5, 331–362.

23. Tiggemann, M. (2005). Television and adolescent body image. The role of program content and viewing motivation. *Journal of Social & Clinical Psychology,* 24(3), 361–381.

24. Rideout, V. J., Foehr, U. G., & Roberts, D. F. (January, 2010). Generation M$^2$: Media in the lives of 8–18 year olds. Henry J. Kaiser Family Foundation [Online: Accessed 4-21-14]. Available: http://kff.org/other/poll-finding/report-generation-m2-media-in-the-lives/

25. Rideout, V. J., & Hamel, E. (May, 2006). The media family: Electronic media in the lives of infants, toddlers, preschoolers and their parents. Henry J. Kaiser Family Foundation [Online: Accessed 4-21-14]. Available: http://www.kff.org/entmedia/upload/7500.pdf.

26. National Association of Theater Owners. [Online: Accessed 4-4-14]. Available: http://www.natoonline.org/data/admissions/.

27. Mutz, D. C., Roberts, D. F., & van Vuuren, D. P. (1993). Reconsidering the displacement hypothesis: Television's influence on children's use of time. *Communication Research,* 20, 51–75.

28. Williams, T. M., & Handford, A. G. (1986). Television and other leisure activities. In T. M. Williams (Ed.), *The impact of television: A natural experiment in three communities.* Orlando, FL: Academic Press.

29. Myers, D. G. (1999). Close relationships and quality of life. In D. Kahneman, E. Diener, & N. Schwarz (Eds.), *Well-being: The foundations of hedonic psychology* (pp. 374–391). New York: Russell Sage Foundation.

30. Putnam, R. (2000). *Bowling alone: The collapse and revival of American community.* New York: Simon & Schuster.

31. Miller, W., & Sparks, G. G. (2008). *Refrigerator rights: Our crucial need for close connection.* Barrington, IL: Willowcreek Association.

32. van der Voort, T. H. A., & Valkenburg, P. M. (1994). Television's impact on fantasy play: A review of research. *Developmental Review,* 14, 227–251.

33. Huston, A. C., Wright, J. C., Marquis, J., & Green, S. B. (1999). How young children spend their time: Television and other activities. *Developmental Psychology,* 35, 912–925.

34. Potter, W. J. (1987). Does television viewing hinder academic achievement among adolescents? *Human Communication Research,* 14, 27–46.

35. Sharif, I., & Sargent, J. D. (2006). Association between television, movie, and video game exposure and school performance. *Pediatrics,* 118(4), 1061–1070.

36. Lee, W., & Kuo, E. (2002). Internet and displacement effect: Children's media use and activities in Singapore. *Journal of Computer-Mediated Communication,* 7(2) [Online: Accessed 4-21-14]. Available: http:// onlinelibrary.wiley.com/doi/10.1111/j.1083-6101.2002.tb00143.x/full.

37. Ferguson, D. A., & Perse, E. M. (2000). The World Wide Web as a functional alternative to television. *Journal of Broadcasting & Electronic Media,* 44(2), 155–174; Kayany, J. M., & Yelsma, P. (2000). Displacement effects of online media in the socio-technical contexts of households. *Journal of Broadcasting & Electronic Media,* 44(2), 215–229.

38. King, D. L., Delfabbro, P. H., Zwaans, T., & Kaptsis, D. (2014). Sleep interference effects of pathological electronic media use during adolescence. *International Journal of Mental Health and Addiction,* 12(1), 21–35.

39. Forrest, D. V., & Ryan, J. H. (1977). *The National Enquirer* TV poll. *Journal of Biological Psychology,* 19, 16–20.

40. Tucker, L. A. (1986). The relationship of television viewing to physical fitness and obesity. *Adolescence,* 21, 797–806.

41. Tucker, L. A., & Bagwell, M. (1991). Television viewing and obesity in adult females. *American Journal of Public Health,* 81, 908–911.

42. Ching, P. L. Y. H., Willett, W. C., Rimm, E. B., & Colditz, G. A. (1996). Activity level and risk of overweight in male health professionals. *American Journal of Public Health,* 86, 25–30.

43. Fitzgerald, S. J., Kriska, A. M., Pereira, M. A., & DeCourten, M. P. (1997). Associations among physical activity, television watching, and obesity in adult Pima Indians. *Medicine & Science in Sports & Exercise,* 29, 910–915.

44. Hu, F. B., Li, T. Y., Colditz, G. A., Willet, W. C., & Manson, J. E. (2003). Television watching and other sedentary behaviors in relation to risk of obesity and type 2 diabetes mellitus in women, *Journal of the American Medical Association,* 289(14), 1785–1791.

45. Bickham, D. S., Blood, E. A., Walls, C. E., Shrier, L. A., & Rich, M. (2013). Characteristics of screen media use associated with higher BMI in young adolescents. *Pediatrics,* 131(5), 935–941.

46. Robinson, T. N. (1999). Reducing children's television viewing to prevent obesity: A randomized controlled trial. *Journal of the American Medical Association,* 282(16), 1561–1567.

47. Epstein, L. H., Roemmich, J. N., Robinson, J. L., Paluch, R. A., Wimewicza, D. D., Fuerch, J. H., & Robinson, T. N. (2008). A randomized trial of the effects of reducing television viewing and computer use on body mass index in young children. *Archives of Pediatrics & Adolescent Medicine,* 3(162), 239–245.

48. Pardee, P. E., Norman, G. J., Lustig, R. H., Preud'homme, D., & Schwimmer, J. B. (2007). Television viewing and hypertension in obese children. *American Journal of Preventive Medicine,* 33(6), 439–443.

49. Parvanta, S. A., Brown, J. D., Du, S., Zimmer, C. R., Zhao, X., Zhai, F. (2010). Television use and snacking behaviors among children and adolescents in China. *Journal of Adolescent Health,* 46(4), 339–345.

# 5

# Effects of Media Violence

Most people know Rod Serling's name because of his brilliant creativity in the hit TV series *The Twilight Zone*. Fewer people know about Serling's unfortunate venture into the world of made-for-TV movies. In a way, Serling's movie *The Doomsday Flight* (1966) was his own journey into the Twilight Zone. The premise of the film was a sure winner for the NBC network. It promised to be a suspense-packed adventure from beginning to end. After a routine passenger jet took off and established its flight path, a report came in that the plane was carrying an altitude bomb. A terrorist had set the bomb to explode if the plane descended below 5,000 feet.

As planned, the movie was a ratings success. In the end, the plane managed to land in Denver, which was barely 5,000 feet above sea level. The plane averted disaster and everyone lived happily ever after. Well, almost everyone. Those who were working in the airline industry on the evening that *The Doomsday Flight* made its debut were not so happy. Even before the movie ended, a bomb threat was phoned in to one of the major airlines. Four more threats were phoned in during the next day, and eight more were reported by week's end. In some cases, the callers threatened to use exactly the same kind of altitude bomb depicted in the movie.

Fortunately, none of these threats turned out to be real. Still, it was a time of tension and high anxiety for airline pilots, crew members, executives, and family members waiting for loved ones. They had been the victims of what media researchers know as the **copycat phenomenon**. People sometimes imitate the exact behaviors that they see depicted in the media. When those behaviors are violent or illegal, this translates into a significant social problem. Rod Serling felt such regret at this unanticipated effect of his movie that he issued a public apology to the nation and requested that the film never be shown again.[1]

Rod Serling was not the first person—or the last—to feel the unanticipated consequences of the copycat effect. Several years before the O. J. Simpson trial turned a spotlight on domestic violence, the ABC network aired a movie depicting spousal abuse. *The Burning Bed* (1984) starred Farrah Fawcett as a battered housewife who felt so desperately trapped by an abusive husband that she did the unthinkable. In what she believed was her only avenue of escape, she soaked her husband's bed in gasoline while he slept. Then, she set the bed—and her husband—ablaze.

In this drama, based on a real-life occurrence, the wife escaped a murder conviction. The court held that she had acted in self-defense. Many experts recognize this movie as one that encourages battered women to seek shelter in the professional help community. Unfortunately, researchers also recognize that the film triggered some rather nasty copycat consequences. In the days following the broadcast, several women around the country who were victims of abuse decided to copy the behavior of the main character in the televised drama. They murdered their husbands. In a few cases, the scenario for the crime was exactly the same as depicted in the movie. Women doused beds with gasoline and set their sleeping husbands on fire.

Scholars have documented the phenomenon of copycat crime regularly since the dawn of TV. Survey results indicate that as many as one-third of the males convicted for felonies admit that they have imitated crime techniques shown on TV. Newspaper reports of early copycat incidents back in the late 1950s helped to trigger a massive effort to investigate the effects of television and movie violence. The controversy over media violence has raged ever since. One incident hit the news in February 2001 and stirred up the controversy anew. According to one report, a young teen set his friend on fire after seeing the same stunt acted out on the MTV program *Jackass*. His friend suffered bad burns over most of his body. Another ongoing concern about copycat violence centers on the potential effects of televised wrestling events. At least four children have died as victims of violence that may have been linked to exposure to professional wrestling. In the case of Lionel Tate, a 13-year-old boy convicted in 2001 for killing a six-year-old girl by lifting her in the air and dropping her onto a table, the legal defense specifically sought to place some responsibility for the incident on televised wrestling events. As you might suspect, World Wrestling Entertainment (WWE) denied any culpability in the girl's death and maintained that Tate's defense was simply a "contrived hoax." In another well-publicized incident, two young people from Oklahoma killed one person and paralyzed another while on a killing spree that was apparently intended to duplicate the behavior that they had seen many times while watching the movie *Natural Born Killers*. In an attempt to hold the makers of the film legally responsible for the crimes, attorneys filed a lawsuit under product liability law—essentially arguing that the movie was a "defective" product that had caused death and injury. During the several years of litigation that ultimately exonerated the moviemakers, additional copycat killings were attributed to the movie.[2] More recently, in March 2011, nine middle school students were expelled after school officials discovered that they were involved in a "fight club" that was apparently inspired by the movie *Fight Club*, which starred Brad Pitt and Edward Norton. The movie has also been blamed for other copycat fight clubs in the last few years.[3] Although it can certainly be difficult to document conclusively that a TV show, movie, or video game actually inspired a copycat incident, this difficulty has not prevented scholars from studying media violence. Of the hundreds upon hundreds of studies that scholars have published on the effects of television and movies, violence is by far the most frequent topic of investigation.

The government's threat in 1996 to introduce a rating system for television programs designed to protect children from the unwanted effects of violence and other objectionable content spurred the networks to act. A new rating system went into effect amid great controversy. Manufacturers now produce TV sets with a V-chip that permits parents to block out programs that contain unwanted violence.

Should we be making all of this fuss over media violence? Are the murder and mayhem on television really to blame for the increased violence in society? Would copycat criminals eventually commit their crimes even if a TV program or movie never inspired them to act? The answers to these questions are not simple. The researchers who have conducted the studies over the years sometimes disagree among themselves. Nevertheless, if one examines the research carefully, it is possible to make some sense of the mountain of data.

What exactly do we know today about the effects of media violence? In this chapter, I have tried to provide brief, accurate summaries of the many dimensions of this complicated body of research.

## THE PRESENCE OF VIOLENT CONTENT

Before his death in 2005, George Gerbner was professor emeritus at Temple University in Philadelphia and former Dean of the Annenberg School of Communication at the University of Pennsylvania. During his career, he directed a series of studies that he designed to tell us something about how much violence there is on television. In short, Gerbner's finding was that there was a large amount of violence on prime-time TV and that, despite public controversy over the years, the level of violence had remained fairly constant.[4] These content analyses were the results of one part of Gerbner's three-part **Cultural Indicators Paradigm** that he used to study media. He called this part **message system analysis**—a strategy that he employed to discover the nature of the actual content on television. Another part of the paradigm, **institutional process analysis**, was designed to discover why media producers produce the content that they do. The main way to accomplish this was to actually *talk with the producers*, and Gerbner did this regularly. The third part of the paradigm, **cultivation analysis**, was designed to explore the effects of media messages on people's beliefs and attitudes about the social world. Gerbner used cultivation analysis to test his well-known **media cultivation theory**. Because Gerbner's content analyses revealed that violence was such a prominent ingredient in prime-time TV, and because his cultivation theory generated so many studies on the effects of media violence, some reviewers of earlier editions of this text recommended that I include a full discussion of media cultivation in this chapter. I'm sympathetic to their point and so you will see Gerbner's name again in this chapter. However, media cultivation theory is about more than just media violence, so I've still included the main treatment in Chapter 8, where you'll read about theories and research having to do with attitude change. For now, the main point to grasp from Gerbner's content analyses is that they left little doubt about the prevalence of media violence in prime-time entertainment.

It isn't difficult to understand why our entertainment media contain a steady staple of violence. Good drama revolves around conflict, and violence is one of the common consequences of conflict. In the early days of the TV medium, however, the notion that people in the average home would have their television set on for more than seven hours per day would have been incomprehensible. As recently as 1950, only one home in 10 even had a TV. A decade later, only one home in 10 was without one. The idea of having more than 50 channels to select from— 24 hours a day—would have been laughable in 1950. By the 1990s, it had become a reality. Today, my local cable system offers channels starting at two and going into the thousands.

As the statistics on TV viewing changed, the sheer amount of violence being beamed into the average American household went beyond what anyone could have imagined. Today's estimates of viewing time, combined with what we know about how much violence is present, produce some very sobering numbers.

Newton Minow, former chairman of the Federal Communications Commission (FCC), noted in his recent book,[5] "By first grade, most children have spent the equivalent of three school years in front of the TV set." By age 18, time spent with TV exceeds time spent in school, time talking with teachers, time talking with friends, and time talking with parents. By age 70, today's average child will have invested more than seven years in TV viewing. Total viewing time varies with age, but the average child, regardless of age, spends more than four hours each day in front of the tube. (See Chapter 4 to review the statistics on time spent with TV.) How much of that viewing time contains violence?

According to George Gerbner's studies, children's shows contain more violence than any other type of programming. He estimated that shows designed for kids average about 32 violent acts per hour. On the basis of a study that spans 15 years, Gerbner estimated that crime is about 10 times more prevalent on TV than it is in the real world. According to the most recent estimates, by age 18 the average adolescent will have viewed over 200,000 acts of TV violence.[6] This is a conservative estimate.

So, there is little question about whether violence saturates our TV screens. No one can dispute this fact. Recent studies have attempted to capture more than just the number of violent acts. In the *National Television Violence Study*[7] researchers examined the context of violence. These data help to give us an even deeper understanding of what is happening on the screen.

The best research on violent content shows that nearly 60% of all television programming contains some violence. One-third of all programs contain nearly 10 violent interactions. These statistics confirm what we knew from earlier research. Violence is prevalent on the tube. But how is it depicted? In nearly 75% of all of the scenes depicting violence, no punishment is given for the violent actions. In one recent study that included an examination of the context of violence, Ron Tamborini and his colleagues studied televised professional wrestling. They found that compared to the way violence is shown in other program genres, the violence in professional wrestling is much more likely to appear justified, go without punishment for the perpetrator, and result in low levels of physical harm. The authors concluded that this combination may mean that viewers of professional wrestling are at higher levels of risk from the violence they witness.[8] These findings take on real significance when they are considered in light of Albert Bandura's theory of social learning, which I discuss later in this chapter.

How realistic are the portrayals of violence? Consistent with Tamborini's findings about professional wrestling, the data show more generally that in more than half of all violent interactions, no character is depicted as experiencing pain. And fewer than half of the violent interactions result in negative consequences for the perpetrator of aggression. There is ample room for concern about the lessons that media violence might be teaching to TV audiences.

While TV may still be regarded as the quintessential electronic entertainment medium, other media have captured significant amounts of our screen time in recent years. For example, YouTube debuted in 2005, and if you're like me, you probably watch short YouTube clips many times during a typical week. Is violence just as prevalent on YouTube as it is on prime-time TV? Andrew Weaver and his colleagues at Indiana University decided to find out. They did a systematic content analysis of the most viewed, the top rated, and the most recently posted videos on YouTube. Their data revealed that the levels of violence on YouTube are considerably lower than they are on prime-time TV. In fact, fewer than 20% of the YouTube videos contained any violence at all. While the overall average number of violent acts on YouTube was relatively high, that was due to a very small proportion of videos (about 1%) that featured constant violence—often taken directly from violent video games.[9] For those concerned about media violence, the YouTube statistics may offer little comfort. TV is still the dominant entertainment medium.

But at this point we have to be careful. Although the content studies clearly show that there is a lot of violence on TV, the studies have *nothing* to say about how that violence may be affecting people. Remember from Chapter 2 that it isn't possible to make inferences about media effects from the content alone. It is at least theoretically possible that all of that TV violence amounts to a kind of warning about how we ought *not* to behave. Maybe the best way to deal with the violent urges inside all of us is to turn on the tube and purge these impulses by indulging our wildest violent fantasies. Over the years, a few scholars have suggested that this idea might have some merit. We will look at this idea in a later section of this chapter. The important point here is that we must resist the temptation to look at the content of the media and assume that it must be having a particular effect on people. People can react to the very same content in a number of different ways. A person might react by walking away from a program and forgetting that it existed. No matter how strong the tendency to think otherwise, it is important to recognize that **content does not equal effect**.

One of my favorite illustrations of the difference between content and effect comes from the world of TV advertising—and probably during a time before you were born. Back in the 1980s, a clever person who was working on the ad campaign for Domino's Pizza invented a strange little cartoon character to star in the pizza commercials. This character was named the Noid, probably because his name sounded like the word *annoy*. The sole purpose of the Noid's existence was to find ways to make pizza cold before people could eat it. Domino's boasted fast delivery times and a special packing method that guaranteed the delivery of hot pizza. Their ad slogan was simple: One could "avoid the Noid" by ordering from Domino's.

The people at Domino's loved the concept and the ads went on the air in the late 1980s. Based on the content of the ad, it seemed easy to speculate about the effect: People would buy more pizza. And that probably was one of the effects of the campaign. But the people at Domino's could not possibly have imagined in their worst nightmare what was to happen next. Out there in the vast urban sprawl lived a man named Kenneth Noid. Mr. Noid was a troubled person, likely suffering from paranoia, who had not yet figured out what TV was all about. When Mr. Noid slouched back on the couch one evening and saw the pizza commercial that told the whole world to "avoid the Noid," he was furious. He couldn't believe the audacity of a major pizza chain taking out national advertising to tell the people of the world to avoid *him*. What could he possibly have done to deserve such treatment? He searched his memory long and hard to try to remember if he had done something to make his local Domino's Pizzeria mad at him. He just couldn't understand why he was under personal attack. He had to do something drastic.

The next thing the people at Domino's knew, one of their pizzerias was making national news. A hostage crisis was under way. On January 30, 1989, Kenneth Noid took hostages at a Domino's pizzeria and demanded that he be given pizza, $100,000, and a getaway vehicle. Mr. Noid didn't kill anyone in the hostage crisis, and was acquitted for his crime by reason of insanity. Things could have turned out far worse than they did.[10] The Noid is still celebrated from time to time in various places as a legendary advertising icon, but Domino's discontinued the campaign in the wake of the hostage incident.

The example of Mr. Noid is one of my favorites because it is so unusual. And in fact this sort of case is not likely to happen often. A more common example of the principle that media effects cannot be inferred accurately from an analysis of content comes from research on the effectiveness of an anti-drug campaign that was aimed at youth. Robert Hornik and his colleagues developed a longitudinal survey (see Chapter 2) to discover if a $1 billion advertising campaign (The National Youth Anti-Drug Media Campaign) was effective in discouraging initial drug use—particularly marijuana—among teens between the ages of 12 and 18. Based on the overall media strategy that involved local and network TV, cable outlets, movies, magazines, and Web sites, it certainly seemed reasonable to think that, if there was any effect on youth, the effect would be in line with the campaign's goals to discourage drug use. But that's not what Hornik's research revealed. In his survey of over 5,000 teens across four time periods between the years 2000 and 2004, he found that exposure to the anti-drug campaign was impressive. At least on that point, the goals of the campaign were met. Teens had been targeted in the campaign and the data revealed that they had definitely been reached. On average, teens saw two to three anti-drug messages per week. However, all of that exposure didn't seem to have the intended impact. The youth who were exposed to the messages actually expressed *fewer* intentions to avoid marijuana use in the future. There was also some evidence suggesting that more exposure to the ads predicted a *greater* likelihood of using marijuana for the first time.[11] Overall, the authors concluded that, "Through June 2004, the campaign is unlikely to have had favorable effects on youths and may have had delayed unfavorable effects" (p. 2229). Hornik and his colleagues speculated that perhaps the effect of seeing so many anti-drug messages in the media was to inadvertently communicate that drug use was a common behavior for teens—leading viewers to the belief that if they didn't have experience with drugs, they weren't normal. While we can't be sure exactly why this campaign appeared to fail, it stands out as an illustration of the principle that media effects cannot be assumed simply by examining media content.

One lesson to be learned from these examples is that the human capacity to react in unanticipated ways to media messages must be carefully respected. For this reason, we have to be cautious about looking at any media content, including violence, and jumping to conclusions about how that content is affecting the viewers. The number of possible effects may be large. Of course, it is also possible that there are no significant effects at all. To find out whether violent content really affects viewers, carefully designed research studies are the most trustworthy sources.

## THE CAUSAL LINK BETWEEN VIEWING VIOLENCE AND BEHAVING AGGRESSIVELY

### The Research of Albert Bandura

Since the late 1950s, researchers have attempted to answer the question of whether viewing media violence actually causes people to behave more aggressively. Albert Bandura, a Stanford University psychologist, designed some of the earliest studies with children. He developed a theory of how TV viewing might cause people to act in particular ways. This theory, known as **social learning theory**, emphasized the importance of **rewards** and **punishments**.

According to Bandura, if a child watched a person on TV who seemed attractive and who received rewards for acting aggressively, then the child would be more likely to imitate that character's behavior. On the other hand, if a child saw a character who received punishment for acting aggressively, then the child might refrain from acting out any aggressive impulses in real life. Bandura's theory did not just apply to TV. It was a general theory about the way people learn behaviors. The basic principles could explain how children learn to help people as well as hurt them. Many of Bandura's experiments used TV and violence to test the theory because the government was giving out grant money to do research on that topic.

In a typical experiment designed by Bandura, he randomly assigned children to watch one of two different videos. In one version, one of the leading characters acted aggressively and received rewards for his actions. In the other version, the same aggressive behavior received punishment. When the video was over, Bandura permitted the children to play freely in a room where his assistants could carefully monitor what happened. They counted the number of times each of the children imitated one of the acts of aggression that they had seen in the video.

The results of these studies are consistent. Children who saw aggressive behavior rewarded were more likely to imitate the aggression than were the children who saw it punished. Critics complained that some of Bandura's early studies used videos that didn't come from actual TV shows. In addition, Bandura considered it "aggressive" when children smacked a large "bobo" doll that toymakers had specifically designed for that purpose. Bandura overcame these early problems in later studies, and scholars around the world now accept the basic principle of social learning.[12]

The results of Bandura's studies should come as no surprise to most parents. When my own nephews were young, I can remember them tuning in religiously to professional wrestling. When the neighborhood children would come over to play afterward, my nephews often pretended to be wrestlers from the show. I watched many a heated argument over who was going to take the role of the wrestler who had just won a shiny new championship belt and who would reluctantly accept the role of his opponent who had just lost the match. If I ever needed to intervene once the play began, it was usually because the person playing the role of the champion was busy performing his heroic—yet very aggressive—actions. The person who was playing the role of champion had a license to be aggressive. After all, the champion had just been publicly recognized and praised for winning his match. He received rewards for his aggressive acts.

Bandura's studies helped researchers to understand a number of things about TV violence and children. First, viewing TV violence could cause children to behave more aggressively, particularly if the violent characters were attractive and received rewards for their actions.

Second, in many of these studies, the effects emerged most strongly for boys, not girls. Many researchers interpret this finding in the context of biological differences between the sexes. Throughout the animal kingdom, nature has programmed the male of the species with a predisposition to behave more aggressively than the female. The researchers thought that perhaps this aggressive predisposition resulted in boys being more sensitive to the impact of media violence. As it turns out, some studies on media violence show that the effects do extend to females as well as males. For a brief description of a recent study that found both sexes affected by media violence, see Study Box 5-1.

A third conclusion that can be drawn from Bandura's social learning effect is that the effect is quite general. It doesn't matter whether researchers make up the videos used in these experiments or borrow them from standard TV programs like old *Batman* and *Superman* cartoons. The principles remain the same. The presence of attractive TV characters who receive rewards for acting aggressively seems to promote more aggressive behavior in children.[13]

Finally, in studies of this type, it is important to understand that differences between the two experimental groups do not necessarily imply anything about a particular child. Not every child who saw the aggression being rewarded behaved aggressively after the video. Some of the children who saw the aggression punished acted aggressively just the same. In fact, as in most experiments of this type, *most* of the aggressive behavior that researchers observed after TV viewing was not the result of watching one of the two videos at all. Many other factors are important in determining aggressive behavior at any given instant. Probably one of the most crucial factors has

## STUDY BOX 5-1 Prolonged Exposure to Media Violence

Dolf Zillmann and James Weaver reported an experiment with college students that was designed to test the impact of prolonged exposure to media violence. They recruited 93 students (53 males, 40 females) to participate in the study. These students were randomly assigned to one of two film-viewing groups. In the "innocuous film" condition, they watched *Little Man Tate, Driving Miss Daisy, Rich in Love,* and *Postcards from the Edge* on successive days. In the "violent film" condition, students watched *Universal Soldier, Under Siege, The Hitman,* and *Excessive Force.* The day after they watched the last movie, the participants were told that they were needed to help identify emotional expressions on the faces of people in photographs. After each participant completed this task, he or she was provided with either positive or negative feedback that was given randomly. Some of the participants were told that they had done a good job. Others were told that their ratings were terrible. After completing this task, each participant was brought to a professor's office and given a form to complete about the experimenter who had provided the feedback. The form asked the participant to rate how deserving the experimenter was of receiving financial support as a research assistant. It also asked the participant, "If you had to make a Yes or No decision [for financial support], what would it be?" These measures were taken by the researchers as an opportunity for the participants to express hostility toward the assistant. The results indicated that both male and female participants who had watched the violent films earlier in the week were much more likely to express hostility in their ratings of the assistant. Of great interest to the researchers, this effect held regardless of the nature of the feedback the assistant had delivered in the ratings task. The researchers concluded that "the findings support the proposal that repeated, prolonged exposure to exceedingly violent drama is capable of facilitating hostile behavior for extended periods after exposure" (p. 159).

SOURCE: Zillmann, D., & Weaver, J. B. III. (1999). Effects of prolonged exposure to gratuitous media violence on provoked and unprovoked hostile behavior. *Journal of Applied Social Psychology, 29,* 145–165.

to do with the years of modeling and teaching that children receive from parents and the other important adults in their lives. Still, although the effect of video violence observed in these experiments is statistically small, it is predictable and reliable.

Although Bandura's studies offered initial insights into the effect of TV violence, many questions remained. One of the most important ones had to do with the type of aggression that researchers were measuring in these studies. Children were doing more hitting, kicking, biting, scratching, and so on in the context of playing with other children. What about more serious acts of aggression? When the government started funding Bandura's research, strong interest was expressed in the possibility that media violence causes an actual increase in the crime rate. Could violence in the media really cause more beatings, robberies, assaults, and murders? This is a more difficult question to answer confidently. A number of researchers have tried to gather data that might help us to provide an answer. What about the possible relationship between media violence and more serious acts of aggression among adults?

# The Long-Term Studies of Leonard Eron and Rowell Huesmann

One of the most impressive lines of research in the area of media violence comes from two psychologists, Leonard Eron and Rowell Huesmann. Working together with other researchers (Lefkowitz and Walder) back in the 1960s, the team studied more than 800 children under the age of 10. There were two things that were of particular interest. First, Eron and Huesmann wanted to know how much violence these children watched on TV. Second, they wanted to know how aggressive each child was in daily life activities. Through conversations and questionnaires given to parents, teachers, and the children themselves, they were able to assign a number to each child that indicated the quantity of violence in that child's daily diet of TV. Higher numbers indicated more violence. They also were able to assign another number to each child that indicated how aggressive the child was in day-to-day situations. After they gathered this information, they looked at the relationship between these two numbers across the entire group of children.

What did they find? Eron and Huesmann found that there was a tendency for those children who watched higher levels of TV violence to also have higher scores on the ratings of aggressive behavior. Researchers now recognize this finding as one that appears again and again in the literature. It might seem straightforward to conclude from this data that children are more aggressive because of their TV diet. Unfortunately, it isn't quite that easy. For one thing, since the researchers measured everything at the same time, there is no way to tell which came first—the TV viewing or the aggressive behavior. Maybe children who behave aggressively like to watch more violent programs because they want to see people who act the way they do.

Even though the researchers found it intriguing that children who watched more violence were also more aggressive, they understood the need for more information. So, they waited. In fact, they waited until the children reached the age of 19. After collecting data on the 19-year-olds, they waited another 11 years, until the children were 30. At each of these two later ages, they gathered some new information about the criminal records that had accumulated over the years. What kinds of crimes and how many crimes did each person commit? How long were the prison sentences that the court assigned? After gathering these data, the researchers went back and examined how much violence these adults had watched on TV when they were children. The findings were interesting, to say the least. The children who had the higher numbers on TV violence also tended to be the adults who became involved in more serious crimes! Huesmann summarized the findings of the study when he wrote:

> Aggressive habits seem to be learned early in life, and once established, are resistant to change and predictive of serious adult antisocial behavior. If a child's observation of media violence promotes the learning of aggressive habits, it can have harmful lifelong consequences. Consistent with this theory, early television habits are in fact correlated with adult criminality (pp. 129–130)[14]

In a study published in 2003, Huesmann, Eron, and their colleagues reported more results from a longitudinal investigation that followed children into adulthood. The findings are the same. Specifically, the authors noted that boys and girls who were in the upper 20% on TV viewing were significantly higher on the measures of adult aggression than were the rest of the study's participants.[15]

Do these findings guarantee that if a child watches TV violence, a life of crime will result? Not at all. First, it is important to understand that, just as in the experiments done by Bandura, not every child who watched large amounts of TV violence ended up getting involved in crime. There was simply a *tendency* for this to be the case. As in Bandura's research, this tendency, although it was definitely present, was small. Knowing the amount of TV violence children viewed enabled the researchers to account for less than 10% of the crimes committed by the children as they matured over the 22-year period. Depending on your perspective, you may believe that we should view this small percentage as an alarming and important statistic, or that we should view it as evidence that TV is not a very strong determinant of criminal behavior. One way to think about these two views is to consider a group of 10 children in your neighborhood. If these 10 children collectively committed 20 acts of aggression over some period of time, then the data indicate that perhaps two of these acts might be attributed to the effects of media violence. On one hand, this sounds like a small and insignificant effect. On the other hand, if this effect is multiplied for the total number of aggressive acts committed in society, it is easy to see reason for concern. One of the most prolific researchers in the media violence area, Ed Donnerstein, attempts to shed light on the size of the effect of media violence on aggression in a recent essay. Study Box 5-2 may help you to get some sense of how important media violence is compared to other factors known to cause aggressive behavior.

Second, even though the researchers could predict a certain number of crimes based on childhood viewing of TV violence, we can't be absolutely sure that the childhood viewing was a causal factor in the later commission of crimes by these adults. Perhaps there was something else about the families of the children that predisposed them to watch either violent or non-violent programs. This same factor may have helped lead the children to either a life of crime or a life of civic responsibility. The researchers tried to measure as many of these other factors as possible. After using some sophisticated statistical analyses, they still concluded that the children's early TV viewing very likely did contribute to criminal activity later in life.

Eron and Huesmann's research is important because it potentially links media violence with real-life violence. They aren't the only researchers to find such a link. More recently, in a study of German adolescents, a research team led by Barbara Krahé used a longitudinal design similar to the ones used by Eron and Huesmann. They measured exposure to media violence and self-reported aggressive behavior over one year in over 1,200 seventh and eighth grade students. They found that reports of exposure to media violence at Time-1 were significantly correlated to reports of aggressive behavior at Time-2. In contrast, the correlation between aggressive behavior at Time-1 was *not* significantly correlated with exposure to media violence at Time-2. What do these results suggest? Correlations between viewing media violence and aggression are always subject to at least two interpretations: (1) viewing violence results in aggression or, (2) people who behave aggressively consume more media violence. In this case, the researchers suggested that the data seem to support the first option—not the second. These findings also held for both boys and girls in the study.[16] Krahé's research

## STUDY BOX 5-2 Comparing Media Violence to Other Risk Factors for Aggression

Ed Donnerstein has recently written a comprehensive overview of the research findings that pertain to the effects of media violence on aggressive behavior. He considers the effects of violence from TV, video games, and the Internet. As part of that overview, he highlights the conclusions from a report of the U.S. Surgeon General in 2001. One of the significant questions treated in that report was the question about risk. What are the "risk factors" that might lead a child to become aggressive? This is the same sort of question that physicians have addressed in trying to understand the likelihood that a person might have a heart attack. There are numerous risk factors for heart attacks such as genetics, obesity, smoking behavior, alcohol consumption, physical exercise, etc. Each of these factors contributes to the risk to some degree. Similarly, Donnerstein reports the data on risk factors for aggressive behavior from the Surgeon General's 2001 study on youth aggression. Just as with heart attacks, there are a number of factors that contribute to the risk that a young person might behave aggressively. In each case, we can actually assign a numerical value to the level of risk that corresponds to a typical correlation coefficient between each factor and aggressive behavior. You may want to go back and review the discussion from Study Box 2-1 in Chapter 2 that gives guidelines on how to interpret values of correlation coefficients in terms of the size of the relationship that they indicate. Based on Donnerstein's essay and the Surgeon General's report, these are some of the risk factors for children in the six to 11 age range along with their typical correlation with aggression and an indication of the size of the effect:

| | | |
|---|---|---|
| Substance Abuse | .30 | (large) |
| Being a Male | .26 | (moderate) |
| Antisocial Parents | .23 | (moderate) |
| Weak Social Ties | .15 | (small) |
| Media Violence | .13 | (small) |
| Low IQ | .12 | (small) |
| Broken Home | .09 | (small) |
| Abusive Parents | .07 | (small) |
| Antisocial Peers | .04 | (small) |

Notice that there are a number of risk factors for aggression that are greater than the risk of consuming media violence. At the same time, media violence is a greater risk factor than coming from a broken home or having abusive parents or antisocial peers. It's important in understanding the possible causal contribution of media violence that the size of the statistical effect is not huge and ranks below several other factors. At the same time, it would be a mistake to dismiss media violence as an inconsequential risk factor.

SOURCE: Donnerstein, E. (2011). The media and aggression: From TV to the Internet. In J. Forgas, A. Kruglanski, & K. Williams (Eds.), *The psychology of social conflict and aggression* (pp. 265–282). New York: Psychology Press.

team extended these results in a more recent longitudinal study on over 1,700 high school students in Germany. Once again, these researchers found that consumption of media violence at Time-1 predicted both self-reported and teacher-rated aggressive behavior two years later.[17] Since one of the criticisms made of many of the experiments in this area is that we cannot extrapolate the results from laboratory studies to the real world, data like these, collected outside of the laboratory context, are also very important. What other evidence might there be that television violence is a culprit in increasing real-life violence?

## The Research of Brandon Centerwall

Dr. Brandon Centerwall graduated from Yale in 1975. He is a medical doctor and teaches at the University of Washington as a psychiatrist in the behavioral sciences. His analysis of crime statistics paints a disturbing picture. In 1945, just before TV emerged on the scene in the United States, statistics show three homicides per 100,000 people. By 1974, that figure had doubled. Similar data emerged for Canada. One could argue that during these years, many changes occurred in addition to the introduction of TV. Centerwall agrees. In an exhaustive series of studies, however, he claims that the data really do point to TV as the major culprit in the rise of homicides.[18]

Centerwall selected other countries that were similar to the United States in a number of ways. South Africa was one such country. When Centerwall examined the homicide rate in South Africa between 1945 and 1974, he discovered that the rate actually dropped by 7% during that time. Centerwall argues that one of the only major differences between South Africa and the United States during those years was the ban on TV imposed by the South African government. What happened in South Africa when the government lifted the ban in 1974? By 1983, the murder rate had increased by 56%. By 1990, the increase registered 130%—the rate had more than doubled in less than 20 years. The pattern of data strongly resembles those for the United States and Canada. To avoid getting a distorted picture of the data in South Africa due to racial tensions, Centerwall excluded all homicides against Blacks in his analysis of that country. Apparently, when racial tension resulted in homicide in South Africa, Blacks were typically the victims.

Although we can't be absolutely certain that Centerwall's analysis is correct, it is difficult to explain his findings without taking TV into account. Centerwall claims that roughly half of all homicides in the United States are a direct result of television watching. Given that Centerwall is not in a position to make a clear causal claim from the type of data he has analyzed, many media scholars conclude that his claim is too extreme. One example is Gary Jensen, a sociologist from Vanderbilt University, who did his own study of the homicide rates in the United States, Canada, and South Africa and concluded that instead of TV as the main culprit, statistics on the ratio of marriages to divorces was a more powerful factor in predicting homicide.[19] As the ratio of marriages to divorces decreases in society (fewer marriages-more divorces), the homicide rate tends to increase. In fact, in his study, once factors like this were incorporated into the analysis, TV vanished completely as a significant predictor of homicide rates. On the other hand, a later study of U.S. homicides by David Perry at the University of Alabama took account of the data on the ratio of marriages to divorces and still found a significant relationship between the permeation of TV and the arrest rate for homicides.[20] At this point, it seems safe to say that we ought to take Centerwall's conclusion seriously about TV's possible contribution to homicide—but also recognize that any final verdict on this thesis is still inconclusive.

## The Catharsis Hypothesis

Even though the research considered so far has tended to indict media violence as a cause of aggression, some researchers were slow to accept this idea. One of the most popular alternative views was advanced by Seymour Feshbach very early in the violence controversy (1960s). Feshbach thought that viewing TV violence could actually be therapeutic for a person filled with anger or frustration. TV could help purge those pent-up emotions. He borrowed this idea from the ancient Greeks. The idea of **catharsis** (meaning "to cleanse or purge; to get rid of") goes back to the Greek culture, which thrived on good drama. The Greeks believed that a person could get rid of grief and misery by going to a play that featured other characters who were grieving.

Feshbach simply extended the idea of catharsis to media violence. He reasoned that a person could cleanse pent-up feelings of anger by watching other people act aggressively. In this view, media violence was actually a positive thing. It could tend to lower the amount of aggressive behavior that might occur if angry people couldn't release their frustrations by watching others act out violence on TV.

Feshbach reasoned that watching TV would tend to calm angry people, making them less likely to react with intense anger. He also believed that watching violence would enable the angry people to engage in aggressive fantasies. If people could act out anger in their heads, they might have less need to act it out in real life. The network executives loved this theory. After all, if Feshbach was right about the effects of media violence, then the networks were actually providing an important public service by serving up a steady diet of TV violence. The crucial task for Feshbach was to prove that his idea had some merit.

The initial evidence that Feshbach offered in support of his theory looked convincing. First, he located a detention facility for boys; he reasoned that the boys who lived in this place would be angry and frustrated about their situation. After gaining the cooperation of the authorities who ran the facility, Feshbach randomly assigned the boys to watch either a violent TV diet or a non-violent TV diet for several weeks. Feshbach carefully monitored the behavior of each boy during the experiment. He relied on reports made by the houseparents of any incidents involving aggressive behavior. At the end of the study, the results were clear: The boys who had watched TV violence behaved less aggressively than the boys who had watched no violence. The results seemed to support the theory of catharsis.[21]

The lesson from Feshbach's research is that we should be slow to arrive at definitive conclusions from any single study. Other researchers who examined what

Feshbach had done were quick to criticize his conclusion. Imagine that you were a boy in this detention facility. Watching TV was one thing you could do to pass the time and entertain yourself. If you were like most of the boys of this age, your favorite programs were the ones packed with violence and suspense. One day, Feshbach's research team arrives and tells you that you can no longer watch your favorite programs because you are participating in a study. To make matters worse, you notice that the researchers permit some of the other boys to watch those shows for no apparent reason. How do you react? Perhaps you feel like hitting someone! If most of the other boys deprived of viewing violence felt like you did, it could easily explain why the boys who watched violence behaved less aggressively than the boys who watched nonviolence.[22]

Feshbach's findings demonstrated that people will act more violently if they can't watch their favorite TV programs than they will if they can watch them. Most researchers now agree that this is the best interpretation of the results of Feshbach's study. The results do not support the catharsis hypothesis.

## A Priming Analysis of the Effect of Media Violence

Over the years, many studies have shown that viewing media violence does not calm people down. In fact, a series of experiments by Leonard Berkowitz and his associates at the University of Wisconsin-Madison shows that angry people and media violence make for an especially volatile mix. Quite the contrary to Feshbach's idea of catharsis, if angry people watch media violence, they are *more* likely to behave aggressively.

Berkowitz and his colleague, Eunkyung Jo, have offered an explanation for how this **facilitating effect** of media violence might operate.[23] The key word in their explanation is *priming*. Priming is a process that can be understood simply in terms of associations. If you read a news story about an airplane crash, the story might "prime" thoughts associated with airplanes that you already have in your mind. You might start thinking about an upcoming trip that you have to take. The story might also prime thoughts about where you will choose to sit on the plane. You might remember that you haven't made your seat reservation yet, so you decide to make a phone call to your travel agent. In short, priming is a process whereby one thing that you think about reminds you of other things in your mind that you associate with the first thing. Berkowitz and his colleagues believe that the mass media are potent sources of images or ideas that can prime our thoughts and actions. According to these researchers, when

> … people witness, read, or hear of an event via the mass media, ideas having
> a similar meaning are activated in them for a short time afterwards, and …
> these thoughts in turn can activate other semantically related ideas and action
> tendencies. (p. 45)

According to this analysis, several things appear likely to happen when people view images of media violence. First, the violence can prime thoughts that are related to hostility. At least for a short period of time, such thoughts might affect the way we see other people and interpret their actions. I was reminded of this process a few years ago when I was out jogging for my daily exercise. As I ran by a parked car, a woman sitting in the driver's seat let out a loud shriek. I had startled her as I ran by the car. As I circled back around toward the car to offer an apology, the woman explained that she was in the middle of reading a newspaper story about a serial killer. The thoughts and feelings that this story had evoked may have primed her to react in a very different way to my presence than she would have otherwise. Second, in addition to priming violence-related thoughts, media violence might prime thoughts that lead one to believe that aggressive behavior might be warranted in certain situations and might bring about certain benefits.

Finally, media violence might prime action tendencies that cause people to be more inclined to act violently. My brothers, who recently retired from their jobs in a state prison system, reported to me that the prison inmates are almost always more unruly and violent immediately after they have watched a violent movie. I expressed some astonishment that the prison administration actually supplied such films for weekend entertainment and was told that this practice is common in many prison systems.

Despite the many studies by Berkowitz and others that clearly show evidence for priming and a facilitative effect of media violence on aggressive behavior, catharsis theory became very popular. This probably had something to do with the TV networks, which had a lot to gain in the violence controversy if the theory was viable. Catharsis is an idea that has died hard. There are still many who espouse this idea in discussions of the effects of media violence. But if the research over the past 30 years tells us anything conclusively, it tells us that we should allow the theory of catharsis to rest in peace. Craig Anderson and his colleagues recently tested the catharsis notion one more time in the context of music that contains violent lyrics. They reported the results of five different experiments conducted with college students and concluded that listening to songs with violent lyrics tends to *increase* aggressive thoughts and feelings—not reduce them.[24] They interpret their findings in the context of what they call the **General Aggression Model (GAM)** which predicts that exposure to media violence is much more likely to lead to a facilitation effect rather than a catharsis effect. The confirmation of that general prediction is now recognized as commonplace in studies of media violence.

## DESENSITIZATION TO VIOLENCE

The research summarized here points to the reasons that there is such a strong consensus among scientists that media violence causes aggressive behavior. We shouldn't conclude our look at this area of research without discussing another powerful effect that seems to be emerging from current studies. Media violence may have a **desensitizing effect**, making us numb to violence in real life so that we don't react to it as we would if we had never seen it on the screen. Before considering the research on this possibility, it's important to understand the basic theoretical process behind desensitization. Essentially, the **law of emotional desensitization** states that when we're exposed repeatedly to the same thing, the initial emotional reaction that we had will tend to decrease in intensity over the course of the repeated exposures. I learned this law well after I rediscovered the joy of riding roller coasters as an adult. After taking about 15 straight rides on a coaster that I found particularly thrilling, I found that the thrill started to diminish. I had to seek a new ride that offered something more. Prospective surgeons can take advantage of the law by desensitizing themselves to the sight of human blood during a surgical procedure. Similarly, a person with a phobia about snakes can effectively reduce their negative emotions when they go through systematic desensitization therapy. In the same way, if a person's initial reaction to seeing violence is fear, anxiety, and upset accompanied by physiological arousal, the law would predict that the intensity of those emotional reactions would diminish with repeated exposure to violence. In the case of media violence, the concern is that repeated exposure might result in such low levels of negative emotion that eventually, exposure to violence—even real-life violence—is accepted casually instead of prompting concern and action. What evidence is there for this effect?

The first type of evidence is anecdotal. Researchers who have taken the time to examine Hollywood movies have noted something interesting about the ones that have sequels. Inevitably, when producers make a sequel to a violent movie, they pack it with more violence than they did in the original film. If one looks only at the number of people killed by violent actions, the statistics are revealing. The first production of *RoboCop* featured 32 dead bodies. The second version featured 81. In *Death Wish,* the body count climbed from nine in the first version to 52 in the second. Rambo killed off 62 people in the initial *Rambo* film. By the time *Rambo III* rolled around, that number had soared to 111. George Gerbner, the researcher who took the time to chart these statistics, noted that the trend is even evident in the critically acclaimed *Godfather* movies. In the first film, 12 people were killed. The second film depicted 18 deaths, and the third installment featured 53![25]

One way to explain the increased violence in movie sequels is that Hollywood is attempting to satisfy the people who bought tickets to the first movie. Producers may intuitively realize that when they keep the same level of violence in the sequel, viewers won't get as great an emotional charge as they did the first time around. As a result, they provide more blood and gore. If this intuition is correct, it points to the possibility that some of our entertainment is actually getting more violent over time. The desensitization idea suggests that there is no easy way to go backward. The entire momentum is toward an ever-increasing level of violence.

Several researchers have accumulated convincing empirical evidence that shows that people do actually become desensitized to media violence. In one study, researchers had over 300 undergraduate students complete a measure that determined the extent to which they were habitual consumers of media violence. Two weeks later, each student watched a violent film clip from either *Casino* (by Martin Scorsese) or *Reservoir Dogs* (by Quentin Tarantino) and a comparison film clip that was either funny or sad. The students who were the heaviest viewers of media violence tended to have the lowest levels of skin conductance response (less physiological arousal) while viewing the violent film clips and they also tended to report higher levels of pleasure. The authors considered this evidence to be consistent with the idea that watching media violence is desensitizing.[26] Another investigation that exposed participants to clips of violence found the same sort of evidence. According to the authors, across nine different scenes of violence, the more violence their participants saw, the more they tended to report both higher levels of enjoyment for the violent clips and lower levels of sympathy for the victims of violence.[27]

While the anecdotal and laboratory evidence seems to support the notion that people desensitize to media violence the more they consume it, there's still another important question to ask: Is there any research to suggest that exposure to media violence may actually desensitize people to violence in real life? To answer this question, two researchers, Ronald Drabman and Margaret Thomas, set up an interesting study.[28] They randomly assigned children to watch either a violent or a nonviolent TV show. After each child finished watching the show, the experimenter drew attention to another TV monitor in the room and told each child that this monitor was displaying pictures of two children who were interacting in an adjacent room. The experimenter also explained that he had to leave the room and would return shortly. Just before leaving, the experimenter instructed the child to watch the TV monitor in case any trouble broke out between the children in the other room. If trouble did break out, the experimenter instructed each child to leave the room and go around the corner to notify him. Actually, the monitor was displaying a videotape in which the two children began fighting. The fighting grew more severe, and eventually, the screen went black. Drabman and Thomas wanted to know if watching a violent video just before receiving these instructions would cause children to be less sensitive to the fighting that they witnessed. The answer they got was clear: Children who had watched the violent video were far less likely than the other children to actually make an attempt to notify the experimenter about the fight that they observed on the monitor. These results support the idea that watching media violence can desensitize one to violence in real life.

The discussion of desensitization to violence goes beyond movies and TV shows. Before we leave the topic of media violence, it is important to recognize that the controversy about violent content extends to new technologies as well.

## WHAT ABOUT VIDEO GAMES? ARE THEY TRAINING KIDS TO KILL?

It doesn't seem like too long ago that my son and I carefully unpacked the newest and hottest toy in all the land—an Atari video game system. Together, we sat transfixed at the TV set and played game after game of *Pong*. We weren't sure that life got any better. What we couldn't have foreseen at the time was that *Pong* was the beginning of a video game revolution that seems to have no end in sight. Over the years, the graphics have become so advanced that it is sometimes difficult to tell whether the person on the screen is an animated image or a real human character from a TV show. The game characters now move in ways that are so close to human movement as to seem almost miraculous.

Although video games have provided hours of enjoyment and entertainment for those who own them, in the past few years the video revolution has shown a darker side. Many of the games seem to be little more than exercises in virtual killing. These games, known as first-person shooters, equip the player with a video gun. The object of these games is to rack up the highest score by blasting various characters to smithereens. The improved graphic technology of these games has enabled the manufacturers to create scenarios that seem quite realistic. The games have fantastic appeal to adolescents—particularly males. They are so much a part of our culture that, as you read these words, you are undoubtedly able to think of specific games and images that perfectly illustrate what I am describing. In fact, video game producers take in *billions* of dollars each year. Over the last few years, some of the games that feature lots of violent action are *Call of Duty, MadWorld, Splatterhouse, God of War III, Grand Theft Auto III,* and *Postal 2*—but by the time you read these words, there will probably be others. Some of these games are actually banned for sale in countries such as Brazil, New Zealand, Australia, and Germany.

Recall from Chapter 1 that in the aftermath of many of the mass shootings over the last few years, violent video games have frequently entered the conversation as a possible culprit in the tragedies. Eric Harris and Dylan Klebold, the two teens who attacked their classmates and teachers at Columbine High School, were supposedly quite fond of playing *Doom.* By this point, you should be able to recognize that a preference for playing a violent video game does not necessarily constitute a cause for violent behavior—even though the individuals who prefer the game and those committing the violent acts are the same. It is quite possible that playing *Doom* had no impact at all on the Columbine murderers. But, once this controversy had started, researchers began to pay more attention to the issues surrounding the incident. Before we look at the academic research, let's briefly look at the rhetoric of Lt. Col. Dave Grossman, a military man who has gone on the record to express his views in the controversy about violent video games.

## An Opinion on Video Games from an Expert on "Killology"

In the 1950s, Dr. Frederic Wertham, a psychiatrist, became convinced that comic books were the ruination of the youth of America. He took his case straight to the public, shunning the peer review process of scholarly research articles. Wertham wrote for popular magazines and published his own book, *Seduction of the Innocent*[29] (see Chapter 3). Although Wertham's analysis of the tremendous negative impact of comic books was never accepted or validated by the research community, he still played a significant role in the public arena and helped to shape standards in the comic book industry itself. When one reads the writings of Lt. Col. Dave Grossman, the similarities with Wertham cannot be ignored. It is almost as if the same basic story is being played out again over 50 years later. Like Wertham, Grossman has a professional credential that gives him some authority with the public and government policymakers. Just as Wertham had a popular book in which he articulated his thesis, so Grossman is the author of his own book on the subject of killing.[30] Whereas Wertham published in popular magazines like *Colliers,* Grossman has had a series of articles in *The Saturday Evening Post.*[31] Most important, Wertham's claims about the effects of comic books were based more on his own private convictions than on solid scientific evidence. Likewise, Grossman seems to be convinced that violent video games are transforming young people into "homemade sociopaths who kill reflexively," a proposition that, as yet, scientists have been unable to confirm. Let's look briefly at Grossman's claims about violent video games.

Grossman claims that the urge to kill is unnatural. He explains that the whole purpose of the military is to use brutalization and desensitization techniques to overcome the natural aversion to killing. He insists that through desensitization, the media have trained children to associate violence and killing with pleasure. Video games that require the player to shoot a gun and react reflexively with the shooting response are, he claims, teaching an entire generation of children to associate shooting with pleasure. Grossman argues that the increases in murder and assault around the world are due largely to violent mass media—and especially to violent video games. You may have heard from news reports over the past few years that violent crime is actually decreasing. Grossman counters that this is only an illusion. Modern medical technology is now so efficient that thousands of assaults that would have ended up as murders years ago never make it into the murder column of today's statistics. Grossman's argument about the illusion created by crime statistics is a point worth pondering. Crime statistics are influenced by many different variables so the arguments based on those statistics about the causal effect of media violence on real-world aggression—or the lack of a causal effect—are properly treated with caution. Study Box 5-3 provides some insight from the field of criminology about why violent crime statistics have shown a decrease in recent years. In any case, Grossman contends that violent assault is increasing because of the increasing violence in our media.

As a good student of media effects, how should you respond to Grossman's contentions? Is it really true that violent video games are transforming our youth into a culture of sociopaths? Grossman is so convinced that this is the case that he has even given a name to what he considers a psychological epidemic. Instead of AIDS (acquired immune deficiency syndrome), Grossman calls this epidemic **AVIDS** (acquired violence immune deficiency syndrome).

## The Research on Violent Video Games

In attempting to evaluate Grossman's position, the first thing that we need to know is whether there are published scientific studies on the effects of violent video games. Because this technology is much newer than TV, the number of available studies is not nearly so large. Nevertheless, over the past few years, the literature in this area has grown steadily. Back in 1988, Nicola Schutte and her colleagues reported the results of a simple study that was reminiscent of the early research of Albert Bandura on social learning theory.[32] Working with young children between five and seven years old, she randomly assigned them to play either a violent or a

## STUDY BOX 5-3 Why Is Violent Crime Decreasing?

According to the Bureau of Justice Statistics, the rate of homicide in the United States dropped nearly 50% from 1992 to 2011. In 1992, the rate was 9.3 homicides per 100,000 residents. In 2011, the rate dropped to 4.7 per 100,000. That's a dramatic decrease and the rates for other violent crimes like rape, assault, armed robbery, etc. followed the same trend. Given that consumption of media violence likely increased or remained stable during these years, doesn't that argue against the notion that media violence causes aggressive behavior? Not necessarily. It's difficult to determine how the consumption of media violence might be related to real-world crime due to the number of factors that affect crime rates. Sociologists and criminologists tend to agree that violent crime has dropped for several different reasons:

1. **Incarceration** – Prisons in the United States are bursting at the seams. Over the last few decades, there's been a concerted effort to put violent criminals behind bars. Once the violent offenders are taken off the streets, there are fewer people left who are inclined to commit violence.
2. **Policing** – It is simply more difficult to commit a violent crime without getting caught. Cameras are popping up everywhere—making it more likely that violent offenders are apprehended.
3. **Demographics** – The population of the United States is growing older. Between 1990 and 2010, the median age has increased by nearly four years to nearly 37 years old. A disproportionate amount of violent crime is committed by young people. As the population ages, there are simply fewer young people left to commit those crimes.

Factors such as these may combine together to exert a strong force on the crime rate in one direction—while other factors such as the consumption of media violence might simultaneously be exerting a force in the opposite direction. If the combined forces on the crime rate are stronger in one direction than the other, they might mask or hide the effects in the opposite direction. But that doesn't mean those effects don't exist. Theoretically, at least, it is quite possible that the consumption of media violence is causally related to real-world crime even though crime rates decrease. Similarly, an *increase* in crime rates shouldn't be taken as clear evidence that media violence causes aggressive behavior. The number of variables that affect crime statistics makes it difficult to tease out the independent contribution of something like media violence. All of this should serve to show that making a definitive case for the effects of media violence on real-world crime is a challenging proposition. Scholars need to use every tool at their disposal in attempting to analyze this important issue.

**SOURCE:** (1) Cooper, A., & Smith, E. L. (2013). Homicide in the U.S. known to law enforcement, 2011. [Online: Accessed 4-14-14]. Available: http://www.bjs.gov/index.cfm?ty=pbdetail&iid=4863, (2) Haq, H. (May 24, 2010). U.S. crime rate is down: Six key reasons. *The Christian Science Monitor*. [Online: Accessed 4-14-14]. Available: http://www.csmonitor.com/USA/2010/0524/US-crime-rate-is-down-six-key-reasons

non-violent video game. The violent game, called *Karateka,* involved a protagonist who was controlled by the player and had a mission to hit, kick, and kill enough villains so that a damsel in distress would be saved. The non-violent game, *Jungle Hunt,* involved a character who would swing from vine to vine in such a way that he would not fall and perish.

After the children had played one of the two games, the researchers observed the children's free play in a large room that was equipped with several toys. One of the toys was a jungle swing with small men attached to vines; another toy was a "bobo" doll that was dressed in a karate-type robe that resembled the garb of characters in the violent video game.

The study produced two main findings. First, the children who had played *Jungle Hunt* tended to play with the jungle swing toy, whereas those who played *Karateka* tended to play with the karate bobo doll. Second, as the authors had predicted, the children who had played *Karateka* tended to play in a more aggressive fashion than the children who had played *Jungle Hunt.* They had significantly higher scores on pushing, hitting, and kicking another child in the playroom as well as higher scores on hitting or kicking the bobo doll.

Considering the results of Bandura's studies, these results really shouldn't surprise you very much. They are consistent with some of the first studies on the effects of televised violence. The results also suffer from some of the same limitations as those of the early studies. We have to be careful about generalizing the results broadly from a single study that used one particular violent game. We also have to be careful about drawing too much from the fact that the children who played the violent video game acted more aggressively toward a bobo doll. Play aggression may have little to do with aggression toward real people. However, the authors did note that these same children were also more aggressive toward other children who were playing in the room.

Two other researchers who study video games, Craig Anderson and Catherine Ford, reported the results of an experiment in which college students played either a high-aggression game (*Zaxxon*) or a mild-aggression game (*Centipede*).[33] Other students were randomly assigned to a no-game control group. Instead of measuring aggressive behavior, the researchers had the students assess their feelings by checking off words that described how they felt after playing the games. The results showed that both of the video games produced higher feelings of hostility than were seen in the control group. In addition, the group that played the high-aggression game reported significantly higher levels of anxiety than either of the other two groups. The authors concluded, "The results indicate that playing aggressive video games can have short-term negative effects on the game-player's emotional state."

An important limitation in Anderson and Ford's study was that aggressive behavior was not measured directly. Placing check marks next to adjectives may have little to do with what someone actually does after playing a violent video game. Anderson tried to address this limitation in a more recent study that he authored with Karen Dill. The authors actually conducted two different types of studies and reported them together in an article in one of the leading journals in psychology, the *Journal of Personality and Social Psychology.*[34]

In their first study, Anderson and Dill had college students respond to some questions about the extent to which they played video games of various types as well as the extent to which they had been involved in aggressive delinquent behaviors in the past. The researchers found that these two variables were significantly related. Students who reported more playing time with violent video games also reported more aggressive delinquent behaviors. Of course, once again, we must be careful in interpreting this evidence. A relationship of this sort does not necessarily mean that playing the games caused increases in aggression. Perhaps some unmeasured variable was causally related to both playing aggressive video games and the tendency to commit acts of delinquent aggression. In fact, the authors gathered some evidence for this possibility. They also had students respond to a number of items that formed a measure of trait aggressiveness. For those students who scored high on trait aggression, the relationship between playing aggressive video games and delinquent acts of aggression was even stronger. One way to interpret these results is that some people are, for whatever reasons, inclined to behave aggressively. They score high on the trait of aggression. These people are also more likely to play violent video games, and they are also more likely to be involved in acts of delinquent aggression when compared to people who do not possess the trait of aggression.

Although the kind of survey data that Anderson and Dill gathered in this first study is certainly informative, it still doesn't help very much in gaining an understanding of the impact of playing violent video games on actual aggressive behavior. To address this issue more precisely, the authors set up a second study, which used an experimental design. Some college students were randomly assigned to play a violent video game (*Wolfenstein 3D*), and some were randomly assigned to play a non-violent game (*Myst*). These two games were chosen because in laboratory pre-tests, they both generated the same amount of physiological arousal during playing even though they differed significantly in terms of their levels of violence. After the game-playing sessions, the students participated in another phase of the experiment that they thought was unrelated to the video game session. They were placed in a situation where they had to react to a stimulus faster than their opponent. If they won the reaction-time test, they could blast their opponent with a loud noise. Not only that, they got to choose, within a certain range, how loud the noise could be and how long the noise would blast.

Imagine that you are a participant in this study and have just lost one of the reaction-time competitions. In the next competition, you win and are now allowed to blast the person who just beat you the time before. You might suspect that under these circumstances, you would send out a particularly loud blast of noise for a relatively long duration. In this respect, the students in the experiment reacted the same way regardless of which video game they had played. All students tended to blast their opponent louder and longer after having lost a reaction-time competition just before winning one. But those who had played the *Wolfenstein 3D* game blasted louder and longer than those who had played *Myst*. To the extent that this blasting behavior can be regarded as aggressive, the results of this experiment might be interpreted as evidence that playing a violent video game actually causes more aggressive behavior. Anderson and Dill certainly believe that these two studies, taken together, provide some insight into the relationship between playing violent video games and actual aggression. They stated:

> In the laboratory, college students who played a violent video game behaved more aggressively toward an opponent than did students who had played a non-violent video game. Outside the laboratory, students who reported playing more violent video games over a period of years also engaged in more aggressive behavior in their own lives. Both types of studies ... have their strengths and weaknesses. The convergence of findings across such disparate methods lends considerable strength to the main hypothesis that exposure to violent video games can increase aggressive behavior.

Of course, the technology improvements that are constantly being made on video game hardware and software create a special challenge for researchers to keep up with the latest innovations.

More recently, Ron Tamborini and his colleagues reported the results of an experiment that made a distinction between people who watched another person play a violent video game and those who actually played either a standard violent video game or one that featured a virtual reality experience.[35] Consistent with past results in this area, those who played the virtual reality version of the game had increased levels of hostility compared to those who only watched the games being played. In one of the most recent experiments along these lines, boys (10-13 years old) who played a violent video game were more likely to behave aggressively in a free-play situation than were boys who merely watched others playing the game.[36] Future studies will undoubtedly test the ways in which the virtual reality experience might lead to different consequences or effects compared to other types of game formats.

In the meantime, a number of recent studies continue to add evidence that playing violent games makes aggressive behavior more likely. In one study, the researchers discovered that when a violent game permitted the player to personalize the game characters, arousal and aggressive behavior increased.[37] The authors of this study used a novel measure of aggressive behavior. Before leaving the laboratory, the game-players were told that the next study in the lab was a taste-test marketing study. After tasting a small sample of hot chili sauce that they were told most people didn't like, each game-player was told that the next participant to enter the lab would have to consume the entire amount of sauce left in a container on the table. The game-players were told that they would determine how much sauce the next participant would have to consume by pouring that amount into a container. Those who played the violent video game poured nearly twice the amount of hot sauce for the next participant. Moreover, those players who got to personalize their game characters in the violent video game poured significantly more hot sauce than those who didn't have the personalizing option.

Back in 2001, John Sherry attempted to summarize all of the known studies on violent video games by using meta-analysis.[38] Recall from Chapter 2 that **meta-analysis** yields general statistical conclusions based on the findings of a large number of individual studies. Sherry was able to estimate the statistical effects uncovered across the entire published literature on this topic. As he notes in his analysis, the sample of studies to draw from is actually pretty small—only about 30 independent investigations—so we should be careful about drawing firm conclusions. Nevertheless, he reports that the data do show "a small but significant overall effect of video game play on aggression." However, he also notes that this effect is smaller than the effect of violent television on aggression. Sherry also concludes that one important variable in the relationship is the type of violence contained in the game. When the violence is related to sports or fantasy, the effect on aggression is smaller than when the violence involves virtual depictions of aggression toward human beings. In another attempt to summarize the literature on violent video games, Craig Anderson conducted a meta-analysis that was published in 2004.[39] According to his analysis, studies like Sherry's may tend to underestimate the effects of violent video games. Anderson contends that the studies with better methodological designs tend to find stronger effects, whereas the studies with more problems tend to show weaker effects. In his analysis, he concluded that exposure to violent video games is causally linked to increased aggressive behavior, increases in aggressive thoughts and feelings, higher levels of physiological arousal, and less helping behavior.

Most recently, Anderson and his colleagues have completed a new meta-analysis that they believed was badly needed because of the number of new studies on violent video games. Their new analysis included 136 different studies that involved over 130,000 participants.[40] This analysis included nearly four times the number of studies than any prior meta-analysis and supports the notion that over the last few years, much more research on this topic is being produced. The authors concluded that, "The evidence strongly suggests that exposure to violent video games is a causal risk factor for increased aggressive behavior, aggressive cognition, and aggressive affect and for decreased empathy and prosocial behavior."

## HOW DO VIOLENT VIDEO GAMES CAUSE AGGRESSION?

The most recent research on violent video games reflects one of the standard goals of science. Recall from Chapter 1 that scientists are not only interested in being able to make predictions—they want to offer explanations for why those predictions work. At this point, the existing data on violent video games look pretty familiar to researchers who have carefully studied the pattern that emerged with TV more than 40 years ago. Although the effects might not be quite as strong, depending on the nature of the game, it is beginning to appear that there may be a causal relationship between playing violent video games and behaving aggressively—just as there is between viewing TV violence and committing aggressive acts. But the similarity in the outcome doesn't necessarily mean the causal mechanisms operating in the video game situation are identical to the ones operating with TV.

Two new studies published in a 2014 article by Tobias Greitemeyer in the *Journal of Experimental Social Psychology* provided evidence that one of the reasons playing violent video games can cause an increase in aggression is because of the contrast between the severe violence in the games and less severe violence in real life.[41]

According to this analysis, those who play violent video games are typically involved in perpetrating very violent actions on other game characters. After blowing someone up or shooting them with an assault weapon, shouting at someone or shoving them in real life seems like a trivial, innocuous action. This perceptual contrast may tend to make it easier to actually engage in the real-life aggression. Doing so just doesn't seem like a very big deal compared to the things that go on in a violent video game.

A third recent study documented another causal mechanism that could be at work: stress. According to the theoretical logic employed by Yussef Hasan, Lauren Bègue, and Brad Bushman, we know that when human beings experience stress, they tend to become more aggressive. These authors wondered whether the well-documented effect of playing violent video games on aggressive behavior might be due to the fact that playing these games actually increases stress. In a study published in 2013 in the journal *Aggressive Behavior*, the authors replicated earlier studies that found that people behaved more aggressively (e.g., blasting loud noise at a competitor in a game) after they played a violent video game instead of a non-violent one.[42] The key finding of the study, however, was that those who played the violent video game also showed higher stress levels during their game play than those who played the non-violent game. In this case, the authors measured stress physiologically with a relatively new measure known as **cardiac coherence**. Cardiac coherence refers to a state in which a person's breathing rhythm and heart-rate rhythm are in sync. When such synchronization occurs, people tend to feel relaxed and report low levels of stress. In contrast, when the two rhythms are out of sync, people report higher stress levels. The fact that cardiac coherence was much lower for those who played the violent video game (lower levels of synchronization and higher stress) suggests that stress may play a crucial causal role in helping to explain why playing violent video games can increase aggressive behavior.

Of course, one bottom-line question that we would really like to answer is how worried we should be about violent video games. Should we let our children play any violent games? Which ones are OK and which should be avoided? One team of researchers recently echoed these questions in the title of their article: "The effect of playing violent video games on adolescents: Should parents be quaking in their boots?"[43] The answer that their article provides is that some children are adversely affected, but many are not. Definitive answers to the real level of risk will emerge more clearly as researchers continue to report the results of new studies during the next several years. For now, it looks as though there is some reason to be concerned that playing violent video games might be associated with the same sorts of effects that are well documented with movies and TV shows. Remember that these effects are definitely causal effects—but they are modest from a statistical standpoint. There are a host of other variables that contribute to aggressive behavior in the real world. It would be a mistake to focus exclusively on any type of media as the sole cause or even the primary cause of aggression in society. Human behavior is complicated and caused by hundreds of factors, only some of which we know about. Given this state of affairs, we shouldn't expect to be able to find easy solutions to the causes of a behavior like aggression.

Some reports out of Littleton, Colorado, have noted that Eric Harris was fond of playing a modified game of *Doom* that had extra weapons, more than one shooter, and a special feature that rigged the game so that the characters on the screen could not shoot back. Some observers suggested that when Harris played the game, he was actually acting out the sort of attack on his classmates that he eventually implemented on that fateful day in April 1999. No amount of evidence from media effects studies will permit us to conclude that the specific acts of a given individual were caused by exposure to violent media. But given what we know so far about the effects of playing violent video games, it surely seems as though Harris's video game habits could have placed him in a high-risk category for translating some of those habits into real-world behavior.

In terms of evaluating the rhetoric of Lt. Col. Grossman, it seems that the current research evidence would hardly support the sweeping claims that he makes about the impact of violent media. His rhetoric may be successful in motivating politicians to pay attention to the problem of media violence, but ultimately, the sorts of "magic bullet" claims of media impact that he suggests are not likely to be supported by scientific research. His claims are probably best regarded as rather gross exaggerations.

## WHY DO PEOPLE LIKE MEDIA VIOLENCE?

As you have made your way through this chapter, perhaps you have wondered why people even watch media violence. There wouldn't be so much controversy about it if people weren't somehow attracted to it. What are they attracted to? This is not an easy question to answer. Researchers who study media effects have devoted much more of their energies to understanding the impact of media violence than they have to the question of the appeal of this sort of entertainment. One thing that we do know is that the assumption that people generally enjoy media violence should not be taken for granted. In one essay, Joanne Cantor pointed out that anyone studying the Nielsen ratings will be struck by the unpopularity of televised violence. The ratings for one season examined in the 1990s showed that among children between the ages of two and 11, situation comedies were much more popular than violent cartoons that were broadcast on Saturday morning.[44] One researcher, Jeffrey Goldstein, devoted an entire book to the appeal of media violence. At one point, he observed: "It is worth remembering that violent entertainment is the preferred form of entertainment only for a minority of the general audience. Most viewers appear to prefer comedies and sitcoms to violent entertainment."[45] Still, the minority of the audience that does prefer violence is a sizable one. What can we say about why they are drawn to this form of entertainment?

Just a few years ago, my wife, Cheri Sparks, who has her doctorate in social psychology, coauthored a book chapter with me in our attempt to analyze the appeal of media violence.[46] We came up with three general reasons people are attracted to this type of entertainment. First, it does seem that violent entertainment may hold inherent appeal for some individuals. There may be some who literally experience a kind of sensory delight when they view mayhem and destruction on the screen. These images may be novel, exciting, and attractive in their own right. Second, some people may experience post-viewing gratification from viewing events, characters, and themes that tend to appear in violent contexts—while not necessarily enjoying the violence itself. For example, one researcher, Dolf Zillmann, has suggested that viewers form alignments with the characters in a movie or program. That is, we decide very quickly whom we like and whom we dislike. When good things happen to the characters we like, we find it enjoyable. Similarly, when bad things happen to characters we dislike, we also experience pleasure. Since a good deal of violent entertainment encourages the viewer to form alignments with different characters, viewers will enjoy violent films to the extent that their favored characters have good outcomes and their disfavored characters have bad ones.[47] Finally, violent media may contain other themes that viewers tend to enjoy. Perhaps violent films tend to contain more sexuality or more suspense. Viewers may be attracted to this sort of media for these factors, rather than for the violence. Although there is some research evidence to support all three of these explanations for the appeal of violent entertainment, researchers need to study these issues much more carefully to come to a better understanding of why violence is so attractive to some people (see Study Box 5-4).

## STUDY BOX 5-4 Is It Violence That People Enjoy?

I became so interested in investigating the appeal of media violence that I decided to team up with my colleagues and study the question using the experimental approach. We randomly assigned college students to watch one of two different versions of the movie *The Fugitive*, starring Harrison Ford. One group watched the movie in its original form. But for the second group, we showed a version of the movie that we had edited. The original version of the film included almost 15 minutes of on-screen violence. Using our digital editing lab, we removed almost all of this violence from the movie in such a way that the casual viewer could not detect that any editing had taken place. We pre-tested this version to make sure that students couldn't detect that the film had been altered. Even students who had seen the movie in years past and saw the edited version in our experiment didn't recall that the movie was any different from the version they had seen before. After participants in each group watched the movie, they responded to a post-viewing questionnaire that contained several questions about their reactions to the film—including a number of items about the extent to which they enjoyed the movie. We also asked them to estimate the number of scenes of violence that the movie contained and asked them to rate the level of violence in the film. The group who watched the edited version of the movie rated it as significantly less violent. But they also reported that they enjoyed the film to the same extent as the group who saw the film in the original, violent version.

Although this finding is limited to only a single movie, it has been replicated in other recent studies.[48] Perhaps Hollywood should examine the common assumption that violence is a popular film commodity. What do *you* think about the extent to which violence, in itself, contributes to the appeal of a movie?

SOURCE: Sparks, G. G., Sherry, J., & Lubsen, G. (2005).The appeal of media violence in a full length motion picture. An experimental investigation. *Communication Reports*, 18(1), 21–30.

## WHERE DOES RESEARCH ON MEDIA VIOLENCE GO NOW?

A steady stream of research on media violence has been ongoing for nearly 50 years. After all of that research energy, are there any directions for the future that still appear to be promising? In addition to some of the themes already covered, two relatively new areas of research appear to be especially exciting. First, scholars seem to be making real progress in understanding the role of **individual differences** in responses to media violence. For example, one team of scholars recently found that children who have been diagnosed as suffering from disruptive behavioral disorders are much more likely to show high levels of physiological reactivity when they are exposed to media violence.[49] This heightened physiological sensitivity may also translate to greater susceptibility to the behavioral effects uncovered in many studies. Perhaps children who suffer from these behavioral disorders are the ones who are most likely to behave aggressively after they watch a violent program or play a violent video game. A second new area of research involves the use of **Magnetic Resonance Imaging (MRI)** to get a visual picture of the areas of the brain that may be most active during exposure to media violence. For example, one team of researchers recently studied a small sample of males while they played a violent video game. They reported that the area of the brain associated with affective or emotional reactions appeared to be significantly suppressed during the video game play.[50] A major challenge in this line of research is to interpret what the results of such studies might mean for our understanding about how media violence affects people. Future studies ought to help scholars to meet that challenge. Research in this area appears to be slow to develop but one recent study does report using MRI with adolescents who played a violent video game and found that playing the game reduced activity in the prefrontal cortex of the brain.[51] More studies using this technology will surely appear in the future literature.

## WHY DO SO MANY PEOPLE DOUBT THE EFFECTS OF MEDIA VIOLENCE?

If you go back to Chapter 4 and review some of the statistics about the time people spend consuming media messages, the notion that all of that media exposure has no effect on the consumers should strike you as strange. Certainly those who are in the advertising business would consider that way of thinking outlandish. After all, advertisers are willing to spend roughly $4 million on 30 seconds of advertising during the Super Bowl. They have good reason to believe in media effects. They see their advertising resulting in more products moving off the shelves. Nevertheless, if you're a typical student, you may find it difficult to believe that media violence has any significant impact on aggressive behavior. You're not alone. Dr. Brad Bushman, one of the leading scholars in the area, wrote an Op-Ed piece for CNN in 2013 about how playing violent video games could affect aggressive behavior. Soon after the piece was published, over 1,400 people made comments that argued against the fact that playing violent games had *any* harmful effects.[52] In fact, such resistance to the idea that media affects people is not limited to the area of media violence. As you read the remaining chapters in the text, my guess is that you'll find yourself expressing some skepticism about effects that have credible evidence in their favor. A skeptical attitude is a healthy thing to cultivate—but it needs to be accompanied by a thorough and nuanced understanding of scientific evidence.

Why is there such resistance to what the science of media effects has clearly revealed? In the case of media violence, part of the problem may be that even teachers and scholars don't understand properly how the large number of studies ought to be interpreted. A small minority of scholars even try to make the case that no causal connection between media violence and aggression exists. In a complicated media environment, separating the wheat from the chaff in the babble of competing voices can be a daunting task even for scholars—much less the public. Three prominent and highly credible voices from the scholarly community recently published an essay that identified no fewer than nine different reasons that help to explain the resistance to what the science of media effects clearly reveals. I've summarized a few of these reasons in Study Box 5-5. One of my goals in writing this book is to

---

## STUDY BOX 5-5 Some Reasons Why People Deny Media Effects

1. **Faulty Reasoning:** People reason that because "I've watched media violence or played violent video games and never killed anyone, media violence must be harmless." The literature on most media effects reveals what statisticians would consider to be "small" effect sizes. That's perfectly consistent with the conclusion of many people that they have not been affected. But it is *not* consistent with the notion that no effect exists.

2. **Stubborn Refusal to Accept the Truth:** For reasons of personal and political identity, some people are hell-bent to express attitudes that are contrary to what is obviously true. Here at Purdue University, every time I walk by the Neil Armstrong Hall of Engineering that was built in honor of one of our favorite alums who walked on the moon, I'm reminded that there are still many people who deny the truth of the moon landing. We shouldn't be surprised. The Flat Earth Society has many members, and an active website too.

3. **Hollywood Denials:** People who work in Hollywood have more channels and opportunities to distribute their viewpoints to the public at large than social scientists. With so much money at stake, the view that frequently comes from Hollywood is that negative media effects—such as the effects of violence on aggression—simply don't exist. At the same time voices from Hollywood might proclaim no connection between media messages and negative effects, they are quick to celebrate the positive effects that media have on society. Having it both ways just doesn't ring true.

4. **News Media Don't Report Negative Effects:** A recent study of news reports about media effects shows that the tone of stories since the year 2000 is even *less* likely to emphasize negative media effects than in prior decades. In addition, the authors noted that when journalists do cover research on negative effects, they often turn to academic sources for commentary that don't match the expertise or credibility of the main researchers.[53] The overall message from such reports leaves an audience confused.

---

SOURCE: Strasburger, V. C., Donnerstein, E., & Bushman, B. J. (2014). Why is it so hard to believe that media influence children and adolescents? *Pediatrics*, 133(4), 571–573.

help you come to an informed perspective about the effects of media. In the concluding remarks in this chapter, I've tried to provide a summary of some of the important points that I hope you remember when the topic of media violence comes up for discussion.

## CONCLUDING COMMENTS

This chapter provides an overview of the research on media violence. This is a challenging task because there are many studies to consider in this literature. When all is said and done, what should you take out of all of the research?

First, the researchers who conduct these studies agree strongly that viewing violence does cause an increase in aggressive behavior. But it is also important to note that, from a statistical point of view, the effect is not very large. People behave aggressively for many reasons. The contribution that media violence makes to aggressive behavior is only one small piece of the puzzle. While the research clearly shows that there *is* a causal connection between consumption of media violence and aggression, that doesn't mean that every person who consumes violence increases their aggressive behavior.

Second, even though the statistical contribution of media violence to aggressive behavior is small, this does not mean that the effect is unimportant. In today's media environment, millions of people may view the same violent program or movie. Even very small statistical effects will translate into large social problems when this many viewers are involved.

Third, the idea that viewing media violence can reduce aggressive behavior is no longer viable. Results from dozens of studies refute this idea. When network executives argue for symbolic catharsis or declare that media violence has no effect, we should believe them to the same extent that we would believe the major tobacco companies if they told us that smoking does not cause lung cancer. In short, we shouldn't believe them at all.

Finally, even though most of the research on media effects deals with violent content, there are many other important effects that scholars have studied. Our picture of media impact would be woefully incomplete if we did not consider these other areas as well.

## SUMMARY

This chapter began by encouraging you to think about copycat crimes and the prevalence of violence in today's media content. In raising the question of the possible causal connection between media violence and aggressive behavior, the chapter reviewed some of the important surveys and experimental research relevant to this issue. It discussed some of the key theoretical concepts, such as priming and desensitization. Finally, you were encouraged to think about why people like media violence and why there's a tendency to resist the notion that media effects exist.

## QUESTIONS TO FOCUS YOUR ATTENTION

1. Do you actively seek out media entertainment to enjoy because of the violence? If not, why not? If so, what is it about media violence that you find enjoyable?

2. Have you ever personally witnessed a person behaving aggressively that you thought could have been fueled to some extent by a media presentation? If so, which theoretical process discussed in the chapter do you think could have been at work?

3. Some scholars have argued that human violence in the world is decreasing and that media violence has become a safer and more acceptable way of expressing aggressive impulses. Their view is that, on the whole, media violence is not something to be concerned about. What do you think of this position in the light of the material covered in this chapter?

## KEY TERMS AND CONCEPTS

| | | |
|---|---|---|
| copycat phenomenon | rewards | law of emotional desensitization |
| Cultural Indicators Paradigm | punishments | AVIDS |
| message system analysis | catharsis | meta-analysis |
| institutional process analysis | facilitating effect | cardiac coherence |
| cultivation analysis | priming | individual differences |
| media cultivation theory | General Aggression Model (GAM) | Magnetic Resonance Imaging (MRI) |
| social learning theory | desensitizing effect | |

## NOTES

1. Liebert, R. M., Neale, J. M., & Davidson, E. S. (1973). *The early window: Effects of television on children and youth*. New York: Pergamon Press.

2. Shapiro, D. M. *Natural Born Killers*. [Online: Accessed 4-21-14]. Available: http://www.crimelibrary.com/notorious_murders/celebrity/natural_born_killers/1.html

3. QMI Agency. Kids expelled over "Fight Club" video. (March 2, 2011). [Online: Accessed 4-21-14]. Available: http://www.torontosun.com/news/weird/2011/03/02/17468226.html

4. Gerbner, G., Gross, L., Morgan, M., & Signorielli, N. (1994). Growing up with television: The cultivation perspective. In J. Bryant & D. Zillmann (Eds.), *Media effects: Advances in theory and research* (pp. 17–41). Hillsdale, NJ: Erlbaum.

5. Minow, N. (1996). *Abandoned in the wasteland: Children, television and the first amendment*. New York: Hill and Wang.

6. Strasburger, V. C. (2007). First do no harm: Why have parents and pediatricians missed the boat on children and media? *Journal of Pediatrics*, 151(4), 334–336.

7. Smith, S. L., Wilson, B. J., Kunkel, D., Linz, D., Potter, W. J., Colvin, C. M., & Donnerstein, E. (1998). Violence in television programming overall: University of California, Santa Barbara Study. In Center for Communication and Social Policy, University of California, Santa Barbara (Ed.), *National television violence study* (Vol. 3, pp. 5–220). Thousand Oaks, CA: Sage.

8. Tamborini, R., Skalski, P., Lachlan, K., Westerman, D., Davis, J., & Smith, S. L. (2005). The raw nature of televised professional wrestling: Is the violence a cause for concern? *Journal of Broadcasting & Electronic Media*, 49(2), 202–220.

9. Weaver, A. J., Zelenkauskaite, A., & Samson, L. (2012). The (non) violent world of YouTube: Content trends in web video. *Journal of Communication*, 62, 1065–1083.

10. I can't remember exactly where I first heard the story of Mr. Noid, and I have had difficulty verifying all of these details since I read the initial account of the incident. I have at least been able to verify that the incident happened. A Web site [Accessed: 4-21-14] (http://tvacres.com/admascots_noid.htm) provides a brief account of the incident that is consistent with mine and cites a story from *Advertising Age* (February 6, 1989).

11. Hornik, R., Jacobsohn, L., Orwin, R., Piesse, A., & Kalton, G. (2008). Effects of the National Youth Anti-Drug Media Campaign on youths. *American Journal of Public Health*, 98(12), 2229–2236.

12. Bandura, A. (2009). Social cognitive theory of mass communication. In J. Bryant & M.B. Oliver (Eds.), *Media effects: Advances in theory and research* (pp. 94–124). New York, NY: Routledge.

13. Stein, A. H., & Friedrich, L. K. (1972). Television content and young children's behavior. In J. P. Murray, E. A. Rubinstein, & G. A. Comstock (Eds.), *Television and social behavior: Vol. 2. Television and social learning* (pp. 202–317). Washington, DC: U.S. Government Printing Office.

14. Huesmann, L. R. (1986). Psychological processes promoting the relation between exposure to media violence and aggressive behavior by the viewer. *Journal of Social Issues*, 42, 125–139.

15. Huesmann, L. R., Moise-Titus, J., Podolski, C. L., & Eron, L. D. (2003). Longitudinal relations between children's exposure to TV violence and their aggressive and violent behavior in young adulthood: 1977–1992. *Developmental Psychology,* 39(2), 201–221.

16. Krahé, B., & Möller, I. (2010). Longitudinal effects of violence on aggression and empathy among German adolescents. *Journal of Applied Developmental Psychology*, (31)5, 401–409.

17. Krahé, B., Busching, R., & Möller, I. (2012). Media violence use and aggression among German adolescents: Associations and trajectories of change in a three-wave longitudinal study. *Psychology of Popular Media Culture*, 1(3), 152–166.

18. Centerwall, B. S. (1989). Exposure to television as a cause of violence. In G. Comstock (Ed.), *Public communication and behavior* (Vol. 2, pp. 1–58). San Diego, CA: Academic Press.

19. Jensen, G. F. (2001). The invention of television as a cause of homicide: The reification of a spurious relationship. *Homicide Studies: An Interdisciplinary and International Journal*, 5(2), 114–130.

20. Perry, D. K. (2007). Does television kill? Testing a period-characteristic model. *Media Psychology*, 9(3), 567–594.

21. Feshbach, S., & Singer, R. (1971). *Television and aggression*. San Francisco: Jossey-Bass.

22. Liebert, R. M., & Sprafkin, J. (1988). *The early window: Effects of television on children and youth*. New York: Pergamon Press.

23. Jo, E., & Berkowitz, L. (1994). A priming effect analysis of media influences: An update. In J. Bryant & D. Zillmann (Eds.), *Media effects: Advances in theory and research* (pp. 43–60). Hillsdale, NJ: Erlbaum.

24. Anderson, C. A., Carnagey, N. L., & Eubanks, J. (2003). Exposure to violent media: The effects of songs with violent lyrics on aggressive thoughts and feelings. *Journal of Personality and Social Psychology*, 84(5), 960–971.

25. Jhally, S. (1994). *The killing screens: Media and the culture of violence* [video]. Northampton, MA: Media Education Foundation.

26. Krahé, B., Möller, I., Huesmann, L. R., Kirwil, L., Felber, J., & Berger, A. (2011). Desensitization to media violence: Links with habitual media violence exposure, aggressive cognitions, and aggressive behavior. *Journal of Personality and Social Psychology*, 100(4), 630–646.

27. Fanti, K. A., Vanman, E., Henrich, C. C., & Avraamides, M. N. (2009). Desensitization to media violence over a short period of time. *Aggressive Behavior*, 35(2), 179–187.

28. Drabman, R. S., & Thomas, M. H. (1976). Does watching violence on television cause apathy? *Pediatrics*, 57, 329–331.

29. Wertham, F. (1954). *Seduction of the innocent*. New York: Rinehart.

30. Grossman, D. (1996). *On killing: The psychological cost of learning to kill in war and society*. Boston: Little, Brown.

31. Grossman, D. (1999, July/August). We are training our kids to kill. *The Saturday Evening Post,* pp. 64–71.

32. Schutte, N. S., Malouff, J. M., Post-Gorden, J. C, & Rodasta, A. L. (1988). Effects of playing videogames on children's aggressive and other behaviors. *Journal of Applied Social Psychology*, 18, 454–460.

33. Anderson, C. A., & Ford, C. M. (1986). Affect of the game player: Short-term effects of highly and mildly aggressive video games. *Personality and Social Psychology Bulletin*, 12, 390–402.

34. Anderson, C. A., & Dill, K. E. (2000). Video games and aggressive thoughts, feelings, and behavior in the laboratory and in life. *Journal of Personality and Social Psychology*, 78, 772–790.

35. Tamborini, R., Eastin, M. S., Skalski, P., Lachlan, K., Fediuk, T. A., & Brady, R. (2004). Violent virtual video games and hostile thoughts. *Journal of Broadcasting & Electronic Media*, 48(3), 335–357.

36. Polman, H., de Castro, B. A., & van Aken, M. A. G. (2008). Experimental study of the differential effects of playing versus watching violent video games on children's aggressive behavior. *Aggressive Behavior*, 34(3), 256–264.

37. Fischer, P., Kastenmüller, A., Greitemeyer, T. (2010). Media violence and the self: The impact of personalized gaming characters in aggressive video game on aggressive behavior. *Journal of Experimental Social Psychology*, 46(1), 192–195.

38. Sherry, J. L. (2001). The effects of violent video games on aggression: A meta-analysis. *Human Communication Research*, 27, 409–431.

39. Anderson, C. A. (2004). An update on the effects of playing violent video games. *Journal of Adolescence,* 27(1), 113–122.

40. Anderson, C. A., Shibuya, A., Ihori, N., Swing, E. L., Bushman, B. J., Sakamoto, A., Rothstein, H. R., & Saleem, M. (2010). Violent video game effects on aggression, empathy, and pro-social behavior in Eastern and Western countries: A meta-analytic review. *Psychological Bulletin*, 136(2), 151–173.

41. Greitemeyer, T. (2014). Intense acts of violence during video game play make daily life aggression appear innocuous: A new mechanism why violent video games increase aggression. *Journal of Experimental Social Psychology*, 50, 52–56.

42. Hasan, Y., Bègue, L., & Bushman, B. J. (2013). Violent video games stress people out and make them more aggressive. *Aggressive Behavior*, 39, 64–70.

43. Unsworth, G, Devilly, G. J., & Ward, T. (2007). The effect of playing violent video games on adolescents: Should parents be quaking in their boots? *Psychology, Crime & Law*, 13(4), 383–394.

44. Cantor, J. (1998). Children's attraction to television programming. In J. H. Goldstein (Ed.), *Why we watch: The attractions of violent entertainment* (pp. 88–115). New York: Oxford University Press.

45. Goldstein, J. (1998). Why we watch. In J. H. Goldstein (Ed.), *Why we watch: The attractions of violent entertainment* (pp. 212–226). New York: Oxford University Press.

46. Sparks, G. G., & Sparks, C. (2000). Violence, mayhem, and horror. In D. Zillmann and P. Vorderer (Eds.), *Media entertainment: The psychology of its appeal* (pp. 73–91). Mahwah, NJ: Erlbaum.

47. Zillmann, D. (1998). The psychology of the appeal of portrayals of violence. In J. H. Goldstein (Ed.), *Why we watch: The attractions of violent entertainment* (pp. 179–211). New York: Oxford University Press.

48. Weaver, A. J., & Wilson, B. J. (2009). The role of graphic and sanitized violence in the enjoyment of television dramas. *Human Communication Research*, 35(3), 442–463; Weaver, A. J., Jensen, J. D., Martins, N., Hurley, R. J., & Wilson, B. J. (2011). Liking violence and action: An examination of gender differences in children's processing of animated content. *Media Psychology*, 14(1), 49–70.

49. Grimes, T., Bergen, L., Nichols, K., Vernberg, E., & Fonagy, P. (2004). Is psychopathology the key to understanding why some children become aggressive when they are exposed to violent television programming? *Human Communication Research*, 30, 153–181.

50. Weber, R., Ritterfeld, U., & Mathiak, K. (2006). Does playing violent video games induce aggression? Empirical evidence of a functional magnetic resonance imaging study. *Media Psychology*, 8, 39–60.

51. Hummer, T. A., Wang, Y., Kronenberger, W. G., Mosier, K. M., Kalnin, A. J., Dunn, D. W., Matthews, V. P. (2010). Short-term violent video game play by adolescents alters prefrontal activity during cognitive inhibition. *Media Psychology,* 13(2), 136–154.

52. Bushman, B. J. (2013). Do violent video games play a role in shootings? *CNN.com*. [Online: Accessed 8-9-14] Available: http://www.cnn.com/2013/09/18/opinion/bushman-video-games/index.html

53. Martins, N., Weaver, A. J., Yeshua-Katz, D., Lewis, N. H., Tyree, N. E., & Jensen, J. D. (2013). A content analysis of print news coverage of media violence and aggression research. *Journal of Communication*, 63(6), 1070–1087.

# 6

# Sexual Content in the Media

## HUMAN SEXUALITY BRINGS OUT PASSIONATE OPINION

R ecall back in Chapter 3 when you read about Edgar Dale's content analysis of movies in the late 1920s. About 75% of the film content he examined could be classified as crime, love, or sex. This should tell us something at the very outset about sexual content in the media. It is not a recent phenomenon. Judging from the controversy that erupted in the United States in early 2011 over MTV's British adaptation series, *Skins*, some may have thought that sexual content in the media was a brand new idea. Several advertisers pulled their sponsorship from the program and the Parents Television Council asked the U.S. government to investigate whether the show violated child pornography laws.[1] As it turns out, the firestorm that erupted over that show is nothing new. In fact, if we wanted to go back centuries, we would find that media dealing with human sexuality in some way are never far from the cultural scene. And controversy is often part of that scene. This should hardly be surprising. The sexual appetite is basic to human existence and future survival. Therefore, it seems reasonable that human sexuality would show up constantly in art and entertainment.

When we consider sexual content in the media and the impact of that content, we enter a highly charged arena that is populated with a number of interest groups. First, more than with any other area of media content, people with religious concerns have historically expressed their views about sexual content with fervor. Back in 1977, when a new sitcom that pushed the envelope, *Soap,* hit the airwaves, the National Council of Churches launched a vigorous campaign that resulted in many letters of complaint being filed with the ABC network and the advertisers who sponsored the program. Just as with MTV's *Skins,* several advertisers withdrew their ads. In the case of *Soap,* some affiliate stations decided not to air the first program of the series. Other stations decided to run the program later in the evening to protect children who might have been in the audience during the earlier time slot.[2]

A second type of interest group that often brings this same type of pressure against the networks is typically not associated with any specific religious group but advocates for the protection of children on behalf of parents who may be generally concerned about broadcast content. The Parents Television Council, which was protesting loudly over *Skins*, is one such group. In 2008, this group applied pressure to affiliates of the CBS network by asking them to pre-empt episodes of the new prime-time show *Swingtown*, which dealt with themes such as spouse swapping. The series was short-lived—it was cancelled early in 2009. There's no way to know if the complaints of the Parents Television Council had any role in the low ratings for the program. But despite protests, sex on TV is hardly disappearing. Early in 2014, Discovery Channel's *Naked and Afraid* was placing high in the Sunday night ratings race with unusually high appeal among young men in the 18–49 demographic.[3] Each episode of the program features an adult male and female who meet for the first time and are then subjected to an adventure that tests their survival skills in remote locations. They face their outdoor challenge wearing no clothes. While viewers do see partial nudity in *Naked and Afraid*, they will only be able to imagine it while watching a pilot episode of a new program that WEtv plans to debut in an adaptation from a program airing in the U.K. The program, *Sex Box*, features real-life couples who agree to come on the show and have real sex with each other while secluded in a soundproof box that is clearly visible to viewers. The premise of the show is that after emerging from their sexual encounter, the couples will discuss their relationship in hopes of a start toward a solution to their various problems.[4]

The Parents Television Council continues to apply pressure about what they deem to be objectionable sexual content. They recently targeted the CW network for plans to make two sexually oriented scenes available online that weren't included in the original TV broadcast of the series *Reign*.[5] But this sort of pressure strikes many as an insidious kind of censorship, even though no laws prohibiting expression are involved. The passion that many bring to this topic based on their religious or moral convictions is matched by the fervor of those who seek to protect free expression under the First Amendment at all costs. The resulting clash of values and voices can make a hotbed (pun intended) of rhetoric. As you might imagine, the TV networks and Hollywood studios want no part of government censorship. They want to be free to produce the content that will make them the most profit—regardless of who might be offended on the grounds of an inappropriate or excessive sexual depiction. They also fear a government that can restrict the flow of any type of information by legal decree.

Despite the fears of Hollywood, U.S. law does permit the government to restrict the flow of certain messages. Complicating matters is the fact that law enforcement officials tend to have strong opinions about sexually explicit media. **Obscenity** is not protected under the First Amendment. If media content is judged as fitting the legal definition of obscenity, it can theoretically be restricted from circulation. Fortunately or unfortunately, depending on your viewpoint, the legal test for obscenity is rigorous, and few judges or courts have been willing to declare many media messages to be obscene. Essentially, to win an obscenity case, a plaintiff must establish that the media message in question was designed primarily to stimulate or appeal to sexual or prurient interests, that it has no redeeming artistic value, and that it violates contemporary community standards. Because all three of these criteria must be met, the history of efforts to declare media legally obscene shows little consistent success. Because of the community standard criterion, it is theoretically possible to have a movie or magazine declared to be obscene in one community but not in another. Despite the legal nightmare involved in tests of obscenity, the legislative branch of government has always had some stake in issues surrounding sexual content in the media.

A variety of competing political interests are evident in the debates about sexual content in the media. Many feminists have been outspoken about the dangers for women of certain types of sexual depictions. Their early voices of concern have been joined by others. Sometimes, strange bedfellows (pun intended again) unite on the same side in debates about sexual content. For example, feminists and members of the religious right often find themselves opposing the same sorts of sexual content in the media. This may be one of the few political issues that they agree on, and they typically find this agreement to be an uncomfortable state of affairs. Other groups have children's interests at the forefront of their campaigns. Believing that early exposure to explicit sexuality can induce various forms of psychological harm for children, these groups fight against public displays of sexually explicit magazines at convenience stores and call for strict enforcement of the MPAA movie code that prevents children from being admitted to watch designated movies without a parent or adult guardian.

Unwary scientific researchers often fail to realize that, in conducting research on the effects of media sex, they enter into a volatile mix of religion, law, and political agendas. It is important to understand at the outset that regardless of the findings of any given study, the researcher who studies sexual content in the media is probably more vulnerable to criticism than in any other area of media studies. There are simply too many passionate voices expressing too many passionate opinions. While few researchers have publicly discussed their apprehensions about conducting research on media sex, there is at least one vivid testimonial that illustrates the point. In 2002, a German publication carried an interview with Dolf Zillmann, who had recently retired as a college dean after a long and illustrious career as one of the most prolific scholars of media effects research in history. Hopefully, you recall his name from the preceding chapters. The interviewer began the conversation by asking Zillmann about his favorite field of media research. Although Zillmann didn't express a favorite, he did express a *least* favorite. He said:

> … I must confess to an anti-favorite domain: erotica. Our research on the effects of pornography triggered an unimaginable avalanche of hostility from those deeming particular findings inopportune—that is, in conflict with their values regarding sexuality. We were attacked in the media for being too liberal (for my theorizing on sadomasochistic interests, I was labeled Marquis de Zillmann) as well as too conservative (it was alleged that I was a born-again Christian marching in anti-porn rallies). Worst of all, my closest collaborator received death threats, along with threats of the sexual abuse of his wife and children. I was ill prepared for assaults of this sort and immediately called off all work on erotica effects. Only recently have we abandoned our moratorium

on such research …. But the disdain for research in this area persists, mostly because the report of any findings is bound to offend the moral sensitivities of some and thus stir controversy devoid of all rationality.[6]

Fortunately, despite the personal aggravations, Zillmann and other scholars have managed to produce a body of empirical research that provides significant insight about the general impact of sex in the media. Before you examine some of that research, it might be helpful to think about exactly what is meant by some of the terms used in discussing this topic.

## SORTING OUT DEFINITIONS AND TERMS

The area of sexual content is fraught with definitional ambiguities. Sexual content is a general label that can refer to something as innocuous as a kiss between two married adults or as horrifying as a brutal rape in a XXX-rated pornographic video. Researchers have struggled with the choice of terms they use to describe the content that is the focus of their investigations. The term *pornography* is often used to refer to almost any explicit sexual depiction. However, in the scholarly community, some use this term to refer to material that features explicit sexual behavior and nudity in a context frequently characterized by depictions of one character exerting physical or psychological dominance over another. Sometimes, this type of material contains explicit violence that is shown along with explicit sexuality. Scholars who use the term pornography in this way tend to reserve the term *erotic media* for material that features explicit sexual content in the absence of violence and without the overt power dynamics that appear in pornography. While this distinction has been useful for scholars, it isn't necessarily shared even in the scholarly community—and it certainly isn't used widely outside the scholarly community where the term *pornography* is applied to a diverse cross-section of media that contains sexual depictions of some sort.

One way to think about media content is to classify media messages according to the quantity and explicitness of both sex and violence. TV soap operas, sit-coms, and prime-time programs may contain lots of sexual content and low to moderate levels of violence. But on each of these dimensions, the content is not very explicit compared to what is offered in movies. Hard-core pornographic films and material found on the Internet typically contain large amounts of very explicit sexuality and sometimes contain explicit violence as well. Erotic films are filled with explicit sexuality but little or no violence, and typically do not show coercive behavior where one character dominates another. Before we can gain an accurate picture of the effects of sexual content in the media, we need to understand what type of content we are talking about. Because the government has been greatly concerned with the effects of pornography, much of the research has concentrated on studying the impact of very explicit sexual material that also features images of dominance, coercion, and/or violence. The research history of this material is tied closely to government-funded efforts. Let's turn our attention to that history and to the research findings that have emerged over the past few decades.

# THE COMMISSION ON OBSCENITY AND PORNOGRAPHY

In 1967, the U.S. Congress established the **National Commission on Obscenity and Pornography**. Formed under the presidency of Lyndon B. Johnson, the commission was put in place because of growing concern about the role of pornography in crime and juvenile delinquency. Part of the charge of the commission was to study existing laws pertaining to pornography and to arrive at a better understanding of the distribution of this material. Media effects scholars were most interested in another aspect of the commission's charge—to study the effects of pornography on the public.[7] On the basis of what was found, specific recommendations for legislation were to be formulated. To meet this charge, the commission sponsored several research projects that examined the impact of sexually explicit materials. University researchers were commissioned to undertake new research designed to answer the question about impact.

It is important to note here that the term *pornography* as it was used in 1967 did not carry the same connotations as it does today, particularly with respect to violent content. Much of the material studied by the commission was sexually explicit but not violent. It is also important to note that much of the material was not nearly as explicit as some of the mainstream material available in today's adult video stores or on the Internet. Nevertheless, the report that was issued in 1970 was the most comprehensive document on the topic up to that time, and it did include study of a wide diversity of sexual content.

## Major Finding

By the time the commission published its report in 1970, Lyndon B. Johnson was no longer president. Richard Nixon had assumed this position, and he was not prepared to hear the findings that were published. The following is a key passage from the report itself:

> The Commission believes that there is no warrant for continued governmental interference with the full freedom of adults to read, obtain or view whatever such material they wish. Extensive empirical investigation, both by the Commission and by others, provides no evidence that exposure to or use of explicit sexual materials play a significant role in the causation of social or individual harms such as crime, delinquency, sexual or nonsexual deviancy or severe emotional disturbances.[8]

Essentially, the commission report stated that there were no known harms caused by pornography for any population studied. President Nixon didn't buy it. He rejected the commission's report—an act that was probably made easier by the fact that the commission had been formed under his Democratic predecessor. But for today's scholars and students of media effects, the important question is this: Does the conclusion of the commission report accurately reflect the state of affairs regarding the effects of pornography? Clearly, Richard Nixon didn't think so, but what about the scholarly community?

## A Reexamination of the Commission's Findings

Two theoretical notions that were widely discussed in the aftermath of the commission report were the **trigger hypothesis** and the **safety valve theory**. The trigger hypothesis essentially claims that exposure to sexually explicit materials will cause a response in some individuals that will provoke them in such a way that it may lead them to commit a sex crime such as rape or indecent exposure. The safety valve theory, in contrast, claims that exposure to sexually explicit material will satisfy whatever urges might cause a person to commit a sex crime. If this second idea has merit, then we might actually see a *decrease* in sex crimes in communities that have ready availability to these materials. Of course, in today's electronic environment, virtually anyone can have access to sexually explicit materials via the Internet, making the concept of availability more difficult to assess for any given community (see Study Box 6-1).

One aspect of the research findings that led the commission to conclude that pornography is not harmful had to do with the findings pertaining to the rate of sex crimes in Denmark following the relaxation of legal restraints on the flow of sexually explicit materials. This evidence could be interpreted as support for the safety valve theory. However, subsequent analysis of this data by one researcher, Berl Kutchinsky, reveals that the decrease in some of the sex crimes may be attributed to the fact that public attitudes became more lenient, resulting in fewer reports to the police. Although this explanation for the decrease could not be applied to every sort of sex crime (it doesn't seem to account for a decrease in molestation of young women), it does seem to call into question the strength of the evidence in favor of the safety valve theory.[9] Following the publication of the commission report, another researcher, J. H. Court, collected data showing inconsistent results across the world in the analysis of sex crimes. Sometimes these crimes seem to decrease with the spread of pornography, sometimes they increase, and sometimes they remain the same.[10] One thing that seems to be relatively stable across countries, however, is that the incidence of rape does not decrease when pornography is permitted to flow freely. One study published over 20 years after Court's data were published analyzed crime statistics from Japan over a 23-year period and found that availability of pornography was definitely correlated with increases in rape and sexual assault.[11] On the other hand, Kutchinsky reported the results of another study in 1991 from Denmark, Sweden, Germany, and the United States from which he concluded that the availability of pornography had no documented detrimental effects on sexual violence.[12] The most recent study of this type was from the Czech Republic, where legal restrictions on pornography were lifted in 1989.[13] The results showed that sex crimes have not increased with the unrestricted flow of sexually explicit material. The data from studies such as these remain inconclusive because of their correlational nature and their reliance upon statistics collected in many different ways across different cultures. This line of research hasn't gone very far in resolving the issue about whether exposure to pornography might be harmful.

As it turns out, the commission noted in its own summary of the data a number of qualifications that serve to caution the reader about accepting the overall

## STUDY BOX 6-1 Old Theoretical Ideas Applied to New Content

As you read about the trigger hypothesis and the safety valve theory, did the ideas seem to have a familiar ring? You should have been able to recognize some similarity between the trigger hypothesis and social learning theory, the facilitating effect, and the idea of priming, all of which you read about in Chapter 5. If you realized that the safety valve theory sounded a bit like the theory of symbolic catharsis, then you probably have a pretty good grasp of these two ideas. In fact, scholars have a tendency to borrow the theoretical ideas that have been applied to one domain of study and apply them to another domain with some modification and a different name. This tendency is so evident that some scholars would suggest that a book like this one could be organized around a basic core set of theoretical ideas instead of being structured according to the different types of media content, as reflected in the chapter titles listed in the table of contents.

An interesting exercise to increase your understanding of the theoretical ideas applied to the study of media effects would be to take several of the ideas explored in different chapters and reflect on the extent to which they are alike or different. Because the text material is organized according to different types of *content*, the connections between theoretical ideas applied across the various content areas might not be immediately evident—even though definite connections do exist.

In the case of social learning theory and priming, these ideas have been used to explain a variety of different sorts of behavior. Although these theoretical ideas often tend to be associated with the effects of media violence, this is mainly because of the large volume of studies done on that topic. The same theoretical principles could be used to explain many phenomena—not just those associated with violence or sexual content. One example comes from a story that I heard reported on a CNN newscast years ago while I was doing my daily jog on the treadmill. The media reported that President Bill Clinton had 90% of his heart arteries clogged and would have to submit to a quadruple bypass surgery. During the period when this was being discussed in the media, health clinics and hospitals reported what they referred to as "Clinton syndrome." In some cases, the number of males in their 50s (Clinton was 58 at the time of his surgery) reporting chest pains and wanting complete exams was triple the typical number. This sort of phenomenon might be explained by appealing to the notion of priming and social learning. Clinton was rewarded for going to the hospital when he had chest pains. His doctors said that he almost certainly would have had a heart attack in a few weeks. Many men who felt some chest discomfort learned this lesson well and decided to do just as Clinton had done ... perhaps a good example of social learning. Or perhaps when some men experienced chest discomfort, the experience primed their recent experience watching the news report about Clinton—which in turn prompted them to seek medical attention.

conclusion too readily. First, the material used in the research was collected over a limited time, and the findings might not generalize to other times and other types of material. Nearly 45 years after the commission report, this limitation seems important. Much has happened in the interim in terms of the type of material generally available to the public and the ease of access to that material. Second, for ethical reasons, the commission could not study the impact of sexually explicit material on children. Thus, although no evidence of harm was reported by the commission, it would make little sense to conclude that children are risk-free if exposed to this kind of media. I personally remembered this point several years ago when I visited a family who lived below me in a two-flat housing unit in a large metropolitan area. Two of the young children in that household, both under the age of 10, were glued to the TV screen during my visit, watching nude women cavort across the screen in a presentation being broadcast on the *Playboy* channel. This is one situation that the commission failed to study—not only because the Playboy channel wasn't available back then—but also because of prohibitions by committees concerning the ethical treatment of human subjects. I don't mean to suggest that nudity is necessarily harmful to young children. But even the programmers at the *Playboy* channel would admit that its entertainment is created for adult viewers. We have little research investigating the meanings and effects that such programs might create for children.

The upshot of the Commission Report on Obscenity and Pornography was that the overall finding triggered controversy among politicians, parents, and researchers alike. As one might expect, the finding was readily embraced by media sources that had a stake in publishing sexually explicit materials. If you go back to the pages of *Playboy* magazine in the early 1970s, you will find frequent mention of the commission report and its overall finding that exposure to sexually explicit materials is harmless. I had the chance to witness firsthand the media industry's reliance on the commission report during the 1980s, when I was called to appear on a TV talk show in Cleveland along with Marilyn Chambers, a star who appeared in many sexually explicit films. At the end of the program, Ms. Chambers retrieved a faded scrap of newspaper from her purse and proceeded to read the final commission report's conclusion about pornography's harmlessness. I had only 15 seconds before the cameras stopped rolling to provide a reaction and refer to the research that followed the commission report. Ms. Chambers seemed uninterested and even annoyed with my response. As the controversy intensified in the 1970s, some researchers renewed their efforts to study the impact of exposure to sexually oriented media. The research that emerged from this renewed effort served to question further the overall conclusion of the commission report. Let's take a brief look at some of the later research.

## RESEARCH FOLLOWING THE COMMISSION REPORT

The 1980s were years of rather intense scholarly study of the effects of sexually explicit materials. For a period of roughly 15 years spanning the late 1970s and going through the early 1990s, many experiments were conducted that manipulated the quantity and type of exposure and studied their impact on a range of attitudes, including attitudes toward women, sexual violence, and family values. James Weaver summarized the evidence from these studies very well in an essay that appeared toward the end of this 15-year period.[14] His summary includes a characterization of the available content and how that content affects the viewer's perceptions and behaviors. While over 20 more years have passed since Weaver summarized the available evidence, the essential points in his summary remain relatively unchanged.

## Content Available

Weaver divided the available content into three categories. First, his analysis revealed that the bulk of material features standard non-violent themes. The content of most films and videos in this category is preoccupied with sexual activity, usually from the masculine perspective. There is a heavy emphasis on heterosexual intercourse, lesbianism, group sex, anal intercourse, and oral-genital contact with visible ejaculation.[15] Weaver notes, "The predominant theme of standard-fare pornography, in other words, spotlights the sexual desires and prowess of men, whereas consistently and persistently portraying women as sexually promiscuous and obsequious."[16]

A second category of material that is much less prevalent involves coercive and/or violent themes. One of the predominant features in this type of material is the "rape myth" scenario. In this sequence of actions, a woman is taken by force and raped against her will. At some point in the sequence, the woman is shown enjoying the rape. There are many variations on this general theme, but the central idea is that the woman enjoys being dominated or abused by violence during a sexual encounter. While Weaver noted that this category of material is much less prevalent, the extent to which pornography should be categorized as containing violence depends upon the way researchers select the material from which to generalize and the way they choose to define violence or aggression. A recent content analysis of over 300 scenes in popular pornographic videos concluded that the violent content was quite high. According to the authors, nearly 50% of the scenes analyzed contained name-calling, which counted as verbal aggression, and about 88% of the scenes contained physical aggression (e.g., spanking, gagging, and slapping).[17] Finally, the third category outlined by Weaver is the idealized world of sexual fantasy, sometimes referred to as "erotic." This category probably includes the smallest number of films and videos.

## Perceptual Consequences of Viewing

Contrary to the Commission Report on Obscenity and Pornography, the newer research on this topic has dramatically changed the way most researchers assess sexually explicit content and its effects on viewers. One line of studies, conducted by Dolf Zillmann and Jennings Bryant, is particularly instructive.[18] The general design of these studies was to expose volunteers to weekly one-hour viewing sessions of mainstream pornography that had been carefully scrutinized by the researchers to make sure that violence and coercion were absent. Following these sessions, the researchers asked the participants questions about relationships and perceptions of women under the guise of conducting another study. Far from indicating the absence of any harmful effects, the findings of these studies show rather conclusively that people who watch mainstream pornography are more likely to think that rape is not so severe a crime, that most sexual practices are more prevalent than they really are, that their own sexual relationships are not particularly satisfying, and that trust in their own partners is misplaced.

Studies conducted by Ed Donnerstein and his colleagues tend to show that all of these perceptual effects are present after viewing sexual depictions that are accompanied by violence and coercion.[19] However, his research does not necessarily reveal these effects for non-violent depictions. The question of whether these effects are typically present after viewing non-violent material still remains controversial; it is a question that future studies may have to address more directly. At present, most of the evidence showing these effects as a result of non-violent material comes from the research by Zillmann and his colleagues. Whatever the ultimate resolution of this issue, both research groups have agreed that depictions of the rape scenario and sexual violence promote attitudes of sexual callousness toward women and cause more lenient attitudes toward the perpetrators of rape. Donnerstein emphasizes that such images are not limited to films and videos that carry the X rating. He argues that they frequently show up in R-rated films. Although the images in these films may be less explicit than ones in X-rated material, the pairing of sex and violence in the R-rated films is often apparent and quite capable of bringing about the effects discussed earlier.

## Behavioral Consequences of Viewing

Think about what would be required to establish a clear cause-and-effect relationship between exposure to sexually explicit materials and some anti-social behavior such as rape. Researchers would need to carefully manipulate exposure to different media content and then provide an opportunity for aggressive behavior. They would then record which participants actually behaved aggressively. Of course, in the case of a behavior like rape, to set up such an experiment would be unthinkable. Researchers run into these ethical issues whenever they think about designing studies that would clearly indict pornography as a causal factor in the increase of sex crimes. For this reason, some scholars take the position that the evidence needed to make a claim for this causal proposition is simply not possible to gather. Other scholars agree but emphasize that there are certainly strong hints available in the present data about the behavioral consequences of exposure to pornography.

One recent study that certainly added to those strong hints reported on a survey of nearly 500 members of fraternities at a large college campus. The results showed that consumption of pornography was common in this population with 83% of the respondents indicating that they had viewed mainstream pornography during the last 12 months.[20] In addition to asking about their consumption, the researchers asked each respondent to imagine themselves as a bystander who witnessed someone in need of help. Respondents indicated the extent to which they would actually be willing to help. In addition, each respondent indicated how willing he would be to commit sexual assault and commit rape if he could be guaranteed that he wouldn't be caught. He was also asked the extent to which he accepted various rape myths.

An example of a **rape myth** is the idea that women really enjoy being raped. While this idea is sometimes depicted in sexually explicit material, it is actually a myth that has no empirical basis in fact. What did the results reveal? Respondents who reported that they had watched mainstream pornography during the last 12 months were more likely than those who reported no such exposure to report a willingness to commit sexual assault and rape if they could be guaranteed they wouldn't be caught. The smaller proportion of respondents in this sample (19%) who reported that they had watched "rape pornography" in the last 12 months also reported greater acceptance of rape myths and less willingness to help someone in need if they were a bystander. The researchers concluded that, "Results of this study showed many effects of fraternity men's exposure to pornography, with increasingly more deleterious effects as the level of violence depicted in it increased" (p. 222). While it might be accurate to say that this study adds to the strong hints in the literature about the behavioral consequences of viewing pornography, careful researchers and students of media effects might disagree. Hopefully, you recognized in reading these results that they were based on a cross-sectional survey (see Chapter 2) and no direction of causality is clearly established. It certainly seems plausible that the various attitudes measured in the study were developed years earlier and played a causal role in motivating exposure to or avoidance of pornographic media instead of the media causing those attitudes. Curiously, the authors of the study failed to discuss this possibility.

How can researchers in this area deal with the problem of correlational data from surveys? While it isn't possible or desirable to set up a situation where real-life sexual aggression might occur, certain types of aggressive behavior can be studied in the laboratory. Over the years in media effects studies, aggression has often been studied in the context of some sort of scenario involving the administration or *perceived* administration of electric shock. The **electric shock paradigm** goes back to the famous experiments done by Stanley Milgram on obedience to authority.[21] In these studies, the participants were ordered by the experimenter to administer electric shocks to another person whenever that person gave a wrong answer on a learning task that was part of the experiment. Real shocks were never delivered, and the person who was supposedly receiving them was actually a member of the team of experimenters. But the participants believed that they were, in fact, administering painful electric shocks to another person. By taking note of how many shocks people were willing to give and how long they held the shock button in the "on" position, the researchers could tell which conditions would generally produce the highest levels of obedience to authority.

When this electric shock paradigm is used in studies on the effects of sexually explicit materials, the findings are quite revealing. In one classic study by Kenneth Leonard and Stuart Taylor, 40 undergraduate males were placed in the presence of a female and viewed slides that were either neutral or erotic.[22] In this case, the female was actually a member of the team of experimenters. When the erotic slides were shown, the female reacted according to one of three different scripts. The males who participated in the experiment were randomly assigned to hear one of these three reactions. In the "no cues" script, she showed no reaction at all.

In the **non-permissive cues** script, she made a variety of disapproving comments about the slides (e.g., "This is disgusting," or "Oh, that's awful"). Finally, in the **permissive cues** script, she made a variety of positive comments (e.g., "That looks like fun"). After the slide-viewing session, the males were told that they were going to take part in a competition with the female that involved reaction times. Each person was given the opportunity to administer a shock to the other. The experiment was rigged such that the males would discover that the female had decided to administer a very high level of shock. The experimenters were most interested in the level of shock that the males would choose to deliver to the female once they discovered this information. Would their chosen shock levels vary as a function of their slide-viewing condition? The results of the study clearly revealed that the answer to this question was yes. Can you guess which group of males delivered the highest levels of shock to the female? Why?

The results of the study showed that the males who had watched the erotic slides in the presence of a female who displayed permissive cues were much more likely to deliver higher levels of shock. The authors reasoned that males in this condition concluded that the female would more easily tolerate inappropriate electric shocks because she had already tolerated the sexually explicit material in the slides. In short, the males adopted calloused perceptions of the female on the basis of the female's earlier tolerance.

What do we learn from this sort of experiment about the effects of sexually explicit media? It appears that males who perceive that females are tolerant of explicit sexuality will be more willing to commit aggressive acts against them if there is provocation to do so. This finding could have implications for the way women are depicted in pornographic films. If male viewers have a steady diet of promiscuous females who are tolerant of and even eager to engage in unusual sexual behaviors, calloused attitudes toward women in general might result. Such attitudes could lead to more severe treatment of women under conditions of provocation. This finding appears consistent with the results of some other studies in the literature conducted by Donnerstein and Zillmann.

One of the big issues in interpreting experimental results like those reported by Kenneth Leonard and Stuart Taylor is trying to figure out how the experiment might apply to behavior that takes place outside of the carefully controlled world of the experimental laboratory. This issue is referred to as one of **ecological validity** (sometimes called *external validity*). Some critics of this type of experiment would argue that it is difficult to know for sure whether we can learn very much about the "real" world from these sorts of studies. After all, how many people have you seen carrying around portable electric shock machines that they use whenever they are angry? According to these critics, if these sorts of details (sometimes referred to as the **mundane realism** of the experiment) don't match situations encountered outside the laboratory, then we know very little about how the results inform our understanding of real-world events. Experimenters answer this criticism by arguing that the details inside the laboratory might not match the details outside the laboratory, but the meaning that people assign to those details is similar to the meaning that people assign to events in the real world. This emphasis on the meaning that is attached to responses in an experiment is referred to as **experimental realism**. Leonard Berkowitz and Ed Donnerstein discuss this issue at length in one of their articles about the effects of media violence.[23]

## THE MEESE COMMISSION REPORT ON PORNOGRAPHY

The wave of research that followed the first Commission Report on Obscenity and Pornography convinced many in the government that a new report was needed on this topic. In July 1986, the Attorney General of the United States, Ed Meese, released the Attorney General's Commission on Pornography Final Report. Although the title of this report was similar to that of the first one, the two reports diverged widely in terms of their purpose, operating procedure, and final conclusion. Unlike the early commission, the **Meese Commission** did not become involved in the conduct of new scientific research on the topic. Instead, it relied on existing studies and anecdotal data gathered from interviews and examinations of the commercial market for pornography. The purpose of this report probably had more to do with an attempt on the part of the attorney general to put some teeth into existing obscenity statutes than it did with arriving at an opinion about the harms of pornography based on science. Several of the commissioners were outspoken opponents of pornography. For example, James Dobson, of the organization Focus on the Family, was a member of the commission. Dobson has long been known in the Christian community as a leading spokesperson for family values and a staunch opponent of pornography. Given this type of constituency, it was inconceivable that the Meese Commission would arrive at any other conclusion except one that asserted the harms of pornography.

### Major Conclusion

Not surprisingly, then, the Meese Commission came to a far different conclusion than the earlier commission about the effects of pornography. In some respects, the summary it offered about the relative harms of sexually violent material, mainstream pornography depicting various degrees of domination, and purely erotic depictions was consistent with the available evidence summarized earlier in this chapter. But the report drew heavy criticism from the scientific community for a number of reasons. First, scientists objected to the weight that the commission seemed to attach to the interviews it conducted with people who were selected through a process that could hardly be called scientific. It appeared that the Meese Commission's procedures included providing an outlet for anyone who had a gripe about the pornography industry. Second, the commission seemed to be confused about how to interpret correlations. Consider this passage from the commission report: [24]

> We recognize, therefore, that a positive correlation between pornography and sex offenses does not itself establish a causal connection between the two. It may be that some other factor, some sexual or emotional imbalance, for example, might produce both excess use of pornographic materials as well as a tendency to commit sex offenses.

The commission would have been wise to stop with this statement, which shows a proper understanding of how to interpret correlations. But the report goes on:

> But the fact that correlational evidence cannot definitively establish causality does not mean that it may not be *some* [emphasis added] evidence of causality, and we have treated it as such.

This statement is, at best, ambiguous. It is true that the presence of a correlation *may* be an indication that a causal relationship is present. But correlations alone cannot be used to establish the case for causality. When the commission members state that they "have treated it as such," it sounds as though they may have actually treated these correlations as some evidence of causality. If they did that, then they misinterpreted the evidence. In fact, the correlations may not be evidence of causality at all. If you've forgotten why this is the case, you might want to go back and review the discussion on correlation in Chapter 2.

In the end, the academic community was not pleased with the Meese Commission report because the report went beyond the scientific evidence in formulating its conclusions. It also seemed to have a strong bias against pornography from the outset. This turned out to be unfortunate, because a strong scientific conclusion regarding the new evidence about sexually explicit materials was desperately needed. Because academic researchers could not fully embrace the Meese Commission report, much of their rhetoric was directed to revealing the scientific shortcomings of the report. Researchers found it extremely difficult to discredit the report while simultaneously emphasizing that many of the studies summarized in it were important and credible. Some of the scientists who had published findings about the harms of sexually explicit materials were seen in the news media criticizing the Meese Commission. Consequently, many of the important studies and their conclusions about the harms of sexually explicit materials got lost in a sea of controversy about the report itself.

Some researchers still describe the proposed relationship between exposure to pornography and aggressive behavior as "equivocal." In a recent summary article on the topic, Michael Seto and his colleagues argued that the multiple definitions of pornography used in the many experiments as well as a heavy emphasis on only one type of effect (male aggression against a female) should lead to caution about the conclusions that we draw from this literature. In any case, Seto points out that the best evidence seems to suggest that the effects of pornography on aggressive behavior appear to be most pronounced with men who are already predisposed to engage in such behavior. The same argument has been made about the effects of violent media as well.[25]

A team of four researchers led by Norbert Mundorf has attempted to make sense of all the published studies on sexually explicit media by conducting a meta-analysis.[26] You have read about meta-analysis in Chapters 2 and 5. Mundorf and his colleagues conducted their analysis after examining 2,200 different manuscripts. On the basis of their results, they made some conclusions about both the attitudinal and the behavioral effects associated with exposure to sexually explicit media.

Regarding attitudes, Mundorf concluded that across all of the studies examined, there is a small statistical effect linking exposure to sexually explicit material with an increased tendency to accept rape myths and interpersonal violence in relationships. Of particular interest is the fact that Mundorf's meta-analysis found that viewing violent material did not increase the size of the attitudinal effect. In other words, the attitudinal effect was just as likely to emerge for non-violent material as it was for violent material. The data pertaining to behavioral effects arc similar. Mundorf found that viewing sexually explicit materials increases the probability of subsequent aggression. Once again, this effect emerged for both non-violent and violent sexual materials. One conclusion from this study is that the findings "run contrary to an argument that the violence in sexual materials causes increases in aggression and not the sexually explicit content." In addition to these conclusions, the meta-analysis examined the effects associated with simple nude pictorials of the sort that might appear in *Playboy* or *Penthouse* magazines. In contrast to the other findings, the data show that in studies that employed this kind of stimulus material, there is actually a small effect in the opposite direction. In other words, exposure to material of this sort actually "diminished the level of subsequent aggressive behavior." It is important to keep in mind that all of the statistical effects that emerged from this meta-analysis were small in magnitude. More recently, another meta-analysis that included studies involving over 2,000 participants in studies that were *non-experimental* found an "overall relationship between pornography consumption and attitudes supporting violence against women …"[27] The researchers conducting this study emphasized that this effect was much more pronounced among men who already had other risk factors for sexual aggression—a view that definitely seems to have empirical support across numerous investigations.

## SEX ON PRIME-TIME TV

To this point, the bulk of this chapter has been about the effects of pornography or highly explicit depictions of sexuality. Although these sorts of depictions are certainly prevalent in movies, videos, and Internet sites, the research on these depictions says little about the more common sexual depictions that appear on prime-time television. The fact that these images are less explicit is not a good reason to ignore their potential influence. Before you finish with this chapter, you should have a clear understanding of the research in this area as well.

One general effect of sexual material that shouldn't be overlooked is its capacity to induce elevated levels of **physiological arousal** and **sexual arousal**. Physiological arousal includes general responses such as elevations in heart rate, blood pressure, and skin conductance (e.g., sweaty palms). Sexual arousal may include some of these general responses but is much more specific to the sex organs. In addition to measuring such arousal with self-report instruments, some researchers have actually measured sexual arousal in males with instruments designed to detect increased blood flow to the penis.[28] Measures designed to detect symptoms of arousal in the vaginal area have also been used for females.[29] As you might imagine, the procedures followed in studies that use these measures are scrutinized carefully by university human subjects committees. Typically, the instruments are self-attached in private and computer readings verify that the instruments are functioning properly. Because of the intrusiveness of these measures, there aren't many researchers who have commonly employed them in their studies. Those who have find that sexual content is arousing.[30] There are a number of questions on which researchers would like to have more data because the current understanding is quite limited. Are males and females aroused by different stimuli? Does arousal vary directly as a function of the level of sexual explicitness? Some scholars have noted that the most arousing material is not necessarily the most explicit.[31] However, there does not appear to be an abundance of research data on this topic. To the extent that low levels of explicitness can induce high levels of arousal, then, TV soap operas and other prime-time offerings that feature verbal and visual depictions of sex are potentially very arousing. What are the implications of this possibility?

## The Dynamics of Excitation Transfer

According to Dolf Zillmann's **theory of excitation transfer** (which you will encounter again in the next chapter), general arousal from any source can intensify an emotional experience and make it much more prominent than it would be ordinarily without the arousal.[32] The implication of this theory is that if people become aroused as a result of watching sex on television, whatever emotions they experience immediately after viewing may be much more intense than they would be ordinarily. For example, if a person became angry right after viewing a sexually provocative show, the anger would be more intense. On the other hand, if a person experienced feelings of warmth and affection toward a viewing partner, those feelings would also be intensified.

The theory of excitation transfer is incredibly flexible. Arousal can intensify both positive and negative emotions. In addition, the source of the arousal can be almost anything. Yes, watching sexual content on television can be arousing, but so can jogging (at least in terms of the general symptoms of increased heart rate, and so on).

According to Zillmann's theory, when something produces arousal in the system, the natural course of that arousal is to decay—to return to the baseline, resting state. If you go out for a jog, your heart will begin to beat faster. But when you stop, your heart rate will gradually return to normal. When your heart rate is clearly elevated and you are aware of the source of the elevation (you jogged), an emotional experience will not be intensified as a result of the jog. Your ability to clearly identify your arousal as coming from the jog enables you to keep it separate from whatever emotional reaction you might have during this time. But as Zillmann's research has demonstrated, there comes a point during the arousal decay where a person *thinks* that arousal has returned to normal when in fact it hasn't. Arousal is still elevated. Joggers can recognize this point easily after exercise, when it feels as though the body is back to resting state but a quick check of the pulse indicates otherwise.

It is during this period of time that the excitation transfer effect can occur. The arousal that is left over from the earlier activity or emotion but goes undetected in the system can transfer to a new emotion and make it more intense.

A former student of mine apparently learned this lesson well and decided to share her experience with me several weeks after the course she took from me was over. She greeted me one day by saying that the theory of excitation transfer had saved her engagement. I was more than a little curious to hear the details. Apparently, every time she wanted to discuss wedding plans with her partner, they got into an argument. Following a lecture on excitation transfer, the student had a light bulb experience. She already knew that her partner was not particularly fond of talking about the details of the wedding. But as she thought back over their discussions, she realized that she was inevitably trying to hold these discussions immediately after her partner's daily jog. The theory predicted that his negative reaction to discussions of wedding plans would be intensified by arousal left over from the jog. Once she realized this, she changed her behavior, making sure that she discussed only pleasant topics after exercise. She saved the wedding plans for more serene moments. According to her report, this single change had made a tremendous difference. It did not change her partner's general attitude toward planning wedding details, but it defused the intensity of that attitude. I don't know how the newlyweds are faring today, but at least in this instance, the theory of excitation transfer turned out to have a practical edge.

## Content Analyses

As it turns out, there have been many more studies about the sexual content of TV than about the effects of that content. One researcher, Bradley Greenberg, studied the content of afternoon soap operas for many years. In one study, he reported that over a 10-year period in the 1980s and 1990s, the number of sexual incidents per hour had increased.[33] Most of the sex centered on incidents of sexual intercourse between unmarried partners or partners who were not attached. Increases were observed in both visual and verbal depictions of sexuality. Greenberg noted that although depictions of sex on the soaps were increasing, many of the incidents of sex outside of marriage were not sanctioned by characters in the program and were portrayed as objectionable. To explain this paradox, Greenberg favored the view that the TV networks attempt to appease multiple audiences. Some people like sexual content. Others will not watch the shows if the attitude toward the sexuality seems to favor promiscuity. By depicting sex and then expressing moral objection, the networks can spike their ratings by appealing to both groups.

Sex on TV is hardly limited to soap operas. One of the reasons sexual content is so controversial is because of its potential impact on children and adolescents and the ready availability of TV content to those younger viewers.

In another content analysis of the most popular prime-time shows viewed by children and adolescents, Monique Ward found that nearly 30% of all the interactions that took place on an average episode contained verbal references to sexual issues.[34] On some episodes, that statistic soared to 50%. A great proportion of the messages related to sexuality emphasized the competitive nature of sexual relations and featured many comments by males about the physical appearance of females. A more recent study directed by Dale Kunkel and his colleagues for the Kaiser Family Foundation emphasized the finding that only 4% of the scenes with sexual content in the programs included in their study contained any mention of sexual risk or responsibility. This was the identical percentage observed in a study conducted seven years earlier. The report concluded:

> ... [A]verage viewers would see roughly one hundred programs with sexual content before they encounter a single one that places strong emphasis through- out the show on sexual risk or responsibility concerns. These odds tell the story of many missed opportunities to increase the visibility of such issues as sexual patience, sexual precautions and the risks of negative consequences of sexual activity, all of which are critical public health concerns.[35]

The conclusion of Kunkel's report sounds all too familiar. Nearly two decades ago, a team of researchers concluded on the basis of their content analysis that ado- lescents were unlikely to learn very much about contraceptives or the risk of sexu- ally transmitted disease from watching TV depictions of sexuality.[36] Historically, the research findings of scholars have tended to have little impact on the practices of the entertainment industry. The report by Kunkel and his colleagues quoted previ- ously was published in 2005. But it is only the most recent of a whole series of reports on sex in the media from the Kaiser Family Foundation that date back into the 1990s. Unfortunately, not many of the statistical trends over the series of reports offer much encouragement of significant and positive changes that might lead to less risky behavior and better health on the part of media consumers. You can read more about the highlights from the 2005 report in Study Box 6-2.

## Sexual Behavior and Viewing

Most of the studies on the impact of sex in the media have taken place on older pop- ulations and have dealt with content that is more explicit than what is typically seen on prime-time TV. This state of affairs is certainly easy to understand. From an ethi- cal standpoint, it is certainly more problematic to study younger viewers in the con- text of a research design that requires exposure to sexual media content. From the standpoint of theory about media impact, it makes sense to study the more explicit depictions of media sexuality, since these would be the materials that one might sus- pect would have the most effects on viewers. Despite the fact that not much research attention has been devoted to the effects of TV sexuality, there are at least a handful of studies that deserve mention here.

One study that was supported by ABC-TV studied how well adolescents (ages 12–16) understood sexual innuendos on prime-time TV. The findings revealed that even the youngest of these viewers understood the innuendos well and felt comforta- ble talking about them.[37] In a second study that used a correlational research design,

## STUDY BOX 6-2 The 2005 Report on Sexual Content in TV

In November 2005, the Kaiser Family Foundation released its most recent content analysis of sexual content on TV. The report was based on nearly 1,000 randomly selected programs from the 2004–2005 TV season. What did the report find? About 70% of all the programs that were included in the analysis contained sexual content of some sort. A similar analysis done in 2000–2001 showed that only 64% of the programs contained sexual content, and back in 1997–1998 the percentage was only 56%. Apparently, sex on TV is clearly on the rise.

One change that the newest study detected was in the age range of the characters who were depicted as having sexual intercourse. In the analysis of the 1997–1998 season, almost a quarter of the characters who were shown engaged in sexual intercourse were young adults (18–24) while only 3% of the characters involved in intercourse were teens. The 3% figure for teens remained unchanged in the 2005 report—but the percentage of those having intercourse who were young adults dropped significantly to only 7%. In general, there seems to be a trend in the direction of older characters (25+ years) being the ones shown having intercourse.

One main emphasis of the 2005 report was on messages about risks and responsibilities associated with sexual behavior. Of all the programs that contained sexual content, only about 11% presented any information about the risks or the responsibilities associated with sexual behavior. That's the same percentage that was found in the content analysis of programs back in 1997–1998. It appears to be a relatively stable statistic.

In general, the authors of the 2005 report concluded that on most of their measures, sexual content on TV is continuing to increase over time. Why might this be happening? One possibility is that as the networks have come under increasing fire for programming violence, they have turned to sex to appease audiences who might be hungry for arousing content. But there might be another principle at work that could help to explain the increase. Recall from the last chapter that the principle of desensitization predicts that once a certain level of explicitness has been crossed, it becomes extremely difficult to reverse direction. Over time, content that initially triggers an intense emotional reaction becomes commonplace. Producers may sense that to keep ratings high, the line needs to be pushed constantly. If this principle holds true, future content analyses of sexual content on TV will find that even more sex is turning up on TV and that the sex is more explicit. If this trend continues, the challenge for researchers of media effects will be to investigate how these changes might make a difference in terms of influencing the beliefs, attitudes, and behaviors of the TV audience.

SOURCE: The Kaiser Family Foundation [Online]. Available: http://kaiserfamilyfoundation.files.wordpress.com/2013/01/sex-on-tv-4-full-report.pdf

pregnant and non-pregnant girls and women between the ages of 13 and 29 were studied. The results of the study revealed that the pregnant girls were more likely to have greater media exposure to those programs and movies that depicted sexual content. They also tended to be more likely to watch these programs and movies in the company of their boyfriends than did the members of the non-pregnant sample. Of course, you know from reading Chapter 2 that there are various pitfalls involved in concluding from this correlation that watching the sex in the media caused these girls and women to have a greater likelihood of becoming pregnant. In this case, the researchers were not even able to establish the time sequence of the relationship (the measure of pregnancy came before the measure of media exposure), much less rule out possible third variables that may have been related to both media exposure and pregnancy status.

In another important study, Rebecca Collins and her colleagues surveyed nearly 1,800 adolescents about their TV viewing habits, with a special focus on the shows that contained sexual content. In this case, the researchers were able to do follow-up interviews one year later. The major finding of the study was that the adolescents who on the first survey reported the highest viewing levels of sexual content were also the ones who were most likely to report that they had initiated an instance of sexual intercourse during the past year. This study established both the relationship between TV exposure to sex and sexual behavior and the time order of the relationship (viewing preceded behavior). In addition, the researchers attempted to eliminate numerous other variables that might have accounted for the relationship. The authors reported that adolescents in the top 10% in viewing sexual content had double the chance of being involved in sexual behavior when compared to the adolescents who were in the bottom 10% on viewing.[38] Of course, as the authors acknowledged, some of this effect could be due to the fact that adolescents who are curious about sex are more likely to watch it on TV and also to initiate sexual behavior in real life.

In another study on the consequences of exposure to sex on TV, Carol Pardun and her coauthors undertook an ambitious project when they had more than 3,200 adolescents in the seventh and eighth grades complete a questionnaire detailing their media use. They also conducted interviews that focused on sexual attitudes and behavior with more than 1,000 of these same adolescents. One strength of this study is that it went beyond TV to include other types of media as well. Based on the responses to the media questionnaire and content analyses of various media, the researchers were able to assign each respondent a value on a measure they called the SMD, or the Sexual Media Diet. This measure reflected the extent to which each respondent was exposed to sexual content in the media (including TV, newspapers, movies, music, and Internet sites). The results of this study showed that the SMD measure was positively correlated with past sexual activity and expressions of intended sexual activity in the future. In particular, when the SMD measure was broken down into media types, the strongest associations were found for music exposure and exposure to movies.[39]

Using a more direct approach, Joanne Cantor and her colleagues asked about 200 undergraduate students to report the details of some past media encounter with sexual content that had affected them strongly.[40] The majority of students reported an instance of media exposure that took place before they were 17 years old and in a viewing environment with no adult present. The most typical content recalled was a movie that was rated R. Viewing tended to occur not because of a deliberate choice to watch—but because of either stumbling upon the movie or because a friend was watching. There was no "typical" effect of the exposure. As the authors stated, "… [T]he most frequent emotional reactions reported were disgust, shock or surprise, embarrassment, and interest …. [T]he most common enduring effect was simply continued thinking about the content, with the next most frequent conse- quences being confusion and unwanted recurring thoughts." There wasn't any indi- cation in these reports that watching the sexual content resulted in any increased desire to engage in sexual behavior. In fact, the study found that for a small number of the respondents, exposure to the movie might have reduced any such desire. The data also showed evidence for the fact that males were more affected by the physical aspects depicted in the movies (e.g., nudity) and were more likely to report sexual arousal than were females. Women's descriptions were more likely to mention rape and feeling sad in reaction to the content. Females seemed to be more attuned to the relational dynamics in portrayals that depicted sex. The researchers concluded that their study provided evidence for the fact that media messages about sex were an important source of information for children and that parents need to be aware of what their kids are seeing and use instances of exposure as "teachable moments" about sexual matters.

One of the more recent studies examining the effects of sexual content in the media employed a longitudinal survey design (panel study) of 501 adolescents. The researchers collected data at two time points that were one year apart. At each point in time, they collected data about exposure to sexual content in TV, music, maga- zines, and video games as well as self-reports of sexual activity. The results of the study showed evidence of a reciprocal relationship between media exposure and sexual behavior. Adolescents who were sexually active at the time of the first survey were more likely to report greater consumption of media with sexual content over the next year. In addition, adolescents who reported higher levels of media con- sumption with sexual content at the time of the first survey were more likely to report an increase of sexual activity over the next year.[41] The authors interpreted these results as evidence for the fact that exposure to sexual content causes sexual activity—and that sexual activity may be causally related to exposure to media that contain sexual material.

Jeffrey Gottfried, a communication researcher at the Annenberg School of Com- munication at the University of Pennsylvania, recently led a research team con- sisting of some of the same researchers who reported the survey on over 500 adolescents. Their study is known in the literature as the Annenberg Sex and Media Study (ASAMS).[42] These researchers believed that the effects of televised sexual content might be different depending on the way the content was depicted. In their survey of adolescents, they asked about exposure to four different program genres: comedy, drama, cartoons, and reality shows. Their content analysis of the four types of programs revealed that there was less sex in reality TV than in dramas. The level of sexual explicitness in reality TV was also lower than any of the other genres. Finally, dramas contained more messages about risk and responsibility than the other genres. Using a sophisticated strategy to analyze the relationships in their data, the researchers reported that overall exposure to TV sex was not associated with any increase in adolescents' reports of having sex. However, when the data were broken down by program genre, exposure to sexual content in comedy shows did predict an increase in having sex; exposure to sexual content in dramas actually predicted a decrease in having sex. These data are not entirely consistent with other published studies (e.g., the survey by Pardun reported above). The authors speculate that the differences might be due to changes in teens' viewing habits over the last decade. They pointed out that the opposite effects of exposure to comedy and drama may be due to the fact that dramas were far more likely to contain messages that emphasized sexual risk and responsibility.

Although the actual amount of research evidence on the impact of TV sex on behavior is modest, the knowledge that researchers have gained from studying other areas of media impact would certainly suggest that there is reason to keep studying this important area. One thing that we can be certain about on this topic is that it will remain controversial. More than any other area of media effects, the number of angles on sexual content in the media (religious, political, scholarly, legal) will continue to make for a hotbed of dispute. As certain as members of these various groups may be about the effects of sexual content on TV, there is no substitute for good research. Often research results challenge existing assumptions. As Study Box 6-3 reveals, research on MTV's show *16 and Pregnant* may actually be *helping* to reduce teen pregnancy.

## SEX AND THE INTERNET

In the past few years, the number of sites in cyberspace has mushroomed tremendously—into the hundreds of millions. At no time in human history have sexually explicit media been so readily available as they are today. We owe that fact—good or bad—to the Internet. A casual perusal of the top 100 Web sites in terms of the heaviest Internet traffic reveals several sites that specialize in sexually explicit material.[43] The significance of this easy availability is that children are part of the consuming audience in a way that they have never been before. Controversies have hit public libraries and schools about whether to load blocking software onto their computers to prevent children from surfing to objectionable sites. Sometimes the blocking software doesn't work properly and screens out material that isn't sexual in nature. Researchers have little to say about the effects of sexually explicit media on children because few committees on the protection of human subjects would ever approve research of this sort. One recent study found that college students perceived the effects of Internet pornography to be more negative for others than for themselves.[44] (This finding is sometimes called the third-person effect and you'll read more about it in Chapter 8). Another recent study documented exposure to sex on the Internet, particularly among males who were 14 years old or older, but the report had little to say about the effects of that exposure.[45] One of the most recent investigations involved more than 2,300 Dutch adolescents.[46] The researchers, Jochen Peter and Patti Valkenburg, designed a longitudinal study to investigate some of the possible effects of exposure to sexually explicit Internet materials (SEIM). They

## STUDY BOX 6-3 Is MTV's *16 and Pregnant* Helping to Reduce Teen Pregnancy?

In January of 2014, two economists, Melissa Kearney and Phillip Levine, made news with the publication of a paper that made a rather provocative claim: MTV's *16 and Pregnant* was actually responsible for a significant drop in the rate of teen pregnancy in the United States. What was the basis for their claim?

- An analysis of the show's content reveals that the vast majority of pregnant teens featured on various episodes weren't attempting to get pregnant; they also reported that they used no contraception prior to their pregnancy. Many of the shows depict C-sections or various health difficulties of the pregnancy to either the mother or the baby. In short, teen pregnancy is *not* depicted in the show as a glamorous proposition.

- An analysis of Nielson TV ratings data revealed that the show was rated #1 in its time slot among the 18–34 age group upon its release. A national random sample of teens in the 12–19 age group revealed that over 70% of the respondents had seen an episode of the program. Fewer than 20% of them perceived the show as one that glamorized teen pregnancy. The bottom line: teens are exposed to the program and aren't encouraged to view teen pregnancy as glamorous.

- An analysis of Google searches and tweets between 2009 and 2012 show statistical spikes around the times associated with the airing of new episodes of the show. The data show an upsurge in the search for information about contraception and birth control strategies. The evidence seems to show that teens were motivated to express interest in learning more about birth control after exposure to the program.

- The data analysis suggests that in the 18 months following the introduction of the program, it was responsible for a 5.7% drop in the teen birth rate during that period. The authors claim that this means that about one-third of the decline in births to teenagers during this 18-month period was due to the influence of the program.

SOURCE: Kearney, M. S., & Levine, P. B. (2014). Media influences on social outcomes: The impact of MTV's *16 and Pregnant* on teen childbearing. *National Bureau of Economic Research,* working paper #19795. [Online: Accessed 5-1-14]. Available: http://www.wellesley.edu/sites/default/files/assets/kearney-levine-16p-nber_submit.pdf

discovered that exposure to such materials caused an increase in what they called "sexual preoccupancy"—the tendency to be preoccupied with thoughts about sex. Their data revealed that those who reported being sexually aroused by Internet material were the ones who were likely to be sexually preoccupied as a result of viewing it. One interesting finding from this study was the fact that there was no difference between males and females in reports of sexual arousal as a result of exposure.

Most recently, Peter and Valkenburg reported another study of nearly 1,000 Dutch adolescents and their use of SEIM.[47] This study was unique in two ways. First, the authors used a panel study in three waves to study how use of SEIM may have changed the users over time (see Chapter 2 for a review of the panel study design). Second, the authors were interested in testing a particular theoretical idea about the impact of SEIM. While the authors don't give a formal name to their idea, it might be referred to as the **sexual uncertainty hypothesis**. Drawing upon studies from sociology, Peter and Valkenburg note that most adolescents are socialized to embrace specific values pertaining to sex: Sexual relationships ought to be characterized by affection and commitment, consensus and mutuality, and an attitude of reciprocity and responsiveness to the wishes of one's partner. This socialization notwithstanding, Peter and Valkenburg point out that "… content analyses of sexually explicit material have consistently found that sex with affection, reciprocal and mutual sexual relations, and gender equality do not occur frequently."[48] A critical question to be answered then is this: What happens when adolescents who have been socialized to embrace these values begin to consume sexually explicit materials that present an alternative and inconsistent social message? According to the sexual uncertainty hypothesis, the answer is that sexual uncertainty will increase in these adolescent users. The results of their survey provided strong support for their hypothesis. They found that over time, adolescents who consumed SEIM expressed greater sexual uncertainty on a questionnaire designed to assess this concept. They also found that the key mechanism underlying this effect might be **involvement** with the material. Their data showed that adolescents who used SEIM the most were much more involved in the material and that the more involved they were the more they expressed sexual uncertainty in their own beliefs or values.

## CONTROL OVER MEDIA CONTENT

The widespread assumption, of course, is that Internet pornography is harmful to children and adolescents. For that reason, solutions to the problem are not typically sought in research. Advocates seeking strategies to control the flow of sexually explicit materials turn instead to **legal, social/economic,** and **education solutions**. From the looks of things, this struggle to control the material is an uphill battle.

### Legal Control

One reason for the heated controversy about media sex is that obscenity does not enjoy protection under the First Amendment. Obscene speech is illegal. Consequently, the government has often attempted to restrict the flow of sexually explicit media that might be judged as obscene. As mentioned earlier, the legal battles against obscenity have not been very successful. Obscenity is a difficult thing to define. Moreover, Americans may object to sex in the media, but they simultaneously tend to defend the right of the media to produce it. The quest for censorship is almost always one that fails to enjoy popular support.

Another legal avenue that has occasionally been tried by opponents of pornography is to claim that certain sexual depictions serve to deprive some members of society (usually women) of their civil rights. These claims have usually met with failure in the courts and state legislatures around the country. One reason for the failure of these efforts is concern about the implications that such rulings would have for other kinds of media content. Do people really want to live in a world where a given group of individuals can lay waste to the media industry by claiming that certain kinds of content injure their civil rights? For now, at least, the courts have answered that question in the negative.

## Social or Economic Control

Instead of passing and enforcing laws against sexual content, some groups pursue a strategy that is based on social norms and economic impact. Religious groups will often launch boycotts of advertisers who try to sell their goods on objectionable programs. Sometimes, groups will boycott particular business establishments that sell sexually oriented material. When I lived in Cleveland, one of the convenience store chains became the target of such a boycott. The stores responded by announcing an open chance for customers to vote on whether they should continue to carry sexually oriented magazines such as *Playboy* and *Penthouse.* Customers had to come into the store to cast their ballots. Since participation in the boycott meant avoiding the stores, it was no surprise when the company announced that the public had overwhelmingly voted to support its policy of continuing to sell the magazines. As a public relations ploy, the strategy worked brilliantly. The stores looked good in the public eye for having an open election. But because the boycott was going on at the same time, the results were virtually guaranteed to support the continued sale of the material—a result that the stores undoubtedly wanted. Eventually, the boycott ended and things returned to normal. Boycotts and economic pressure sometimes work in isolated cases over the short term. But history shows them to be relatively ineffective over the long haul.

## Control Through Education

In a free society that protects freedom of speech and expression, the preferred form of control over media content is probably education. If people learn about media impact, they can take steps to deal with it and manage it in their daily lives. As evidence for this fact, Ed Donnerstein has shown that participating in his experiments can actually be beneficial—despite the fact that male college students who go through his experiments are exposed to violent pornography.[49] Compared to males who don't have the chance to participate in the studies, those who do actually become more sensitive to issues involving rape myths after they have gone through the instructional debriefing required by human subjects committees. Research by Neil Malamuth shows similar findings.[50] In this case, education turns out to be effective. When you finish this course on media effects, you will be in a far better position to think through the issues of media impact in your own life. You will then be better able to make informed choices about your own media diet and, in the future, the media diets of your children.

# SUMMARY

Few topics stir such passionate opinion as sexual content in the media. Researchers have tended to distinguish between pornography, violent sexuality, and eroticism as they have studied media impact in this domain. Early evidence from the *Report of the Commission on Obscenity and Pornography* led to the conclusion that this material was relatively harmless. Subsequent reanalysis of some of the data in the report, combined with a new wave of research that followed its publication, modified this conclusion. The Meese Commission report reversed the conclusion of the first commission report, but, for a variety of reasons, it was widely criticized by social scientists. Nevertheless, the broad consensus of the scientific community is that exposure to sexually explicit material is associated with a host of negative perceptual and attitudinal consequences. Some research also suggests that negative behaviors might also be more likely following exposure. Research on sexual content on TV has concentrated mainly on content analyses rather than studies of impact. The main concern is with *how* sex is depicted rather than with *how much* is depicted. More research needs to be done on the impact of less explicit media sex such as the depictions on soap operas and prime-time TV. Sex on the Internet is a current concern that ought to attract considerably more research attention in future years. Recent studies suggest that adolescents who consume sexually explicit Internet material may develop higher levels of sexual uncertainty that challenge the values that they were socialized to embrace. Evidence also supports the notion that consumption of media containing sex leads to increases in sexual activity. However, research on MTV's *16 and Pregnant* reveals that the way in which sex is depicted may lead to very different effects than might be expected. The relationship between consumption of sexually explicit media and sexual activity may also be reciprocal. Those who engage in more sexual activity may be more curious about sexual depictions in the media and consume more of that sort of content.

## QUESTIONS TO FOCUS YOUR ATTENTION

1. Sexual content in the media has nearly always been associated with controversy. Do you think that as this material becomes more available through the Internet, controversy will increase, decrease, or remain unchanged? Why?

2. Research on the effects of consumption of sexually explicit material— particularly on young consumers—is scrutinized so carefully that fewer studies are conducted in this area of media research relative to others. To what extent do you think this is a problem? Is there any solution?

3. Should sexual content in the media be controlled at all? If so, which of the various strategies of controlling the content do you think is best? Why? If you think no control is the best option, how would you defend that position?

<table>
<tr><td colspan="3" align="center">KEY TERMS AND CONCEPTS</td></tr>
<tr>
<td>obscenity<br>pornography<br>erotic media<br>National Commission<br>  on Obscenity and<br>  Pornography<br>trigger hypothesis<br>safety valve theory<br>rape myth</td>
<td>electric shock paradigm<br>permissive cues versus<br>  non-permissive cues<br>ecological validity<br>mundane realism<br>experimental realism<br>Meese Commission<br>physiological arousal</td>
<td>sexual arousal<br>theory of excitation transfer<br>sexual uncertainty<br>  hypothesis<br>involvement<br>legal, social/economic and<br>  education solutions</td>
</tr>
</table>

# NOTES

1. George, S. (2011). Latest MTV Show Skins Struggles Amidst Controversy. The Lafayette On-Line Edition. [Online]. Available: http://media.www.thelaf.com/media/storage/paper339/news/2011/02/04/Ae/ Latest.mtv.Show.Skins.Struggles.Amidst.Controversy-3973316.shtml

2. Liebert, R. M., Sprafkin, J. N., & Davidson, E. S. (1982). *The early window: Effects of television on children and youth*. New York: Pergamon Press.

3. Arellano, J. (2013). "Naked and Afraid" ratings: Surprise! Dudes love the stripped-down survival show. *Entertainment Weekly*, July 13. [Online: Accessed 4-26-14]. Available: http://insidetv.ew.com/2013/07/30/naked-and-afraid-ratings/

4. Robbins, S. (2014). Couples will have sex in a box for reality show. *Entertainment Weekly*, March 11. [Online: Accessed 4-26-14]. Available: http://insidetv.ew.com/2014/03/11/sex-box-reality-show-we-tv/

5. Oliver, K. (2013). PTC condemns CW network for plans to air uncut episode of Reign's sex scenes online. *Parents Television Council Press Release*, March 6. [Online: Accessed 4-26-14]. Available: http://w2.parentstv.org/Main/News/Detail.aspx?docID=3034

6. Schramm, H. (2002). Interview with Dean Emeritus, Dolf Zillmann, College of Communication and Information Sciences and Department of Psychology, University of Alabama, on occasion of his recent retirement. *Zeitschrift fur Medienpsychologie,* 14(N.F.2), 2, 90–92.

7. Ibid.

8. Commission on Obscenity and Pornography. (1970). *Report of the Commission on Obscenity and Pornography*. New York: Bantam Books.

9. Kutchinsky, B. (1973). The effect of easy availability of pornography on the incidence of sex crimes: The Danish experience. *Journal of Social Issues, 29*, 163–181.

10. Court, J. H. (1977). Pornography and sex crimes. *International Journal of Criminology and Penology, 5*, 129–157.

11. Diamond, M., & Uchiyama, A. (1999). Pornography, rape, and sex crimes in Japan. *International Journal of Law and Psychiatry, 22*, 1–22.

12. Kutchinsky, B. (1991). Pornography and rape: Theory and practice? Evidence from crime data in four countries where pornography is easily available. *International Journal of Law and Psychiatry, 14*(1–2), 47–64.

13. Diamond, M., Jozifkova, E., & Weiss, P. (2011). Pornography and sex crimes in the Czech Republic. *Archives of Sexual Behavior*, 40, 1037–1043.

14. Weaver, J. B. (1994). Pornography and sexual callousness: Perceptual and behavioral consequences of exposure to pornography. In D. Zillmann, J. Bryant, & A. C. Huston (Eds.), *Media, children and the family: Social scientific, psycho dynamic, and clinical perspectives* (pp. 215–228). Hillsdale, NJ: Erlbaum.

15. Hebditch, D., & Anning, N. (1988). *Porn gold: Inside the pornography business*. London: Faber & Faber.

16. Brosius, H., Weaver, J., & Staab, J. (1993). Exploring the social and sexual "reality" of contemporary pornography. *Journal of Sex Research, 30*, 161–172.

17. Bridges, A. J., Wosnitzer, R., Sharrer, E., Sun, C., & Liberman, R. (2010). Aggression sexual behavior in best-selling pornography videos: A content-analysis update. *Violence Against Women*, 16(10), 1065–1085.

18. Zillmann, D., & Bryant, J. (1988). Effects of prolonged consumption of pornography on family values. *Journal of Family Issues, 9*, 518–544.

19. Donnerstein, E. (1984). Pornography: Its effect on violence against women. In N. M. Malamuth & E. Donnerstein (Eds.), *Pornography and sexual aggression* (pp. 53–81). Orlando, FL: Academic Press.

20. Foubert, J. D., Brosi, M. W., & Bannon, R. W. (2011). Pornography viewing among fraternity men: Effects on bystander intervention, rape myth acceptance and behavioral intent to commit sexual assault. *Sexual Addiction & Compulsivity*, 18, 212–231.

21. Milgram, S. (1963). Behavioral study of obedience. *Journal of Abnormal and Social Psychology*, 67, 371–378.

22. Leonard, K. E., & Taylor, S. P. (1983). Exposure to pornography, permissive and nonpermissive cues, and male aggression toward females. *Motivation and Emotion*, 7, 291–299.

23. Berkowitz, L., & Donnerstein, E. (1982). External validity is more than skin deep: Some answers to criticisms of laboratory experiments. *American Psychologist*, 37, 245–257.

24. U.S. Department of Justice. (1986). *Attorney General's Commission on Pornography: Final report* (Vol. 1). Washington, DC: U.S. Department of Justice.

25. Seto, M. C, Mane, A., & Barbaree, H. E. (2001). The role of pornography in the etiology of sexual aggression. *Aggression and Violent Behavior*, 6(1), 35–53.

26. Mundorf, N., D'Alessio, D., Allen, M., & Emmers-Sommer, T. M. (2007). Effects of sexually explicit media. In R. W. Preiss, B. M. Gayle, N. Burrell, M. Allen, & J. Bryant (Eds.), *Mass media effects research: Advances through meta-analysis* (pp. 181–198). Mahwah, NJ: Erlbaum.

27. Hald., G. M., Malamuth, N. M., & Yuen, C. (2010). Pornography and attitudes supporting violence against women: Revisiting the relationship in nonexperimental studies. *Aggressive Behavior*, 36(1), 14–20.

28. Eccles, A., Marshall, W. L, & Barbaree, H. E. (1988). The vulnerability of erectile measures to repeated assessments. *Behavior Research and Therapy*, 26, 179–183.

29. Sintchak, G, & Geer, J. (1975). A vaginal plethysmograph system. *Psychophysiology*, 12, 113–115.

30. Allen, M., Emmers-Sommer, T. M., D'Alessio, D, Timmerman, L., Hanzal, A., & Korus, J. (2007). The connection between the physiological and the psychological reactions to sexually explicit material: A literature summary using meta-analysis. *Communication Monographs*, 74(4), 541–560.

31. Harris, R. J. (1999). *A cognitive psychology of mass communication*. Mahwah, NJ: Erlbaum.

32. Zillmann, D. (1983). Transfer of excitation in emotional behavior. In J. T. Cacioppo & R. E. Petty (Eds.), *Social psychophysiology* (pp. 215–240). New York: Guilford Press.

33. Greenberg, B. S., & Busselle, R. W. (1996). Soap operas and sexual activity: A decade later. *Journal of Communication*, 46, 153–160.

34. Ward, M. L. (1995). Talking about sex: Common themes about sexuality in the prime-time television programs children and adolescents view most. *Journal of Youth and Adolescence*, 24, 595–615.

35. Kunkel, D., Eyal, K., Finnerty, K., Biely, E., & Donnerstein, E. (2005). *Sex on TV: 2005*. The Henry J. Kaiser Family Foundation [Online]. Available: http://kaiserfamilyfoundation.files.wordpress.com/2013/01/sex-on-tv-4-full-report.pdf.

36. Brown, J. D., Childers, K. W., & Waszak, C. S. (1990). Television and adolescent sexuality. *Journal of Adolescent Health Care*, 11, 62–70.

37. Liebert, R. M., Sprafkin, J. N., & Davidson, E. S. (1982). *The early window: Effects of television on children and youth*. New York: Pergamon Press.

38. Collins, R. L., Elliott, M. N., Berry, S. H., Kanouse, D. E., Kunkel, D., Hunter, S. B., & Mm, A. (2004). Watching sex on television predicts adolescent initiate on of sexual behavior. *Pediatrics*, 14(3), 280–289 [Online]. Available: http://pediatrics.aappublications.org/cgi/content/full/114/3/e280

39. Pardun, C. J., L'Engle, K. L., & Brown, J. D. (2005). Linking exposure to outcomes: Early adolescents' consumption of sexual content in six media. *Mass Communication and Society*, 8(2), 75–91.

40. Cantor, J., Mares, M. L., & Hyde, J. S. (2003). Autobiographical memories of exposure to sexual media content. *Media Psychology*, 5, 1–31.

41. Bleakley, A., Hennessy, M., Fishbein, M., & Jordan, A. (2008). It works both ways: The relationship between exposure to sexual content in the media and adolescent sexual behavior. *Media Psychology*, 11(4), 443–461.

42. Gottfried, J. A., Vaala, S. E., Bleakley, A., Hennessy, M., & Jordan, A. (2013). Does the effect of exposure to TV sex on adolescent sexual behavior vary by genre? *Communication Research*, 40(1), 73–95.

43. Alexa. The top 500 sites on the web. [Online: Accessed 5-1-14]. Available: http://www.alexa.com/topsites

44. Lee, B., & Tamborini, R. (2005). Third-person effect and internet pornography: The influence of collectivism and internet self-efficacy. *Journal of Communication*, 55(2), 292–310.

45. Ybarra, M. L., & Mitchell, K. J. (2005). Exposure to internet pornography among children and adolescents: A national survey. *Cyber Psychology & Behavior*, 8(5), 473–186.

46. Peter, J., & Valkenburg, P. M. (2008). Adolescents' exposure to sexually explicit internet material and sexual preoccupancy: A three-wave panel study. *Media Psychology,* 11, 207–234.

47. Peter, J., & Valkenburg, P. M. (2010). Adolescents' use of sexually explicit internet material and sexual uncertainty: The role of involvement and gender. *Communication Monographs,* 77(3), 357–375.

48. Peter & Valkenburg (2010), p. 359.

49. Donnerstein, E., & Berkowitz, L. (1981). Victim reactions in aggressive erotic films as a factor in violence against women. *Journal of Personality and Social Psychology,* 41, 710–724.

50. Malamuth, N. M., & Check, J. V. P. (1980). Sexual arousal to rape and consenting depictions: The importance of the woman's arousal. *Journal of Abnormal Psychology,* 89, 763–766.

# 7

# Media That Stir Emotions

I will never forget the night from my childhood when my parents made a fateful decision that they could never have known would affect me for the rest of my life. It was a Friday evening, and my older brothers had gathered around the TV set in keen anticipation of their favorite weekly program, *The Twilight Zone.* Up to this point, my parents had insisted that I could not watch the show because it came on after my bedtime. But on this particular evening, for whatever reason, my parents relented and allowed me to join my brothers in front of the set. I was six years old. By the end of the program, I was certain that I would never be able to walk into a department store again. The program depicted department store mannequins that turned into real people and then back into mannequins. I was quite literally terrified! (After writing these words, I went to the Internet and found the details of the particular episode that frightened me. My memory was accurate. The episode, "The After Hours," was broadcast on Friday, June 10, 1960. It was the first season of the program. Perhaps I was allowed to watch it because the school year was ending and my parents were less concerned about bedtime.)

Despite the fact that numerous cable stations run old episodes of *The Twilight Zone,* I have never cared to re-watch the particular episode that scared me that night. When I have described the episode to my students, many of them shake their heads in that knowing way. Some have even tried to fill me in on some of the plot details that have become fuzzy in my mind over the years. I don't really care to know. What I do know is that when I watched that program as a child, my mind could not have dreamed that a TV show could depict such a spooky and terrifying scenario. Even today, I get a slightly negative feeling when I walk into a department store that has mannequins standing around. *The Twilight Zone* may be one of the oldest classic examples of how **paranormal media content** can terrify people.[1]

Perhaps in part as a result of my intense personal experience with a frightening TV program, I ended up devoting a large portion of my research career to studying the effects of frightening media on children. This has been rewarding. Perhaps if

I had not suffered such intense fear myself, I wouldn't have felt so drawn toward this topic. The research on frightening media really didn't get started in earnest until the late 1970s. At that time, a researcher at the University of Wisconsin-Madison, Joanne Cantor, received a major grant from the National Institute of Mental Health to study the emotional impact of frightening movies and TV programs on children. I was fortunate enough to work with Professor Cantor on this research. Cantor and I, along with a few other researchers (Barb Wilson and Cindy Hoffner), continued to study frightening media for many years and continue to have an interest in the topic today. Cantor has even published a children's book, *Teddy's TV Troubles,* which is based on key research findings and is designed to help parents deal with their children's emotional reactions to frightening media.[2]

What has the research on this topic uncovered? In the remainder of this chapter, I attempt to provide a brief summary of the theory and research findings in this area and in other areas concerning the emotional reactions that people experience from exposure to media. One thing clearly emerges from this research: Paranormal themes are often the most terrifying for both children and adults. After years of research, we think we know why.

## FRIGHT REACTIONS TO MEDIA ARE PREVALENT

In considering the effects of media violence on aggressive behavior, the most frequently researched media effect in the literature, it is important to note that the statistical effect definitely exists, but the size of the effect is small (see Chapter 5). Not many people become more aggressive because of something they see in a movie or TV show. In contrast, the emotional effects of frightening media are far more prevalent, even though they tend to receive less attention in the research literature.

Anecdotes of copycat crimes clearly support the notion that media violence sometimes affects aggressive behavior. Similarly, there are many anecdotes about the emotional impact of frightening films. When the film *Jaws* made its debut, tourism in ocean resort towns plummeted. People expressed terror at the prospect of becoming the victim of a "great white" attack. On the paranormal front, an issue of *The Journal of Nervous and Mental Disease* in 1975 carried reports of clinical psychiatric patients who had to seek hospitalization and months of treatment after viewing the movie *The Exorcist.*[3] Apparently, images of demon possession haunted these patients to the point of social and emotional malfunction. In the case of the film *Silence of the Lambs,* one graduate student in my department reported to me that she had been unable to eat meat for many weeks after viewing the film. And a remarkable number of adults reported that they suffered trauma as children from viewing the Winged Monkeys and the Wicked Witch of the West in that all-time classic *The Wizard of Oz.* Anecdotes of intense fright reactions to media are common. I am almost certain that if you are reading this book, you can pause and think of at least one instance in your media experience where you found yourself frightened, anxious, spooked, or otherwise disturbed by some media image. The chances are also good that this image was part of a movie or TV show that depicted something from the realm of the paranormal. You are not alone in your experience.

As early as 1933, a researcher named Herbert Blumer found that 93% of the children in his sample reported having experienced fright caused by a movie.[4] In a classic study of the effects of television published in 1958, another researcher, Hilde Himmelweit, found that one-third of the children in her study reported having been frightened by something seen on television.[5] More recent data reveal that about 75% of elementary school children report fright from something seen in a movie or TV program.[6] In interviews about TV and children, parents often express concern about children's fright reactions. They frequently report that their children suffer nightmares as a result of watching frightening programs. Interviews with children confirm that this topic is an important one. In one study conducted in 1983 by researchers Palmer, Hockett, and Dean, more than one-third of the children interviewed reported that there were specific scenes or programs that they were sorry they had ever seen.[7] Fortunately, the research goes beyond the documentation of the prevalence of these responses and offers some explanation and understanding of what is happening. One of the most important findings to emerge from this research is that the media content that frightens children varies, depending on the age of the child.[8]

## DEVELOPMENTAL THEORY: WHAT SCARES ONE CHILD MAY NOT SCARE ANOTHER

Research on children's fright reactions made a breakthrough with the insight of Joanne Cantor. Cantor noticed that the developmental psychology of Jean Piaget helped her sort out reports of fright that she recorded from children and their parents. According to Piaget's theory, children pass through a series of stages in their cognitive development. The way they process, interpret, and think about the world around them depends on where they are in this sequence of stages. Children in the general age range of two to seven years old think **perceptually**. The concrete, visual appearance of things tends to dominate the child's interpretation of and reaction to the world. In contrast, children older than seven years begin to make a shift toward more **conceptual** or **abstract thought**.[9]

After studying these distinctions in Piaget's theory, Cantor realized that they might help explain her data on fright responses. Children in the younger age group tended to show fright in response to scenes and characters that looked grotesque and menacing (e.g., the wicked queen in *Snow White,* the Wicked Witch in *The Wizard of Oz,* or the Incredible Hulk). The fact that many of these characters appear in cartoon form and could never occur in the real world didn't seem to make any difference. The young child was not able to focus on this more conceptual or abstract observation.

In contrast to the younger children, older kids tended to report fright from movies and TV shows that featured events and characters that *could* actually occur in the real world. Their fears tended to involve scenes depicting violence or bodily harm to a character. They also included depictions of natural and technological disasters such as floods, fires, storms, earthquakes, or nuclear holocaust. Cantor reasoned that because of the older child's focus on the conceptual or abstract instead of the visual, the really scary media to them was that which depicted threatening things that might actually happen. Complicating the situation for these older children is the fact that they don't understand the low probability of many of the "real" events that they see in the media. They have a hard time telling themselves that these things won't really happen to them. They also haven't lived long enough to develop a sophisticated set of coping skills that enable them to deal with the harsh images of reality they see in the media.

Upon viewing a scene from a movie about a child kidnapping, children at eight or nine years of age may understand that kidnappings are real and could actually happen. They may also fail to comprehend that the probability of a kidnapping occurring in their neighborhood is low. At the same time, they may realize all too well that kidnappings are serious business and potentially life threatening. This combination of ingredients makes it particularly likely that older children will react with emotional distress to this sort of media depiction. For an older child, this kind of depiction has much more fright potential than the wicked queen in *Snow White*. The older child simply writes off the queen as pretend or impossible. In contrast, young children, who tend to operate at the perceptual level, may find the wicked queen far more disturbing than the kidnapping movie. To them, the real possibility of a kidnapping is simply beyond their comprehension. And if the movie never actually showed physical injury, the young children would probably not react strongly to the content.

## EXPERIMENTING WITH THE INCREDIBLE HULK

When I worked with Cantor on this research, I decided to do my doctoral dissertation on children's reactions to *The Incredible Hulk*. Although this may sound like an unusual topic for scholarly study, the experiment I conducted was logistically quite complex, and the findings were important in supporting Cantor's extensions of Piaget's theory. After screening nearly every episode in the series, we elected to show children of both older and younger ages a brief segment that depicted a hospital employee becoming injured in an explosion. David Banner, played by the late Bill Bixby, witnessed the explosion and ran into a burning storage room to rescue the worker. While Banner was dragging the worker to safety, a subsequent explosion hurled him up against a wall, making him very angry. When David Banner becomes angry, he undergoes his strange metamorphosis into the huge, monstrous Hulk. Although the Hulk's transformation might not be called paranormal, it certainly falls into the more general category of "weird" or "strange." After showing the transformation (which included his eyes turning green, his shirt tearing, and his shoes ripping), the segment concluded by showing the Hulk gently lifting the worker to safety. In the closing scene, the camera followed the Hulk down a hallway and showed him jumping out of a window and growling ferociously.

Why did we show this segment to children, and what did we learn as a result? Following Cantor's logic, we reasoned that older children would show more fright than younger children would during the first part of the segment. The prospect of an explosion and fire would frighten them because these were events that could really happen. Because of their appreciation for the distinction between fantasy and reality, older children would be able to understand the dangers confronted by the characters in this crisis. However, once David Banner began to transform into the Hulk, we thought that the pattern of fright reactions would change. Older children would recognize that the Hulk, despite his monstrous appearance, was really a "good" guy who would probably save the day. These children could discount the ugly visual appearance and focus on the more abstract reality that the Hulk was the answer to the problem. We reasoned that younger children would view the situation very differently. When the Hulk appeared, we thought that these children would be unable to think about very much except the fact that the Hulk's appearance was scary. We expected that the younger children would show more fright at this point in the program. We also expected that this would last until the end of the segment because the Hulk was present right up until the closing shot.

When children watched this segment, we had them come to a room in their school building that teachers had set aside for our research. Each child came separately, and we were able to monitor their heart rate and other physiological reactions as they watched. These reactions helped us interpret what the child felt during the show. The results were just as we had expected. The older children showed more fright during the explosion and fire and calmed down as the Hulk appeared. Younger children showed just the opposite tendency. They were calmer at the beginning of the show and got much more upset at the appearance of the Hulk.[10]

Perhaps you are thinking that researchers should not be going around scaring little kids. We couldn't agree more. We deliberately chose a program that most children were familiar with before the experiment. None of the emotional reactions we observed were extreme. We also made sure that parents and children agreed to participate in the procedure and that the Human Subjects Committee at the University of Wisconsin-Madison approved of everything in the experiment. Finally, we talked with each child afterward and made sure that no harmful emotional reactions had occurred. Actually, children seemed to enjoy these procedures. In Study Box 7-1, I detail a little more about the exact procedures that we went through to make sure that children suffered no harm from participating in this experiment with viewing clips from *The Incredible Hulk*.

What have we learned from experiments like this one? First, Cantor's ideas about the kinds of media that frighten children at different ages are confirmed. For younger kids under age seven, if it looks scary, it probably will be scary. For older kids, if the depiction could really happen and the consequences are physically threatening, it probably will generate some fear. Although most fear reactions tend to be short-lived, in some cases children can suffer media fear that lasts long beyond the program. Coping with these fears can be a real challenge for the parent.[11]

## STUDY BOX 7-1 Research Procedures for Protecting Children

As you might imagine, studies of children's fright reactions must be undertaken with great care. This care is taken from the very beginning of planning a study. In getting ready to run the study that called for preschool and elementary school children to view a clip from *The Incredible Hulk,* meticulous planning started with the choice of video material. Here, I detail the various steps and considerations that went into planning this experiment. As you can see, minimizing the risk to children was paramount throughout the procedure.

1. At the outset, we looked for a program that was sufficiently frightening to induce a detectable level of fear—but not one that was so intense that it would terrorize children. It was important to select a program that children were familiar with so that they wouldn't feel too frightened by some completely unknown scenario. In the case of *The Incredible Hulk,* the program was being broadcast on weekday afternoons in Madison, Wisconsin, during the time of the study. We reasoned that there was a good chance that many children had seen an episode once or twice and that they would have some familiarity with the general plot.
2. After selecting the program, we had to secure the permission of a local preschool and an elementary school to cooperate with us in conducting the study. This meant making sure that each school facility had a room that could be dedicated to data collection during the day. More important, it meant securing the approval of school administrators to show the children the video material. The school administrators had to watch the video and give their official approval before we could move ahead.
3. In the case of the elementary school, the local school system had its own review board for all research conducted in the district. We had to submit a full proposal to this board and give the board members the opportunity to view all of the video material before we could proceed with our plans.
4. In addition to the approvals required from the participating schools, the University Human Subjects Committee had to give its own approval to our procedures and materials. Once all of these approvals were in place, we could proceed with the mechanics of the procedure. But at each step of the process, the children's welfare was paramount.
5. First, parents of all of the school children received a letter describing the research project. A permission slip was enclosed for their signature if they agreed to permit their child to participate. Parents who knew that their children might be particularly sensitive to programs like *The Incredible Hulk* simply didn't sign the permission slip, and their children were never considered for participation in the study.
6. After the permission letters were sent to parents, we set up times for parents to come to the school, preview the video material, and meet the experimenters. Parents who viewed the material and thought that it might be too intense for their children could simply refrain from turning in the permission forms.
7. Once the permission forms were submitted, the research team visited the school classroom and gave a general demonstration of the experimental procedure. We

watched a few programs together with the class while one of the children wore the physiological electrodes we used in the procedure. These electrodes were attached to the fingers of one hand. We showed the class how a computer monitored the children's heart rate during the TV viewing. This was an educational time for all of the children—not just those who ended up participating in the study.

8. Before any individual child participated in the study, he or she had to agree to go through the procedure. In some cases, children whose parents had already given consent to participate decided on the day of the study to decline participation. Of course, if a child showed any reluctance to participate, the child was encouraged *not* to go through the procedure.

9. During the procedure, if a child showed any signs of genuine distress, the procedure would have been discontinued. Probably because of the elaborate screening procedures, all of the children who started the procedure watched the program to the end. We did not have to discontinue the viewing because of signs of distress.

10. After each child had finished viewing the video material and answering questions, we offered that child a "scratch 'n sniff" sticker in the aroma of their choice. The key principle in dismissing children from a study of this type is to make sure that they leave happy. Our major concern was that no child would suffer any lingering distress as a result of the procedures. Parents of participating children were encouraged to contact us if they had concerns after the study was completed. As far as we know, none of the children who participated suffered any lingering reactions.

In general, guidelines followed by university human subjects committees have grown even stricter since the time that this study was done. In the final analysis, these guidelines help to protect not only the participants but the researchers as well. No researcher would want to be responsible for inducing severe emotional trauma in a child. By following the guidelines of human subjects committees, researchers have at least some protection from having to bear such a burden.

## WHY IS THE PARANORMAL SO SCARY?

Ironically, the seeds of understanding why paranormal media depictions are so often experienced as frightening and upsetting are contained in my early experience with *The Twilight Zone*. At the age of six, I had come to understand the difference between reality and fantasy. At precisely the point in my life where I thought I had this distinction sorted out, along comes Rod Serling to toy with my mind. The transformation of people into mannequins looked as if it could actually happen in a real department store. I was just uncertain enough about this possibility that I found it to be terrifying.

Some of the most frightening movies that deal with paranormal themes are those that deftly juxtapose reality with the paranormal world. In a survey of college students that I did some 20 years after *The Exorcist* was first released, this film was still the most frequently mentioned as a movie that had induced enduring fright.[12] In follow-up interviews, I discovered that students often expressed the idea that the film had made them feel as if demon possession was real. And if it was real, many felt vulnerable and unprepared to deal with it. This is the nature of the paranormal world, almost by definition. If it does exist, most of us would confess to understanding it very poorly. And how can we control or protect ourselves against something we don't understand? We can't, and that's one of the things that makes us afraid. It is no wonder, then, that many a director intent on scaring the audience has turned to the paranormal for the horror film's basic ingredient. If the film can convince the viewer that it might just be possible in real life, then the rest of the task is easy. The mystery and uncontrollability inherent in the paranormal take over from there and finish the job of terrorizing the viewer. Not only is this a particularly deadly combination for young children who have just begun to sort out the difference between fantasy and reality, but it is also extremely potent for adults, many of whom carry a fair amount of uncertainty about the existence of paranormal phenomena.[13]

## The Law of Apparent Reality

Back in 1988, Nico Frijda, a psychologist at the University of Amsterdam, published an important paper titled, "The Laws of Emotion."[14] One of the laws that he identified was the **law of apparent reality**. Frijda stated the law simply: "Emotions are elicited by events appraised as real, and their intensity corresponds to the degree to which this is the case." The implications of this law for understanding fright reactions to media presentations are quite clear. If the material that viewers encounter in a TV show or movie is potentially threatening but is dismissed by viewers as complete fantasy, the law predicts that the intensity of viewers' fear will be low. In contrast, if viewers perceive the material to be "real," higher levels of fear should be the result. Perceptions of the reality of media content can be discussed in different ways. Viewers might perceive a news report of radiation leaking from a nuclear reactor to be "real" because the event is actually happening at the time of the report. Obviously, that's a very different case than when viewers watch a fictional depiction of demon possession in *The Exorcist*. But even though viewers may distinguish between these types of "reality," there may still be a sense in which the depiction of demon possession is perceived by viewers to be "real." While viewers may know the possession is not actually happening at the time they are watching the movie— and they may recognize that the depiction is a dramatic one that only involves actors and actresses—they may still perceive the depiction to have some degree of reality. That perception could be based upon a belief that something like the depiction *could* happen. Frijda's law may be an interesting theoretical foundation for future testing that examines the intensity of emotions that result from different sorts of media presentations. James Potter, a communication scholar, reviews a number of empirical studies that appear to be consistent with Frijda's law. As he stated, the results of these studies:

> ... lead to the conclusion that when reality cues about a mediated message are made very explicit, people who see the real material will be more likely to exhibit changes in behaviors and attitudes in the direction of the depiction than those who see the fictional material. (p. 34)[15]

When I look back over the films that are mentioned again and again by college students as those that terrified them and caused them to experience lingering anxiety and fear, many of them depict paranormal phenomena in a context that strongly suggests the events could actually happen. There is no better way to do justice to the nature of these fear responses than to report them verbatim as they were originally reported in my research. The following descriptions are the recollections of college students from film experiences that they had in their childhood—usually around the ages of nine to 11.

## *Poltergeist*

**[A family experiences the horror of discovering that their house is built on a burial ground. Ghosts arrive through the fuzziness of the TV screen and proceed to haunt the family in various ways.]**

**Respondent #1** *"This movie made me so scared that I felt like my heart froze, like I sort of went into shock. I totally remember this feeling of almost having a heart attack because I still get it now when I'm scared. I hate that feeling. I feel so uneasy. I'm like a basket case. Till this day that movie stayed with me. There are little things from the movie I can identify with when I see them now, and I'll get flashback feelings of how scared I felt. For example: clowns, closets, a fuzzy TV, and that little girl's voice all give me the willies. I really feel that that movie has scarred me for life."*

**Respondent #2** *"I was 10 years old, and, of course, my imagination went wild. At the end of the film, I went to my room quietly ... and being a pretty spoiled kid, I had my own black-and-white TV in my room. Well, needless to say, it was unplugged and hauled into my closet with blankets piled on top of it. To this day, I still unplug the TV every night before I go to bed. The idea of static in the reception magically appearing on the screen still frightens me."*

**Respondent #3** *"I still get chills when I remember the part where the little girl in the movie looks at the snowy TV set and says, 'They're here!' I think the greatest effect of this experience is the fact that no one ever reassured me that events in this movie weren't real. This is probably the most important factor that shaped my belief that supernatural beings probably do exist."*

**Respondent #4** *"The lingering effects of the fear I experienced that night are numerous. Because the haunting situation, in my mind, is not entirely impossible, I still find myself worrying about it at times. I feel the same fear emotions and reactions, like increased heart beat and paranoia, when I am confronted with some of the film's major symbols. Seeing a snowy TV screen at night, worrying that the tree outside my brother's window will attack him whenever it storms, thinking our house might have been built over a graveyard, clowns, and closets are all residual effects of my frightening media experience."*

## The *Nightmare on Elm Street* Series

**[Freddy Krueger returns from the grave to kill young children. He is able to get them only while they are sleeping. He comes to them in their dreams with sharp knives in place of fingers.]**

**Respondent #1** *"When the movie was over, I went home petrified to death. For about the next month and a half, I was terrified of going to sleep. I was afraid that if I went to sleep Freddy Krueger was going to kill me in my dreams. The first night I didn't sleep a wink. The next night I had trouble falling asleep and staying asleep once I got there."*

**Respondent #2** *"There were many times during the movie that I thought about things such as whether or not the door was locked, or if these things could really happen. My aunt had a basement door that I continually kept an eye on to see if Freddy would come out of it. During the movie I convinced myself that I could not ever fall asleep again, because Freddy would get me. I remember this movie as being the most scary thing I have ever experienced, even to this day. To this day I seem to be afraid of dark unfurnished basements, and I do not think I will ever get over that."*

**Respondent #3** *"I knew the part about the dreams was purely fiction, yet I could not make myself fall asleep that evening or for several evenings following that one. To this day, I am still especially disturbed when I hear about kids being abducted or killed."*

**Respondent #4** *"This movie has a scene in it that I will never forget. It is the one where Freddy's arms stretch out to an arm span of some 30 feet and then slash someone to pieces. The reason why this scene scared me so bad is still unclear to me, but I think it might have something to do with Freddy having the superhuman ability to stretch out his arms and catch me no matter how far away I get and that it looked pretty creepy. For many nights after that I could not sleep without having a dream about Freddy reaching out and slashing me. Even now, I could do without alleys, because I am afraid if I look back I might see Freddy waiting for me with open arms, so to speak."*

## *The Exorcist*

**[A young girl is possessed by a demon and a local priest must perform an exorcism as the only remedy.]**

**Respondent #1** *"As I viewed this movie, I was filled with fear and terror. I had never been so frightened by a movie before. I thought that I was going to be possessed. I prayed throughout the entire movie that this would not happen to me. I tried to go to sleep, but I was too worked up to relax. By the time it was over, I was very exhausted. I finally fell asleep. That night, I had nightmares that I was possessed. When I went home the next day, I forgot all about the movie. Until I went to bed, that is. That night, I was paranoid. Every noise I heard was what I thought was the devil in my house. Every once in a while I have a nightmare still, or become a bit frightened by an unfamiliar noise. Still, to this day, I will not watch* The Exorcist.*"*

**Respondent #2** *"Never in my life had I been so afraid to go to sleep. This insomnia lasted for about a week before I finally got a good night's sleep, with the assistance of a trip to church. I have yet to watch a movie that has even remotely compared to the fear I felt when I watched* The Exorcist. *To this day, I have still never seen the last ten minutes of that movie, simply because I don't ever want to see it again. I also refuse to watch the second and third parts of this movie as well. I must also have a Bible or a crucifix in the room that I sleep in before I go to bed. I will never play with or purchase a Ouija board or even be in the same room with someone who is. All this results from my most traumatic experience in my life, watching* The Exorcist.*"*

**Respondent #3** *"After seeing* The Exorcist, *I was literally afraid that if I didn't go to church every week, and do only right, this could actually happen to me."*

**Respondent #4** *"The music played a tremendous part in building the evil tone of the movie. For years, whenever 'Tubular Bells' would be played over the radio I would quickly switch stations or shut off the radio completely. In Indianapolis, on I-65, there was a business that had its name printed in large letters on the side of its building. Whenever we were traveling and went past this spot, I looked the other way. I knew exactly where this building was located and knew when to avert my gaze to the opposite side of the road. I went so far as to turn my whole body away from the building. The name of the business was Tubular Sales. Close enough for me!"*

Clearly, based on these descriptions, one area that has been overlooked in all the controversy about paranormal media and the promotion of belief in weird things is the fact that the images and plots contained in these movies and TV shows are often scary—particularly for children.[16]

## WHY DO SOME MEDIA FEARS LINGER FOR SO LONG?
## A THEORY OF DIFFERENTIAL BRAIN PROCESSING

When confronted with experiences like the one I had with *The Twilight Zone,* some researchers have been especially curious about why an early fear response from childhood would linger so long—even well into adulthood. Joanne Cantor provided a good answer to this question by drawing on the work of another scholar, Joseph LeDoux. LeDoux makes a distinction between **implicit memories** and **explicit memories** that are stored in the brain.[17] Explicit memories concern the particular details of an event and are stored in the **hippocampus**. Apparently, these memories are more susceptible to change and decay. As I mentioned earlier in the chapter, I don't remember the key details about the program I watched back in 1960. In contrast, implicit emotional memories of a frightening event are stored in the **amygdala**—a completely different part of the brain. These memories are designed to be recalled quickly. In the case of fear, the memory might simply contain a negative association with a particular object. When we encounter that object years later, the negative feeling stored in the amygdala is activated to signal us that there might be some danger lurking. In my case, perhaps this is why I have some feelings of discomfort when I see mannequins in a department store. The feeling arises quickly with no conscious thoughts about the episode of *The Twilight Zone* that I watched years ago. Cantor thought that the way LeDoux described the brain's processing of fear memories in the following passage was a good summary of what may happen when people become intensely scared by a movie or TV program:

> Unconscious fear memories established through the amygdala appear to be indelibly burned into the brain. They are probably with us for life. This is often very useful, especially in a stable, unchanging world, since we don't want to have to learn about the same kinds of dangers over and over again. But the downside is that sometimes the things that are imprinted in the amygdala's circuits are maladaptive. In these instances, we pay dearly for the incredible efficiencies of the fear system.[18]

In my case, the fear of department store mannequins is very mild and I wouldn't say that I'm paying "dearly" for being exposed to *The Twilight Zone.* On the other hand, if LeDoux is correct, it looks as if the mild discomfort I feel whenever I go into a department store at the mall is something I shouldn't expect to go away any time soon.

Kristen Harrison, a researcher at the University of Michigan, teamed up with Joanne Cantor to find out more about enduring fright responses to media. As it turns out, my experience with *The Twilight Zone* is not unusual. After surveying over 153 college students, Harrison and Cantor reported that nearly everyone in their survey sample wrote about at least one program or movie that had frightened them so much that their fear had endured after the viewing experience ended.[19] In fact, about 26% of the sample reported that their fright had endured for over a year after the viewing experience and was still part of their life at the time of the survey. What sorts of post-viewing symptoms were reported? Study Box 7-2 provides a summary of the sorts of responses and their frequencies that were reported in this study.

**STUDY BOX 7-2 Symptoms Reported by College Students in Harrison and Cantor's Survey**

- Crying or Screaming – 26.8%
- Trembling or Shaking – 23.9%
- Nausea or Stomach Pain – 20.3%
- Clinging to a Companion – 18.1%
- Freezing or a Feeling of Paralysis – 17.4%
- Fear of Losing Control – 10.9%
- Sweating – 6.5%
- Chills or Fever – 6.5%
- Fear of Dying – 5.8%
- Shortness of Breath – 4.3%
- Feeling of Unreality – 3.6%
- Dizziness or Faintness – 2.2%
- Numbness – 0.7%

Over 80% of the sample reported feeling at least ONE of these symptoms.

SOURCE: Harrison, K., & Cantor, J. (1999). Tales from the screen: Enduring fright reactions to scary media. *Media Psychology*, 1, 97–116.

## Theory about Emotional Coping: What's a Parent to Do?

Cantor's research team has also addressed the issue of what parents should do to help their children through frightening experiences that come during or after media exposure. One thing she discovered was that parents inevitably resort to what seems like a logical approach to dealing with children's fright reactions to TV and movies. They tell their children, regardless of age, that what they are seeing is "not real" or "just pretend." Actually, the research shows that this strategy can be effective with older children who have come to distinguish between **reality** and **fantasy**.[20] The problem is that parents also tend to use the strategy with younger children (under age seven) who often are not capable of comprehending why this should cause them to be less afraid.[21] If something *looks scary,* the fact that Mom or Dad is saying "it isn't real" doesn't seem to matter much. Younger children may come to understand that their parents believe that labeling something "not real" should make it less threatening. And they do acquire some superficial knowledge about the difference between reality and fantasy. Usually, however, this knowledge is not sufficient to make much difference in processing media images.

To illustrate the young child's difficulty with the concept of reality, I often relate a family incident that occurred when my daughter Erin was four years old. My wife, Cheri, wanted to demonstrate that Erin understood the difference between reality and fantasy. As we drove around the neighborhood at Christmastime, Cheri spotted a large plastic statue of Rudolph the Red-Nosed Reindeer. She called the statue to Erin's attention and asked, "Is that Rudolph *real?"* Erin answered promptly, "Of course not, Mom." It certainly appeared as if Cheri had made her point. But, just to make sure, I asked one more question: "Erin, did that Rudolph eat breakfast this morning like you did?" Erin's response was just as prompt as her first one: "Of course, Dad!"

Erin's understanding of the plastic Rudolph is typical of how young children understand their parents upon hearing that certain TV characters are not real. Children may be able to correctly label the character as pretend, but this label does not mean quite the same thing that it does to an adult. For Erin, Rudolph wasn't real, but he still ate breakfast. In the case of the Wicked Witch, young children may say that she's not real, but this doesn't tend to reduce fright reactions because the witch *looks so scary.*

The research on helping children to cope yields a number of practical conclusions. For older children, it may be very helpful to talk about the fact that media productions contain staged scenes for entertainment purposes and that the characters are not real. When the older child shows fright at viewing events that could actually happen, some attempt to work through the low probability of these events in the child's life may be helpful. Researchers refer to this approach as employing cognitive strategies. **Cognitive strategies** encourage children to think about the things they already know and relate those things to the aspects of the movie that are scary. A few years ago, a professor of chemistry at my university phoned me to seek my advice on how to handle the fears of his 10-year-old son. Apparently, his son had seen some doomsday preaching on a religious channel and had become terrified of the idea that the world would end soon. This kind of fear—fear that something seen on TV might actually happen—is typical for a child of this age.

My advice was to tell the child two things simultaneously. First, I advised that whenever the child vocalized his fear, the parent should tell him matter-of-factly that the world was *not* going to end soon. Second, I advised that the child be reminded of how many days had passed since the last conversation without the world ending. Gradually, I predicted that the fear would diminish as the boy came to understand through his own experience that the world was unlikely to end soon. That's exactly what happened. It isn't clear from the excerpts included earlier in this chapter, but most of the students who reported being scared by a paranormal depiction also noted that their fears diminished over time.

For younger children, the best strategy in coping with media-induced fears is to prevent them in the first place. To do this, parents need to heed the research findings. Hollywood is of little help here. In fact, movie advertising can be misleading when it comes to children's fright reactions. Many of the films that carry a G rating and promise "family entertainment" are also films that feature characters who look scary. Unfortunately, unwitting parents who strive to treat their young child to a movie often find that the only thing they have succeeded in doing is scaring the child. My own daughter expressed fear of the Jabberwocky in *Alice in Wonderland*—one of Showtime's special Fairy Tale productions that targeted an audience of children. The research data reveal hundreds of reports from parents about scenes and characters from "family"-oriented films that scared their children. Many of these scenes are from animated classics produced by none other than the

Disney studios. The key thing for parents to think about in avoiding this kind of entertainment for their young child (especially in the two to five age range) is *how the characters look.* Even slight variations in normal appearances (e.g., long fingernails, beady eyes, or sharp teeth) can be enough to trigger a fear reaction. Of course, parents also need to know their own children. Some kids are much more sensitive to these visual features than others. There is no substitute for spending time with a child during viewing to become more familiar with how emotional reactions are likely to vary.

If a young child does become scared of something seen on TV or in a movie, parents should not hesitate to turn the set off at the first sign of trouble. As logical as this advice is, some parents become convinced that their children need to continue to watch the program to "conquer" their fear. But there is no research evidence to support such behavior. And it is probably better to avoid extensive discussions with a very young child about the frightening show. It is better to cuddle the child and distract him or her from the program by reading a book or playing a game. Consistent with the young child's tendency to process things perceptually, there may be some truth to the maxim "out of sight—out of mind." Researchers summarize this type of strategy with the young child as a non-cognitive strategy. **Non-cognitive strategies** refrain from trying to encourage the child to think about the source of their fear. They work instead to distract the child or avoid the object of fear altogether.

## IS IT FUN TO BE SCARED?

Although the research reveals that many people regret having seen certain scenes in TV shows or movies and suffer long-term fright reactions, this is hardly the complete picture. In nearly every study conducted in which people are asked if they like to watch this type of media, the distribution of responses is similar. Roughly one-third of respondents report that they do not enjoy this kind of entertainment and will avoid it at any cost. Another one-third report that they enjoy this kind of entertainment and actively seek it out. The last group of people report that it depends on the content. There are certain themes that they find enjoyable and other themes that they can't take very well.[22]

### Frightening Films and Roller Coaster Rides

Researchers were intrigued by the findings on enjoyment of frightening films. *Fear is a negative emotion.* A person who feels scared is a person who is experiencing a negative feeling. Fear, by definition, is unpleasant. How can it be that people experience frightening films as enjoyable?

Actually, there are several possible answers to this question. One answer comes from Dolf Zillmann's **theory of excitation transfer**,[23] which you encountered in the last chapter. Zillmann's idea is that when people become scared while watching a movie, their entire arousal system kicks into high gear. Heart rate and blood pressure increase, as do muscle tension and other physiological indicators. During the movie, the arousal helps to intensify the negative emotion of fear. But what about after the movie is over? Recall from the last chapter that physiological arousal normally does not return to baseline levels quickly. The arousal lingers for a while. But the fear that people experience while viewing is usually replaced with feelings of relief and even joy. The threatening scenes are over and the film's protagonist may have emerged victorious. So a person may leave the film feeling a positive emotion. Because physiological arousal intensifies any emotion that a person feels, this positive emotion at the end of the film can be intense. There is usually a high level of arousal left over from the fright. The end result is that even a mild feeling of relief that the film is over can be experienced as a kind of euphoria. A person may leave the frightening film feeling elated—even though during the film, the only feeling was terror. Over the long run, instead of remembering the terror, a person tends to remember the last feeling experienced—euphoria.

The dynamics of excitation transfer that may take place in a scary movie are similar to what may happen during a roller-coaster ride. A person may not actually enjoy the feeling that results from thinking about the possibility that the coaster will fall from the track and plunge the riders to their deaths. But after the ride is over, the arousal generated during the terror transfers to feelings of relief and creates a kind of euphoria. There is also solid evidence for the process of excitation transfer while people are viewing films.[24] And so, it may be that people don't really like feeling scared, but they do like the feeling of euphoria that follows. As in the case of roller coasters, not everyone experiences scary movies the same way. For some, the terror of the ride outweighs any feelings of relief that follow. But for others, the transfer of arousal to a feeling of relief provides an experience that outweighs the terror. Of great interest to researchers is the fact that there is a relationship between the enjoyment of scary movies and the tendency to enjoy roller coasters. People who enjoy one also tend to report that they enjoy the other.

## The Sexual Dynamic in Viewing Frightening Films

One research finding that emerges over and over again is that males enjoy scary movies much more than females do. Why might this be so? According to Zillmann, it might have something to do with the ancient tribal practice of male initiation rites. For thousands of years, society has socialized males to conquer threatening stimuli and act as the protector. Modern society has discontinued this practice, but strong remnants remain. Fraternity hazing on college campuses is a constant problem. Viewed from the perspective of the tribal initiation rite, it is no wonder that colleges have been unable to eliminate this practice. College administrators are attempting to buck several thousand years of male socialization. Zillmann believes that scary movies may also serve as an informal replacement of the ancient initiation right. Males can test their masculinity by exposing themselves to the most horrible images that Stephen King can dream up. If they are able to emerge from the theater victorious, they have proved their masculinity once and for all. According to Zillmann, females also participate in this rite. By withholding affection to the males who are not able to conquer the film's threatening images, females help to contribute to the ongoing socialization pattern. Females also participate in the rite by displaying the appropriate signs of discomfort and their need for protection during a scary film. This idea is sometimes referred to as **gender role socialization**.

To test this idea, Zillmann and his colleagues carried out a fascinating experiment.[25] Females who participated in the study believed that their viewing partner was just a random male participant in the study. Actually, the male participant was one of the experimenters. During the movie, the male engaged in certain behaviors that the experimenters described as either "conquering" or "escapist." For half of the female participants, the male exhibited only "conquering" behaviors. He commented on how silly the film was and how it wouldn't scare anyone. For the other half of the female participants, the male exhibited "escapist" behaviors. He placed his hands over his eyes at the scary parts of the film. He commented on how he wished the film would end soon. At the end of the experiment, the females rated their male viewing partners on attractiveness. Can you guess what happened? Females rated the male as being very attractive when he expressed conquering behaviors. When he expressed escapist behaviors, they rated him as unattractive.

The researchers repeated this same experiment on male participants using a female experimenter. The results in this case were completely opposite to those for the females. Males found the females more attractive when they displayed the classic fear response indicating that they wanted to escape. Males rated the females very unattractive when they showed conquering behaviors. There was one very interesting limitation to the experimental results. The pattern of findings emerged only for people who were ordinary in terms of physical attractiveness. Opposite-sex viewing partners still found those rare males and females who were judged to be gorgeous by their peers to be attractive, regardless of how they responded to the frightening film. The results of this study show that enjoyment of frightening films may reflect deeply ingrained socialized sex roles.

Two communication researchers, Cynthia Hoffner and Kenneth Levine, decided to conduct a meta-analysis (see Chapter 2) in order to gain insight about the variables that contributed to the enjoyment of frightening and violent media.[26] Their analysis of 38 different studies revealed that viewers who tended to empathize with media characters enjoyed frightening media *less* than those who weren't particularly empathic. Apparently, empathizing with characters who are frightened and distressed takes its toll on enjoyment. But Hoffner and Levine did find some clear patterns in the research in terms of enjoyment. Those who tended to enjoy frightening media were males, adolescents, those inclined toward aggressive behavior, and those higher on the sensation-seeking measure (see Chapter 4). There was also some support across the studies for the process of excitation transfer outlined by Zillmann. The more frightening a program or movie was during viewing, the more viewers reported afterward that they enjoyed it.

## BEYOND FEAR: OTHER EMOTIONAL REACTIONS TO MEDIA

The possibility of feeling euphoric after a frightening movie or of feeling attracted to a viewing partner serves to illustrate only a couple of specific emotional reactions among many that might occur when people use media. During the past two decades, probably more studies have been published on human emotion than were published in the entire century up to that point. As a result, many theoretical ideas about emotion have been tested in the context of media and have helped scholars to understand the different ways that our feelings are inextricably tied to the media we consume. Before concluding this chapter, let's consider just a few of the important ideas about emotion and the media that have helped to shape the way scholars now understand this topic.

### Empathy: I Feel What You Feel

If you've ever watched any of the U.S. television coverage of the Olympic Games, you'll have no trouble recalling what has now become a familiar pattern in the way the networks put together a typical segment. Just before presenting the culminating event in a particular sport, the coverage will focus on a specific athlete's personal struggle to reach what is now the climactic moment of his or her career—or even his or her life. After learning about what the athlete has gone through to make it to the Olympics, it is difficult for most people to keep themselves from feeling joyful if the person featured is shown smiling in victory with a gold medal hanging around the neck. Alternatively, if the athlete fails and we see feelings of distress and pain etched on his or her face, viewers tend to experience a profound sense of disappointment. The process that occurs in both cases can be described as **empathy**—the tendency for viewers to feel the same feelings as another person they are watching or thinking about. One important thing to notice about the process of empathy is that viewers can experience virtually *any emotion* as a result of consuming media depictions of other people. Empathy is especially likely to occur if you have formed a positive view or bond with the person projected by the media. Once that bond is in place, whatever the media character feels, the tendency will be strong for viewers to feel the same thing. Is there any evidence that this sort of process actually takes place? You can probably think of examples from your own viewing experiences that confirm this kind of empathic process. It should come as no surprise, then, to discover that the process has been documented systematically in the research laboratory (see Study Box 7-3).

The fact that exposure to media messages can bring about feelings of empathy with particular characters shouldn't be too surprising. On the other hand, the fact that certain media messages might actually cause people to show more empathy for other people in general—people who are completely unrelated to anyone depicted in the message—is a more provocative finding. That's exactly what some researchers discovered when they studied the effects of listening to songs that contained "prosocial" lyrics.[27] After listening to either a prosocial song that referred to people helping others or a neutral song that didn't contain those sorts of lyrics, Tobias Grei-temeyer had his 38 experimental participants read essays which told of the author's experience of being dropped by a romantic partner, or the experience of suffering a physical injury and being unable to participate in a sport that he passionately loved. After reading the essays, those who had listened to the song that had prosocial lyrics expressed significantly more empathy for the author of the essay than those who had listened to the neutral song. In a follow-up experiment, Greitemeyer wondered if listening to a prosocial song could actually increase altruistic behavior. When his participants who listened to either a prosocial or neutral song were given a chance to donate to a non-profit organization before leaving the laboratory, 53% of those who had heard the prosocial song chose to make a donation—compared to just 31% who heard the neutral song. While this sort of effect certainly needs to be replicated, it does highlight the potential of media messages to foster more or less interpersonal empathy for others.

## STUDY BOX 7-3 Empathic Responses to Media

In a study designed to test the notion of empathy in the media context, Dolf Zillmann and Joanne Cantor wanted to see if the empathic process took place even in children. They were able to test this idea with third-grade boys and girls. Using different films, the researchers created two conditions. In one, they presented a child who was very nice in interacting with his friend, his pet, and his brother. In the second condition, they presented a child who acted in just the opposite way. After establishing that children who viewed these films expressed liking for the nice child and dislike for the mean one, the researchers presented different endings to the two scenarios. In the happy-ending film, the child received a new bicycle and was shown in a state of glee; the sad ending showed the child getting onto an old bicycle and having an accident. The camera focused on the child's face, which cringed with pain. The researchers watched the facial expressions of the children who viewed these films and also inter-viewed them afterward. What did the results show? If children viewed the film about the nice child who expressed glee at the film's conclusion, they also reported that they felt gleeful. Upon viewing the nice child who ended up in pain, emotional reactions were quite the opposite—the children felt sad and pained as well. In short, children empathized with the nice child and took on his feelings whether they were positive or negative.

Also of interest were the responses of children who watched the mean child. Their emotional reactions might be described as anti-empathic. When the mean child showed glee at receiving a new bike, the children felt bad. On the other hand, when the mean child was shown in pain after crashing his old bike, children felt a great sense of satisfaction. This study suggests that feelings of empathy apply across a wide range of emotions and are seen even in very young viewers.

SOURCE: Zillmann, D., & Cantor, J. R. (1977). Affective responses to the emotions of a protagonist. *Journal of Experimental Social Psychology*, 13, 155–165.

In another more recent pair of studies, Greitemeyer studied how cooperative team-play in a violent video game affects empathy.[28] He assigned participants to one of three experimental conditions. In the first condition, players played a violent video game alone; in the second condition they played the same violent game with another player—a teammate who helped to kill the monsters in the game; in the third condition players played a neutral game alone. After playing the game, the participants read a story about a family in Bangladesh who had endured many hardships. Participants were asked to indicate the extent to which they empathized with the family members. The results were intriguing. Participants who played the violent game alone were significantly less empathetic than those who played with a teammate or played a neutral game. Greitemeyer concluded that playing cooperatively on the same team increases empathy and can erase the negative effects of playing a violent video game alone. In a second study, Greitemeyer showed that playing a neutral game with a cooperative teammate increases empathy when compared to playing a neutral game alone. These studies indicate that cooperative videogame play could serve to increase empathy to various situations beyond the videogame setting.

## Using Media to Manage Your Mood

Have you ever found that you weren't "in the mood" to go to a particular type of movie or watch a particular TV show? According to Dolf Zillmann's **theory of mood management**, this experience is not only common—it is quite predictable.[29] According to the theory, our entertainment choices are often a function of how we're feeling at the present moment and how we anticipate that exposure to certain media content is likely to make us feel during and following that exposure. One proposition from this theory is that when people find their emotions to be at a low ebb, they will make entertainment choices designed to lift their spirits. This proposition has been tested with female viewers in a most interesting fashion. Jean Meadowcroft and Dolf Zillmann asked women to indicate their viewing preferences for different types of TV programs at the time that they completed a questionnaire. In addition to the women's viewing preferences, the researchers also were able to gather information on exactly where the women were in their monthly menstrual cycles. Although this might seem like an odd piece of data to gather in a study of media preferences, there was actually a good reason for getting this information. The chemistry of the menstrual cycle is well documented. When women experience a premenstrual syndrome, levels of progesterone and estrogen take a precipitous drop. These chemical changes typically trigger emotional changes as well—often leading to bad moods and even depression. In contrast, when women are in the middle of their cycles, progesterone and estrogen are high and typically are accompanied by more positive mood states.

When the researchers examined their data, they discovered a systematic difference in the program preferences of the women in their sample. The women who were at the premenstrual point in their cycle and presumably experiencing lower moods were much more likely to report a preference for watching situation comedies. Women who were in the middle of their cycles, presumably having no bad moods to manage, tended to prefer dramas over situation comedies.[30] The findings of this study were essentially replicated by other researchers who studied women during and after pregnancy, when these same hormones vary in the body. Once again, women with low levels of the hormones who felt more depressed expressed a strong preference for watching comedies.[31]

It isn't accidental that the experiment I chose to illustrate mood-management theory was one that used only female participants. Quite a few studies in the literature appear to show that males don't necessarily behave in the same way that females do when it comes to using media to alter mood states. In fact, there's also evidence that females don't always behave in the way that they did in the study by Meadowcroft and Zillmann. While the evidence often indicates that females will choose game shows and comedies when they are feeling bad, men, in contrast, are more likely to choose violent or action shows. The fact that the theory doesn't always seem to be supported in the way that Zillmann predicted has led scholars to describe the supporting evidence for the theory as "mixed."

One researcher, Silvia Knobloch-Westerwick, has sought to clarify this state of affairs by noting that men and women tend to handle their stress differently. It may be that females prefer to initially ruminate on their negative moods and choose media that are not very absorbing; males in contrast may tend to choose absorbing media that serve to distract them initially from their negative mood state. Knobloch-Westerwick also noted that based on past research, the mood-management process is probably more complicated than the theory first proposed. While people might initially choose one type of media in response to their current mood, they might change their mood-management strategy at some later point in time. For example, females who initially choose media that will not distract them much from their current mood may eventually prefer something more distracting. Males might show just the opposite pattern. As a result, depending on when researchers measure media choices after a mood induction, different results might be observed. Using voluntary exposure to different types of music after a mood induction, Knobloch-Westerwick was able to gather data that offered some support for these ideas.[32] While the overall evidence on the theory of mood management seems to suggest a more complicated set of processes at work that scholars are still in the process of understanding, there seems to be little doubt at this point that people do use their media selections to alter or manage their moods.

Part of the complication surrounding the theory of mood management has to do with the various dimensions of media content that are relevant to the mood-management process. Knobloch-Westerwick recently reviewed the four dimensions of media that Zillmann pointed out as those that were potentially at work.[33] First, media have **excitatory potential**. That is to say, they can influence our levels of physiological arousal. Think about a fast-paced song as opposed to a calm, serene melody. Or think about an erotic film as opposed to an episode of *Meet the Press*. People can select media to have an arousing effect or a calming effect.

Second, media have **absorption potential**. In other words, some media presentations totally absorb us in the content, and other presentations don't really draw us in very much. If you're in a negative mood, the theory suggests that you'll want to stop ruminating about your feelings and select media that have high absorption potential. You might select a juicy drama that permits you to lose yourself and forget about your negative mood. On the other hand, if you are feeling upbeat and positive, you'll want to avoid highly absorbing media that could take your mind off of how good you feel.

Third, media have more or less **semantic affinity** with a person's thoughts that are associated with positive and negative moods. Imagine that you have just had a huge argument with your romantic partner and you're not feeling very happy. The theory of mood management would predict that you might want to seek out a movie with high absorption potential to keep your mind from ruminating on the unpleasant residue of the conflict. But the last thing you'd probably want to watch is a classic romantic drama. The theme of romance would simply remind you of your own situation and make you feel worse. In this case, semantic affinity would override the general absorption potential of the film.

Fourth, media have **hedonic valence**. In general, pleasant media depictions should cause people to feel happier; unpleasant or disagreeable media depictions should sour the mood. Of course, what counts as pleasant or unpleasant media is often a matter of personal interpretation. What one person finds to be disagreeable may cause another to laugh with delight. When these four dimensions of media are considered together, it isn't difficult to see how researchers studying the theory might sometimes encounter a pattern of results that weren't initially predicted.

## Does Mediated Emotion Disrupt and Confuse Our Emotional Well-Being?

So far, this chapter has outlined both negative and positive emotions that people experience from media exposure. Although some types of media can terrify viewers, other types can induce positive moods and even move people to experience euphoria. As we've seen, people deliberately seem to use the media to manage their emotional states. Nevertheless, some lines of analysis suggest that the most profound effects of electronic media on human emotion may be more disturbing than helpful. A woman who lives in my local community (Dr. Sally Miller) is well known for her work with people who are grieving the loss of a loved one. One of the problems that she frequently confronts is the expectation that media messages often convey about how quickly people deal with the emotional trauma of a loss. She points out that just 24 hours after the attacks on September 11, 2001, some media commentators were already referring to people who had "started the recovery process." Miller found such phrases to be incredibly inappropriate—almost ludicrous. First, Miller points out that people who lose loved ones don't really ever "recover" from their loss.

Instead, they find ways to deal with it. Second, she notes that people who lose someone have rarely even begun to comprehend the reality of their loss during the first
24 hours. They are still in a state of shock. They haven't even had time to *begin*
grieving.

I find Miller's observations interesting in the light of speculations from Dolf
Zillmann about what modern media may be doing to our emotions. Consider the following provocative comments from an essay that Zillmann wrote in 1991:

> [T]he pace that characterizes contemporary audiovisual storytelling and report-
> ing is likely to produce affective confusion and shallowness in both children
> and adults…. The rapid pacing of affect-inducing effects in modern media pre-
> sentations, then, appears to minimize affective and, especially, empathetic reac-
> tions (a) by preventing the complete unfolding of the response because
> distracting, competing information is provided too soon after the elicitation of
> affect; and (b) by creating affective confusions through the intensification (by
> excitation-transfer) of subsequent, potentially non-empathetic affect. Empa-
> thetic reactions, in short, are often deprived of their inherent intensity, while
> other reactions are often artificially intensified.[34]

Zillmann seems to be suggesting that by depicting a wide range of human emotional reactions over such a fast-paced medium like TV, new technology may dis-
rupt and confuse the human tendency to experience emotions more slowly in a
process that gradually unfolds over a longer period of time. When excitation transfer processes are also considered, things can really get quite confusing. A viewer
may find that a more minor emotional reaction to a depicted event is intensified by
arousal left over from a preceding emotional reaction just a few minutes earlier.
The emerging picture of our emotions when we are subjected to a stream of TV
images is that we run through different affective states at highly artificial speeds
and often get confused about which emotions we initially reacted to with greatest
intensity. Moreover, this mediated world of emotions may be increasingly the one
we're turning to as a source for learning how we ought to respond emotionally to
the events around us. Is it possible that the media may be conditioning us not to
linger too long in any one emotional state? Could this be one reason why Dr. Sally
Miller observes such a preoccupation in our culture with "getting over" the loss of
a loved one?

While I know of no empirical research on the topic, I hear more and more people talking in casual conversation about their disdain for network news. When I listen closely to these conversations, I often hear complaints about how watching the
news is emotionally distressing. I hear people complaining about the steady stream
of tragic events that come at them at lightning speed. Part of the complaint has to do
with the unwanted negative mood that is induced. Another part of the complaint
seems to be about the pace of the events that are presented. One hardly has time to
adjust to one tragedy and react to it before being presented with another one. Given
that our emotional life is a key component of our overall health, do the news media
play an important role in the epidemic levels of anxiety and depression that are

being recorded in recent years? These sorts of questions about media impact may ultimately be difficult to test. Nevertheless, they may be extremely important for researchers to address in future studies.

## SUMMARY

In this chapter, you have seen some facets of the research on frightening media and on media that induce other emotional reactions. One thing that emerges clearly is that paranormal themes are often front and center when fear reactions occur. Although the emotional effects of this type of media are not nearly as sensational as the effects of media violence, these effects may be far more common. For children, the research shows that there is a wide range of material capable of inducing emotional upset at various points in the child's development. For young children two to five years old, animated features hold the potential to terrify. For older children and even for adults, fictional violence represented in a realistic fashion or themes of the paranormal may be emotionally disturbing. News reports of war, famine, and other disasters may be distressing as well. By focusing on the research in this area, you should be a little better prepared to manage these emotional reactions in children entrusted to your care.

It would be too simplistic, though, to dismiss frightening films by focusing only on their capacity to induce negative emotions. As Zillmann's research shows, these films may be popular for good reason. They help to reinforce important patterns of socialization. It is also possible that, in some cases, a person experiences a frightening film therapeutically. The viewer is able to compare real-life circumstances favorably with the dread and horror in the lives of the film characters. Although there is less research to substantiate this point, this possibility certainly seems reasonable.

In concluding these thoughts about frightening media, I would call attention to the fact that the MPAA movie ratings and the new system for TV ratings are terribly vague when it comes to warning parents about frightening content. The wise consumer realizes that a movie like *The Sixth Sense* is going to be potentially frightening to children. But fewer people may realize that Walt Disney's *101 Dalmatians* may also be upsetting to preschoolers. One reason to call attention to the research studies on children is to let Hollywood know that it is time for the industry to create program and movie labeling that draws directly from the academic research. The vast majority of parents want a more specific labeling system that gives information about the specific content. Researchers agree that this seems like the best approach. Now the message has to get through to the people in Hollywood who can do something about it.

Finally, this chapter encourages you to think about emotional reactions other than fear. The media present a rich, fast-paced tapestry of characters who experience a wide range of emotional reactions and, through empathy processes, induce various emotions in viewers. This sort of entertainment is unprecedented in the history of the human race. Perhaps the ways in which we are expected to respond emotionally are being shaped daily by our media experiences.

## QUESTIONS TO FOCUS YOUR ATTENTION

1. Can you recall watching a TV program or movie that caused you to suffer fear after the program was over? If so, how does your experience fit with the ideas about frightening media that were discussed in this chapter?

2. How frequently do you use media to manage your mood? What media do you choose and how effective is your strategy?

3. Why do you think that playing a video game with a teammate increases empathy for other people after the game is over?

## KEY TERMS AND CONCEPTS

| | | |
|---|---|---|
| paranormal media content | hippocampus | empathy |
| developmental theory | amygdala | theory of mood management |
| perceptual thought | reality | excitatory potential |
| conceptual thought | fantasy | absorption potential |
| abstract thought | cognitive strategies | semantic affinity |
| law of apparent reality | non-cognitive strategies | hedonic valence |
| implicit memories | theory of excitation transfer | |
| explicit memories | gender role socialization | |

## NOTES

1. The term *paranormal* has been defined in many ways in the scholarly literature. I use it here to refer to events that clearly violate the known laws of nature. Such events might include extrasensory perception (ESP), astrological forecasts, prophetic dreams, psychic detectives, space aliens, UFOs from outer space, palm reading, astral projection, psychokinesis (moving objects just by thinking about them), and so forth.

2. Cantor, J. (2004). *Teddy's TV troubles.* Madison, WI: Goblin Fern Press.

3. Bozzuto, J. C. (1975). Cinematic neurosis following "The Exorcist." *Journal of Nervous and Mental Disease,* 161, 43–48.

4. Blumer, H. (1933). *Movies and conduct.* New York: Macmillan.

5. Himmelweit, H. T., Oppenheim, A. N., & Vince, P. (1958). *Television and the child.* London: Oxford University Press.

6. Cantor, J. (1994). Fright reactions to mass media. In J. Bryant &. D. Zillmann (Eds.), *Media effects: Advances in theory and research* (pp. 213–245). Hillsdale, NJ: Erlbaum.

7. Palmer, E. L., Hockett, A. B., & Dean, W. W. (1983). The television family and children's fright reactions. *Journal of Family Issues,* 4, 279–292.

8. Cantor, J., & Sparks, G. G. (1984). Children's fear responses to mass media: Testing some Piagetian predictions. *Journal of Communication,* 34(2), 90–103.

9. Flavell, J. (1963). *The developmental psychology of Jean Piaget.* New York: Van Nostrand.

10. Sparks, G. G., & Cantor, J. (1986). Developmental differences in fright responses to a television program depicting a character transformation. *Journal of Broadcasting and Electronic Media,* 30, 309–323.

11. Cantor, J. (1998). *"Mommy, I'm scared": How TV and movies frighten children and what we can do to protect them.* San Diego, CA: Harcourt Brace.

12. Sparks, G. G. (1997). Unpublished raw data.

13. Sparks, G. G., Nelson, C. L., & Campbell, R. G. (1997). The relationship between exposure to televised messages about paranormal phenomena and paranormal beliefs. *Journal of Broadcasting & Electronic Media,* 41, 345–359.

14. Frijda, N. H. (1988). The laws of emotion. *American Psychologist,* 43(5), 349–358.

15. Potter, W. J. (1988). Perceived reality in television effects research. *Journal of Broadcasting & Electronic Media,* 32(1), 23–41.

16. For years, the Committee for the Scientific Investigation of Claims of the Paranormal (CSICOP) has published *Skeptical Inquirer,* a journal devoted to scientific skepticism concerning paranormal claims. CSICOP often takes the media to task for exploiting paranormal themes to make a profit. Rarely, however, has the committee considered the fright potential of paranormal depictions.

17. Cantor, J. (2006). Long-term memories of frightening media often include lingering trauma symptoms. Poster presented at the Association for Psychological Science convention, New York, May 26, 2006. Available: http://yourmindonmedia.com/wp-content/uploads/longterm_memories.pdf

18. LeDoux, J. (1996). *The emotional brain: The mysterious underpinnings of emotional life.* New York: Simon & Schuster.

19. Harrison, K., & Cantor, J. (1999). Tales from the screen: Enduring fright reactions to scary media. *Media Psychology,* 1, 97–116.

20. Cantor, J., & Wilson, B. J. (1984). Modifying fear responses to mass media in preschool and elementary school children. *Journal of Broadcasting,* 28, 431–43.

21. Wilson, B. J., & Cantor, J. (1987). Reducing children's fear reactions to mass media: Effects of visual exposure and verbal explanation. In M. L. McLaughlin (Ed.), *Communication yearbook* 10 (pp. 553–573). Newbury Park, CA: Sage.

22. Sparks, G. G. (1986). Developmental differences in children's reports of fear induced by the mass media. *Child Study Journal,* 16, 55–66.

23. Zillmann, D. (1980). Anatomy of suspense. In P. H. Tannenbaum (Ed.), *The entertainment functions of television* (pp. 133–163). Hillsdale, NJ: Erlbaum.

24. Sparks, G. G. (1991). The relationship between distress and delight in males' and females' reactions to frightening films. *Human Communication Research,* 17, 625–637.

25. Zillmann, D., Weaver, J. B., Mundorf, N., & Aust, C. F. (1986). Effects of an opposite-gender companion's affect to horror on distress, delight, and attraction. *Journal of Personality & Social Psychology,* 51(3), 586–594.

26. Hoffner, C. A., & Levine, K. J. (2005). Enjoyment of mediated fright and violence: A meta-analysis. *Media Psychology,* 7, 207–237.

27. Greitemeyer, T. (2009). Effects of songs with prosocial lyrics on prosocial thoughts, affect, and behavior. *Journal of Experimental Social Psychology,* 45(1), 186–190.

28. Greitemeyer, T. (2013). Playing video games cooperatively increases empathic concern. *Social Psychology,* 44(6), 408–413.

29. Zillmann, D. (1988). Mood management: Using entertainment to full advantage. In L. Donohew, H. E. Sypher, & E. T. Higgins (Eds.), *Communication, social cognition, and affect* (pp. 147–171). Hillsdale, NJ: Erlbaum.

30. Meadowcroft, J., & Zillmann, D. (1984, August). *The influence of hormonal fluctuations on women's selection and enjoyment of television programs.* Paper presented at the meeting of the Association for Education in Journalism and Mass Communication, Gainesville, Florida.

31. Helregel, B. K., & Weaver, J. B. (1989). Mood-management during pregnancy through selective exposure to television. *Journal of Broadcasting & Electronic Media,* 33, 15–33.

32. Knobloch-Westerwick, S. (2007). Gender differences in selective media use for mood-management and mood adjustment. *Journal of Broadcasting & Electronic Media,* 51(1), 73–92.

33. Knobloch-Westerwick, S. (2006). Mood management: Theory, evidence, and advancements. In J. Bryant & P. Vorderer (Eds.), *Psychology of entertainment* (pp. 239–254). Mahwah, NJ: Erlbaum.

34. Zillmann, D. (1991). Empathy: Affect from bearing witness to the emotions of others. In J. Bryant & D. Zillmann (Eds.), *Responding to the screen: Reception and reaction processes* (pp. 135–167). Hillsdale, NJ: Erlbaum.

# 8

# Persuasive Effects of the Media

## WHAT IS PERSUASION?

What does it mean to say that the media have persuasive power? Scholars have identified at least three dimensions of **persuasion** that help to answer this question. First, when you are persuaded, there is a change in your **attitude**. You feel differently about something as a result of being exposed to a message. I can remember a conversation with my older brother several years ago in which he told me that he had changed his attitude about smoking cigarettes. He no longer felt good about his smoking habit and had resolved to change it. One sure sign that a person has experienced a genuine change in attitude is when other related beliefs and attitudes surrounding the one that's been changed also seem to be affected. In my brother's case, I expected that if his attitude toward smoking had really been changed, he would also show some concern for the fact that his wife was a smoker too. When I checked back with him a few months later, I discovered that he was still expressing his new attitude about smoking and, indeed, he was still concerned about his wife's smoking habit. But, unfortunately, he was still smoking just as much as he had been before he adopted his new attitude. This helps to illustrate the fact that a change in attitude is only part of what is involved in persuasion.

In addition to attitude change, significant persuasion also results in changes of **behavior**. It wasn't until my brother actually started to alter his smoking behavior that I became convinced that he had been persuaded by antismoking messages. A few weeks after he started smoking less, he found the new behavior difficult to maintain. Nicotine has addictive properties, and, as almost any smoker will testify, the habit is not easily broken. After battling the urge to smoke for months, my brother finally kicked the habit. He hasn't smoked in over 15 years. Truly significant persuasion results in behavior that persists over time. Together, these three features (attitude change, behavior change, and **persistent change**) help to define what we mean by persuasion.

189

It is important to mention here that the "attitude change-behavior change-persistent change" definition of persuasion omits one ingredient that some communication scholars would insist should be part of the definition. These scholars would argue that true persuasion doesn't occur unless someone has made a deliberate attempt to change attitudes or behavior. According to this view, persuasion really involves a transaction between a source and a receiver—a transaction that is quite deliberate on the part of the source. While it's true that most persuasion does involve that sort of transaction, sometimes people change their attitudes or behavior when the source of the message might not be clear or the idea of a deliberate attempt to persuade may be at least debatable. In this chapter, I take a broad view of the persuasion process and consider scenarios in which persuasive attempts are quite deliberate as well as ones in which that might not be the case.

As you read in Chapter 3, the history of media effects research revolves around the idea that media messages exert persuasive influence on people. In this chapter, we will explore the basis for this assumption in more detail. Are the media really persuasive?

## HOW MEDIA MESSAGES PERSUADE WITHOUT EVEN TRYING

Although we usually think of persuasion as an intentional action on the part of a "persuader," it is quite possible to persuade someone to change an attitude or behavior without even consciously trying to do so. In fact, numerous examples seem to show that people are often persuaded by media messages that weren't even designed explicitly to change attitudes or behavior. A high proportion of media messages are designed to entertain. Over the years, scholars have learned that these entertainment messages can exert a powerful influence on attitude and behavior. Let's take a brief look at some of these examples.

One example of unintended media influence involved the controversial 1983 broadcast by the ABC-TV network, *The Day After*. This movie depicted the aftermath of a nuclear war in the United States. The movie was designed primarily for entertainment purposes, not persuasion, but researchers discovered that exposure to the movie was sufficient to change attitudes about the seriousness of nuclear war. People who watched the movie were especially likely to change their attitudes and express the view that nuclear war was a critical concern. They also expressed their intent to take some action to help prevent nuclear war.[1]

During the summer of 2004, researchers in England decided to investigate the impact of the movie *The Day After Tomorrow* while it was playing commercially in movie theaters. The film depicts a scenario in which global warming ultimately produces another ice age over just a few days. The film shows such disasters as a major tidal wave plowing into New York City. Interviews were conducted with movie patrons either before or after seeing the movie, and their responses were compared. The researchers reported that those questioned after seeing the film were willing to give 50% more toward efforts to mitigate changes in climate than those questioned before seeing the film. While exposure to the film sensitized people to the importance of the climate issue, it also produced less realistic expectations about the climatic effects that scientists had actually predicted for England. The researchers wondered whether this type of movie portrayal could be made more accurate and still maintain its appeal to audiences seeking suspenseful and dramatic entertainment.[2]

The persuasive impact of *The Day After* was not very controversial. Few people could get upset about people wanting to do something to curb the risk of nuclear war. Sometimes, however, the impact of entertainment media is not so positive. Consider the well-known case of the CBS movie *Cry Rape*. As social psychologist Elliot Aronson describes the situation, this movie depicted a rape victim who discovered that pressing charges against her rapist could result in an ugly ordeal that only prolonged her suffering.[3] In the weeks following the broadcast of the movie, actual rape reports to law enforcement authorities decreased significantly. Apparently, viewers were persuaded by the nature of the rape victim's experience in the film and learned the lesson of the high emotional cost of pressing charges.

What can we learn from these examples of persuasion that occurred in the context of entertainment programs? Think about the last time you went to a movie or watched your favorite TV program. The chances are good that, as you sat back in your seat to relax, you were not preparing to process a persuasive message. As psychologists have studied the persuasion process, they have discovered that ordinarily people approach a persuasive situation with their defenses up. Richard Petty and John Cacioppo describe this situation in their **elaboration likelihood model (ELM)** of persuasion. According to them, there are two main routes by which people might be persuaded. One of these is called the **central route to persuasion**. The central route is a highly rational or cognitive route to persuasion. People scrutinize the message carefully and tend to think up many counter arguments that the persuader must defeat to be successful.[4] This route to persuasion is especially likely if people know that the message they will hear is **counter-attitudinal** (i.e., different from the position they hold themselves). Persuasion through the central route is more difficult for the would-be persuader to achieve than other methods. Whenever a salesperson calls me on the telephone, I find that I am ready to resist the message no matter how good it sounds. I am motivated to think up one counterargument after another. If the salesperson is persistent, I may just decide to say goodbye and hang up the phone. But when I sit down to watch a movie or TV show, I am not planning on having to do a careful analysis of a persuasive message. In the entertainment context, all sorts of messages can get through my normally strong defense system and exert their influence. Persuasion that takes place with less careful scrutiny of the message is referred to by Petty and Cacioppo as **peripheral-route persuasion**. In persuasion by the peripheral route, certain cues in the message lead people to accept the persuasive proposition with little cognitive thought or scrutiny. When people are persuaded while watching movies and programs that are designed to entertain, any influence that occurs is likely to be peripheral-route influence. From the perspective of advertisers who attempt to use the media to sell their products, the biggest obstacle to success is the fact that people recognize a TV commercial or a magazine ad as an attempt to influence attitude or behavior. This recognition can trigger central-route processing, which is a more difficult path to influence. This may be one reason that many advertisers use creative ways to entertain their audience rather than using a strong persuasive appeal. If people process an ad as another entertaining bit of media, they may be more willing to change their attitudes or behaviors with little thought or scrutiny instead of carefully weighing the relative advantages of a particular product. Perhaps this helps to explain why advertisers were willing to pay roughly $133,000 per *second* for an ad in the 2014 Super Bowl game. Over the years, people have become accustomed to processing the ads during this game as entertainment instead of persuasion. Advertisers may realize that this state of affairs is favorable for their purposes—which, ultimately, are persuasive.

Of course, if advertisers follow the logic of the elaboration likelihood model of persuasion, they will also have to face one daunting proposition from the ELM: the more important an issue is for a person, the less likely persuasion is to occur through the peripheral route. Change on important issues must go through the more deliberate and rational process associated with the central route to persuasion. Peripheral cues may work to get me to try a new brand of toothpaste, but if I'm asked to consider changing my political position on an issue I care about, I'm going to be motivated to carefully scrutinize the arguments.

## Product Placement in Entertainment Programming

An even better alternative to paying high advertising rates during the Super Bowl game might be to pay for "**product placements**" that appear within movies or TV programs as more or less incidental to the plot. You might remember seeing the classic movie, *ET*, and recall that the extra-terrestrial character enjoyed eating Reese's Pieces candy. Product placements like this one are commonplace throughout the entertainment industry today. Advertisers clearly believe that the money they pay to have their products featured in movies or TV shows is well worth it. From the perspective of the research scholar, information about the profitability or persuasive effectiveness of these product placements is difficult to obtain. Advertisers are generally protective of any information about the impact of their advertising strategies.

Given the proprietary nature of the data pertaining to the effectiveness of product placements, two communication scholars decided to run their own experiment to see if they could establish evidence in favor of the persuasive impact of this advertising technique. Moonhee Yang and David Roskos-Ewoldsen designed their experiment according to the theoretical logic of the **landscape model**.[5] According to this approach, the authors explain that:

> When people watch a movie, their primary focus is on comprehending the story. What viewers cognitively do with different information in a movie—including brand placements—depends on the implications of the information for comprehending the movie. (p. 471)

As viewers watch a movie, you might think of them as "surveying the landscape" of the movie plot in order to comprehend the story. If product brands like Reese's Pieces in the movie *ET* or Fed-Ex packages in the movie *Castaway* play a major role in the plot, viewers are likely to process the brands and be able to recall them when asked. On the other hand, if a product brand only occurs incidentally in the background of a scene and plays no central role in the plot, viewers may not be able to explicitly recall the brand (**explicit memory**), but they may still have some recognition of the brand that has been stored in **implicit memory**. A common test of implicit memory is to present word fragments (words with missing letters) and ask respondents to fill in the blanks to spell the complete word. If respondents can correctly complete word fragments for product brands seen in a movie more often than for brands not featured in the movie, researchers assume that implicit memory was at work.

In their experiment, Yang and Roskos-Ewoldsen randomly assigned nearly 375 participants to one of three movie-viewing conditions. In one condition, product brands appeared only in the background in an incidental way. In a second condition, the product was actually used by the main character in the movie. Finally, in the third condition, the product brand was centrally connected to the main story of the film. When the participants were tested after they watched the movie, they were asked to indicate whether they recognized specific product brands from the film. The highest levels of recognition were observed when the brand was centrally connected to the main story. Participants who viewed the main character using the brand were lower on recognition compared to the central story condition—but higher than those who viewed the brand as only an incidental product placement.

On the test of implicit memory, it didn't matter which type of brand placement participants had seen—they completed the word fragments for the product brands equally well—but at a significantly higher rate than people who had not seen the movies at all. Finally, participants were given a choice to choose a product from the same brand category featured in the movie. For example, if Pepsi had been seen in the film, the participants were given a choice to choose among a number of soft drinks. The results on this test mirrored those on the implicit memory test. There was no difference in the product choices between the three viewing conditions—but those who watched one of the three versions of the film were more likely to choose the featured brand than were people who never saw the movie clips. In one last analysis, the researchers also measured attitudes toward the brands depicted in the movies. Those who saw the product used by the main character expressed significantly more positive attitudes toward the brand than those who saw the incidental placement of the brand or those who saw the brand as integral to the story plot. In general, the authors concluded that product placements seem to be an effective technique in that they can increase recognition and familiarity with a product that may translate into brand preference over the long run.

## The Theory of Media Cultivation: Cultivating Attitudes Is Attitude Change

The idea that consumption of entertainment media can change people's attitudes is an idea that has been formalized in one of the major theoretical perspectives of mass communication. George Gerbner's **theory of media cultivation** does not use the term *persuade* to describe the impact of media, and his theory is often treated in the context of discussions of media violence or media stereotypes. You may recall that I mentioned the theory in the context of media violence in Chapter 5. Because so many of the studies on cultivation are concerned with how consuming media violence affects attitudes, some readers expect to see Gerbner's theory treated under media violence. Nevertheless, the theory is all about the cultivation of attitudes *in general*, which is, after all, another way of talking about attitude change. According to Gerbner, the cultivation process is gradual and cumulative. Many people tend to think of persuasion in terms of a direct response to a single message. This is one reason that Gerbner's theory is not typically presented in the context of persuasion. But, Gerbner's perspective does fit well into a discussion about the media and persuasion defined broadly. According to Gerbner, the world of media entertainment presents a particular view of **social reality**. For example, content analyses of prime-time TV programs reveal that about 12% of the male characters holding jobs work in law enforcement. This proportion is a gross exaggeration; in reality, only about 1% of employed males hold jobs in the general area of law enforcement.[6]

What happens to the person who makes a steady habit of watching prime-time TV? According to Gerbner, this person gradually becomes "cultivated" into the television view of social reality. Even though there is no particular intent on the part of the creators of the media messages to change attitudes or beliefs, over time, the heavy viewer will begin to believe that the real world resembles the world presented in the media. **First-order cultivation** refers to the process in which heavy viewers come to believe that the real world is like the TV world. For example, according to Gerbner, the heavy TV viewer tends to believe that the world is a more violent place than it really is. Such a person might believe, for example, that many more people actually die as a result of being murdered than is actually the case. **Second-order cultivation** refers to heavy viewers adopting a particular attitude as a result of their media exposure. For example, Gerbner maintained that heavy TV viewers are more likely to express **fear of criminal victimization** and to express more concern about their safety and welfare. While the theory of media cultivation emphasizes gradual changes in beliefs and attitudes, some of Gerbner's studies show behavior changes as well. According to some of the results, heavy TV viewers are more likely to purchase home security devices because of their beliefs in the high probability of criminal victimization. Gerbner summarizes his view in the following way:

> The repetitive "lessons" we learn from television, beginning with infancy, are likely to become the basis for a broader world view, making television a significant source of general values, ideologies, and perspectives as well as specific assumptions, beliefs, and images.... One example of this is what we have called the "mean world" syndrome.... [W]e have found that long-term exposure to television, in which frequent violence is virtually inescapable, tends to cultivate the image of a relatively mean and dangerous world. Responses of heavier viewers compared to matching groups of lighter viewers suggest the conception of reality in which greater protection is needed, most people "cannot be trusted," and most people are "just looking out for themselves."[7]

Gerbner and his colleagues believe that they have uncovered evidence in several studies for two processes that show evidence of media cultivation. The first process, **mainstreaming**, refers to what happens when people of different groups are exposed to the same media. Over time, Gerbner believes that the differences that might be expected on the basis of group membership become less pronounced because everyone is being similarly cultivated by media messages. The second process, **resonance**, refers to what happens when a person's real-life environment strongly resembles the environment depicted in the media. Such a person receives a "double dose" of the same message, making the impact of media cultivation particularly likely. For example, a person who lives in a high crime neighborhood might naturally fear criminal victimization. If that person also consumes heavy doses of the violent world of TV, the cultivating effect of the media would be particularly powerful because the message is already consistent with the person's real-world experience.

Gerbner's theory of cultivation has certainly had its critics over the years. One major constraint that causes reservation among media scholars is that the theory describes processes that seem to defy conclusive testing. Gerbner maintains that the process of media cultivation occurs gradually over time. Consequently, researchers conducting laboratory experiments—which by their very nature observe changes over short time intervals—are not able to shed any light on the process. Unfortunately, this leaves the survey method as the only major methodological tool for testing the theory. As you know from Chapter 2, the survey method is limited in its ability to document causal relationships with certainty. Typically, evidence for media cultivation is presented with positive correlation coefficients between TV exposure and some particular belief about the world. As you will see in the following example, such correlations are difficult to interpret unequivocally as evidence of a causal process.

In an effort to explore the evidence in favor of media cultivation, two researchers, Anthony Doob and Glenn Macdonald, conducted a survey in the city of Toronto.[8] When they examined their data, they found the same basic relationship between TV exposure and fear of criminal victimization that Gerbner had found in many of his studies. The relationship was positive and statistically significant, showing that heavy TV viewers were more likely to fear being the victims of crimes. Whereas Gerbner tends to interpret such a relationship as evidence for media cultivation (viewing TV causes fear of victimization), Doob and Macdonald wondered whether the relationship wasn't due to a variable that Gerbner had ignored in previous studies: level of crime in a person's neighborhood. They reasoned that people who live in high crime neighborhoods might naturally fear criminal victimization because crime is indeed a high risk. Moreover, they thought that such people might also tend to stay inside their homes more than people who live in safer places. As a result, the people in high crime neighborhoods might naturally tend to watch more TV. According to this scenario, the correlation observed by Gerbner between TV viewing and fear of victimization might not be the result of a cultivation effect. Instead, it might result from the fact that both of these variables are simultaneously affected by the level of crime in one's neighborhood. When Doob and Macdonald divided the city of Toronto into four areas (high- versus low-crime areas in both the city and its suburbs), they found that the relationship between TV viewing and fear of victimization was no longer present in three of the four areas. They interpreted this result as evidence in favor of the role of the neighborhood variable and against the media cultivation hypothesis. Gerbner might interpret the same result as evidence for the resonance hypothesis. As it turned out, in the high crime area of the city, there was still a significant relationship between TV viewing and fear of victimization. This is exactly where Gerbner would expect the strongest relationship to exist between the two variables, as a result of the double dose of the message received by residents of this type of neighborhood.

A few years ago, I teamed up with my colleague Bob Ogles to investigate what we thought was another important methodological issue in Gerbner's research program on media cultivation. When Bob and I examined the published research, it appeared to us that when Gerbner and his colleagues claimed to measure "fear of victimization," they were often measuring **perceptions of the probability of being victimized**. We thought these two concepts were obviously very different. A person might believe that the probability of being victimized is relatively high—but that same person might also believe that there is no shortage of personal strategies for dealing with such an occasion. For example, a truck driver who makes daily deliveries in a high crime area of a city might believe that the chances of being assaulted in any given month are high. But if that same truck driver carries various weapons for personal defense and feels capable of dealing with any dangerous situation, the level of fear associated with driving into high crime areas might be relatively low. To demonstrate this distinction, we surveyed random samples of the population in two Midwestern cities and asked them about their media consumption, their estimates of the probability of being victimized by crime, and their reports of their actual fear of criminal victimization. In support of the conceptual distinction between estimates of the probability of victimization and actual fear of victimization, we found that the measures for these two concepts were not correlated with each other. When we tested the media cultivation hypothesis, we found the typical low to moderate significant positive correlations between media exposure and actual fear of victimization—but we found no evidence for media cultivation when we used the traditional measure containing items about the probability of criminal victimization.[9]

## If Cultivation Works—*How* Does It Work?

One of the ongoing problems in the literature on media cultivation surrounds what happens when people become cultivated by media messages. Exactly how does that process work? One scholar who has tried to answer that question is L. J. Shrum. His answer revolves around the **accessibility principle**.[10] In order to understand this principle, imagine that you were asked to estimate the percentage of Americans who held the job of an attorney. According to Shrum, when you are asked a question like this, you tend to rely upon information that is most accessible—or the information that tends to pop into your mind first. Where does this information come from? If you've just had an appointment with an attorney to go over your estate, your recent experience might lead you to inflate your estimate when you're making your judgment. Similarly, if you have a long-standing habit of watching *LA Law,* you're quite accustomed to spending time watching attorneys practice law. While you might not be consciously aware of the fact that you're drawing upon this information to make your judgment about how many people hold that job, your recent experience seeing attorneys and thinking about them might lead you to increase your estimate when you're making your judgment. Most cultivation researchers tend to subscribe to something like the accessibility principle as a likely theoretical mechanism for explaining cultivation effects. By the way, the actual percentage of Americans who hold the job of attorney is *less than 1%.*[11]

Over the past few decades, Gerbner and his colleagues have produced enough data to keep the theory of media cultivation alive and well. Most researchers do give some credence to the idea that media messages unintentionally exert an influence on the attitudes and beliefs that people hold about the real world. Notice, however, that the theory of media cultivation is not really the right theory to invoke in trying to explain the sort of effect described earlier in the chapter where watching a single TV movie, *The Day After*, caused viewers to become more concerned about the possibility of nuclear war. According to Gerbner's theory, media cultivation occurs as a result of *gradual* media exposure that takes place over long periods of time. In contrast, when viewers watched *The Day After*, the resulting effect was immediate. One media scholar, Bradley Greenberg, might explain what happened with *The Day After* by appealing to what he calls the **drench hypothesis**. Where media cultivation tends to emphasize the effects of repeated exposure to the same sorts of images over a long period, the drench hypothesis emphasizes the power of "critical images" to overwhelm the stereotypical ones that appear regularly. According to Greenberg, critical images are ones that "stand out, are deviant, are intense, and thus are more important viewing experiences."[12]

Consider the possible, unintended effects of the classic movie *Jaws*. I'm unaware of any systematic data collection on this point, but as mentioned in Chapter 7, tourism at beach resorts supposedly declined noticeably after the film's debut and scientists attributed increased public interest in sharks to the stir that the film created.[13] The film's images of happy-go-lucky swimmers attacked viciously by a killer shark certainly meet Greenberg's criteria of ones that "stand out, are deviant, and intense." In contrast to what might be called the **"drip-drip-drip" hypothesis** of media cultivation or effects that emerge after steady, long-term exposure, the examples of *The Day After* and *Jaws* were clearly ones in which the intense images "drenched" viewers and may have caused an immediate and rather dramatic effect.

## Do Media Messages about the Paranormal Influence Paranormal Beliefs?

In the previous chapter, you read about the research on frightening mass media and the intense emotional effects that scary films have on children and adults. I was personally involved in conducting many of these studies. After a number of years,

I started paying more attention to the actual content of the movies that people reported as scary. One of the themes noted in the Chapter 7 discussion was that many scary movies have paranormal content. Depictions of the paranormal might include ghosts, witches, devils, psychics, extrasensory perception (ESP), UFOs and space aliens, and people who claim they can talk to the dead. I became interested in the question of whether these depictions, quite apart from their capacity to scare people, could change people's beliefs. Are you more inclined to believe in the existence of space aliens after watching a movie like *Close Encounters of the Third Kind*? Just as Gerbner was concerned about the possibility that media messages might cultivate beliefs about the level of crime in the real world, I became concerned about the possibility that media depictions of the paranormal might cultivate beliefs about the existence of a paranormal world. Once again, just as in the case of media cultivation, this type of persuasion is not necessarily intentional on the part of the media source—but the persuasive effect might be an important one to understand.

To study this possibility, I began with a simple experiment.[14] College students were randomly assigned to watch a 30-minute episode of the program *Beyond Reality*. This episode depicted people who could "astral-project" themselves to different locations. What is astral projection? According to those who practice it, it is the ability to leave one's body through deep meditation or a drug-induced state and transport one's spiritual essence to some other location in the universe. Opportunities abound to pay hundreds of dollars to learn how to master this incredible skill. (My personal advice would be to save your money.) I was interested in whether seeing such behavior depicted in a fictional entertainment program would affect what people believe about the reality of astral projection.

When the USA network aired this episode, they started it off with an announcer's voice saying, "The following incidents are based on actual reports." In my experiment, I decided to assign the students to watch the program in one of four conditions. In the first condition, the "reality" condition, I included a tag that emphasized the fact that the actors and actresses in the show were fictitious, but that the events shown were based on actual reports and were real. In the second condition, the "fiction" condition, the preliminary tag emphasized that the events were completely fictitious. In the third condition, the "impossible" condition, the tag emphasized that the events were completely fictitious and also impossible from a scientific perspective. It included a statement that events like this had never actually happened and that if they had happened, it would violate the known laws of nature. In a fourth condition, the "no tag" condition, the students watched the program without any tag at all. Finally, in a control group condition, some students watched an episode of the situation comedy *Perfect Strangers,* which had no references to any paranormal phenomenon.

A few weeks before the students watched the program, I measured the extent to which they believed in astral projection and other paranormal activities. After the program was over, I once again measured these beliefs to see if there was any change. Of course, to be careful about tipping the students off to what I was studying, I took steps to draw their attention to the fact that I was not very interested in their reactions to the program. Instead, students were led to believe that I was really interested in what they thought about the commercials in the program. At the very end of the study, I asked the students what they thought the study was about. The nearly unanimous verdict was that the study was concerned with reactions to advertising. Most students expressed surprise to learn later about the true purpose of the experiment.

What did the results of the study reveal? Figure 8-1 shows a graphic representation of what happened. The major results concerned the students who watched the program with no tag at all and those who watched the program with either the fiction tag or the impossible tag. The beliefs in astral projection of the students who saw no tag *increased* over their pre-viewing levels; the beliefs in astral projection of the students in both of the other two conditions *decreased*. The difference between the groups was statistically significant ($p < .05$; see Chapter 2 for a review of this concept). You might expect that the students who were told that the program was real would have increased their beliefs the most. That's not what happened. In fact, there was a slight decrease in belief in astral projection among these students, although the decrease was not statistically significant. It could be that telling these students that the events were real caused them to wonder about why they had been told this. As they thought about it, they ended up doubting the veracity of the events more than if they had been told nothing at all. This experiment demonstrated that, depending on the information included in a program, viewers' beliefs about a paranormal phenomenon could be affected. I have now completed several studies that

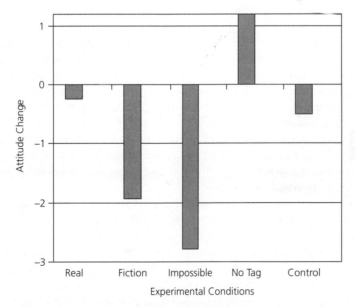

**Figure 8-1  Change in Paranormal Beliefs after Watching a Paranormal TV Show**
Note: The values on the y-axis indicate the amount of change on the measure of paranormal beliefs after the program was over. Changes on the negative side indicate less belief following the program; changes on the positive side indicate more belief following the program.

investigate the relationship between media depictions of the paranormal and para-normal beliefs.[15] Taken together, these studies show that media messages do exert an influence on what people believe. Depending on the message, people may be persuaded to change their beliefs.

## INTENTIONAL PERSUASION IN THE MEDIA

So far in this chapter, we have defined persuasion and seen how it might occur as a result of media exposure to entertainment messages that are not designed particu-larly to change attitudes and behaviors. One implication of the fact that entertain-ment messages can persuade unintentionally is that media practitioners could study these instances and learn to master the principles of persuasion so that they could be applied in an intentional way. Clearly, many messages that appear in the media are designed explicitly with persuasion in mind. How well do these messages work? If they do work, what are the theoretical principles behind their success? Let's consider these two questions.

### Using Entertainment to Improve Public Health

If a single viewing of a movie like *The Day After* can increase concern and change what people plan to do about nuclear war, can entertainment programs be used deliberately to persuade people to adopt behaviors that contribute to their overall health? The answer, based on recent attempts to try this strategy, seems to be yes. According to Jane Brown and Kim Walsh-Childers, when the entertain-ment program *Felicity* decided to treat the topic of date rape in a special two-part episode, the producers of the program advertised a telephone number at the end of the show that would connect callers with a rape hotline. More than 1,000 calls were received. Viewer reactions to the program *ER* were also studied after that program showed a victim of date rape being treated with the morning-after pill. Viewer knowledge of this type of contraceptive treatment increased 17% after the show—even though a follow-up study showed that this knowledge might not have persisted for long.[16]

This sort of persuasive effort is often referred to as **entertainment-education**. In 2004, the Kaiser Family Foundation issued a brief report on a variety of differ-ent entertainment-education efforts that have been implemented.[17] There is no doubt that this method can be persuasive. Why? How does this type of persuasion really work? Two communications scholars, Emily Moyer-Gusé and Robin Nabi, recently reported an experiment that they designed to gain some answers to this question.[18] They randomly assigned 353 college students to watch one of two dif-ferent TV programs that depicted the problems of teen pregnancy. One was a news-style show that featured various interviews with teens and parents. The other show was an episode of *The OC*, a program designed for teens that originally aired on the FOX network. One of the main purposes of the experiment was to test the notion that in contrast to the news program, the entertainment narrative of *The OC* would draw people into the story line in such a way that their natural persuasive defenses would be lowered. This idea is referred to as the **Entertainment Overcoming Resistance Model (EORM) to persuasion**. Consistent with the predictions of this model, those who watched the episode of *The OC* reported that they were more likely to change their sexual behavior to reflect "safe-sex" practices. While this finding held only for females, the authors reasoned that because the major character most affected by teen pregnancy was female, this result makes sense. An additional finding from this study was that those who watched the narrative version of the program perceived less persuasive intent in the message. Those who did perceive high levels of persuasive intent tended to be more resistant to the message to adopt safe-sex practices.

Despite the apparent effectiveness of entertainment education, the news is not all good. Susan Morgan and her colleagues have discovered that the effects of entertainment education are often less than positive. For example, despite the fact that the public seems to hold favorable attitudes toward organ donation, there is still significant reluctance for many to actually sign up for donating organs upon one's death. Morgan's research team found that upon content-analyzing all of the TV storylines from CBS, NBC, ABC, and FOX during a recent season, organ donation tends to be presented in terms that would discourage people from agreeing to donate their organs.[19] Notice that while in this case, scholars might view the possible persuasive impact of entertainment education to be negative, the example still suggests that entertainment education does hold persuasive power. But one problem with using entertainment in a deliberate way to persuade the audience is that these techniques may not always be met with enthusiasm on the part of the creators or the producers. They may tend to view such efforts as interfering with their creative license and ultimately turning entertainment into more advertising. Although these "embedded health messages" will undoubtedly continue to appear in various forms, most future persuasion efforts probably will still be more direct. An advantage of studying embedded messages is that it provides a chance to see persuasion occur in the natural environment. The next section describes an important study that looked at persuasion outside of the typical laboratory setting that most researchers use to study persuasion.

## An Unusual Study: The Great American Values Test

One of the major weaknesses of academic research on media effects is that too many of the studies are conducted in the carefully controlled confines of the laboratory. Although much is learned from this approach about whether certain message features can cause specific effects, there is the inevitable limitation in generalizing the effects to what happens in a more natural environment (see Chapter 2). For this reason, three researchers, Sandra Ball-Rokeach, Milton Rokeach, and Joel Grube, decided to break away from the confines of the laboratory to test the persuasive impact of TV in the real-world setting. The findings of their study, "the great American values test," are undoubtedly among some of the most important findings on the persuasive impact of the media.[20] You'll notice that the study was completed a few decades ago, and a natural reaction to that fact might be to conclude that it is no longer relevant or informative. I've resisted making that conclusion for two reasons. First, I can think of no other study that has managed to implement the methodological procedures that these researchers employed. In fact, given today's media environment, it is difficult to imagine that something like what they did could ever be accomplished again. For that reason alone, I believe the study is something of a landmark and ought to be included in your media effects education. But the study is also noteworthy for the findings that were uncovered. They leave little doubt about the potential promise of using media messages to change attitudes and behavior. Let's look briefly at what these researchers managed to do.

Back in 1979, the research team was able to produce a 30-minute program designed solely for the purpose of their experiment. The program was co-hosted by Ed Asner of the old *Lou Grant* show, and Sandy Hill of ABC's *Good Morning America*. The program was structured such that the co-hosts presented viewers with national survey results showing that Americans ranked "freedom" very high as a value priority but ranked "equality" quite a bit lower. The first part of the program was designed to encourage viewers to think about both of these values and to consider renewing their commitment to each one. The second part of the program was designed to convince viewers to likewise place high value on the importance of the environment and living in a "world of beauty."

The real masterstroke that the researchers were able to pull off in this study came with the broadcast of the program. It aired on the evening of February 27, 1979, at 7:30 P.M. Somehow, the researchers were able to get all three commercial channels in Richland, Pasco, and Kennewick (the Tri-Cities area in eastern Washington State) to air the program at the same time. This essentially guaranteed that if anyone in those cities watched TV during the 7:30–8:00 P.M. time slot, they would be exposed to the persuasive message. At the same time that the program was aired in the Tri-Cities, the authors managed to arrange for the show to be totally blacked out in the city of Yakima, a comparable city about 80 miles away. In advance of the program's broadcast, they were also able to promote the show in *TV Guide* and commercial spots that appeared on the stations. Given today's radically changed television environment compared to the pre-cable days in which this study was conducted, it might be an impossible challenge for researchers to ever duplicate what this study managed to accomplish.

Through a combination of phone calls to randomly selected households in the four cities, follow-up opinion surveys, and mail solicitations from organizations that promoted the values of freedom, equality, and a world of beauty, the researchers were able to determine whether their program had any persuasive impact. The results were nothing short of impressive. On the mail solicitations that were sent out to random recipients in the four cities, significantly more people from the Tri-Cities area donated to the causes than did the people from Yakima, the city where the program was not shown. Of particular interest in the study was a comparison between those people who reported that they watched the program without interruption versus those who never saw the program and those who were interrupted during the program by such events as phone calls or an unexpected visitor. The uninterrupted viewers responded to the mail solicitations with anywhere from four to six times the amount of money contributed by the non-viewers. They gave about nine times as much money as the interrupted viewers. In general, the uninterrupted viewers also changed their value structure so that freedom, equality, and a world of beauty were all elevated as a result of exposure to the program.

Just as laboratory experiments have limitations in terms of generalizing results beyond the experimenter's carefully controlled research situation, natural experiments such as the one conducted by Ball-Rokeach, Rokeach, and Grube are also limited in terms of reaching conclusions about the exact reasons for the results. Perhaps the differences in the amount of money given by the various groups had little to do with the fact that some people were interrupted during the program and others were not. Maybe there was something different about the people who reported interruptions in viewing (e.g., living in a busier household) that made it less likely that they would give money to *any* solicitation. Nevertheless, despite the study's limitations, it is clear that the broadcast did exert a powerful influence on the audience. Advertisers probably were not surprised by the results.

## How Does an Advertiser Determine Success?

As we address the question of persuasive effectiveness of the media, it is important to keep in mind that *effectiveness* is a relative term. If you were an advertiser who paid for a 30-second ad on TV, how would you decide if the ad was worth the cost? One criterion that advertisers use is the cost-per-person statistic. Because national TV ads reach millions of people, the cost per person for the ad is often extremely low (just pennies per person), even though the total cost of the ad might be more than $1 million. Of course, even if the cost per person is extremely low, the investment would not be worthwhile if no one responded to the ad by purchasing the product. How many purchases need to result from one ad to make the advertising venture worthwhile? When millions of people are in the audience, a very small response rate might still make the ad cost-effective. The point here is that, from the advertising perspective, a relatively small effect can transfer into profits. An ad is often deemed to be an effective example of persuasion when 99% of the audience fails to respond. The 1% who do respond are more than enough to offset the cost of the ad.

## Evidence for the Effectiveness of Advertising

Having recognized the important point that advertising effectiveness may not always be overwhelming in terms of the percentage of people who respond to the message, it is still instructive to contemplate some of the impressive results that have been achieved with persuasive campaigns in the media. Years ago, when I taught an advertising class, I invited an executive from an ad agency to be a guest speaker, and he told me that a single-page ad in a large metropolitan newspaper is expected to yield a minimum revenue equal to 10 times the cost of the ad. Thus, if the ad costs $15,000, the department store that runs the ad expects revenues to increase $150,000 over the amount that would have been received if the ad had not appeared. If you're in the advertising business, these figures translate into the realization that newspaper advertising is a powerful persuasive technique.

Many other companies have also recognized that media advertising is a powerful choice. A few years ago, the executives of the Northwest Mutual Life Insurance Company discovered that their company had poor name recognition. In fact, people tended to have better recognition of 33 other insurance company names than theirs. But after two weeks of advertising on TV, they improved their name recognition so that only two company names were recognized ahead of theirs. It cost the company $1 million to accomplish this feat, but the effort was considered to be cost-efficient.[21]

Advertisers discovered the power of television to increase sales back in the 1950s. That's when the Mattel toy company decided to pour money into a TV ad campaign. The results of that campaign are now legendary. The company increased its value by a factor of about 25![22]

The effectiveness of campaigns like Mattel's raised a number of issues related to children. For the most part, Mattel was advertising to the children in the TV audience. Studies by Charles Atkin reveal that children who are heavy viewers of TV ads are more likely to consume the products in those ads and more likely to ask their parents to buy the products that they see advertised.[23] A political action organization, Action for Children's Television (ACT), actively lobbied Congress for years to prohibit advertising directed to children. Even though the data point clearly to the conclusion that children are heavily influenced by advertising, lawmakers found the proposals by ACT to be unworkable. The Saturday-morning time slot is still an advertising bonanza directed to children. The fact that advertisers continue to pay huge sums of money for their messages should be instructive. Advertising works. It is persuasive. This point was reiterated recently by a team of scholars from the fields of psychology and communication in a report of the American Psychological Association's Task Force on Advertising and Children.[24] Study Box 8-1 describes a recent experiment that shows how advertising specific products to children is effective in shaping children's preferences.

## KEY PRINCIPLES OF MEDIA PERSUASION

If media messages are persuasive, what are the key ingredients that contribute to their power? Psychologists have studied the persuasion process scientifically for more than 50 years. As a result of their study, much has been learned about the

## STUDY BOX 8-1 French Fries or Apple Dippers?

Christopher Ferguson and Monica Muñoz, two behavioral scientists, reported the results of a simple experiment that showed how advertising can affect children's preferences. They recruited 75 children between three and eight years old and had them watch two *Tom and Jerry* cartoons that were interrupted three times with 60-second commercial messages. The first and third commercials were always the same—for LEGO and the *Cars 2* movie, respectively. The second commercial was for a McDonald's food product and was different depending upon the group that children were randomly assigned to at the beginning of the experiment. Half of the children saw a commercial for French fries and the other half saw a commercial for apple dippers.

After the cartoons were over, children were permitted to select a food coupon to cash in at McDonald's. They could choose a coupon for French fries or one for apple dippers. In addition to their interest in which coupon was chosen, the researchers were also interested in whether or not the child's parent could influence the coupon choice. Parents were randomly assigned to either encourage the child to select the coupon they wanted the most—or to select the coupon for apple dippers—the healthier choice.

The results of the experiment showed clearly that children's preferences were different depending upon the commercial they had seen. Without respect to the advice their parents gave, children who saw the ad for French fries chose a French fries coupon by a margin of 62% to 38%. Those who saw the ad for apple dippers chose an apple dippers coupon by a similar margin of 59% to 41%. Parents weren't very effective in influencing their children's coupon choice. A few more children who saw the apple dippers ad chose a French fries coupon if their parent told them to choose the coupon they wanted most. Similarly, a few more children who saw the French fries ad chose the apple dippers coupon if their parent told them to choose the coupon for the healthier food. Nevertheless, the statistical effect of the parental recommendation was not significant. The authors noted that outside the laboratory, parents might be able to exert greater persuasive pressure than they were in this experiment (they were required to adhere to a simple script in giving their comments). Nevertheless, they concluded that their results show how commercials directed to children can be effective.

SOURCE: Ferguson, C. J., & Muñoz, M. (2011). Advertising influences on young children's food choices and parental influence. *Journal of Pediatrics*, 160(3), 452–455.

dynamics of persuasion. Study Box 8-2 details some of the common principles of persuasion identified by Robert Cialdini in his classic text on the subject. Let's take a brief look at what the research has discovered about how people change their attitudes and behavior.

## The Power of the Source

Back in the 1950s, Carl Hovland and Walter Weiss reported a groundbreaking experiment that is now famous in the annals of persuasion research.[25] In this simple

## STUDY BOX 8-2 Weapons of Influence

In his analysis of persuasion, Robert Cialdini has identified at least six principles that he claims are ubiquitous in daily life. By learning to recognize these principles, you may be able to guard against the bombardment of persuasive attempts from the mass media. After you read about the principles, see if you can identify how they are used in the media. The principles are as follows:

1. **Reciprocity:** If someone does something for you, you usually feel that you need to reciprocate and do something in return. This principle can be used to persuade you. When some charity group sends you free address labels with its logo and slogan to place on your mailing envelopes, you may be more vulnerable to the charity's persuasive pitch. Because the group has given you something, your automatic response may be that you need to give something back in return. The dangers, of course, are that you end up giving much more than you received and you could end up giving to a group that you wouldn't typically support.

2. **Commitment and consistency:** People strive for consistency in their behavior. Sometimes your desire to be consistent can be used against you. Suppose you resist the reciprocity rule and decide to use your address labels without sending any money to the charity. You might not be off the hook just yet. As you continue to attach the address labels to your envelopes, you realize that every piece of mail you send out is an expression of support for the charity. A few months later, when the charity solicits you for a donation, you may feel more inclined to give to maintain consistency with your prior commitment.

3. **Social proof:** When we are not sure how to behave, we look to others around us for guidance. Producers of TV sitcoms know that their programs will be perceived as funnier if they include laugh tracks. Apparently, people are persuaded that the content of the show is more humorous if they hear other people laughing at the one-liners.

4. **Liking:** If we like someone, we are more susceptible to being influenced by that person. One car salesman attributes his great success to the cards he sends his customers that simply say "I like you." The power of this strategy may reside in the fact that few people want to believe that such an expression of affection could be disingenuous. After all, you are a very likeable person, aren't you?

5. **Authority:** We tend to respond more readily to messages delivered by people whom we regard as authority figures. Who would you tend to believe more about the virtues of spending money to travel to Mars—the author of this textbook or Leonard Nimoy, who played Spock in the *Star Trek* episodes? You may have found yourself instantly wanting to go with Leonard Nimoy. But does playing a part on a TV show make one an authority? Persuasive practitioners often try to capitalize on our urge to be persuaded by an authority figure by presenting us with messages from people who only appear to be authorities. Appearances can often be deceiving.

6. **Scarcity:** We tend to go after things that appear to be in high demand. If everyone wants it, it must be good. How many advertisers use the scarcity appeal by telling

us that their offers are good "only while supplies last"? This phrase gives the impression that people are going to be beating down the door to obtain the product. If the product is in such high demand and will soon be gone, it must be worth whatever price is being charged. Right? Well, maybe. The danger of relying exclusively on the scarcity of a product to determine its worth is that you might soon discover that the true merits of the product weren't worth the price you paid.

**SOURCE:** Cialdini, R. (1985). *Influence: Science and practice.* Glenview, IL: Scott Foresman.

experiment, they exposed people to a persuasive message that argued that atomic-powered submarines were perfectly feasible for future development. At the time they ran the experiment, such submarines were nonexistent and little more than a fanciful dream. It might be similar to arguing today for the feasibility of establishing a city on Mars. Hovland and Weiss set up the experiment so that some of the participants received the message from the official newspaper of the Communist Party Pravda. The rest of the participants received the message from J. Robert Oppenheimer, a well-known and well-respected atomic physicist. Prior to the experiment, the participants indicated their opinions on this topic. After they read the message, they indicated their opinions once again. You can probably guess which group of participants was more persuaded about the feasibility of atomic-powered subs. The participants who heard the message from Oppenheimer were much more likely to change their view. Why? As it turns out, the key reason has to do with the **credibility** of the source. Oppenheimer was a much more credible source than Pravda.

What makes a source more or less credible? Two of the chief components of source credibility are **expertise** and **trustworthiness**. Expertise has to do with the extent to which people perceive that the source of the message is an expert on the topic that he or she is speaking about. **Trustworthiness** has to do with the extent to which people find the source of the message to be reliable or truthful. If advertisers can find sources who have both of these characteristics, they stand a good chance of putting together a persuasive ad. One practitioner of persuasion, Tony Schwartz, was able to design an antismoking commercial for the Foundation for a Smoke-Free Indoor Environment. The brief spot simply featured a man talking to the camera. The spot worked because the man was not just any man. He was a source who had maximum expertise and trustworthiness. I have included the text of this ad so you can see a vivid example of source credibility in action:

My name is Patrick Reynolds. My grandfather, R. J. Reynolds, founded the tobacco company which now manufactures Camels, Winstons, and Salems. We've all heard the tobacco industry say that there are no ill effects caused by smoking. Well, we have plenty of cigarette-caused disease and death right here in the R. J. Reynolds family itself. My grandfather, R. J. Reynolds, Jr., smoked heavily and died of emphysema. My mother smoked and had emphysema and heart disease. And two of my aunts, also heavy smokers, died of emphysema and cancer. Three of my older brothers who smoke have emphysema. I smoked for 10 years and have small airways lung disease. Now tell me, do you think the cigarette companies are truthful when they tell you that smoking isn't harmful? What do you think?[26]

This spot managed to combine expertise and trustworthiness in a single source. Who would be perceived as more of an expert on the effects of smoking than a member of a family who owned a tobacco company? As for trustworthiness, by appearing to speak against the financial interests of his own family, the message delivered by Patrick Reynolds seemed particularly reliable. When the audience perceives that the source of the message has little to gain by delivering a particular message, then the source is more likely to be perceived as trustworthy.

## Message Features: Simplicity and Repetition

Bill Moyers, an award-winning journalist who has made a series of videos for the Public Broadcasting Company, conducted an interview in one of his documentaries with Fritz Hippler, the mastermind of most of the German propaganda films made during Adolf Hitler's reign of terror.[27] When asked what made propaganda so effective, Hippler didn't hesitate. The two principles he identified were simplicity and repetition. These were essentially the same principles noted in another interview that Bill Moyers did, this one with Rosser Reeves, the advertising man who developed campaigns for Dwight Eisenhower, M&M candies, Bic pens, and Anacin pain reliever, to mention just a few. Reeves stated that too many advertising people "get tangled up in their own underwear" instead of communicating messages that are simple and to the point.[28] Both Hippler and Reeves had discovered something that researchers have documented in laboratory experiments. John Cacioppo and Richard Petty showed that a repeated message was more persuasive than one that was heard only once. But repetition does have its limits. After about three exposures, Cacioppo and Petty found, people started to become bored by the same message, and persuasive impact started to decrease.[29] Commercial advertisers who use radio and TV often fail to appreciate how quickly a commercial message "burns out" with the audience. The research suggests that campaigns need regular infusions of new life to prevent consumer boredom.

## More Message Features: Fear, Guilt, and Humor

If you think about some of the commercials that you have seen or heard over the years, you will probably have little trouble identifying messages that used one of the three appeals just listed: fear, guilt, or humor. Let's look briefly at each of these message features from the perspective of persuasion research. How effective are they?

Fear appeals have been a standard part of the persuader's arsenal for as long as persuasion has been practiced. Not long ago, I saw a commercial for a children's fever-reducing remedy. The commercial seemed designed to induce a mild level of fear about what might happen if my child's fever went too high. Of course, use of the advertised pain reliever was presented as the remedy. Do such appeals work? In their exhaustive review of the theory and research results pertaining to fear appeals in persuasion, psychologists Alice Eagly and Shelly Chaiken answer the question:

> What is the effect of fear or threat on persuasion? ... For the applied health professional, then, the most important question about public health communications is whether scare tactics enhance or inhibit their efficacy. On this bottom line issue, the research findings are fairly clear: The vast majority of experiments have found that higher levels of threat lead to greater persuasion than lower levels.[30]

Fear appeals do tend to increase persuasion. Although this conclusion seems simple enough, the theory and research behind the conclusion are anything but simple. Over the years, researchers have had to wade through many studies appearing to contain inconsistent findings. The theories in the area are quite diverse, yet no particular theory seems to enjoy clear support. One example of the complexity involved in predicting the success of fear appeals is the **protection motivation theory**.[31] According to this view, to the extent that fear appeals convince an audience of the severity of a threat, their vulnerability to the threat, and their ability to respond effectively to the threat, they will be persuasive. On the other hand, to the extent that the audience perceives that yielding to the persuasive message will be costly in some way, even high-fear appeals might not be effective.

Sometimes media messages bypass the strategy of inducing fear in favor of trying to make you feel *guilty* for not responding to a persuasive appeal. One reason for the prevalence of guilt appeals is that it is relatively easy to make people feel guilty. Parents who have their children's welfare at heart are easy prey for the persuader who wants to induce guilt. As a parent, how can I live with myself if I don't have the very best tires on my car to keep my child as safe as possible? Or how about the very best computer for my child's pursuit of education? Advertisers are well aware that it is relatively easy to play on feelings of guilt. Does it work? According to communication researcher Em Griffin, guilt appeals are certainly persuasive—at least in the context of interpersonal communication.[32] If you feel guilty and I am standing in your face asking you to comply with a request, the chances are good that you will comply. People can be motivated to do many things because they feel guilty. But Griffin warns about some side effects of the guilt appeal that persuaders would do well to consider carefully. He maintains that most people tend to avoid and devalue those who make them feel guilty. This would seem to hold important implications for using guilt in a mass media campaign. Because there is no individual person who has to be confronted directly, media campaigns that are based on guilt may tend to backfire. Indeed, there is evidence that consumers respond with anger when a media advertisement makes them feel guilty.[33] Consistent with Griffin's analysis, recent research from Australia shows that guilt is an over-used marketing technique that in the long run may cause people to comply less with a persuasive request.[34]

The final message ingredient examined briefly in this chapter is humor. If you've ever had the chance to see the annual Clio Awards given for outstanding achievement in advertising, then you know that many of the award winners are commercials that feature some type of humorous appeal. Practitioners of persuasion have long believed that being funny makes them more persuasive. The idea is based on the notion that humor tends to attract attention to the message, creates a more favorable attitude toward the source of the message and the product, and may produce a general orientation toward the message that is less critical. In other words, if people are laughing, they can't be thinking too hard about the arguments against your message.

Perhaps the really funny thing in all of this is that researchers have had a difficult time documenting the superiority of humorous messages in persuasive campaigns. There may be good reason for this. Although humor may attract attention, it may attract attention to itself instead of to the persuasive message. People may remember the joke—but not what product they're supposed to buy. It may also be the case that humor tends to discourage the consumer from taking the product very seriously. It may be true that people who are laughing are not thinking up reasons they shouldn't buy the product, but on the other hand, they may not be thinking seriously about buying the product at all. They are simply too busy laughing. Still, advertisers continue to use humor in campaign after campaign. Why? One reason may be that humor is tolerated much more easily with repetition. It wears well. Another reason may be that advertisers are convinced that people feel positive sentiment toward the source that makes them laugh. In today's competitive media market, positive sentiment is a precious commodity. Regardless of the research findings, it is a relative certainty that advertisers will continue to pack their ads with humorous appeals. Actually, some recent research indicates that the advertising money spent on humor might pay sales dividends. A study by Robin Nabi, Emily Moyer-Gusé (the same two researchers who studied the EORM model), and Sahara Byrne confirmed some of the basic beliefs that persuasive practitioners have about why humorous messages are so effective.[35]

## The Health Campaign

It is one thing to use the media to persuade people to buy products. It is another thing to use the media to persuade them to adopt healthy behaviors. Earlier in the chapter, you read about how entertainment media can sometimes be used to promote healthy behaviors. But what about more deliberate advertising that attempts to persuade people to change their behaviors for their own health? Over the years, advertising messages have often brought consumers conflicting messages about appropriate health-related behaviors. Up until 1971, when cigarette ads were banned from the public airwaves, TV and radio saturated the culture with commercial messages designed to encourage smoking behavior. More recently, the airwaves have been used to deliver a very different message about smoking. Study Box 8-3 explains the curious case of cigarette advertising that saw tobacco sales increase after the law went into effect banning cigarette ads from radio and TV. At the same time that the government

## STUDY BOX 8-3 Why Did Cigarette Sales Increase after Cigarette Ads Were Banned from Radio and TV?

In 1967, the Federal Communications Commission (FCC) made a landmark ruling when they applied the fairness doctrine to cigarette advertising. The fairness doctrine (removed from broadcast law in 1987) required broadcasters to afford reasonable time for the discussion of different views on matters of public controversy. The FCC's application of the fairness doctrine to advertising was a first. Reasoning that smoking was a controversial issue of public health, the FCC required broadcasters to give *free airtime* for one antismoking commercial for *every three* cigarette ads. Although the ruling was challenged in federal court by the broadcasters and tobacco companies, their legal efforts failed. The late 1960s were years in which antismoking messages saturated the airwaves alongside the numerous ads for cigarettes.

The bad news for tobacco companies was that their sales dropped when the antismoking ads started to run. Research on smoking statistics and the economic impact of the antismoking ads revealed that smoking dropped each year the ads ran by 531 cigarettes per person. Since the impact of cigarette ads over the same time period was estimated to *increase* smoking by 95 cigarettes per person, the net loss for the tobacco industry was 436 cigarettes per person. The magnitude of this loss in sales was simply unacceptable for the tobacco companies. After considering various options, they finally lobbied Congress to pass a law banning the advertising of their own product on radio and TV. The law went into effect on January 2, 1971, and it released the broadcasters from the obligation to provide free time for antismoking messages. Consequently, the antismoking messages disappeared from the airwaves too. The organizations that had produced them didn't have the money to begin paying for airtime that had previously been free. Once that happened, cigarette sales increased again. Over the long run, as the health evidence associated with smoking continued to grow and various social movements against smoking took hold, per capita sales of cigarettes decreased. But one thing that we learned from the era of free airtime for antismoking ads was that these ads *worked*. Electronic media could be used to persuade people to change unhealthy behavior.

SOURCE: Tobacco Industry Efforts to Influence Tobacco Control Media Interventions. [Online: Accessed 5-16-14]. Available: http://cancercontrol.cancer.gov/brp/tcrb/monographs/19/m19_13.pdf

wants to invest in persuasive messages to reduce drug use, the commercial messages during sporting events sell young people on the virtues of alcohol consumption. Is there any evidence that media messages can be used to change public health behavior for the good? As it turns out, persuasive principles are persuasive principles. The same principles that persuade people to engage in unhealthy behavior can also be used to persuade them to engage in healthy behavior.

Some of the most impressive data sets that argue in favor of using the media to address public health problems come from other countries. Working in Bolivia, researchers Thomas Valente and Walter Saba reported the results of two surveys taken a year apart and involving more than 3,000 respondents. The goal of these surveys was to evaluate the effectiveness of a major campaign to encourage positive reproductive health practices (the use of safe contraception, etc.). The campaign included 11 different TV and radio spots, and the researchers measured how the campaign affected both information acquisition and behavior. The results indicated that people who were exposed to the mass media campaign were more likely to adopt contraception into their sexual practices. There was also some evidence that the media campaign was likeliest to have an effect on those who did not have a rich interpersonal network. It is worth noting here that the effect of exposure to the campaign was not particularly large in statistical terms, but it was statistically significant (see Chapter 2 for a review of these concepts).[36]

Similar to the findings in Bolivia, another survey of over 1,200 mothers in the Philippines found evidence that exposure to a media campaign about preventing the measles had a significant impact on increasing specific knowledge about the disease. Once again, the media—and not interpersonal networks—seemed to be the source of the information gains.[37] A study of nearly 1,700 smokers and ex-smokers by researchers working on the Finnish North Karelia Project also found that for the men in the study, weekly exposure to mass media health messages was significantly correlated with attempts to stop smoking. Unlike the studies in Bolivia and the Philippines, interpersonal communication also had an impact on efforts to quit. The respondents who received both media and interpersonal communication were the most resistant to the temptation to smoke.[38]

The effects of successful health campaigns are not limited to countries outside the United States. The National Diabetes Education Program launched a campaign in 1998 called Control Your Diabetes for Life. In 2007, researchers noted that more than half of the diabetics surveyed said that they were familiar with the campaign. The data also indicate a number of positive trends in the care with which diabetics monitor their daily glucose levels.[39] Another campaign that met with some success was reported in a 2008 issue of the *American Journal of Health Promotion.* Using an experimental approach, researchers ran an eight-week media campaign in Morgantown, West Virginia, that was designed to increase the perceived importance of moderately intense daily walking. No such campaign ran in the control group community—Huntington, West Virginia. Baseline measures were taken from policy makers in each of the two communities about the problems that were being faced in each city. At the end of the media campaign, the policy makers in Morgantown had elevated daily walking to a significant issue to be addressed. There was no such change in Huntington.[40] Health communication is now one of the most active research areas to emerge in the larger discipline of communication. Early on, much of the research was correlational. You know from the preceding chapters that we must be careful about assuming that the media exert a causal force if we don't have the data needed to make that conclusion. As the literature develops, experiments like the one done on the walking campaign in West Virginia are becoming more prevalent. Evidence does seem to be mounting in favor of the idea that persuasive health campaigns using the mass media can have an effect on individual behavior. Researchers at the University of Kentucky have done a number of investigations that look at how individuals differ in their response to media health messages. They have found that sensation seekers are more likely to use drugs and are more likely to respond well to media messages that are high in novelty and action.[41] Another researcher, Richard Perloff, has recently summarized research on media campaigns designed to convince people to have safer sex.[42] The implication that this research holds for addressing the AIDS crisis and other sexually transmitted disease is obvious. We shouldn't be surprised to find that research on media health campaigns is turning up evidence that persuasive tactics work. If the media are able to persuade people to buy products, laugh, and adopt attitudes of fear toward their environment, they should be able to influence people to change their health habits.

As much as researchers have learned about health campaigns, a recent overview of the research by Charles Salmon and Charles Atkin reveals that we still have quite a bit of progress to make in this area.[43] In a major meta-analysis that was conducted on this research over nearly 50 different campaigns, media effects were discovered to be quite modest.[44] Compared to the control conditions where people didn't receive the health messages, the people in conditions that received the health messages resulted in behavior changes in only about 7% to 10% more of the people. Another important finding from this literature is that it seems a bit easier to persuade people to *adopt a new behavior* such as beginning an exercise routine or changing dental care practices than it is to persuade them to *stop an unhealthy practice* such as smoking or engaging in risky sex. To highlight some of the unknowns about health campaigns and to help set the agenda for future research, Salmon and Atkin raised several critical questions that future researchers need to attempt to answer (see Study Box 8-4). On the other hand, scholars have already learned plenty about how to conduct persuasive health campaigns. Study Box 8-5 provides a recent summary of some of the key principles for success.

Most recently, a team of researchers in England was able to assess the effectiveness of a media campaign designed to curb smoking behavior.[45] The campaign,

---

**STUDY BOX 8-4 Questions about Media Campaigns for Future Research**

1. How much message-exposure is needed to get behavior change?
2. Exactly when does message "burnout" occur? How much message exposure is too much?
3. What is the optimum mix of persuasive strategies? What sort of balance should messages contain between positive incentives and negative appeals like fear?
4. What is the best balance of channels for a campaign? To what extent should a campaign rely on paid ads or public service announcements? To what extent should the campaign rely on TV, radio, print, or Web sites?
5. What is the latest research on new communication technologies and health campaigns? Given that technologies are evolving so quickly, how are we to understand these changes in terms of their effects on campaign strategies?

---

SOURCE: Salmon, C. T., & Atkin, C. (2003). Using media campaigns for health promotion. In T. L. Thompson, A. M. Dorsey, K. I. Miller, & R. Parrott (Eds.), *Handbook of health communication* (pp 449–472). Mahwah, NJ: Erlbaum.

**STUDY BOX 8-5 Conducting Campaigns Based upon Communication Research**

Three communication scholars (Seth Noar, Nancy Grant Harrington, and Donald Helme) recently featured some of the key, research-based principles that have emerged from communication research about successful health campaigns. They mentioned:

1. Divide one's audience into one or more audience segments.
2. Conduct formative research with the audience segments.
3. Apply a theory to the population and behavior under study.
4. Use a message design that is targeted to the audience segment.
5. Place the message in channels frequently used by the audience segment with high reach and frequency.
6. Conduct process and outcome evaluation.

SOURCE: Noar, S. M., Harrington, N. G., & Helme, D. W. (2010). The contributions of health communication research to campaign practice. *Health Communication,* 25, 593–594.

named Stoptober, was designed to encourage people to stop smoking in unison on October 1 for one entire month. One of the principles used in the campaign was consistent with advice from the recent meta-analytic studies—the notion that supporting a new desired behavior would be more effective than simply trying to get people to stop smoking. The campaign itself was truly multi-media and included messages on TV, radio, Facebook, and Twitter. People who signed up for the campaign received a free support pack in the mail, access to a Web site with information on how to stop smoking, a motivational text messaging program that encouraged people to continue to resist the urge to smoke, and a smartphone app designed to encourage users and permit self-monitoring toward the no-smoking goal. The researchers reported that over 300,000 people attempted to quit smoking during the campaign. While it is difficult to know which media and which messages were the most effective in achieving the persuasive goal, the researchers concluded that the campaign "... provided excellent value for money as a life-saving public health intervention. Designing a national public health campaign with a clear behavioural target (making a serious quit attempt) using key psychological principles can yield a substantial return in terms of behaviour change and public heath impact" (p. 57). Clearly, the evidence in the area of health shows that media messages can be effective.

## SUBLIMINAL PERSUASION: THE MAGIC KEY?

Before concluding the discussion on the persuasive effects of media, there is one topic that we dare not ignore because it is one of the most interesting to think about, and it holds a special place in the history of advertising. Shortly after I earned my master's degree in communication (1976), I took a part-time teaching job that required me to teach a course on persuasion. One of the questions that arose in the class at the very outset was about the effectiveness of something called **subliminal persuasion**. I knew a little about the topic from my graduate studies but not enough to feel competent teaching a class of curious undergraduates who wanted the truth about this persuasive technique. My students' curiosity was fueled by two books published in the 1970s by Wilson Bryan Key.[46] Key argued that media advertising contained hidden or subliminal appeals that penetrated into the unconscious mind of the consumer. Because these messages presumably bypassed the conventional process of rational scrutiny that people typically give to persuasive messages, they were supposedly particularly effective in motivating human behavior. According to Key, advertisers were so committed to the technique that occasionally they even put subliminal messages on the product itself.

After reading about the contention that a popular brand of cracker had the word *sex* hidden on the surface of the product, I became suspicious. I purchased a box of the crackers and proceeded to spread them out over the kitchen table at the home of my mother-in-law. With a magnifying glass in hand, I examined each cracker carefully to see if I could find evidence of the subliminal technique. As I was deeply engaged in my search, my mother-in-law came into the room and asked me what I was doing. Without batting an eye, I replied, "I'm looking for sex." Only after I uttered these words did I realize that I had a lot of explaining to do. At that point in my study, I was prepared to explain much more than I had been ready to explain to my persuasion class.

As it turns out, the academic study of subliminal persuasion is a fascinating one. Let's take a brief look at some of the highlights.

## Early History

Subliminal messages are messages that presumably enter the unconscious mind without being detected. The primary example of such a message was outlined in 1957 by an advertising expert, James Vicary. Vicary claimed that in extensive tests he designed for movie audiences watching the film *Picnic,* he had clearly established that subliminal messages were persuasive. He claimed that by splicing into the film the phrases "Eat popcorn" and "Drink Coke," he dramatically increased the sales of these products at the concession counter. Even though the phrases were on the screen for only one-third of one millisecond (too brief to be perceived consciously), they registered in the brain and stirred the urge to eat and drink. According to Vicary, after people were exposed to the subliminal messages, Coke sales increased 18% and popcorn sales increased 58%.[47] As you might imagine, this revelation caused quite a controversy. Articles appeared in popular magazines that scorned this technique as highly unethical. In an article that appeared in the *Saturday Review*, Norman Cousins wrote that subliminal persuasion was so insidious that we should "take this invention and everything connected to it and attach it to the center of the next nuclear explosive scheduled for testing."[48] Even before any supporting data could be examined on the effect that Vicary announced, the Federal Communications Commission threatened that any use of the technique by broadcasters would result in loss of their broadcasting license. The National Association of Broadcasters also prohibited the practice of subliminal persuasion for any of its members, which included nearly every broadcast facility in the United States. The advertising community wanted to see the supporting data from Vicary's study before it rendered a final opinion about subliminal persuasion. The little-known truth about the history of this topic is that James Vicary confessed in 1962 that the study reported in 1957 was, in fact, a fabricated account that was intended to increase the number of customers for his marketing business.[49] But the confession appeared in an advertising trade journal, and the word never seemed to circulate very widely. The notion of subliminal persuasion had taken on a life of its own. Despite Vicary's confession, the idea was so intriguing that it just wouldn't go away.

## The Presumed Mechanism

How is subliminal persuasion supposed to work? When Key popularized the notion of subliminal persuasion in the 1970s, he argued that many of the subliminal messages in advertising revolved around two themes: sex and death. Any casual reader of Sigmund Freud would recognize these two themes instantly. According to Freud, the death wish and thoughts about the sexual appetite are repressed in the unconscious mind because there are few socially acceptable outlets for their expression. Subliminal messages, which directly enter the unconscious mind, unlock these repressed urges and motivate a person to purchase the particular product that the unconscious has linked with those urges. It is no accident that many supporters of the notion of subliminal influence in the psychological community are those who take a **psychoanalytic** or **Freudian perspective** in their general outlook on human behavior.

## Two Important Questions

Two important questions need to be answered regarding subliminal persuasion. First, to what extent are subliminal messages actually present in today's mass media? Second, if they are present, are they persuasive? The first question is difficult to answer. The advertising community is not particularly interested in confessing to the use of subliminal messages, and there appears to be no good source to document their prevalence. Back in the 1980s, I asked an advertising executive at Wyse Advertising if he had any insights into the use of subliminal messages in advertising. His answer was only an estimate, but it was more concrete than anything I had encountered up to that point or have encountered since. He estimated that about 10% of all ads use some form of subliminal technique. Of course, there are also various audiotapes and videotapes marketed to the public that supposedly encourage weight loss, relaxation, avoidance of tobacco use, and similar behaviors. So, even though we can't be certain about the exact prevalence of subliminal messages, we can be confident that at least some messages attempt to employ the subliminal strategy.

Are subliminal messages effective? To answer this question, two psychologists, Anthony Pratkanis and Anthony Greenwald, decided to run an experiment that tested the power of subliminal tapes marketed to the public to increase self-esteem and memory.[50] The tapes that they used contained classical music that was clearly audible, or **supraliminal**. The manufacturer had altered the tapes to include subliminal audio that could not be perceived consciously. Some of the tapes contained messages designed to enhance the listener's self-esteem (e.g., "I have high self-worth and high self-esteem"); others contained messages designed to improve memory (e.g., "My ability to remember and recall is increasing daily"). After testing volunteers on measures of self-esteem and memory, the experimenters randomly assigned them to listen to the tapes daily for five weeks. There were four experimental conditions. Each of the four groups received tapes that contained labels indicating the type of subliminal content that they would hear. For two of the groups, the labels were correct and indicated either the memory or self-esteem message. For the other two groups, the labels were incorrect. For one group, the tapes labeled "self-esteem" actually had subliminal messages about memory. Likewise, for the final group, the tapes labeled "memory" actually had subliminal messages about self-esteem.

The results of the study were clear. First, the authors found absolutely no evidence that the subliminal messages were effective in changing self-esteem or memory. Second, the study revealed what the authors dubbed as an **illusory placebo effect**. The volunteers who listened to the tapes labeled as self-esteem tapes thought that the tapes had increased their levels of self-esteem. The volunteers who listened to the memory tapes thought that the tapes had increased their memory ability. This happened regardless of the actual subliminal content of the tapes. Thus, the effect that emerged here was a placebo effect because the volunteers expressed opinions that were based on the labels on the tapes. The effect was illusory because, in fact, actual levels of self-esteem and memory were unaffected by any of the tapes.

The study by Pratkanis and Greenwald is typical of many that scholars have published over the past 40 years. There is virtually no evidence that subliminal messages are capable of influencing the kinds of large changes in attitude and behavior that marketers of products attempt to bring about in consumers.

As Pratkanis concluded in a recent article on this topic, "Perhaps now is the time to lay the myth of subliminal sorcery to rest and direct our attention to other, more scientifically documented ways of understanding the causes of human behavior and improving our condition."[51] It is worth noting that there are still some cognitive psychologists who believe that subliminal persuasion is a possibility that may be documented in future research.[52] Until more confirming data appear in the literature, however, the consensus of scholars is probably best summarized in the statement by Pratkanis. From the perspective of a consumer who might wonder about whether to buy a subliminal tape to facilitate weight loss, relaxation, or some other desirable result, it is important to realize the inherent inconsistency in such marketing strategies. The effectiveness of subliminal messages is predicated on the notion that the messages enter the mind undetected. When a consumer buys a tape that promises to deliver subliminal messages of a certain type, then the process is no longer under cover. Once the nature of the subliminal message is known, the entire presumption of the message's effectiveness is undone. It is no longer subliminal. Any positive benefits that listening to such tapes might produce cannot be attributed to the subliminal nature of the messages. Following the study by Pratkanis, these effects are more plausibly due to the power of prior expectations, or the placebo effect.

A final warning about claims for the effectiveness of subliminal persuasion is in order. As I have taught classes in persuasion over the years, I occasionally have heard or read about fantastic claims that seem to support the notion that subliminal appeals are effective. For example, a TV program on the PBS network reported that some department stores incorporate subliminal messages about honesty into their music systems as a way of reducing shoplifting. One store supposedly reported that the move had saved them hundreds of thousands of dollars. The problem with such claims is that the data do not come from carefully controlled laboratory experiments. We have no way of knowing whether the department stores in question took other security measures at the same time that they implemented subliminal messages. Perhaps the reduction in shoplifting was due to changes in the economy or the time of year. In the end, these kinds of anecdotal reports fail to meet the strict rigors of scientific testing. For that reason, you should be careful about attaching too much significance to them.

## A Caveat: Research on Subliminal Priming

While the evidence pertaining to subliminal persuasion is certainly lacking, there is now quite a bit of evidence in the literature to show that **subliminal priming** is an effect that can be demonstrated reliably. One common method of demonstrating the effects of subliminal priming is to show that people can recognize certain words much faster if they have been exposed to a prior subliminal stimulus word that is related. For example, imagine that you are sitting in front of a computer screen and told that you are going to be presented with a string of letters. For each string of letters, you are instructed to press the "Y" key (for "yes") on your keyboard if the letters spell a real word. If the letters you see don't spell a real word, you are told to press the "N" key (for "no"). You are told to make your judgment as quickly as you can without making an error. Just prior to the words appearing (referred to as target words), you are presented with the word *Florida*—but the presentation is subliminal. That is, the word *Florida* appears so quickly on the screen that you can't consciously report that you saw it. Now, the letter strings appear and you begin to respond to the target words or the target letters that sometimes don't form any recognizable word. The data from numerous experiments suggest that if you are presented with words like *sun, sand, beach,* or *ocean,* the time it takes you to hit the "Y" key is significantly shorter than if you had been exposed to a subliminal word like *Alaska*. Presumably, the word *Florida* is much more likely to be related to the concepts of sun and sand than the word *Alaska*. It serves to prime those other concepts, making them more accessible as you perform the task you were instructed to do. Even though the exposure to the word *Florida* was subliminal, it still influences the time of your response.

Some researchers believe that the existence of subliminal priming effects might mean that subliminal stimuli could theoretically be used to enhance persuasion in the proper context.[53] For example, a team of social psychologists recently demonstrated how using the appropriate priming words in a subliminal priming experiment can affect desirability ratings of consumer products, which could result in increased purchasing behavior.[54] However, the subliminal priming effect appears to decay quite rapidly in the experiments that have been reported. That is, once the length of time between the subliminal word and the target word or product increases to even a matter of a few minutes, the effect seems to decay substantially. It should also be noted that identifying a string of letters or a target word—or even expressing a temporary desire for a product—is hardly the same as changing one's behavior. At this point, most scholars would probably agree that the degree of precision required to actually apply the subliminal priming effect to produce significant persuasion is so high that it would be practically impossible— or at least extremely difficult.

## The Third-Person Effect

As you've read through this chapter, you may have thought a bit about the extent to which the people you know have actually been persuaded to change their attitudes or their behaviors as a result of exposure to media messages. Suppose someone asked you if you thought that the mass media persuaded people to change their attitudes and behavior. What would you say? Suppose someone asked you if you thought that the mass media persuaded *you* to change your attitudes and behavior. If you are like many people, you will agree that the media influence others. When the question turns in a personal direction, however, you will resist admitting that you are personally affected. This tendency to think that media influence is stronger for other people than it is for oneself is a phenomenon that media researchers have documented in several studies.[55] A recent meta-analysis of the literature found clear evidence for the **third-person effect** across nearly three dozen different studies.[56] More recently, two researchers, Erica Scharer and Ron Leone, documented the presence of the third-person effect among a group of adolescents with respect to the effects of playing video games. Specifically, they found that the size of the effect grew as a function of the rating of the video game. The more restrictive the game was in terms of its intended audience, the greater the third-person effect. In addition, the size of the effect grew as a function of the age of the game-players. The younger the perceived "other" player was, the greater the effect was.[57]

The third-person effect has been studied for several decades and appears in the context of many different types of possible media impact. A perusal of recent literature shows the breadth of different types of media effects that turn up in this literature. In one study with over 1,000 college students in Taiwan, researchers found the third-person effect in the domain of news. Students estimated the effects of news reports about the avian flu would affect others more than themselves.[58] In another study that showed how one's sex might play a role in third-person effects, males expressed the opinion that the effects of media depictions of the idealized body image would be much greater on their female friends than on themselves.[59] Finally, a recent study with participants who were affected by depression in daily life showed the participants advertisements for various antidepressants. As predicted, the participants thought that the ads would affect other people with depression problems—but not themselves.[60]

Years ago, a psychologist named Phillip Zimbardo noticed this same phenomenon when he studied persuasion in the context of cult groups that employ brainwashing. He referred to this tendency as the **illusion of personal invulnerability**. He discovered that students of persuasion tended to think of themselves as people who would never succumb to the pressures of brainwashing. At the same time, they found it easy to assume that the same brainwashing techniques would work on others. Zimbardo noted that this attitude was not particularly healthy. To maximize resistance to persuasion, it is best to have a proper understanding of one's own vulnerability.[61]

In concluding this chapter, it is important to note that persuasion in the media is a topic that goes well beyond a single chapter in a text like this one. About all we can do here is touch on some of the highlights. The next chapter explores some other dimensions of this topic when it takes up research on politics in the media. In politics, persuasion is the name of the game, and we will take a closer look at how that game is played.

## SUMMARY

Significant persuasion involves attitude and behavior changes that persist over time. In the 1950s, James Vicary made claims about the effectiveness of subliminal advertising in the media. Although such advertising is practiced today, research studies have generally failed to find evidence that it works effectively. There is no doubt that media messages persuade, however. Much of this persuasion is unintentional. Gerbner's theory of media cultivation claims that media messages cultivate particular views of social reality. The theory is somewhat controversial but does enjoy some empirical support. Of course, the media are full of persuasive messages that are deliberately designed to influence. Researchers have studied the influence process and have identified many important variables and developed theoretical ideas to explain how persuasion works. Much of the research has concentrated on understanding how the source of a message affects persuasion and how particular message factors contribute to the process. Recent research in the field of health communication shows promise for documenting how media messages are capable of improving people's health habits.

## QUESTIONS TO FOCUS YOUR ATTENTION

1. Can you think of an example of when you were persuaded to change your attitude or behavior while you were watching entertainment media? What specific aspects about the media that you watched were persuasive? What was the outcome of your persuasion?

2. To what extent does reliance upon the survey method by media cultivation researchers cause you some reluctance about accepting Gerbner's notions of media cultivation as ones that are clearly established?

3. Are you able to identify any commercial messages that you believe were designed to induce feelings of guilt? Were the messages effective in accomplishing the persuasive goal? Why or why not?

## KEY TERMS AND CONCEPTS

| | | |
|---|---|---|
| persuasion | social reality | credibility |
| attitude | first-order cultivation | expertise |
| behavior | second-order cultivation | trustworthiness |
| persistent change | fear of criminal victimization | protection motivation theory |
| elaboration likelihood model (ELM) | mainstreaming | subliminal persuasion |
| | resonance | psychoanalytic or Freudian perspective |
| central route to persuasion | perceptions of the probability of being victimized | supraliminal |
| counter-attitudinal | | |
| peripheral-route persuasion | accessibility principle | illusory placebo effect |
| | drench hypothesis | subliminal priming |
| product placements | "drip-drip-drip" hypothesis | third-person effect |
| landscape model | entertainment-education | illusion of personal invulnerability |
| explicit memory | Entertainment Overcoming Resistance Model (EORM) to persuasion | |
| implicit memory | | |
| theory of media cultivation | | |

## NOTES

1. Schofield, J. W., & Pavelchak, M. A. (1989). Fallout from "The Day After": The impact of a TV film on attitudes related to nuclear war. *Journal of Applied Social Psychology*, 19, 433–448.

2. Balmford, A., Manica, A., Airey, L., Birkin, L., Oliver, A., & Schleicher, J. (2004). Hollywood, climate change and the public. *Science*, 305, 1713.

3. Aronson, E. (1995). *The social animal*. New York: W. H. Freeman.

4. Petty, R. E., & Cacioppo, J. T. (1986). The elaboration likelihood model of persuasion. In L. Berkowitz (Ed.), *Advances in Experimental Social Psychology* (pp. 123–205). Hillsdale, NJ: Erlbaum.

5. Yang, M., & Roskos-Ewoldsen, D. R. (2007). The effectiveness of brand placements in the movies: Levels of placements, explicit and implicit memory, and brand-choice behavior. *Journal of Communication*, 57, 469–489.

6. Dominick, J. R. (1999). *The dynamics of mass communication*. Boston: McGraw-Hill.

7. Gerbner, G., Gross, L., Morgan, M., & Signorielli, N. (1994). Growing up with television: The cultivation perspective. In J. Bryant & D. Zillmann (Eds.), *Media effects: Advances in theory and research* (pp. 17–41). Hillsdale, NJ: Erlbaum.

8. Doob, A. N., & Macdonald, G. E. (1979). Television viewing and fear of victimization: Is the relationship causal? *Journal of Personality & Social Psychology*, 37, 170–179.

9. Sparks, G. G., & Ogles, R. M. (1990). The difference between fear of victimization and the probability of being victimized: Implications for cultivation. *Journal of Broadcasting & Electronic Media*, 34(3), 351–358.

10. Shrum, L. J. (2009). Media consumption and perceptions of social reality: Effects and underlying processes. In J. Bryant, & M. Oliver (Eds.), *Media effects: Advances in theory and research* (pp. 50–73). New York: Routledge.

11. The Law School Tuition Bubble. [Online: Accessed 5-15-14]. Available: http://lawschooltuitionbubble.wordpress.com/original-research-updated/lawyers-per-capita-by-state/

12. Greenberg, B. S. (1988). Some uncommon television images and the drench hypothesis. In S. Oskamp (Ed.), *Applied social psychology annual* (Vol. 8, pp. 88–102). Newbury Park, CA: Sage.

13. Lovgren, S. (2005). "Jaws at 30": Film stoked fear, study of great white sharks. *National Geographic News* [Online: Accessed 5-15-14]. Available: http://news.nationalgeographic.com/news/2005/06/0615_050615_jawssharks.html

14. Sparks, G. G., Hansen, T., & Shah, R. (1994). Do televised depictions of paranormal events influence viewers' paranormal beliefs? *Skeptical Inquirer*, 18, 386–395.

15. The main studies that I have conducted on this topic include the following: Sparks, G. G., Nelson, C. L., & Campbell, R. G. (1997). The relationship between exposure to televised messages about paranormal phenomena and paranormal beliefs. *Journal of Broadcasting & Electronic Media*, 41, 345–359; Sparks, G. G., & Pellechia, M. (1997). The effect of news stories about UFOs on readers' UFO beliefs: The role of confirming or disconfirming testimony from a scientist. *Communication Reports*, 10, 165–172; Sparks, G. G., Pellechia, M., & Irvine, C. (1998). Does television news about UFOs affect viewers' UFO beliefs? An experimental investigation. *Communication Quarterly*, 46, 284–294; Sparks, G. G., Sparks, C. W., & Gray, K. (1995). Media impact on fright reactions and belief in UFOs: The potential role of mental imagery. *Communication Research*, 22, 3–23; Sparks, G. G, & Miller, W. (2001). Investigating the relationship between exposure to television programs that depict paranormal phenomena and beliefs in the paranormal. *Communication Monographs*, 68, 98–113.

16. Brown, J. D., & Walsh-Childers, K. (2002). Effects of media on personal and public health. In J. Bryant & D. Zillmann (Eds.), *Media effects: Advances in theory and research* (pp. 453–488). Mahwah, NJ: Erlbaum.

17. Kaiser Family Foundation (Spring, 2004). Issue Brief on entertainment education. [Online]. Available: http://kaiserfamilyfoundation.files.wordpress.com/2013/01/entertainment-education-and-health-in-the-united-states-issue-brief.pdf

18. Moyer-Gusé, E., & Nabi, R. L. (2010). Explaining the effects of narrative in an entertainment television program: Overcoming resistance to persuasion. *Human Communication Research*, 36, 26–52.

19. Morgan, S. E., Harrison, T., Chewning, L., Davis, L., & DiCorcia, M. (2007). Entertainment (mis)education: The framing of organ donation in entertainment television. *Health Communication*, 22(2), 143–151.

20. Ball-Rokeach, S. J., Rokeach, M., & Grube, J. W. (1984, November). The great American values test: Can television alter basic beliefs? *Psychology Today*, 34–41.

21. Aronson, E. (1995). *The social animal*. New York: W. H. Freeman.

22. Liebert, R. M., & Sprafkin, J. (1988). *The early window. Effects of television on children and youth*. New York: Pergamon Press.

23. Atkin, C. K. (1978). Observation of parent-child interaction in supermarket decision making. *Journal of Marketing*, 42, 41–45.

24. Kunkel, D., Wilcox, B. L., Cantor, J., Palmer, E., Linn, S., & Dowrick, P. (2004). *Report of the APA task force on advertising and children*, American Psychological Association [Online]. Available: http://www.apa.org/pi/families/resources/advertising-children.pdf; pp. 1–64

25. Hovland, C., & Weiss, W. (1951). The influence of source credibility on communication effectiveness. *Public Opinion Quarterly*, 15, 635–650.

26. Hoffman, D., & Duggan, W. (Producers). (1989). Guerrilla media: A citizen's guide to using electronic media for social change. The inside story from Tony Schwartz [video recording]. Princeton, NJ: Films for the Humanities.

27. Moyers, B. D. (Producer). (1988). *World War II: The propaganda battle* [Video recording]. Washington, DC: PBS Films.

28. The 30-second president. An episode of the series *A walk through the twentieth century with Bill Moyers* [video recording]. A presentation of WNET and KQED in association with the Corporation for Entertainment and Learning. Washington, DC: Public Broadcasting Service.

29. Cacioppo, J. T., & Petty, R. E. (1979). Effects of message repetition and position on cognitive response, recall, and persuasion. *Journal of Personality and Social Psychology*, 37, 97–109.

30. Eagly, A. H., & Chaiken, S. (1993). *The psychology of attitudes*. Fort Worth, TX: Harcourt Brace Jovanovich.

31. Rogers, R. W. (1975). A protection motivation theory of fear appeals and attitude change. *Journal of Psychology*, 91, 93–114.

32. Griffin, E. (1976). *The mindchangers: The art of Christian persuasion*. Wheaton, IL: Tyndale.

33. Pinto, M. B., & Priest, S. (1991). Guilt appeals in advertising: An exploratory study. *Psychological Reports*, 69, 375–385.

34. Brennan, L., & Binney, W. (2010). Fear, guilt and shame appeals in social marketing. *Journal of Business Research*, 63(2), 140–146.

35. Nabi, R., Moyer-Gusé, E., & Byrne, S. (2007). All joking aside: A serious investigation into the persuasive effect of funny social issue messages. *Communication Monographs*, 74(1), 29–54.

36. Valente, T. W., & Saba, W. P. (1998). Mass media and interpersonal influence in a reproductive health communication campaign in Bolivia. *Communication Research*, 25(1), 96–124.

37. McDivitt, J., Zimicki, S., & Hornick, R. C. (1997). Explaining the impact of a communication campaign to change vaccination knowledge and coverage in the Philippines. *Health Communication*, 9(2), 95–118.

38. Korhonen, T., Uutela, A., Korhonen, H. J., & Puska, P. (1998). Impact of mass media and interpersonal health communication on smoking cessation attempts: A study in North Karelia, 1989–1996. *Journal of Health Communication*, 3(2), 105–118.

39. Gallivan, J., Lising, M., Ammary, N. J., & Greenberg, R. (2007). The national diabetes education program's "Control Your Diabetes for Life" campaign: Design, implementation, and lessons learned. *Social Marketing Quarterly*, 13(4), 65–82.

40. Leyden, K. M., Reger-Nash, B., Bauman, A., & Bias, T. (2008). Changing the hearts and minds of policy-makers: An exploratory study associated with the West Virginia Walks campaign. *American Journal of Health Promotion*, 22(3), 204–207.

41. Donohew, L., Palmgreen, P., & Lorch, E. P. (1994). Attention, need for sensation, and health communication campaigns. *American Behavioral Scientist*, 38(2), 310–322.

42. Perloff, R. M. (2001). *Persuading people to have safer sex: Applications of social science to the AIDS crisis*. Mahwah, NJ: Erlbaum.

43. Salmon, C. T., & Atkin, C. (2003). Using media campaigns for health promotion. In T. L. Thompson, A. M. Dorsey, K. I. Miller, & R. Parrott (Eds.), *Handbook of health communication* (pp. 449–472). Mahwah, NJ: Erlbaum.

44. Snyder, L. (2001). How effective are mediated health campaigns? In R. E. Rice & C. K. Atkin (Eds.), *Public communication campaigns*, 3rd ed. (pp. 181–190). Thousand Oaks, CA: Sage.

45. Brown, J., Kotz, D., Michie, S., Stapleton, J., Walmsley, M., & West, R. (2014). How effective and cost-effective was the national mass media smoking cessation campaign, 'Stoptober'? *Drug and Alcohol Dependence*, 135(1), 52–58.

46. Key, W. B. (1973). *Subliminal seduction*. Englewood Cliffs, NJ: Signet; Key, W. B. (1976). *Media Sexploitation*. Englewood Cliffs, NJ: Signet.

47. Pratkanis, A. R. (1992). The cargo-cult science of subliminal persuasion. *Skeptical Inquirer*, 16, 260–272.

48. Cousins, N. (1957, October 5). Smudging the subconscious. *Saturday Review*.

49. Danzig, F. (1962, September 17). Subliminal advertising: Today it's just historic flashback for researcher Vicary. *Advertising Age*.

50. Pratkanis, A. R., & Greenwald, A. G. (1988). Recent perspectives on unconscious processing: Still no marketing applications. *Psychology & Marketing*, 5, 339–355.

51. Pratkanis, A. R. (1992). The cargo-cult science of subliminal persuasion. *Skeptical Inquirer*, 16, 260–272.

52. Epley, N., Savitsky, K., & Kachelski, R. A. (1999). What every skeptic should know about subliminal persuasion. *Skeptical Inquirer*, 23, 40–45.

53. Strahan, E. J., Spencer, S. J., & Zanna, M. P. (2005). Subliminal priming and persuasion: How motivation affects the activation of goals and the persuasiveness of messages. In F. R. Kardes, P. M. Herr & J. Nantel (Eds.), *Applying social cognition to consumer focused strategy* (pp. 267–280). Mahwah, NJ: Erlbaum.

54. Loersch, C., Durso, G. R. O., & Petty, R.E. (2013). Vicissitudes of desire: A matching mechanism for subliminal persuasion. *Social Psychological and Personality Science*, 4(5), 624–631.

55. Shah, D. V., Faber, R. J., & Youn, S. (1999). Susceptibility and severity: Perceptual dimensions underlying the third-person effect. *Communication Research*, 26, 240–267.

56. Paul, B., Salwen, M. B., & Dupagne, M. (2007). The third-person effect: A metaanalysis of the perceptual hypothesis. In R. W. Preiss, B. M. Gayle, N. Burrell, M. Allen, & J. Bryant (Eds.), *Mass media effects research: Advances through meta-analysis* (pp. 81–102). Mahwah, NJ: Erlbaum.

57. Scharrer, E., & Leone, R. (2008). First-person shooters and the third-person effect. *Human Communication Research*, 34(2), 210–233.

58. Wei, R., Lo, V. H., & Lu, H. Y. (2008). Third-person effects of health news: Exploring the relationships among media exposure, presumed media influence, and behavioral intentions. *American Behavioral Scientist*, 52(2), 261–277.

59. Chia, S. C., & Wen, N. (2010). College men's third-person perceptions about idealized body image and consequent behavior. *Sex Roles*, 63(7–8), 542–555.

60. Taylor, L. D., Bell, R. A., & Kravitz, R. L. (2011). Third-person effects and direct-to-consumer advertisements for antidepressants. *Depression and Anxiety*, 28(2), 160–165.

61. Zimbardo, P. G., Ebbesen, E. B., & Maslach, C. (1977). *Influencing attitudes and changing behavior*. Reading, MA: Addison-Wesley.

# 9

---

# The Effects of News and Political Content

## THINKING ABOUT THE NEWS

On March 8, 2014 something very strange happened that captured the interest of the entire world. That was the date that a Malaysia Airlines jumbo jet Flight #370 disappeared from radar during its flight and vanished. I'm writing these words over 70 days later and the plane—along with its 227 passengers and 12 crew—is still missing. Millions of dollars have already been spent searching the floor of the Indian Ocean but so far, there's not a trace. Perhaps by the time you read these words, the world will know what happened to the plane. Time will tell. One thing that's fairly certain is that the news folks at CNN believed that the plane would be found almost immediately after they reported the plane's disappearance. When it wasn't located, CNN's coverage began to focus almost exclusively on the story. The casual viewer who flipped onto CNN at any time of the day or night was greeted for several weeks with the headline "Breaking News" or "Developing Story" related to the missing plane. After a while, the breaking news was that there was no news. While the story is still mentioned each day, CNN has moved on to other stories for its central focus. No news is only news for so long.

By the beginning of May, the story was beginning to fade from the public's consciousness. At about that time, my family celebrated Mother's Day and my wife's two brothers came to town for our usual gathering of food and fun. While I was not surprised at the theme of our family's conversation that weekend, I did recognize that it was rather unusual. Between my wife, Cheri, her brothers, her father, and me, there was nonstop analysis, exchange of opinion, and even argument about what happened to Malaysia Airlines Flight #370. But after spending almost 40 years at family gatherings with Cheri's family, I knew that if the discussion topic hadn't been Malaysia Airlines Flight #370, it would have been something else. When it comes to politics, mysteries, and potential conspiracies, it seems to me that Cheri's family can generate more lines of analysis on a given topic in five minutes than most people can do in five days. Clearly, some people are more highly motivated than others to think about the stories they hear in the news. Perhaps this is because of a particular interest in the news—or perhaps it has something to do with more general individual differences that apply across a variety of different domains.

## Need for Cognition

In the 1950s, Arthur Cohen and his colleagues demonstrated the presence of a psychological variable that they called the **need for cognition**. They conceived of this variable as "a need to structure relevant situations in meaningful, integrated ways ... a need to understand and make reasonable the experimental world."[1] Years later, John Cacioppo and Richard Petty, in their research on attitude change, modified the concept and showed that it was helpful in some studies on media effects. These researchers noted that certain people have a higher need for cognition than others.[2] That is, some people are simply motivated to think a lot. They *enjoy* thinking. Consequently, if there is an opportunity to think about a topic, people with a high need for cognition will be inclined to take it. Study Box 9-1 provides an example of some of the statements used to measure a person's need for cognition when researchers study this concept. With respect to political events, mysterious stories, and conspiracy theories, Cheri's family members are surely among the group of people who would measure high on the need for cognition scale. One media

---

### STUDY BOX 9-1 How Is "Need for Cognition" Measured?

When researchers measure "need for cognition," they typically ask people to indicate the extent to which they agree with different statements such as the ones below. For each statement, a person might indicate agreement with a number on a scale from 1 to 10. A "1" might indicate strong disagreement and a "10" would indicate strong agreement. A "5" might indicate neutrality—neither agreement nor disagreement. Scores on the items are added together and provide a numerical indication of one's general "need for cognition."

1. I usually end up deliberating about issues even when they do not affect me personally.
2. I really enjoy a task that involves coming up with new solutions to problems.
3. I prefer my life to be filled with puzzles that I must solve.
4. I find satisfaction deliberating long and hard for hours.

SOURCE: Ho, S. S., Peh, X., & Soh, V. W. L. (2013). The cognitive mediation model: Factors influencing public knowledge of H1N1 pandemic and intention to take precautionary behaviors. *Journal of Health Communication*, 18, 773–794.
The four items shown were used in this study to measure need for cognition and were adapted from a measure reported in another study: David, C. C. (2009). Learning political information from the news: A closer look at the role of motivation. *Journal of Communication*, 59, 243–261.

scholar, Elizabeth Perse, thought that Cacioppo and Petty's concept might be useful for predicting who pays attention to local television news. In a survey of more than 300 people, she found a statistically significant correlation between need for cognition and attention paid to news about the government.[3] This general finding was replicated in 1992 by Mollie Condra, who found that people with a higher need for cognition were more likely to be interested in media dealing with politics.[4] More recently, in a study of Flemish television viewers, additional evidence emerged for the notion that people with a high need for cognition prefer public television and news programming.[5] In another recent study that involved over 1,000 adults surveyed in Singapore, the authors found that those who had high need for cognition tended to pay closer attention to news stories about the H1N1 flu pandemic. They also tended to think more about the pandemic after their news exposure. In addition, those with high need for cognition tended to talk more with their friends and co-workers about the pandemic.[6]

The need for cognition concept suggests that some people may be more likely to think about a news report and ruminate on it after exposure. But it may suggest even more than that. Being the news junkie that she is, I can often find my wife Cheri watching news shows that feature people who I know she holds in very low regard. She distrusts their motives, often makes fun of them, and tends to be highly skeptical of whatever they report. On more than one occasion, our conversation has gone something like this when I walk into the room while she's watching the news:

CHERI:     Can you believe him? I don't know how he gets away with that stuff. He shouldn't even be allowed on the air.

ME:        You sound like you're pretty upset.

CHERI:     Well, I *am* upset. I mean—just listen to what he's saying. It's enough to upset anyone.

ME:        Well, why don't you just change the channel and watch something else?

CHERI:     Because then I'd miss what he was saying.

This conversation captures the essence of a situation that two researchers, Yariv Tsfati and Joseph Cappella, investigated in a survey of more than 400 people. They were interested in why people watch news that they don't trust.

Data consistently tend to show that regardless of how much people trust or distrust the news, they still watch it. In statistical terms, the correlation between level of trust about the news and levels of consumption are often lower than .20 (see Chapter 2 for a refresher on how to interpret correlations). In short, there are many people like my wife who don't particularly trust certain news shows, yet they continue to watch. Why? One reason seems to be related to need for cognition. Tsfati and Cappella discovered that for people who had high need for cognition, skepticism about the news had little impact on their overall news consumption.[7] Like my wife, these people continue to soak up the news stories even though they may be skeptical or distrust the person delivering the story. Trustworthy or not, the news gives these high-need-for-cognition folks stuff to think about. In contrast, for those who had low need for cognition, skeptical attitudes and distrust were much more of a factor in the decision to consume news. Those who were skeptical about the accuracy of information consumed far less news than those who weren't skeptical. One way to summarize what the data show is that, as you'd expect, people who distrust the news don't consume as much of it—*unless* those people have high need for cognition. In that case, attitudes of skepticism and distrust fall by the wayside and cease to matter. I'm sure that Cheri has a high need for cognition. I also believe that this helps to explain how she is able to continue to sustain deep thought about a news story—even when she's skeptical about its accuracy—when most of the public have nearly forgotten that the story ever existed.

**Need for Cognition and Internet News** Two researchers from South Korea, Eun-Ju Lee and Yoon Jae Jang, recently expanded the research on need for cognition by studying how it affected the process of reading news stories on the Internet. As you probably have noticed, one of the unique features of many Internet news stories is that readers can see more than just the news article—they can also read the comments and opinions of other readers who post their personal reactions. In addition, these online stories will often include a summary of the percentage of readers who have expressed opinions on the subject of the article. In their experiment, Lee and Jang randomly assigned 252 undergraduate students to one of three conditions. Those in the first condition simply read two different Internet stories that were slanted toward specific viewpoints—one of the articles was about animal testing and the other was about regulation of TV content. In a second condition, readers read the same articles but also read seven different individual comments from readers—six of which expressed disagreement with the slant taken in the article. In the third condition, readers read the same articles but instead of the individual comments from readers, they were provided with a statistical summary of the number of readers who either approved or disapproved of the slant taken in the articles. The summary reflected the identical proportion (six out of seven) of individual comments that expressed disagreement in the second experimental condition. For example, for one story in the third condition, readers were told that 48 people disapproved of the slant in the article while eight people approved (six out of every seven people disapproved). Among the many interesting results that were observed in this study, one in particular stands out. In contrast to those high on the need for cognition measure, participants who were low on need for cognition were more likely to express personal views on the issues that were consistent with the views expressed by other readers. The participants who were high on need for cognition were far more likely to express personal views that disagreed with the views of others.[8] Apparently, those high on need for cognition continue to think beyond the views of other people and are more likely to come up with an independent conclusion.

## Political Sophistication

Another concept related to the need for cognition was introduced into the communication literature by June Rhee and Joseph Cappella.[9] These authors were interested in trying to explain why some news viewers come away from a story having learned very little information while other viewers have learned quite a bit. Working in the realm of politics, these authors developed the concept of **political sophistication**. One's level of political sophistication is a function of knowledge and political ideology. A person who knows very little and doesn't have a well-developed political ideology has a low level of sophistication. In contrast, a person who knows a great deal and has definite political views has a high level of sophistication. Rhee and Cappella found that after exposure to news stories about healthcare reform and a mayoral election campaign, those viewers who were politically sophisticated had learned more and had higher quality arguments about the issues when they were given a chance to write about their own views.

The studies that link need for cognition with a preference for viewing news seem to suggest that the news media may naturally tend to appeal to those with a disposition to think about ideas, concepts, or implications. The research on political sophistication seems to suggest the same kind of news effect on certain individuals. But is there any hard evidence that exposure to news in the media has a definite impact on what people are actually thinking? For the answer to that question, we need to look no farther than the theory and research associated with the notion of agenda setting that was introduced years ago by two journalism professors, Maxwell McCombs and Donald Shaw.[10]

## Agenda-Setting Theory: A Theory about Thinking

For years, the **agenda-setting theory** of the press has been summarized succinctly in a single quotation from political scientist Bernard Cohen: "The press may not be successful much of the time in telling people *what to think,* but it is stunningly successful in telling its readers *what to think about.*"[11] The idea here is that the news media set the public agenda. Their coverage of issues helps to define for the public what they should be thinking about on a given day. As you read these words, the chances are good that you have heard or read at least one reference to the possibility that climate change may pose a variety of problems for the way people live in the coming years. The extreme winter of 2014 drove some of the news coverage but as winter ended, the extreme drought in the western United States and the early fire season in California kept stories about the climate in a prominent position. The theory of agenda setting would predict that if a survey of public opinion had been taken during the past few months, the problem of climate change would emerge as a serious concern. A core notion in the theory of agenda setting is that public opinion about what should be an important concern is heavily influenced by the topics and issues that appear in the news. News coverage may not determine exactly what position people take on a given issue, but it helps to guarantee that the issue is considered to be an important one. Is there any evidence to suggest that this might be true?

The theory of agenda setting has by now spawned many individual research studies that support the basic idea of media influence. McCombs and Shaw first sought to test the theory in the context of the 1968 presidential campaign (Richard

Nixon versus Hubert Humphrey). Their study included an exhaustive analysis of the media agenda that included four newspapers from North Carolina, *Time* and *Newsweek*, CBS and NBC television news, and *The New York Times*.[12] According to the results, the five issues given the most prominent coverage by the press were foreign policy, law and order, fiscal policy, public welfare, and civil rights. When McCombs and Shaw asked voters to identify the key issue of the campaign, quite apart from their perceptions of what the candidates had been saying, there was a remarkable convergence with the issues that emerged from the media analysis. Indeed, just as the theory predicted, the media agenda and the public agenda tended to correspond.

Of course, the mere fact that the media's agenda corresponded with the public's agenda does not really provide the most powerful evidence in favor of agenda-setting theory. Recall from Chapter 2 that to establish a causal relationship between two variables, it isn't sufficient simply to establish a relationship between them. It is also important to establish that the causal variable precedes the other in time. Researchers who study agenda setting are most interested in documenting that the media agenda actually precedes the public agenda. Is there any evidence that it does?

In one of the experimental tests of the theory, Shanto Iyengar and Donald Kinder studied this question by exposing people to one of three different presentations of the news over a four-day period.[13] The presentations differed according to the topic of one of the stories placed in the newscast on each day. For one group, the topic focused on pollution. For the second group, it focused on national defense. For the third group, the story dealt with inflation. After the four days of exposure, the researchers found that the experimental groups expressed greater concern about the issue that had been featured in their respective newscast.

The research by Iyengar and Kinder should remind you of some of the research covered in Chapter 8. Recall the "great American values test" in which the researchers used a TV program to heighten viewers' awareness of certain values. Not only did the program succeed in changing the priority that viewers assigned to those values, it also triggered a number of behavioral changes. Although the show wasn't a news program in the strict sense and clearly had a persuasive edge, you might wonder if a continued focus on particular issues in the news could do more than just set the agenda about what topics people think about. Couldn't the news also have an impact on what people actually think about those topics?

## Framing the News

In a revision of the agenda-setting theory, McCombs and Shaw believe that the answer to this question is a distinct yes. How do the media do this if they are not intentionally trying to persuade consumers? The answer may be found in a concept known as **framing**. As James Tankard defines this term, framing is "the central organizing idea for news content that supplies a context and suggests what the issue is through the use of *selection, emphasis, exclusion,* and *elaboration*" [emphasis in the original].[14]

One of my favorite parts of the local newspaper in the wintertime is the coverage of the aftermath of a big snowstorm. Consider how the media might frame such news coverage. In the wake of a huge snowfall, the news could concentrate on winter recreation and the fun that children in the area have playing with snowballs and sledding down steep hills. On the other hand, the media could focus on how slowly snow removal is progressing and attempt to track down local government officials to comment on the problem. Depending on which way the story of the snowstorm is framed, consumers may have different thoughts as a result of reading the news. Traditionally, this effect might be described in the standard agenda-setting terminology: "The media don't tell us what to think, they tell us what to think about." But a closer inspection of what goes on here suggests that there is more to it. By framing the story in terms of poor snow removal instead of recreational activities, the media are doing more than just telling us *what to think about.* In a very real way, they are telling us *what to think* by focusing attention on one particular angle of the story. I can remember years ago when I lived in the Chicago area, the city changed mayors because of what many perceived as the failure of the administration to set up adequate snow removal. The press helped to frame the poor snow removal as a major failure in planning, and the public apparently accepted the frame. As McCombs has recently suggested, "the media may not only tell us what to think about, they may also tell us how and what to think about it, and perhaps even what to do about it."[15] In the case of the Chicago snowstorm, the people may have voted out one mayor and voted in another, in part, because of the media framing of the event.

If framing news about snowstorms can have important political consequences, what about news framing of even more important topics—like war? Have you even wondered whether news stories about a war were very different depending upon the news organization covering the story? Two researchers asked that question about the war in Iraq in March and April of 2003. They compared the TV news coverage coming out of five different countries—including the news from ABC, NBC, and CBS in the United States as well as the Al-Jazeera network in Qatar. Their study was a content analysis (see Chapter 2 for a review) of thousands of statements and pictures that the news organizations produced. Perhaps not surprisingly, the study found that over 55% of the news content from U.S. networks depicted Iraqis in a negative way. In Germany, the United Kingdom, and the Czech Republic, only about 25% of the news depicted Iraqis in a negative way. Al-Jazeera had only about 10% of its coverage of Iraqis coded as negative. Although a content analysis isn't capable of documenting any effects of the content, the authors concluded their report by saying that:

> These findings suggest that the reporting of the war was conditioned by the national political contexts in which it was produced. The cross-country comparisons raise serious questions about the credibility and impartiality of TV news in the reporting of the war. (p. 654)[16]

As Em Griffin concludes in his discussion of agenda setting and framing, "McCombs and Shaw have established a plausible case that some people look to print and broadcast news for guidance on which issues are really important. Agenda-setting theory also provides a needed reminder that news stories are just that—stories. The message always requires interpretation."[17] In the end, the way a story is framed by the media can have great impact on the interpretations that people carry away from the message.

The theory of agenda setting is currently recognized as one of the tried-and-true theoretical contributions to the literature in mass communication. It continues to spawn new research projects on a variety of topics. In a longitudinal study of agenda setting reported by Spiro Kiousis, news coverage of the sex scandal during Bill Clinton's presidency was linked to changing interpretations of President Clinton. Depending upon how old you are and how much you remember about Clinton's presidency, you may not be familiar with Clinton's affair with White House Intern Monica Lewinsky that threatened to undo his presidency. The news coverage of the scandal tended to lead to increases in favorability toward Clinton while simultaneously leading to decreases in his job approval rating.[18] In another study, based on a random-digit-dialing telephone survey in Washington, D.C., Kimberly Gross and Sean Aday discovered that people who watched TV news were much more likely to have higher estimates than people who didn't watch TV news of the importance of local crime. Apparently, the preoccupation with crime in local news reports helped to set a public agenda about this issue's overall importance.[19] The most recent research also tends to support an agenda-setting effect on the Internet. When researchers tracked discussions on electronic bulletin boards, the topics discussed corresponded with the topics that had appeared days earlier in the news.[20] Some researchers have argued that the new media environment is relatively free of the formal gate-keeping structures of the old media.[21] That is, political information is now available from a nearly limitless number of sources when one considers the Internet. If this is true, perhaps strong agenda-setting effects might be more difficult to find. Some evidence consistent with this notion was reported by Scott Althaus and David Tewksbury in an experiment with print and online versions of *The New York Times*.[22] Students were assigned to read either a print version or an online version of the newspaper every day for five days. The researchers discovered that the readers of the traditional print version of the paper were more likely to recall the content of what they had read and were also more likely to assign personal importance to the issues that were heavily featured in the newspaper. Perhaps the ability to navigate away from an online story and explore a side link diminishes the time spent with the main news story. But with the rise of Internet news sources and increasing amounts of time consumers spend on these sites, this may be the new pattern of news consumption. Although the data from future studies will tell the tale as to the validity of these ideas, it certainly appears as if the theory of agenda setting is alive and well in the first decade of the twenty-first century. In a recent meta-analysis that included nearly 100 studies on agenda setting, Wayne Wanta and Salma Ghanem concluded that the agenda-setting influence of the news media is "wide ranging"— yielding significant effects across different types of studies using different methodologies. It doesn't seem to matter whether the "agenda" in these studies consists of a single issue or multiple issues—the agenda-setting effect is still quite evident.[23] In support of this conclusion is another recent study that found clear evidence in favor of agenda setting that resulted in more people visiting certain museums. Highly visible museums—as measured by the number of times they were mentioned in newspapers—were much more likely to be visited the month after they were mentioned in the news than were museums that weren't mentioned as frequently.[24]

Based on the results of one recent study, not only can newspaper coverage cause visits to museums to increase—it can also cause an increase in visits to the doctor. Craig Trumbo, a researcher at Colorado State University, wanted to see if news stories about the spread of the flu virus resulted in more people actually visiting the doctor with flu-like symptoms.[25] Using agenda-setting theory, he expected that reports of flu in the newspaper would elevate concern about the flu—which, in turn, would cause more people to visit their doctor when they felt sick. Trumbo examined newspaper coverage in 32 large metropolitan newspapers between 2002 and 2008 and found over 7,000 stories about the flu. Using data from the Centers for Disease Control, which tracks statistics on doctor visits for flu-like symptoms, Trumbo was able to establish a clear pattern. Using a sophisticated statistical analysis, he was able to take account of the real prevalence of the flu virus in each of the six flu seasons included in his study. Regardless of the seriousness of an outbreak, he found that newspaper stories about the flu were associated with increased doctor visits due to flu-like symptoms. Trumbo recognized the key issue in doing this kind of research on agenda-setting: correlation is not causality. Using a technique known as **time-series analysis**, Trumbo was careful to test whether increased doctor visits led to increased news coverage or whether the news coverage led to more doctor visits. The clear verdict from his analysis was in favor of agenda-setting. The news coverage was followed by increases in doctor visits—evidence that the media had set a behavioral agenda. There was no evidence for the reverse direction of causality. Increases in doctor visits for the flu did not lead to more news coverage about a flu epidemic.

## The Spiral of Silence

Visiting museums and going to the doctor with flu symptoms are not very controversial behaviors. The last time I took my grandson, Caleb, to the Chicago Aquarium, I had the sense that I was doing something that most people would do if they had the opportunity. I had no feeling that I was going against the grain of popular opinion by spending a day looking at fish. But let's suppose that based on my impression of news coverage, I concluded that a position I held was distinctly out of step with the mainstream and few people shared my position? How would I react? One media theorist, Elisabeth Noelle-Neumann, believes that the media's impact on the interpretations that people carry away from a story can have a dramatic effect on the entire course of public opinion in the culture.[26] Her **spiral of silence** theory is based on the idea that most of us don't feel comfortable speaking out about our views if we perceive that we are in the minority. If we think that our view is really the minority view, we would rather keep quiet than risk being isolated or rejected by those to whom we wish to feel attached. This **fear of isolation** is an important motivating factor in an individual's decision to be quiet. The process can eventually gather steam and spiral into a relative silence when it comes to certain minority views. That is, the more often people who feel as if they are in the minority decide not to speak their views, the less we hear those views, and the more we tend to believe that most people agree with the majority viewpoint. According to Neumann, this process can lead to views that eventually die out and exert little influence, even though they are actually held by substantial numbers of people. Once those large numbers of people get the impression that their views are not widely shared, they stop talking, and this reinforces the notion that their views are *not* widely shared. And so on. According to Neumann, this process is particularly likely to happen when the issue in question is a moral one. People who don't share the majority view on such issues don't want others to think of them as "bad" people because they hold the "wrong" position on something of moral importance.

Sei-Hill Kim, a communication researcher, recently studied the spiral of silence process in South Korea in the context of people's willingness to share their views on genetically modified food. The study supported Neumann's contention that fear of isolation was a significant factor in the process. Kim found that those who tended to express higher levels of fear of isolation were the least likely people to share their views on genetically modified food. The data also revealed that those with high levels of fear of isolation were more likely to be influenced by the opinions of others.[27]

The role of the news media in this spiral of silence can be quite dramatic. To the extent that people tune in to TV news and perceive that most people hold a particular opinion or viewpoint on a given issue, the spiral of silence can be off and running. Media researchers William Eveland, Douglas McLeod, and Nancy Signorielli found evidence supporting the spiral of silence theory when they conducted a sample survey on attitudes toward the Gulf War in 1991.[28] In contrast to the strong consensus in favor of the war that the news media reported, the survey revealed that very few people actually expressed strong support in their answers to the questions. In fact, whereas less than 7% of the respondents expressed strong support for the war, more than half of the respondents expressed neutrality, disagreement, or strong disagreement. When the researchers examined how the supporters differed from the non-supporters, they found that their perception of public opinion was a key variable. The people who tended to express the strongest support for the war were those who thought that public opinion was running in that direction. The people who were most willing to express neutrality or disagreement were those who thought that public opinion was mixed or was, at least, not so strongly in favor of the war. This close link between how people perceive public opinion and the attitudes they are willing to express is a fundamental prediction of the spiral of silence. The fact that media coverage of the war was decidedly distorted in favor of support may have contributed to the unwillingness of many to speak out publicly against the war effort. After people watched the news coverage, they carried away an interpretation of the events that suggested that public opinion was heavily in favor of what the United States was doing.

More recent evidence on the spiral of silence suggests that the effect cuts across decades of research. Dan McDonald and his colleagues went back to an old, but infamous, set of data collected during the presidential campaign of 1948 (recall the People's Choice study discussed in Chapter 3). When they analyzed that data, they found evidence for a spiral of silence effect.[29] Today, most researchers acknowledge that the spiral of silence is more than just a theoretical idea. It also has some empirical teeth. However, the strength of those teeth is still a matter of some controversy.

First, in the wake of many studies on the spiral of silence—some of which offer support for the theory—Noelle-Neumann has suggested that much of the research has actually misinterpreted what the theory really says. At issue seems to be the assumption implicit in many of the studies that people are able to *consciously* detect and talk about the ebb and flow of public opinion and clearly articulate a view about which opinion is dominant and which is in the minority. A standard procedure in the research is to explicitly ask people if they hold the majority view, or to estimate the percentage of the population that holds a particular position. According to Neumann, this procedure is inconsistent with the theory. She maintains that the perceptions that people have of whether their personal views are gaining or losing ground in the public arena is a perception that takes place *unconsciously*. People may keep quiet in the public arena once they've made these unconscious perceptions—even if they report to researchers that they believe their views are widely shared.[30] What counts, according to Neumann, is the objective *fact* about which view is on the rise or on the wane in the arena of public discourse. This position suggests that rather than asking people for their conscious perceptions about the popularity of different views, researchers need to incorporate objective barometers of those views into their studies. Neumann's assertion that people perceive the popularity of different views through an unconscious process may seem curious. How is it that these unconscious perceptions can lead to the concrete behavior of remaining quiet (a behavior that seems to be in the realm of conscious self-awareness and self-perception)—yet these same unconscious perceptions simultaneously fail in the research studies to produce valid self-reports of perceptions about public opinion? Based on the current literature, the answer to that question doesn't seem obvious.

A second point to make here is that the overall empirical support for the spiral of silence idea may not be particularly overwhelming. Some scholars concluded that the body of evidence based on survey studies "was not very convincing."[31] One improvement that some scholars offer for future research is to change the measure of how willing a person is to speak up about his/her opinion of a given issue. Often, past research has relied on the **train test** as a valid measure of this variable. Respondents are asked to imagine that they are on a train ride and are seated with a person who holds a view on some issue that is very different from their own. Then they are asked to indicate how likely they would be to articulate their view on the issue to this hypothetical stranger. A better measure might be one that actually measures real behavior instead of reports of hypothetical behavior. Most recently, a team of communication scholars collected some data that seems to indicate that the spiral of silence process doesn't apply to everyone.[32] For people who are highly certain about their views on an issue, perceptions of the majority opinion don't matter in terms of their willingness to express those views. They'll tell anyone how they feel at any time even if they know that their view represents a small minority. Some of my family members might serve as a good example when they shared their belief that Malaysia Airlines Flight #370 probably didn't crash in the ocean. In contrast, people who are less certain about their viewpoints may be those most likely to fall silent when they think their views are out of step with the majority.

One last thought about the spiral of silence theory has to do with the explicit role assigned to media. The role of media in the theory is often presumed to be uniform and unambiguous. The audience presumably tunes into the media and receives a message that permits clear inferences about public opinion. Rarely are distinctions made between different media audiences. How do people who watch all of their news on MSNBC differ in their perceptions of the majority opinion when compared to people who watch all of their news on FOX? What about people who rely on their Facebook network or their contacts in the Twittersphere for most of their news? Do those media habits affect perceptions of the opinions held by the majority? At least one researcher has suggested recently that people who consume their news in the online environment may tend to perceive that the opinion climate is consistent with their own views—thus reducing fear of isolation and encouraging opinion expression.[33] Clearly, there may be different spiral of silence processes taking place simultaneously—depending on where one consumes their news. Despite these limitations, the spiral of silence theory continues to generate significant research about how media coverage of issues might affect public opinion.

## How Much of the News Do We Remember?

With a story like the missing Malaysian airliner that appeared day after day for months, the public gradually comes up to speed on the basic facts and begins to comprehend and commit to memory certain details. When we speak of people "carrying away" an interpretation of a message that has been framed in a particular way, we are talking about memory. The question that is raised here has to do with how well people typically remember the information that they are exposed to in a newscast. As it turns out, the answer may be different depending on the nature of the newscast and how many times a person hears the story. In most cases, unlike coverage relating to the missing Malaysian flight, we are exposed to a story just a single time.

A few years ago, I was contacted by an attorney who wanted me to provide an expert opinion on a legal matter that arose out of a TV newscast. Her client, a TV station, had recently broadcast a story that clearly identified by name a young man who was in his late twenties. According to the report, which relied heavily on information provided by the local law enforcement authorities, the man had gone to a suburban home, knocked on the door, and shot the young teenager who answered the door in the stomach. A day or two later, law enforcement authorities discovered that the man had an airtight alibi and could not possibly have been at the boy's home at the time the crime occurred. The young teenager who had been shot also confessed that he had lied about the incident. As it turned out, he was a disturbed young boy who, in fact, had turned a gun on himself. In the aftermath, the man who had been identified in the TV news story filed a lawsuit against the TV station, charging that they had libeled his good name. The case was settled out of court and never went to trial. But if it had, I might have been called to give an opinion about the extent to which the man who sued the TV station had really been injured by the news report. Two of the issues that would have entered into my analysis would have been the extent to which people comprehend the news they are exposed to in an average newscast and the extent to which they retain information or remember it after the newscast is over. What does the research reveal about these two issues?

Two researchers, John Robinson and Dennis Davis, provided some insights on these issues in their article "Comprehension of a Single Evening's News."[34] In tracking the responses of a group of people who watched the evening news on one particular night, the authors used an eight-point coding scheme to assess how well the news was recalled. If a viewer's recall was rated as a 0, it indicated recall of the wrong story or information that was not even contained in the newscast. Inability to recall a story, no reply, or a "don't know" response rated a 1. On the other end of the scale, a 7 indicated recall of the central point of the story plus two additional important details. Recall of the central point plus three or more additional details rated an 8. After coding the data, the researchers noted that, on average, viewer response to stories fell between 2 and 3 on the eight-point scale. Viewers who could "recall something but then can give no details" from the specific news broadcast were rated at 2. Viewers who could provide only "vague, general responses related to the story" were given a 3.

If these results surprise you, think about the way most people probably watch the news. Only rarely do people give their undivided attention to the TV screen during a newscast. The news usually comes into the home amid a host of daily activities that might include meal preparation, conversations with family members, and other routine tasks. People are more likely to monitor the news audio and engage in the well-documented practice of selective exposure to news material. The principle of **selective exposure** emphasizes that people come to any communication message with their own attitudes, interests, beliefs, and values (see Chapter 3). These attitudes and interests help to guide attention to particular messages. If a person is especially interested in the news story, attention will be high. But if a story is perceived as uninteresting, a person will be more inclined to tune out. During an average newscast, a person's attention may fluctuate from low to high and back to low many times as the stories change. Many news stories are simply not attended to very well because viewers find them to be irrelevant, uninteresting, or too demanding in terms of the effort required to comprehend fully the major points. Consistent with this point of view, Hans Kepplinger and Gregor Daschmann recently presented a model for how people process news content. In summarizing their understanding on this topic, they stated: "… much information is avoided, much is misunderstood, and only some is adequately retained."[35]

If I had been called on to give testimony about the man who was concerned about his reputation after the TV news broadcast his name as a potential gunman, I might have pointed out that, in light of what we know from research on news, the chances are high that most of the viewers probably didn't even remember the alleged gunman's name. If this were the case, his reputation might not have been damaged to nearly the extent that he thought it was. On the other hand, a news story about a shooting incident might be a story of greater than average interest. It also might have an unusual emotional impact on local viewers. In this type of situation, sorting out the effects of the messages on comprehension can be pretty difficult. Researchers have only begun to discover how emotions, vivid images, and standard news content might mix together to produce different results in terms of overall comprehension.

John Newhagen and Byron Reeves attempted to study how vivid or intense images might affect what people remember from a news story. Their findings were intriguing. When they asked people to recall news topics and facts from the news stories six weeks after exposure to a newscast, the researchers found that people were able to recall the facts and topics better if they had been presented without a vivid visual. However, when vivid visuals were included, people definitely remembered the visuals.[36] These results support a type of **dual-coding theory** of news content. Images might be processed differently than verbal information. When a vivid image is presented alongside verbal information, it might actually tend to distract people from processing the verbal information efficiently. On the other hand, the vivid images themselves prove to be highly memorable and might even enhance memory for the information that comes right after the images appear.

There is probably some practical wisdom that news directors can glean from these results. If, for example, a station wants to give verbal instructions about how to avoid being killed in a tornado, it probably wouldn't be a good idea to show dramatic video footage of a tornado destroying buildings at the same time the instructions are being given. Newhagen and Reeves's results indicate that tornado footage offered at the same time as instructions might actually prevent effective processing of the instructions. However, it might be a good idea to catch viewers' attention with the tornado footage and then, after it was over, immediately follow up with the verbal instructions for safety. Recent research with children conducted by Barrie Gunter and his associates also found evidence for dual coding of news. Children learned more information from television news than they did from print or audio versions of the same material. However, this advantage was only found when the pictures on TV were completely redundant with the verbal information in the news story.[37] The impact of pictures and words has also been studied in the context of newspapers. Results from a recent experiment show that photographs can actually change what people think they read. For example, in a story about a hurricane, some readers saw a picture of a village prior to the hurricane's arrival; other readers saw a picture of the same village after the hurricane had blown through. Neither story included any mention of physical injuries or death due to the storm. Nevertheless, those who read the story with the picture of the aftermath of the hurricane were more than three times likely to say that they specifically remembered reading details about physical injury and death.[38]

**Do Sexually Attractive TV Anchor Women Cause Better Memory for the News?** Maria Grabe, a professor at Indiana University, and a graduate student, Lelia Samson, decided to focus their research on a fascinating question that has practical implications for TV news consumption. Does the source of the news story make any difference in how well the news content is remembered? Specifically, suppose you sat down to watch the news and found yourself watching a female reporter who wore a tight, figure-flattering dress, lipstick, and a necklace? Would you remember more or less of the news she delivered if she wore, instead, a loose fitting, formless dress, no lipstick, and no necklace? Grabe and Samson decided to find out by carrying out an experiment.[39] They had the same female newscaster deliver five short news stories that were shown to both males and females who were randomly assigned to watch one of two versions of the news report. The only difference in the two versions was the newscaster's physical appearance that varied according to dress, lipstick, and necklace just as I described. What did the research reveal?

First, a group of viewers who watched both versions of the newscast side-by-side with the sound off answered the same questions about each version of the video. The newscaster wearing the tight dress, lipstick, and necklace was rated sexier by general standards, more feminine, more attractive, and more likely to receive a date invitation from a heterosexual male. Second, Grabe and Samson were interested in how these differences affected the processing of the news. They summarized their results by stating that:

> Men paid attention to the visual appearance of the sexualized anchor to the detriment of encoding the news information she delivered. When the sexual cues were absent, men performed better on recognition memory for news facts and showed fairly poor encoding of visual information about her appearance. On the other hand, sexual cues prompted women to encode more news content whereas they maintained relatively high levels of visual encoding across the two grooming versions. (p. 489)

Grabe and Samson were careful to note that the effects they found in this experiment need to be replicated in additional studies with different news anchors and different news stories. Until that research is carried out, this study provides a strong case that memory for news content depends upon the physical appearance of the newscaster as well as the gender of the news consumer.

## THE ROLE OF EMOTION

One reason vivid images may tend to be memorable is that they evoke more intense emotional reactions than spoken words or plain written text. Of course, there may be exceptions to this rule. If you were highly involved with a particular issue, mere words in the newspaper or words spoken by a newscaster might be more than enough to set your emotions stirring. Generally speaking, however, vivid images have a more direct pathway to the emotions. John Newhagen recently reported new research from his program of studies on emotional media images. Using news images, he found that those that provoked anger in viewers were the most memorable, followed by images that induced fear. Finally, people had the worst memory for images that they had found to be disgusting. Newhagen pointed out that these findings may have practical implications for the way news stories are put together.

He stated, "[P]roducers can use such images to first draw attention to a story, and then insert information they think viewers will want to remember right after them. Images that elicit disgust, on the other hand, inhibit memory late in the stories" (pp. 274–275).[40] Another recent study completely confirms Newhagen's findings: when consumers find a news image to be disgusting, this interferes with the overall depth of processing devoted to the story.[41]

The research on emotional news images and memory is becoming a well-developed literature. Newhagen's research findings are not the only ones that point to the memory-enhancing effects of some types of negative news stories. In a study reported by Annie Lang, John Newhagen, and Byron Reeves, negative news stories increased memory for news items.[42] Lang and her co-authors speculated that the primary function of negative news video might be to heighten the overall emotional impact of a story. The greater impact of the story shows up in a person as increased physiological arousal. That arousal results in increased memory. When I first began writing this section of the chapter for an earlier edition of the text, the news media all across the state of Indiana as well as the CNN Headline news were replaying the last lap of the 2001 Daytona 500 NASCAR race. Even if you're not a race fan, you may still know what happened in this fateful contest. Racing star Dale Earnhardt Sr. was killed instantly when he crashed into a wall at 180 miles per hour. The news footage of this crash was dramatic and highly emotional. I am certain that if I had been wired to sensors monitoring my physiological state, I would have shown clear signs of arousal upon watching the tragic crash footage. Thanks to new video technology, viewers were actually able to see what the crash looked like from Earnhardt's perspective from inside his car. According to the research findings, my heightened physiological response was probably typical. People who watched this coverage were probably likely to remember the news material that was reported during the video footage and directly following it.

You may have noticed that instead of avoiding news stories that feature violent events and images, the news media provide us with a steady stream of this sort of content. One study showed that violent news stories are most likely to trigger reactions of anger and contempt instead of sadness, fear, or empathy for victims.[43] When these findings are combined with the findings of Lang and Newhagen, it would seem to suggest that in terms of overall impact on news viewers, the industry practice according to the slogan, "if it bleeds—it leads," may hold some practical wisdom. Violent news images may induce physiological arousal and anger—emotions that help to guarantee that viewers become involved in stories and recall them better.

Nowhere is the role of emotion in news more important than in politics. One of the first demonstrations of the potential role of emotion from TV images in politics came from the first presidential debates between the Republican candidate, Richard Nixon, and the Democratic candidate, John Kennedy, in the 1960 election. Even though 90% of Americans had a TV set in 1960, radio was still a popular medium for political news. Many people listened to the debates on the radio instead of watching them on TV. According to Sid Kraus, who may be the only communication researcher who has been in attendance at every presidential debate since they began in 1960, the people who listened to the debates on radio were more inclined to perceive Nixon as the winner, while those who watched the debates on TV thought that Kennedy had the upper hand. Although the integrity of the supporting data for this conclusion has been debated through the past few decades, Kraus concludes after his exhaustive review of the data that "[M]y own observation on the night of the debate in 1960, and my consultations with scholars conducting debate research at that time, convinced me that the finding was a credible one."[44] In support of Kraus's conclusion, the following excerpt from *Broadcasting* magazine, a leading trade journal in the broadcasting industry, states the finding clearly: "In answer to the question who won the debates, 48.7% of the radio audience named Mr. Nixon and only 21% picked Mr. Kennedy. Among those who watched the debates on TV, 30.2% named Mr. Kennedy the winner and 28.6% picked Mr. Nixon."[45] Since the TV audience was so much larger than the radio audience, the advantage that Kennedy had on TV presumably meant a narrow victory. There is also another very recent source of support for Kraus's conclusion on this debate. In an experiment reported by James Druckman, subjects in the United Kingdom, who knew nothing of the history of the Kennedy–Nixon debates, were randomly assigned to either watch the debate on TV or listen to an audio version.[46] Druckman's conclusions about the impact of the television images are completely consistent with Kraus's conclusions that viewers who watched the debate were more likely to conclude that Kennedy won, whereas viewers who heard the debate were more likely to conclude that Nixon won.

The fact that TV images of political debaters may exert greater influence on voters than the actual words spoken has been reinforced by more recent research by Michael Pfau and Jong Kang. These authors emphasized that on TV, political candidates with a "softer, warmer communication, similar to communication in an interpersonal context" will be more influential among the voters.[47] One of the first political ads that demonstrated how images may be more powerful than words was the now infamous "Daisy Girl" commercial designed by the late advertising genius Tony Schwartz, for Lyndon Johnson's 1964 presidential campaign against Barry Goldwater. Schwartz's obituary recently appeared in virtually all the nation's leading newspapers and the Daisy Girl spot was prominently featured in each description of Schwartz's career—even though it was just one spot among thousands that he had made.[48] The ad began by showing a young girl picking petals from a daisy and counting (incorrectly) from 1 to 10. When she reached the number 10, the camera slowly zoomed in on the child's eye and then farther into the pupil of the eye as a cold, military-sounding voice began a countdown from 10 to 1. The pupil of the girl's eye became transformed into a window where the viewer saw a nuclear explosion. As the screen went black, an announcer's voice said, "These are the stakes, to make a world in which all God's children can live, or to go into the darkness. Either we must love each other or we must die."[49] The ad aired only one time, but it caused a national discussion about political advertising techniques. Most political analysts agree that it virtually ended Barry Goldwater's campaign without even mentioning him by name. Schwartz believed that the ad used powerful images to connect to the deep-seated emotions that people had about nuclear war. By surfacing the fears associated with the possibility that Goldwater might actually be inclined to use nuclear weapons to settle global conflict, the ad drove people to vote for Johnson in packs. In a documentary on political advertising made for public television, news commentator Bill Moyers complained that he found it troubling to note that Johnson was portrayed as the peacemaker in the 1964 election and Goldwater as the warmonger.[50] This image was effectively exploited with the Daisy Girl commercial. But, Moyers noted, it was Johnson who committed the country to the bloody conflict in Vietnam that we eventually lost. Not a single spot, according to Moyers' recollection, even touched on the Vietnam issue in 1964. The Daisy Girl ad may have been a triumph of image over issue, pictures over words, and emotions over deeper thinking. Study Box 9-2 focuses on the advertising philosophy of Tony Schwartz, considered by some to be a modern-day media guru. The fact that I have chosen to introduce Schwartz in this chapter and feature some of his ideas reveals the high regard I have for his professional insights about media. My hunch is that when Schwartz passed away in June 2008, the world lost a person who understood the working dynamics of mass media better than a barrelful of media scholars.

### STUDY BOX 9-2 Who Is Tony Schwartz?

Tony Schwartz used electronic media to influence the political process for several decades until his death in 2008. He worked for countless candidates and created public service campaigns for police departments, fire departments, the American Cancer Society, and many other organizations. He also did numerous product campaigns. Schwartz believed that many people who use the media to influence others have a poor understanding of how media work. Here, I have listed some of the key principles that Schwartz relied on when he worked on a political campaign.

1. **Use PRE-search—not research.** Schwartz believed that most politicians create campaign material and then test the effects of that material before they decide to put it on the air. This, according to him, is totally backward. He didn't test ad material. Instead, *before* he created an ad, he conducted research to find out what people were thinking and feeling about the candidates in a campaign. Once he knew their feelings, he could design media that tap into those feelings easily. He felt no need to test his commercials. When his pre-search in the 1968 presidential campaign revealed that many people thought that the idea of Spiro Agnew as a vice presidential candidate was a joke, Schwartz made an ad that consisted of little more than a voice laughing in the background while viewing Agnew's name on a TV screen.
2. **Create "resonance" between the message and the audience.** Schwartz was a big believer in the notion that the audience has a lot to say about whether or not it is influenced by a message. The goal of a campaign message, he said, was to resonate with voters' inner feelings. A good campaign ad will take advantage of these feelings, stir them up, and then use them ever so gently to nudge the receiver in the desired direction. Schwartz was no fan of "hard-sell" advertising. He preferred the term *deep sell*. The Daisy Girl ad discussed in this chapter is a good example.
3. **Use the audience as "workforce," not as a target.** Many practitioners of advertising treat the audience as a target. They just throw information at the receiver as if they

were throwing darts at a dartboard. Schwartz rejected this practice. For him, the feelings and information that existed in the hearts and minds of the audience were the most powerful forces that he had at his disposal. If he could draw those feelings out, then the audience began to work for his cause. They became his "workforce." In Schwartz's view, the goal of any commercial was not to put information inside of the audience. Instead, he tried to use commercials to draw information out of the audience. One way he knew what was inside of the audience was from news reports. If a jumbo jet crashed and killed hundreds of people, he might create a spot that asked people to think of that tragedy. Then he would follow by asking people to think about the fact that tobacco use annually kills the equivalent of three fully loaded jumbo jets going down each day.

Even though the Daisy Girl commercial never mentioned Goldwater's name, some analysts labeled it as an example of negative advertising because it implied that Goldwater was comfortable with the possibility of blowing up little girls. Since that time, there have been a number of studies on the effects of negative campaign ads. One of the main questions surrounding this type of political advertising is whether they backfire and essentially turn the public off completely so that they don't even vote. Some recent research seems to suggest that attack ads may lead consumers to conclude that politics is too complicated, and individuals can't really make a difference.[51] But two other studies suggest that while consumers often become disgusted with campaigns that feature negative ads, it is difficult to find evidence that the negative advertising actually leads to either voter apathy or decreases in voter turnout.[52]

## Is News on Twitter Packed with More Emotion?

According to a recent report by the Pew Research Center (see Study Box 9-3), the way news is consumed is changing rapidly.[53] More and more people report that they trust traditional news outlets less than they used to and they consume more and more of their news on the Internet and on social media platforms. The report specifically mentions that Twitter serves as a crucial information source in major emergencies. This fact was confirmed recently by two researchers, Zizi Papacharissi and Maria de Fatima Oliveira, who studied the Twitter traffic in January and February of 2011 that related to the political upheaval in Egypt.[54] They were able to collect and analyze over a million individual messages about the political crisis. The findings revealed that many of the messages conformed to traditional news values. The researchers noted, "...Twitter streams tended to revolve around larger scale events, in proximate locations, were intent on providing clarity and accuracy, prioritized more recent events, were reflective of drama and action, and associated specific persons with aspects of a story" (p. 272). However, in addition to including features of traditional news reports, the Twitter posts differed from traditional news reports in significant ways. One major characteristic as described by the researchers was that "Tweets blended emotion with opinion, and drama with fact, reflecting deeply subjective accounts of interpretations and events, as they unfolded" (p. 277). If the news on Twitter, at least in emergency situations, carries more of an emotional and dramatic punch than conventional news, could this be one of the ingredients that is fueling the increase in news consumption on social media platforms? Is it possible that social media is conditioning consumers to prefer news with a higher level of emotional involvement than has typically been present in traditional news presentations? These may be some of the questions that future research will address.

---

### STUDY BOX 9-3 The Move to Online News Consumption

The way Americans get their news is changing fast. Consider these statistics:

- In 2001, 74% said a main source for news was TV—in 2013 that's down to 69%.
- In 2001, 13% said a main source for news was the Internet—in 2013 that's up to 50%.
- 71% of those in the 18–29 age group say the Internet is a main source of news—only 55% in that age group say the same for TV.
- In just two years (2010–2012), the percentage who say they saw news on a social network "yesterday" has more than doubled—from 9% to 19%.
- In the 2012 presidential election, 47% said the Internet was a main source of campaign news—more than newspapers (27%), radio (20%), and magazines (3%)—but still less than TV (67%).

SOURCE: Caumont, A. (2013). 12 Trends shaping digital news. Pew Research Center [Online: Accessed 5-21-14]. Available: http://www.pewresearch.org/fact-tank/2013/10/16/12-trends-shaping-digital-news/

---

In thinking about issues of news consumption, political campaigns, and voter participation as I was preparing my notes for this chapter, one of the things that struck me in the final analysis was how little attention research on news receives from the popular press relative to research on topics like violence, sex, and fright. It is important to note, however, that popular press coverage is a relatively poor barometer for determining the importance of a research topic. Media messages about news and politics potentially help people to understand the world and know how to respond to various social and political problems. Increasingly, media messages help shape the contours of leadership by determining who gets elected to public office. News content does not tend to be associated with the most dramatic and sensational effects. Because news is designed to inform readers, listeners, and viewers, its effects are generally taken to be functional rather than dysfunctional. This may predispose the press and even those of us who conduct research on media effects to de-emphasize the topic.

Perhaps the interesting trend in exposure to news that has been documented recently will serve to draw more attention to the study of news. As recently as the year 2000, survey results reported by the Pew Center for the People and the Press revealed that only 9% of people in the 18–29 age group relied on comedy shows for their news content—with 39% mentioning the more traditional network newscasts. However, just four years later, 21% of the respondents in this age range said that they relied on *The Daily Show* on Comedy Central as well as *Saturday Night Live* for their news. This percentage is nearly equal to the percentage who reported reliance on the traditional networks (23%).[55] In past editions of this text, I raised the question, "Will this trend continue?" The answer at this point seems to be, "yes."[56] If it continues this way, what will the impact be on the level of information that Americans have about their government and important social and civic affairs? One possibility is that the shrinking percentage of network news consumers is related to the fact that people are getting more and more of their serious news about public affairs from Internet sources. Although this certainly sounds plausible, the recent data would at least caution against this conclusion. David Tewksbury has studied the behavior of people who consume news online.[57] On the basis of a survey of more than 3,000 adults, he reports that "the chief conclusion one may take away from this research is that online news readers do not select public affairs content as often as they select other news content" (p. 705). Perhaps heavy reliance on *The Daily Show* by younger news consumers shouldn't be viewed as all that disturbing. A media industry report recently reported that *The Daily Show* presents the same amount of news on policy and international affairs as the traditional cable news channels. It also presents less news than traditional outlets that deal with sensational events.[58] Future studies will probably help scholars determine whether current news trends indicate that something dysfunctional is occurring with respect to news consumption—or whether the changes are more benign. After reading this chapter, you may come away with some sense of how important media effects in this area can be.

## ANOTHER VIEW OF NEWS: DO CERTAIN NEWS REPORTS CAUSE MORE PEOPLE TO DIE?

Several years ago, soon after I had left a job at Cleveland State University for my current position at Purdue, I received a phone call from a news reporter who worked for *The Cleveland Plain Dealer*. Usually, phone calls from reporters mean that someone has read a press release from my university that gives details on one of my studies. In this case, however, the reporter was not interested in my research. Instead, he wanted to know my opinion about whether an article that he was about to submit for publication in the newspaper would increase deaths in the city of Cleveland. He believed that he was in an ethical dilemma. He wanted to report the news, but he also didn't want to bring about unnecessary harm to the city that he loved.

This reporter's concern was not typical. I had never before received a phone call quite like his and I have not received one since. Why did this reporter think that his article might cause an increase in deaths in the city of Cleveland? Was there any basis for his concern? As it turns out, there certainly was! The article he planned to submit was a news report that told about the death of a well-known city official who had committed suicide.

## Imitative Suicides and the News

Nearly 30 years ago, a sociologist, David Phillips, published an article that presented a provocative set of findings. Phillips took note of the dates on which suicide stories appeared in newspapers. Then he went to the statistical archives for the area served by the newspapers and discovered that a few days after these stories appeared, the number of automobile fatalities in the area increased.[59] Phillips also noticed that the more publicity the suicide story received (front page versus succeeding pages), the greater the increase in automobile fatalities. Could it be that the publication of a suicide story in the newspaper actually served as a trigger for other people to commit suicide themselves? As incredible as it might seem, the more data that Phillips examined, the more convincing the case became. Phillips reasoned that if people were really using their cars to commit suicide, there should be more of an increase in single-car accidents than in other types of accidents after the suicide stories appeared. This is exactly what he found.

The increase in fatalities following newspaper suicide stories may not be limited to automobiles. In another study, Phillips discovered the same kind of effect for fatal crashes involving private, business, and corporate-executive airplane crashes.[60] Again, the more publicity given to the suicide, the greater the number of plane crashes that occurred. The increase in crashes was limited to the states in which the suicide story was most heavily publicized.

A prominent social psychologist, Robert Cialdini, is convinced that Phillips has unveiled an important media effect. He summarized his views in his own popular book on the subject of influence:

> The influence of suicide stories on car and plane crashes, then, is fantastically specific. Stories of pure suicides, in which only one person dies, generate wrecks in which only one person dies; stories of suicide-murder combinations, in which there are multiple deaths, generate wrecks in which there are multiple deaths.... I am left wholly convinced and, simultaneously, wholly amazed by it ... Phillips' findings illustrate a distressing tendency for suicide publicity to motivate certain people who are similar to the victim to kill themselves—because they now find the idea of suicide more legitimate.[61]

Phillips reasoned that if the statistics he examined really indicated that news stories about suicide were causing an increase in suicides, the same effect might be observed with other types of media messages. He turned to the world of soap operas and found the same effect. Documented suicides and automobile accidents both increased immediately after soap opera story lines included plots that involved a suicide.[62] The sort of media effect that Phillips's data seem to support has turned up before in the context of books. In 1774, when Johann Wolfgang von Goethe published his book *The Sorrows of Young Werther*—in which the major character takes his own life—suicides increased in Europe to such a degree that the book was banned in several countries. Apparently, some empathetic readers decided to imitate the fictional character—but more recent scholarship suggests that there was hardly an epidemic of suicide as a result of the book.[63] Media effects scholars sometimes commemorated the European experience with this novel by referring to the imitative-suicide effect documented by Phillips and others as the **Werther effect**.

If you still are having a little trouble believing that news reports of suicides can trigger an increase in the suicide rate, consider the recent evidence documented by Elmar Etzersdorfer and Gemot Sonneck on the Vienna experience.[64] In the late 1970s, it apparently became quite common for people to use the new subway system in Vienna as a way to commit suicide. The news media organizations adopted the practice of reporting on these suicides in a dramatic way. Consistent with Phillips's data, suicide rates spiraled upward. To address this situation, the Austrian Association for Suicide Prevention developed guidelines for media reporting of suicides that discouraged such dramatic reporting. The suicide rate promptly dropped more than 80% and remained low for years. A good portion of this drop was probably the result of a media campaign aimed at discouraging suicide, but some of the decrease could have been related to the news media's change in reporting suicide stories with such sensation.

A team of scholars in Japan wanted to study the possibility of news coverage influencing suicides after they noticed an alarming increase in teen suicides by use of hydrogen sulfide following the first reported suicide of this type in January of 2008. In the next 10 months, there were over 1,000 suicides that used this method— 35 times more than had occurred in the same period a year earlier. In order to see whether there was any connection between newspaper coverage of these suicides and a subsequent increase after the articles appeared, the authors' content analyzed both national and local newspapers over a 56-day period in 2008. They found over 700 suicide stories reporting the use of hydrogen sulfide. Using a very sophisticated time-series analysis of their data, the authors concluded that there was definitely a statistically significant link between the appearance of newspaper articles about hydrogen sulfide suicides and subsequent suicide attempts using this method. Their data also indicated that the size of the statistical effect was four times greater when the news story appeared on the front page than when it appeared elsewhere in the paper.[65]

One important question that arises about the Werther effect is whether the effect is just a **repositioning or rescheduling effect** as opposed to an **additive effect**. That is, think about the situation where suicides increase after a well-publicized suicide story. Would the people who committed suicide after the news story decide to commit suicide anyway at some later point in time? If so, then over the long haul, we would expect to see some decrease in the normal rate of suicide such that the overall rate remained predictably stable. The media story in this case would simply cause a rescheduling of suicides. But when Phillips examined his data, he discovered that this was not what tended to happen. Instead, it appears that the sudden increases in suicide following a media story about a suicide result in a genuine addition to the number of suicides that would have occurred had the story never been published. Elmar Etzersdorfer recently documented a strong connection between the reports of celebrity suicide in Austria and subsequent suicides over the next several weeks. Of particular interest is the fact that these subsequent suicides used the same method as reported for the celebrity (in this case, a gun).[66]

Given the research findings, you might be wondering what I told the conscientious reporter from *The Cleveland Plain Dealer*. I told him about Phillips's research and gave him some of the original study citations. Then I cautioned him about placing the story on the front page of the newspaper. Phillips's work definitely suggests that the imitative suicide effect decreases if the stories do not receive wide publicity by appearing on page one. I never received a copy of the reporter's story, but he told me that he would recommend to his editor that it appear somewhere other than the front page. In retrospect, I could have probably benefited from some new guidelines that have been developed to help the press in reporting on suicide stories (see Study Box 9-4). Of course, when a celebrity like Robin Williams commits suicide, the press may find these guidelines to be challenging to follow. Phillips would undoubtedly predict an increase in the suicide rate in the wake of the publicity about Robin Williams. Researchers will be able to test that prediction.

---

### STUDY BOX 9-4 Guidelines for Reporting on Suicide Stories

Researchers concerned about public health have recently noted that different countries have developed a number of guidelines for the press when they report suicide stories. I've listed some of these guidelines below. Even though these guidelines are in place, more research is needed to evaluate the extent to which the press follows them—and the extent to which they have any real impact.

1. **Avoid sensationalizing or glamorizing suicide or giving it undue prominence.** My caution to the journalist about placing the story on the front page is consistent with this guideline.
2. **Avoid providing specific detail about the suicide.**
3. **Recognize the importance of role models.**
4. **Take the opportunity to educate the public.**
5. **Provide help/support to vulnerable readers/viewers.**
6. **Consider the aftermath of suicide.**
7. **Acknowledge that journalists are vulnerable too.**

**SOURCE:** Pirkis, J., Blood, R. W., Beautrais, A., Burgess, P., & Skehan, J. (2006). Media guidelines on the reporting of suicide. *Crisis: The Journal of Intervention and Suicide Prevention*, 27(2), 82–87.

---

Phillips's studies on the impact of news stories about suicide do have a few important limitations in terms of documenting clear evidence for media effects. First, it isn't possible to know for sure that any of the people involved in the automobile or plane fatalities actually were exposed to the media suicide story. The only data Phillips presents are raw statistics. Some sociologists also note that the theoretical process behind this effect is not particularly clear. Why do some people commit suicide and not others? How can we understand the factors that bring about this effect? Although there is a need to develop in more detail the theory behind Phillips's data, one of the first things that happens after people process news reports is something relatively simple: thought or rumination. It seems clear that if a person reads a news story about suicide or hears a brief account on TV, the story may or may not trigger additional thoughts or ruminations. Some people may shake their heads and forget the story in an instant. Others may be struck about some feature of the story and begin to ruminate in a way that connects the story with their own personal experiences. What determines the amount of thought a person devotes to a news story?

In concluding the discussion on news reports and imitative suicide, it is important to note that from the very first studies reported by Phillips, there was controversy about whether all of the appropriate statistical procedures had been followed in arriving at the conclusions.[67] Controversy about the effect remains today. One researcher claims that in a re-analysis of some of the classic data, the Werther effect is only partially supported.[68] Nevertheless, the preponderance of evidence does seem to suggest that the media have the capacity to induce imitative suicides in the population.

## SUMMARY

In this chapter, we have examined a number of effects of media news content. As we have seen, certain types of news content (suicide stories) actually may trigger imitative behavior in the population. This effect emerges because some people ruminate about the news stories they have read or seen. People with a high need for cognition are particularly likely to ruminate and think about the things they have processed in the news. Agenda-setting theory postulates that the media actually affect what people think about. Research on the theory is supportive. Through the process of framing, the media may not only affect what people think about; they may also affect what we think. What we think helps to determine public opinion. The spiral of silence theory details one way the media may affect public opinion by giving sanction to the expression of certain viewpoints. Still, one of the issues that emerges in the study of news content has to do with how much people actually remember from their news exposure. Emotion may be one key variable that helps to determine what we remember. In politics, emotional reactions to debates and short commercial messages can often play a pivotal role in election outcomes.

### QUESTIONS TO FOCUS YOUR ATTENTION

1. Are you a person with high or low "need for cognition"? Do you consider yourself to be a news "junkie" or a person who doesn't consume very much national and international news? Do you think your answers to those two questions are related to each other?

2. Can you think of instances in which the media didn't just tell you what to think about—but also told you what to think? How susceptible are you to the media's suggestions about what to think about and what to think?

3. Is news reporting today becoming more emotional? What examples would you cite to support your answer? What do you believe the overall impact might be if the trend in news was toward more emotionality? Explain.

| KEY TERMS AND CONCEPTS | | |
|---|---|---|
| need for cognition | spiral of silence | Werther effect |
| political sophistication | fear of isolation | repositioning or |
| agenda-setting theory | train test | rescheduling effect |
| framing | selective exposure | additive effect |
| time-series analysis | dual-coding theory | |

# NOTES

1. Cohen, A. R., Stotland, E., & Wolfe, D. M. (1955). An experimental investigation of need for cognition. *Journal of Abnormal & Social Psychology,* 51(2), 291–294.
2. Cacioppo, J. T., & Petty, R. E. (1982). The need for cognition. *Journal of Personality and Social Psychology,* 42, 116–131.
3. Perse, E. (1992). Predicting attention to local television news: Need for cognition and motives for viewing. *Communication Reports,* 5, 40–49.
4. Condra, M. B. (1992). The link between need for cognition and political interest, involvement, and media usage. *Psychology—A Quarterly Journal of Human Behavior,* 29, 13–18.
5. De Pelsmacker, P., & Geuens, M. (1998). Television viewing behaviour, program preference and individual differences: The role of affect intensity and need for cognition. *Communicatie,* 27, 2–19.
6. Ho, S. S., Peh, X., & Soh, V. W. L. (2013). The cognitive mediation model: Factors influencing public knowledge of H1N1 pandemic and intention to take precautionary behaviors. *Journal of Health Communication,* 18, 773–794.
7. Tsfati, Y., & Cappella, J. N. (2003). Do people watch what they do not trust?: Exploring the association between news media skepticism and exposure. *Communication Research,* 30(5), 504–529.
8. Lee, E. J., & Jang, Y. J. (2010). What do others' reactions to news on Internet portal sites tell us? Effects of presentation format and readers' need for cognition on reality perception. *Communication Research,* 37(6), 825–846.
9. Rhee, J. W., & Cappella, J. N. (1997). The role of political sophistication in learning from news: Measuring schema development. *Communication Research,* 24, 197–233.
10. McCombs, M., & Shaw, D. (1973). The agenda-setting function of the mass media. *Public Opinion Quarterly,* 37, 62–75.
11. Cohen, B. (1963). *The press and foreign policy.* Princeton, NJ: Princeton University Press.
12. McCombs, M., & Shaw, D. (1973). The agenda-setting function of the mass media. *Public Opinion Quarterly,* 37, 62–75.
13. Iyengar, S., & Kinder, D. (1987). *News that matters.* Chicago: University of Chicago Press.
14. Tankard, cited in Griffin, E. (1999). *A first look at communication theory.* Boston: McGraw-Hill.
15. McCombs, M. (1997). New frontiers in agenda setting: Agendas of attributes and frames. *Mass Communication Review,* 24, 4–24.
16. Kolmer, C., & Semetko, H. A. (2009). Framing the Iraq war: Perspectives from American, U.K., Czech, German, South African, and Al-Jazeera news. *American Behavioral Scientist,* 52(5), 643–656.
17. Griffin, E. (1999). *A first look at communication theory.* Boston: McGraw-Hill.
18. Kiousis, S. (2003). Job approval and favorability: The impact of media attention to the Monica Lewinsky scandal on public opinion of President Bill Clinton. *Mass Communication & Society,* 6(4), 435–451.
19. Gross, K., & Aday, S. (2003). The scary world in your living room and neighborhood: Using local broadcast news, neighborhood crime rates, and personal experience to test agenda setting and cultivation. *Journal of Communication,* 53(3), 411–426.
20. Marilyn, R., Wanta, W., & Dzwo, T. H. (2002). Agenda setting and issue salience online. *Communication Research,* 29(4), 452–465.
21. Williams, B. A., & Carpini, M. X. (2004). Monica and Bill all the time and everywhere: The collapse of gatekeeping and agenda setting in the new media environment. *American Behavioral Scientist,* 47(9), 1208–1230.
22. Althaus, S., & Tewksbury, D. (2002). Agenda setting and the "new" news: Patterns of issue importance among readers of the paper and online versions of *The New York Times. Communication Research,* 29, 180–207.

23. Wanta, W., & Ghanem, S. (2007). Effects of agenda setting. In R. W. Preiss, B. M. Gayle, N. Burrell, M. Allen, & J. Bryant (Eds.), *Mass media effects research: Advances through meta-analysis* (pp. 37–51). Mahwah, NJ: Erlbaum.

24. Bantimaroudis, P., Zyglidopoulous, S., & Symeou, P. C. (2010). Greek museum media visibility and museum visitation: An exploration of cultural agenda setting. *Journal of Communication,* 60, 743–757.

25. Trumbo, C.W. (2012). The effect of newspaper coverage of influenza on the rate of physician visits for influenza 2002–2008. *Mass Communication and Society,* 15, 718–738.

26. Noelle-Neumann, E. (1991). The theory of public opinion: The concept of the spiral of silence. In J. A. Anderson (Ed.), *Communication Yearbook,* 14 (pp. 256–287). Newbury Park, CA: Sage.

27. Kim, S.H. (2012). Testing fear of isolation as a causal mechanism: Spiral of silence and genetically modified (GM) foods in South Korea. *International of Public Opinion Research,* 24(3), 306–324.

28. Eveland, W. P. Jr., McLeod, D. M., & Signorielli, N. (1995). Actual and perceived U.S. public opinion: The spiral of silence during the Persian Gulf War. *International journal of Public Opinion Research,* 7, 91–109.

29. McDonald, D. G., Glynn, C. J., Kim, S., & Ostman, R. E. (2001). The spiral of silence in the 1948 presidential election. *Communication Research,* 28(2), 139–155.

30. Noelle-Neumann, E. (2001). Commentary. *International Journal of Public Opinion Research,* 13, 59–60.

31. Shanahan, J., Glynn, C., & Hayes, A. (2007). The spiral of silence: A meta-analysis and its impact. In R. W. Preiss, B. M. Gayle, N. Burrell, M. Allen, & J. Bryant (Eds.), *Mass media effects research: Advances through meta-analysis* (pp. 415–427). Mahwah, NJ: Erlbaum.

32. Matthes, J., Morrison, K. R., & Schemer, C. (2010). A spiral of silence for some: Attitude certainty and the expression of political minority opinions. *Communication Research,* 37(6), 774–800.

33. Schulz, A. (2012). The spiral of silence and the Internet: Selection of online content and perception of the public opinion climate in computer-mediated communication environments. *International Journal of Public Opinion Research,* 24(3), 346–367.

34. Robinson, J., & Davis, D. (1986). Comprehension of a single evening's news. In J. P. Robinson, & M. R. Levy (Eds.), *The main source: Learning from television news* (pp. 107–132). Beverly Hills: Sage.

35. Kepplinger, H., & Daschmann, G. (1997). Today's news—tomorrow's context: A dynamic model of news processing. *Journal of Broadcasting & Electronic Media,* 41, 548–565.

36. Newhagen, J. E., & Reeves, B. (1992). The evening's bad news: Effects of compelling negative television news images on memory. *Journal of Communication,* 42, 25–41.

37. Gunter, B., Furnham, A., & Griffiths, S. (2000). Children's memory for news: A comparison of three presentation media. *Media Psychology,* 2, 93–118.

38. Garry, M., Strange, D., Bernstein, D. M., & Kinzett, T. (2007). Photographs can distort memory for the news. *Applied Cognitive Psychology,* 21(8), 995–1004.

39. Grabe, M.E., & Samson, L. (2011). Sexual cues emanating from the anchorette chair: Implications for perceived professionalism, fitness for beat, and memory for news. *Communication Research,* 38(4), 471–496.

40. Newhagen, J. E. (1998). TV news images that induce anger, fear, and disgust: Effects on approach-avoidance and memory. *Journal of Broadcasting & Electronic Media,* 42, 265–276.

41. Miller, A., & Leshner, G. (2007). How viewers process live, breaking, and emotional television news. *Media Psychology,* 10(1), 23–40.

42. Lang, A., Newhagen, J., & Reeves, B. (1996). Negative video as structure: Emotion, attention, capacity, and memory. *Journal of Broadcasting & Electronic Media,* 40, 460–477.

43. Unz, D., Schwab, F., Winterhoff-Spurk, P. (2008). TV news—the daily horror?: Emotional effects of violent television news. *Journal of Media Psychology: Theories, Methods, and Applications,* 20(4), 141–155.

44. Kraus, S. (1996). Winners of the first 1960 televised presidential debate between Kennedy and Nixon. *Journal of Communication,* 46, 78–96.

45. Debate score: Kennedy up, Nixon down. (1960, November 7). *Broadcasting,* 27–28.

46. Druckman, J. N. (2003). The power of televised images: The first Kennedy-Nixon debate revisited. *Journal of Politics,* 65(2), 559–571.

47. Pfau, M., & Kang, J. G. (1991). The impact of relational messages on candidate influence in televised political debates. *Communication Studies,* 42, 117.

48. Obituaries from *The New York Times* and *Washington Post* appear on the official Web site of Tony Schwartz—a site well worth visiting to learn more about his genius when it came to media: http://www.tonyschwartz.org

49. Schwartz, T. (1973). *The responsive chord.* New York: Anchor Books.

50. CEL. (1984). The 30-second president. In *A walk through the 20th century with Bill Moyers*. Washington, DC: Public Broadcasting Service.

51. Dardis, F. E., Shen, F., & Edwards, H. H. (2008). Effects of negative political advertising on individuals' cynicism and self-efficacy. The impact of ad type and message exposures. *Mass Communication and Society,* 11(1), 24–42.

52. Clinton, J. D., & Lapinski, J. S. (2004). "Targeted" advertising and voter turnout: An experimental study of the 2000 presidential election. *Journal of Politics,* 66(1), 69–96. Pinkleton, B. E., Um, N., & Austin, E. W. (2002). An exploration of the effects of negative political advertising on political decision making. *Journal of Advertising,* 31(1), 13–25.

53. Caumont, A. (2013). 12 Trends shaping digital news. Pew Research Center [Online: Accessed 5-21-14]. Available: http://www.pewresearch.org/fact-tank/2013/10/16/12-trends-shaping-digital-news/

54. Papacharissi, Z., & Oliveira, M.d.F. (2012). Affective news and networked publics: The rhythms of news storytelling on #Egypt. *Journal of Communication,* 62, 266–282.

55. Associated Press. (2004). And now for the news: For many young viewers, it's Jon Stewart [Online: Accessed 5-21-14]. Available: http://www.today.com/id/4400644/ns/today-entertainment/t/now-news-many-young-viewers-its-jon-stewart/#.U30MdFGZhVA

56. Pew Research Center. (2008). Journalism, satire, or just laughs? "The Daily Show with Jon Stewart," Examined [Online: Accessed 5-21-14]. Available: http://www.journalism.org/2008/05/08/whats-onand-whats-not-onthe-daily-show/

57. Tewksbury, D. (2003). What do Americans really want to know? Tracking the behavior of news readers on the Internet. *Journal of Communication,* 53(4), 694–710.

58. Weir, D. (2008). No Joke: The best news strategy is at "The Daily Show" [Online: Accessed 5-22-14]. Available: http://www.cbsnews.com/news/no-joke-the-best-news-strategy-is-at-the-daily-show/

59. Phillips, D. P. (1979). Suicide, motor vehicle fatalities, and the mass media: Evidence toward a theory of suggestion. *American Journal of Sociology,* 84, 1150–1174.

60. Phillips, D. P. (1978). Airplane accident fatalities increase just after newspaper stories about murder and suicide. *Science,* 201, 748–750.

61. Cialdini, R. B. (1988). *Influence: Science and practice*. Glenview, IL: Scott Foresman.

62. Phillips, D. P. (1982). The impact of fictional television stories on U.S. adult fatalities: New evidence on the effect of the mass media on violence. *American Journal of Sociology,* 87, 1340–1359.

63. Thorson, J., & Oberg, P. A. (2003). Was there a suicide epidemic after Goethe's Werther? *Archives of Suicide Research,* 7(1), 69–72.

64. Etzersdorfer, E., & Sonneck, G. (1998). Preventing suicide by influencing mass-media reporting: The Viennese experience 1980–1996. *Archives of Suicide Research,* 4(1), 67–74.

65. Hagihara, A., Abe, T., Omagari, M., Motoi, M., & Nabeshima, Y. (2014). The impact of newspaper reporting of hydrogen sulfide suicide on imitative suicide attempts in Japan. *Social Psychiatry and Psychiatric Epidemiology,* 49(2), 221–229.

66. Etzersdorfer, E., Voracek, M., & Sonneck, G. (2004). A dose-response relationship between mutational suicides and newspaper distribution. *Archives of Suicide Research,* 8(2), 137–145.

67. Wasserman, I. M. (1984). Imitation and suicide: A reexamination of the Werther effect. *American Sociological Review,* 49(3), 427–436.

68. Hittner, J. B. (2005). How robust is the Werther effect? A reexamination of the suggestion-imitation model of suicide. *Mortality,* 10(3), 193–200.

# 10

# The Effects of Media Stereotypes

## STEREOTYPICAL REPRESENTATIONS IN THE MEDIA

In February 2012, Kimberly-Clark released a new video advertising campaign for their popular disposable diapers, Huggies. Company executives obviously had no idea what was coming next. The campaign was titled "Have Dad Put Huggies to the Test" and it attempted to be humorous by depicting fathers as less than competent when it came to the business of changing diapers. The five million stay-at-home-dads were not amused. The Twittersphere lit up immediately with a protest petition and Kimberly-Clark issued a statement admitting that it had failed to communicate its message effectively. In conjunction with that statement, they pulled the ads and ended the campaign. In an ABC news story about the offensive ad campaign, one father asked, "Who are they talking to here? It felt like this was an ad from three generations ago." Another father complained that the ads "…played up the stereotype while claiming to celebrate fatherhood."[1]

The stereotyped ads for Huggies was hardly the first time that an advertiser has run into trouble with the images associated with a campaign designed to sell products. Less than a year before the diaper debacle, the Cadbury candy company released a new print advertisement for their Bliss chocolate candy bars. The slogan of the ad was simple. It said: "Move over Naomi, there's a new diva in town." Under the slogan was a picture of the Bliss chocolate bar. If you don't recall reading anything about the controversy sparked by this ad campaign, you might recognize that the ad slogan invokes the name of Naomi—an unmistakable reference to Naomi Campbell, the Black British supermodel. Almost immediately after the ad appeared, Naomi Campbell released a statement that expressed her shock and emotional upset at being compared to a chocolate bar. She complained that the ad was "insulting and hurtful."[2] In her full statement, she said, "It's upsetting to be described as chocolate, not just for me but for all black women and black people … I do not find any humor in this."[3] The campaign group, Operation Black Vote, lodged a formal complaint about the ad to the Advertising Standards Authority (ASA), claiming that the ad was racist. The ASA rejected the complaints and decided not to investigate the campaign in order to determine whether the ad was a violation of the advertising code. Nevertheless, Cadbury issued a public apology and pulled the ad from its campaign.[4]

A few other advertising incidents are worth mentioning to highlight how stereotypes can blow up and cause a campaign to be scrapped in an instant. In 2008, the popular chef Rachael Ray appeared in an advertisement on the Dunkin' Donuts Web site. She was holding a cup of iced coffee and endorsing the product for Dunkin' Donuts—the company that undoubtedly hoped consumers would transfer her culinary credibility to their product. About two weeks later, a conservative blog site made the observation that the black and white scarf that Ms. Ray wore in the ad looked much like the sort of scarf worn by Muslim extremists (a keffiyeh). Specifically, the blog charged that by running this ad, Dunkin' Donuts had deliberately done something to "casually promote the symbol of Palestinian terrorism and the intifada, the keffiyeh, via Rachael Ray."[5] Once the controversy started, Dunkin' Donuts realized, just as the Cadbury candy company realized in the Naomi Campbell case, that it had little choice but to pull the ad and start over. In yanking the ad, the company pointed out that absolutely no symbolism had been intended with the choice of the scarf for Ms. Ray. It was simply a nice scarf that the stylist thought looked becoming. They decided, however, that they had to pull the ad just the same because the controversy had created the possibility of a misperception on the part of the public. But the decision to pull the ad didn't end the controversy. Many observers contended that by responding to the criticism, the company was simply reinforcing a bad stereotype that only terrorists wore this type of garment.

The Dunkin' Donuts example is a bit of a twist on the common theme of advertisers running into trouble with stereotypes in their advertising. In this case, the company was criticized for perpetuating a bad stereotype by *canceling* the ad. Typically, companies come under fire for perpetuating damaging stereotypes in their ad content, and cancelation is seen as the heroic remedy. The Cadbury case might fall into this more conventional category. Also consider the TV commercials run by Taco Bell that featured the dog named Dinky. Dinky was a Chihuahua, and the commercials were presumably successful at selling Taco Bell's products. They were also successful at stirring controversy about Latino stereotypes. Gabriel Cazares, the former mayor of Clearwater, Florida, and former president of the Tampa, Florida, chapter of the League for United Latin American Citizens (LULAC), complained about the content of some of the Dinky ads. Instead of using a talking dog to depict Mexicans as was done in some of the ads, Cazares pointed out, Taco Bell could have used any number of Mexican artists, singers, dancers, or other celebrities who would have had even greater selling impact when they uttered the famous lines given to Dinky—*"Yo quiero* Taco Bell." Apparently, part of the controversy had to do with the fact that it was felt the ads encouraged people to associate Mexicans with dogs. In addition, in some of the commercials, Dinky scampers around looking for food—an image that infuriated many Latinos who perceived that Dinky's actions were being taken as the actions of the entire race. On the other hand, in one ad, Dinky answered a question correctly on *Jeopardy* to get food. Some thought that this ad depicted Dinky as a clever dog and that this image was not offensive.

The controversy surrounding Huggies, Rachel Ray's scarf, Dinky the dog, and how commercials might convey subtle messages about groups of people raises the issue of media stereotypes. When media representations tend to depict groups of people in particular ways, they may play an important part in determining how media consumers come to think about individuals who are members of those groups. Social psychologists do not necessarily agree on how to think about stereotypes, but Susan Fiske and Shelly Taylor offer an approach that seems clear and sensible. They say, "One can think about stereotypes as a particular kind of role schema that organizes people's expectations about other people who fall into certain social categories."[6] If, for example, you tended to think that a male was more likely than a female to be an attorney, we might say that you had a **role schema** that was part of your thought processes when it came to thinking about men and women. Schemas help to organize thoughts. In the case of a role schema, the thoughts and expectations you have for a specific person are guided by a general set of expectations that you might have for people who hold the same role as the specific person you're thinking about. If you think that females are not as likely as males to be attorneys, then your expectations for females are **stereotyped** in a particular way.

One's expectations about someone else's role may be based on accurate data. That is, it might be the case that males really are more likely to be attorneys than females. However, one negative consequence of holding a stereotype, even if it is accurate, is that it may function to reinforce the status quo and unfairly restrict the diversity of social roles that individuals might hold. Think about what might happen if most people held the stereotype that males were more likely to be attorneys than females. To the extent that people had such expectations, females might not be socialized into career paths that would lead them to law school. In this way, stereotypes, even if accurate at a given point in time, can serve to perpetuate the status quo and be unduly restrictive for various groups of people. Of course, inaccurate stereotypes produce false expectations.

The media may generally depict people in stereotypical ways such that consumers are encouraged to adopt expectations about the roles that those people occupy. Following the example of female attorneys, if the media depicted few females in the role of attorney, then consumers of the media might come to think of males as much more likely to be attorneys. The media would be engaging in a stereotypical depiction that has an impact on media consumers.

If this is the case, then there are two fundamental issues to be addressed in any discussion of the media and stereotypes. First, one might ask about the particular role expectations that the media encourage. In other words, how do the media actually depict certain groups of people? Second, once we know the answer to the first question, we might ask whether these depictions actually affect the role expectations that media consumers have for those same people. As it turns out, there is much more data available for the first question than the second. Nevertheless, both questions are important to examine.

## Sex Role Stereotypes

One of the most repeated findings from content analyses of TV programs is that men far outnumber women. Summarizing across a number of different studies, Tannis MacBeth Williams observed: "[T]here are more than twice as many male as female models on TV, and when women do appear, they are most frequently found on comedy and light entertainment programs. Furthermore, this situation has remained constant over time."[7] One of the few consistent exceptions to the strong tendency to employ males more than females in the world of TV is found in the content of afternoon soap operas. Research by Natan Katzman confirms that the proportion of male and female characters in the soap opera genre is roughly equal.[8] In a review of some of the more recent content analyses on the frequency with which males and females appear in the media,[9] Richard Jackson Harris pointed out that males are three times more likely to appear in children's cartoons,[10] twice as likely to appear in music videos, and four to five times more likely to be featured as voice-over announcers—even though they aren't any more persuasive than female voice-overs.[11] For many researchers, the fact that males outnumber females in the TV world is a troubling finding that may suggest to viewers that males, by virtue of their greater presence, should be considered more important or more significant. Of course, researchers must be extremely careful at this point. Remember that in previous chapters, the point was made that media content cannot be assumed to cause any particular effect. It is important to distinguish carefully between the two questions about content and effect. Media effects researchers cannot speak about the effects of any particular stereotype without having evidence of an effect. The mere presence of a stereotype does not constitute evidence for an effect.

In addition to documenting the fact that females don't appear on TV as frequently as males do, researchers have found a full range of other stereotypical depictions. Tannis MacBeth Williams reviews evidence showing that married females on TV are far less likely to be employed than females in the actual population. Moreover, when females do hold jobs on TV, they tend to be restricted to a more narrow range of occupations than males. George Gerbner (discussed in Chapters 5 & 8) has also contributed some interesting insights about sex role stereotyping from his research on media violence. He maintains that women are much more likely to be depicted as victims of crime and violence than males. Although males are depicted in violent scenarios more frequently as the perpetrators or the aggressors, females are depicted more frequently as the victims. To Gerbner, these sorts of systematic distortions communicate a strong message about who has power in the culture. According to him, the predominant message of TV is that males have power over females; males are relatively powerful, and females are relatively powerless.[12]

It is interesting to note that during the past decade or so, content studies on sex role stereotypes seem to have decreased in frequency. This may be partially due to the fact that researchers have expanded their focus of concern to other sorts of stereotypical depictions. Harris provides brief reviews of research on depictions of African Americans, Latinos, Native Americans, Asian Americans, Arabs, Arab Americans, gays and lesbians, the elderly, the physically disabled, those suffering from psychological disorders, police officers, lawyers, psychologists and psychiatrists, farmers, and college students.[13] The list of possible stereotypes in media content is quite lengthy and research resources are relatively limited. As scholars have turned their attention to other possible stereotypes, the fact of stereotypical depictions in the area of sex roles has been taken to be relatively well established.

In one of the most recent studies, a team of researchers (Martha Lauzen, David Dozier, and Nora Horan) examined 124 prime-time programs that appeared on six networks during the 2005–2006 TV season.[14] Consistent with past studies, they found that of the 1,342 characters that they analyzed, 60% were male and 40% were female. They also found that male characters were more likely to appear in roles that focused on work while females were more likely to appear in roles related to family, friends, and romance. Of particular interest, the researchers found that the role portrayals varied depending on the sex of the program writers. Compared to programs that had both male and female writers, programs that had only male writers were much more likely to feature both male and female characters in work roles instead of more relational roles within a family, friendship, or romance. When all of the content studies are considered together, there seems to be little doubt about the appropriate conclusion when it comes to sex role stereotypes. Two researchers, Jennifer Herrett-Skjellum and Mike Allen, used **meta-analysis** to examine this issue. They summarized the data in the following way: "Television programming generally portrays men and women in traditional gender stereotypical roles.... All content analyses illustrate the consistent finding that men are more often on TV, in higher status roles as characters, and are represented as having greater power than women."[15]

Before he died, cultivation theory author George Gerbner appeared in a number of videos and summarized many of his findings about media content. With respect to sex stereotypes, Gerbner pointed out that the imbalance of males and females (he contended that males outnumbered women 3:1) and the nature of their media portrayals had significant and problematic implications for female actresses who aspired to long and prosperous careers. As females age, the number of roles available to them in dramatic productions declines. According to Gerbner's study commissioned by the Hollywood Screen Actors Guild, women's roles start to decline precipitously once they reach 35 years old. In contrast, male roles remain prevalent throughout the lifespan and even increase after age 35. Gerbner also contends that when females do appear as older characters, they lose their sex appeal and are frequently limited to depictions that are evil- or witch-like.[16] That's not the case for male characters.

An important question for our purposes is: So what? Why should stereotypical presentations of men and women be of concern? Aside from some of the employment difficulties for female actresses, are there any effects associated with these portrayals? That is, do the media stereotypes actually cause people's perceptions to change or cause them to act any differently? As it turns out, several researchers have attempted to answer the question of media impact with respect to gender role stereotypes. Let's take a look at some of the findings.

## Effects of Sex Role Stereotypes

Over a decade ago, my daughter Jordan, then a sophomore in high school, was preparing to attend a weeklong computer camp at Purdue University. Over the course of the week, she was to learn various things about computers and actually compete in some computer projects with the other campers. Just before camp was to begin, we checked with the camp registration just to make sure things were in order and we discovered a shocking statistic. There were 19 girls signed up for the camp—along with 98 boys. Although Jordan and her female friends found this statistic to be quite exhilarating, the camp leaders would probably have preferred a better balance of girls to boys. But recruiting girls to computer camp is quite a challenge. Somehow, adolescent girls just don't seem to be that attracted to computers.

Even though some time has passed since Jordan's computer camp adventure, the problem of recruiting girls into the world of computers has persisted. When Trina Finton majored in management of information systems at the University of Arizona at about the same time Jordan was in computer camp, she was the only female in the program. A few years ago, she created a Web site, GamingAngels.com, designed to interest young girls in the world of computer gaming. In the summer of 2011, for the first time, the Gaming Angels helped to sponsor a camp scholarship for almost $1,000 for a young girl to attend a computer camp for a week. I wish my daughter Jordan had been able to apply for such a scholarship.[17] While some progress is being made to recruit young girls into computer-related careers, the gender gap is slow to close. Why might this be? One likely reason has to do with the way young girls construct their social reality. Many have adopted beliefs about the social world around them that do not leave much room for females being attracted to computer camps. Study Box 10-1 provides some information that seems to support the notion that early role socialization may play a huge role in the computer career gender gap. Obviously, there are many things that might affect a young person's view of his or her social world, but the media messages that are consumed might be one important factor. Two communication researchers who are concerned about how media messages influence the **construction of social reality** are Robert Hawkins and Suzanne Pingree. In one study that they reported with their co-author, Ilya Adler, they surveyed more than 1,300 adolescents, most of whom were from Australia. The most important general finding from their investigation was that heavy TV viewers tended to have beliefs about the world that were consistent with the messages of TV.[18]

**STUDY BOX 10-1 The Problem of Attracting Women to Careers in Computer Science**

- When boys and girls are in elementary school, they express interest in computer science in nearly equal numbers (boys, 68%; girls, 66%).
- When they take the AP computer science exam, girls and boys score equally well.
- Girls do significantly worse on computer science exams if they are told beforehand that boys are naturally better in computer science. There's no disparity in scores if they aren't given such information.
- Most girls (90%) express a desire to enter careers that help people, and they don't consider computer science to be a good fit with that desire.
- Most college students (57%) are female but few (18%) are computer science majors.
- Since 1980, the percentage of females enrolled in the computer science major has actually decreased.

SOURCE: Lepi, K. (2013). Why are girls not pursuing computer science degrees? *Edudemic*. [Online: Accessed 6-19-14]. Available: http://www.edudemic.com/girls-computer-science-degrees/

We might be able to get some insight into this question by looking at the natural experiment that Tannis MacBeth Williams conducted in Canada. You may recall reading about this study in Chapter 4. Along with her colleague Meredith Kimball, Williams examined what happened to boys' and girls' job expectations over a two-year period in a town that initially had no access to television (Notel) and then received access to one TV channel. Even though the study is now decades old, the results were enlightening and very pertinent to understanding the effects of media stereotypes.

The researchers had two main hypotheses, both of which were confirmed. First, Kimball and Williams believed that children who lived in Notel would hold fewer stereotypical attitudes about the appropriateness of various behaviors than would the children who lived in towns that did have TV access. The researchers measured stereotypical attitudes by having children in the sixth and ninth grades fill out the Sex Role Differentiation Scale. As expected, the results showed that the children in the town with no access to TV (Notel) did not differentiate behaviors according to sex to the same extent as the children in the TV towns. Given that the towns were chosen to be similar in almost every other respect except TV access, the authors interpreted this as evidence in favor of the idea that children develop sex-stereotyped attitudes as a result of watching TV.

But the evidence is even more compelling when the second hypothesis is examined. Immediately after the first hypothesis was tested, the children who lived in the town with no TV gained access to TV reception. Two years later, when the researchers returned and administered the Sex Role Differentiation Scale once again to children in the same grades, they found that the pattern of the results had changed. In contrast to the scores two years earlier, now that the children in Notel had TV access, their scores on the Sex Role Differentiation Scale changed to show a dramatic increase in stereotyped attitudes. Given that the only major change over the two-year period was access to TV, the researchers felt comfortable interpreting this evidence as a clear media effect. In drawing implications about these findings, the researchers stated the following:

> Several studies, including this one, have documented links between TV viewing and stereotyped sex-role attitudes. The evidence for same-sex preferences in viewing television, greater recognition of same-sex characters and behaviors, and the role of gender schemata in processing sex-role information probably account for the effects of TV viewing. In light of this information, we recommend that more female characters be portrayed in more varied roles on television. This may be particularly important for young children.[19]

A meta-analysis by Patrice Oppliger found only 31 studies on the effects of gender stereotyping—and most of those were completed prior to 1990, indicating once again that research in this area has not been overly popular of late among media effects scholars. Oppliger's study found that there was a statistically significant effect of sex role stereotypes across all of the published studies—indicating that stereotypical depictions do influence attitudes and behavior in a direction consistent with the stereotype. She stated that "Results of the meta-analysis show a consistent, positive correlation; as exposure to gender stereotyping increases, sex-typed behavior and sex-role stereotyped attitudes increase."[20] It wouldn't be good science to conclude that the great disparity between males and females who registered for the Purdue computer camp was due to the impact of media messages. But could media images have contributed in part to this enrollment pattern? Extending the conclusions from this research, it certainly seems like a plausible idea.

## Media Images of Thin Bodies and Effects on Body Image

If sexual stereotypes in the media might have an impact on the socialization of young boys and girls that in turn might affect enrollment patterns at computer camps, then perhaps there are other important areas of media impact related to sexual stereotypes. One such area that has received a fair amount of research attention over the past decade is the way in which female bodies are represented and the impact of those representations. In contrast to what appears to be a decline in general research that focuses on sex-role stereotypes and their effects, studies on body image in the media—particularly female body image—and the effects of body image depictions seem to have increased. The journal *Media Psychology* devoted an entire issue to studies on body image and media in 2014. So, what do we know?

In one important content analysis on this topic, Gregory Fouts and Kimberley Burggraf studied 18 situation comedies from prime-time TV.[21] Their findings were striking. First, they discovered that the females in these programs were far more likely to be judged as being "below average" in weight as opposed to "average" or "above average." This finding is consistent with the results of other research that shows that media images of females tend to place a heavy emphasis on an idealized, overly thin standard compared to males.[22] Second, and even more important, the higher the weight of the female character depicted, the more likely it was that negative comments were made by other characters about her or directly to her. Moreover, these negative comments were often followed by a laugh track that suggested to the audience that these negative comments were funny. The authors speculated that the combination of programming that presents a disproportionate emphasis on overly thin female bodies and creates a context that explicitly reinforces the value and attractiveness of this standard may amount to a huge social problem. If young girls internalize the idea that females should be thin, then the media might have some role in creating **body dissatisfaction** or **body image disturbance** among females. That is, because of their natural tendency to engage in **social comparison**, young female viewers may compare their own bodies with those frequently depicted and reinforced in the media. To the extent that there is a perceived mismatch, young girls might start down a road that could lead to eating disorders such as bulimia or anorexia nervosa. Such a path might jeopardize the health, or even the life, of young girls. Some researchers believe that these risks aren't limited to young girls but extend to older women—particularly those who are exposed to older females in the media who have body shapes and sizes more typical of younger women. Programs like *Cougar Town* and *Desperate Housewives* might be good examples of this kind of media.[23]

Of course, these presumed effects require evidence. Is there any research to suggest that overly thin females in the media actually have an impact on the way young girls or older women think or behave? The answer to this question is yes. Let's take a brief look at some of the studies that have been reported.

In one of the experiments on this topic, two researchers, Eric Stice and Heather Shaw, randomly assigned 157 female college students to view pictures in magazines that contained either thin models, average models, or no models.[24] Immediately after viewing the pictures, the students responded to a number of items on a questionnaire. The results revealed that the students who had viewed the thin models were more likely to report a variety of negative emotions such as stress, shame, guilt, depression, and insecurity. They also indicated higher levels of body dissatisfaction. A second finding of the study was that, in general, students who reported high levels of body dissatisfaction, regardless of their experimental condition, were more likely also to report that they suffered from the symptoms associated with bulimia. More recently, Kristen Harrison and Joanne Cantor surveyed more than 400 college students and asked questions about media consumption, body dissatisfaction, drive for thinness, and various symptoms related to eating disorders.[25] Their results, though not conclusive in terms of causality, were consistent with the experimental results reported by Stice and Shaw. For the female students, media consumption was related to higher body dissatisfaction, a drive for thinness, and reports of symptoms that suggest eating disorders. For the male students, media consumption was related to the tendency to endorse thinness and dieting for females. Harrison has reported the results of yet another study that replicates and extends these same findings.[26] Two researchers from the United Kingdom ran a small experiment that included 42 female participants who were exposed on two occasions to magazine images of either thin models or overweight models. Following each exposure, those who had seen the thin models expressed greater body dissatisfaction while those who saw the overweight models expressed greater satisfaction with their own bodies. While there wasn't any effect of exposure on a measure of disordered eating, the authors noted that participants were exposed only briefly to the images.[27]

One particularly interesting investigation was reported by Duane Hargreaves and Marika Tiggemann.[28] These authors attempted to explore the possibility of a cumulative effect of media exposure to ideal body types. They randomly assigned 80 adolescents, both boys and girls, to watch either 20 commercials that contained "female thin ideals" or 20 commercials that featured no physical appearance at all. As many studies have shown, exposure to the thin body ideals produced small changes in body dissatisfaction. The really interesting aspect of this study was that the authors came back to these adolescents two years later and again had them respond to measures on body dissatisfaction and drive for thinness. This type of longitudinal study is not so common, and the results can often be particularly illuminating. In this case, they found that the girls who were most affected by the commercials when they first viewed them were more likely to express body dissatisfaction and a drive for thinness than the group who had seen the neutral ads. This same effect was also observed for boys on the measure of a drive for thinness, but not on the measure of body dissatisfaction. The authors interpret these results as evidence for cumulative media effects. Apparently, the initial media effect continued to produce changes in body image that were detectable two years later.

The study by Hargreaves and Tiggemann is one of the few in the literature to include boys as well as girls. However, researchers appear to be more interested now than in years past in studying these sorts of body image effects on males. In a recent study reported by Daniel Agliata and Stacey Tantleff-Dunn, 158 males were randomly assigned to watch either neutral television commercials or ones that featured male ideal body images.[29] The authors reported that the group who watched the ideal body images reported significantly higher levels of depression and muscle dissatisfaction. One of the most recent studies also yields more evidence for females that points in this same direction in terms of an effect. Nearly 100 Australian undergraduate females participated in an experiment in which they viewed magazine ads. The women who were randomly assigned to view a "thin-idealized" woman in the ads were significantly more likely to report body dissatisfaction, negative moods, and anxiety about their appearance with respect to their overall bodily weight.[30] In a meta-analysis that included nearly 80 studies, Shelly Grabe, Monique Ward, and Janet Hyde reported that "The findings support the notion that exposure to media images depicting the thin-ideal body is related to body image concerns for women."[31] This conclusion is consistent with ones from other scholars and some of the most recent data. In a major review of the literature published in 2010, researchers concluded that "evidence is accumulating that repeated exposure to media and to both the direct and indirect (via media's effects on peers, parents, physicians, etc.) pressure from media to be thin constitute a risk factor for body dissatisfaction, concerns over weight, and disordered eating behaviors in adolescent girls and young women" (p. 406).[32] Most recently, in a correlational study involving 189 older women (average age of about 45 years old), a team of scholars from Chapman University in California concluded that "...exposure to aging media is related to midlife women's eating disorder symptomology, body image perceptions, and food choices around others" (p. 200).[33]

## How Important Are Media in Promoting Body Dissatisfaction?

While there's certainly plenty of evidence to warrant concern about the media's role in promoting body dissatisfaction and eating disorders, without more systematic experimental and longitudinal data, caution is probably warranted before proclaiming a strong scientific consensus. Alan Roberts and Emily Good reported recently that their research suggested that the harmful effect of media images seemed to occur mainly for women who scored high on a measure of neuroticism.[34] While media still played a role in the effects uncovered in their study, the authors interpreted their results by suggesting that media impact in this area may not be nearly as "widespread" as once believed. Two other researchers who studied eating disorders in China made similar conclusions. While not ruling out the media as a potential influence in this area, they identified other psychological factors as more important in their model of statistical predictor variables.[35] In a 2014 study, a team of researchers at Texas A&M University led by Christopher Ferguson studied nearly 240 mostly Hispanic girls between the ages of 10 and 17 years old and followed them over a six-month period. They assessed the role of TV, social media, and peer competition in creating body dissatisfaction and eating disorders. They found no direct media effects—but they did find that peer competition was negatively related to body dissatisfaction and eating disorders.[36]

Finally, in a paper published in the *Review of General Psychology,* Ferguson and two other colleagues considered the evidence supporting the link between media and female body dissatisfaction. They noted that "The relationship among media exposure, body dissatisfaction, and disordered eating is complicated and requires a more sophisticated answer than just 'yes/no there are causal effects.'"[37] In Study Box 10-2, you can read some of the key points of their more sophisticated answer to the question.

To summarize the research on this topic, it appears that a number of studies document that media images of females are stereotypical in that they tend to represent females with idealized, overly thin bodies. These depictions may be important because a number of studies do conclude such images may have negative effects on both males and females. Females may be encouraged to internalize the ideal image and may strive to attain it even in the face of suffering from various eating disorders. Males may be encouraged to reinforce the ideal image and thus may create additional social pressure on females to conform to this ultrathin body standard. There is still more research to be done on this topic. Even though the literature does reveal a connection between media exposure and body dissatisfaction, some scholars believe that connection is not very large. Other researchers are beginning to investigate the

## STUDY BOX 10-2 A More Sophisticated Answer to the Supposed Link between Media and Body Dissatisfaction

After their review of the evidence, Christopher Ferguson, Benjamin Winegard, and Bo M. Winegard made some specific conclusions about the relationship between media, body dissatisfaction, and eating disorders among females. Some of their points are summarized below:

1. There is a small relationship between media exposure and body dissatisfaction—but the emphasis should be on the word "small." In fact, the relationship is so small that it doesn't reach the level of practical significance.

2. Most women aren't affected by media exposure to thin body images. Those who are affected tend to be dissatisfied with their bodies prior to any media exposure and may have neurotic tendencies.

3. Women who are satisfied with their bodies may tend to have positive outcomes associated with media exposure.

4. Both the popular and scientific literatures on body dissatisfaction have tended to over-emphasize the role of media as a causal contributor.

5. The relationship between body dissatisfaction and the development of an eating disorder is not well established—particularly for anorexia nervosa.

SOURCE: Ferguson, C. J., Winegard, B., & Winegard, B. M. (2011). Who is the fairest one of all? How evolution guides peer and media influences on female body dissatisfaction. *Review of General Psychology,* 15(1), 11–28.

extent to which some program types may be more likely than others to produce these effects (see Study Box 10-3).

One question that has surely occurred to you by now is what one can do about a negative media effect such as this one. Researchers and scholars recommend teaching students to engage in **critical media consumption**. One of the hoped-for consequences of writing a textbook like this one is that college students will become more sensitive to media stereotypes and the possible effects of media exposure on attitudes and behavior. Many media scholars recommend that elementary and secondary schools explicitly teach children about these sorts of media stereotypes and their effects on viewers. Research on high school females strongly suggests that school curricula designed to expose sexual stereotypes in the media are effective in reducing the extent to which young girls embrace the idealized, overly thin body standard that consistently shows up in magazines, movies, advertisements, and TV shows.[38] Consistent with this idea, two researchers from the University of Amsterdam reported the results of an experiment in which they either informed or explicitly warned adolescent girls about the health risks of viewing pictures of models who were underweight. The results of the experiment showed that simply providing information about the models was more effective than a heavy-handed warning in inoculating the girls to the negative effects of viewing overly thin models.[39]

One organization that is dedicated to teaching students to consume media more critically is the Media Education Foundation. You can find its Web site by

**STUDY BOX 10-3 Do Sports Programs Promote Body Dissatisfaction?**

In one of the classic studies on the relationship between media exposure and body dissatisfaction, two communication researchers, Kimberly Bissell and Peiqin Zhou, administered a questionnaire to 218 female college students. The students were asked to report the frequency of their exposure to 40 different TV programs that were on the air in 2001 when the study was conducted. Independent coders rated these programs on a scale designed to assess the "dominant body shape" seen in the program. On the scale, a 1 indicated that the dominant body shape was "conspicuously thin"; a 5 on the scale indicated "conspicuously fat." Numbers between 1 and 5 were used to indicate varying levels from thin to fat. After each program was rated, the researchers examined the programs that were the most popular among the sample of respondents. Eight programs were identified: *Friends, Dawson's Creek, Will & Grace, 7th Heaven, Felicity, ER, Dharma & Greg,* and *Gilmore Girls.* For each of these programs, coders had rated the dominant body shape as conspicuously thin. Each respondent was assigned a total exposure score for these conspicuously thin programs based on their reports of how frequently they watched the shows. The researchers also measured reports of body dissatisfaction and drive for thinness, as well as the experience of two eating disorders—anorexia and bulimia. They computed correlations between the measure of TV exposure and these four measures. In each case, the correlation was positive and statistically significant (see Chapter 2 for a refresher on correlations and statistical significance). Higher levels of exposure to these programs were associated with the experience of anorexia ($r = .22$), bulimia ($r = .24$), a drive for thinness ($r = .21$), and body dissatisfaction ($r = .17$). Finally, the researchers computed correlations between the exposure that respondents reported to sports programs on TV and these same four measures. Unlike the results for the entertainment programs, none of these measures were significantly related to exposure to TV sports. Thus, the answer to the question posed in the title to this study box seems to be no.

SOURCE: Bissell, K., & Zhou, P. (2004). Must-see TV or ESPN: Entertainment and sports media exposure and body-image distortion in college women. *Journal of Communication,* 54(1), 5–21.

typing the foundation name into a search engine. One aspect of the foundation's teaching mission is to produce videos that seek to reveal the way in which certain types of media depict stereotypes that are potentially harmful. For example, in a series of videos (*Dreamworlds*) on the way music television stereotypes both males and females, Sut Jhally has presented brief clips that encourage the viewer to see these videos in a new light.[40] Similarly, Jean Kilbourne's *Killing Us Softly* series examines how women are depicted in advertising in ways that are demeaning and stereotypical.[41] Although these videos are valuable instructional aids, their focus, like much of the research on stereotypes, is on the nature of media content—not on the scientific investigation of the effects of that content. Consequently, some social scientists find these videos to be long on claims and short on supporting evidence.

# RACIAL STEREOTYPES

As the earlier example about Dinky the Chihuahua illustrated, sex stereotypes are not the only area of research that concerns the student and scholar of media effects. Several years ago, the Frito-Lay company introduced a cartoon character in its advertising that was supposed to convey the message that Fritos corn chips are delicious. The character was dubbed the Frito Bandito, and his role was to run around stealing bags of Fritos because he couldn't resist the taste. He wore a big yellow hat, and a gun on either side of his waist. His long mustache and his accent clearly identified him as Mexican. The company thought that it had come up with a smashing advertising campaign until the Mexican community began to protest. Their argument was simple and reduced to two points: (1) The frequency of media depictions of Mexicans is so low that any depiction is crucially important in terms of the overall image it represents to the masses of media consumers; and (2) the image of the Frito Bandito, as one of the few media representations of Mexicans, was an image that encouraged consumers to adopt an undesirable stereotype, associating this ethnic group with crime and thievery. The storm of controversy surrounding the cartoon icon reached such a fever pitch that the Frito-Lay company decided to put the Frito Bandito in his grave. They abandoned the use of the bandito in all of their advertising.

Although the Frito Bandito certainly stirred controversy, perhaps the greatest concern over the years about stereotypes in U.S. media has been about the representation of African Americans. In his brief discussion of the history of how African Americans have been portrayed over the years, Richard Jackson Harris noted that, "Until the 1960s, there were almost no African Americans as models in mainstream U.S. advertising … and the only African Americans in prime-time TV programming were limited to a few stereotyped and demeaning roles …"[42] Although the situation has certainly changed over the past four decades and the presence of African Americans is now much more commonplace in advertising and serious dramatic roles, a recent content analysis, discussed in the next section, reveals that negative media stereotyping of African Americans is still taking place in a surprising and dramatic way.

## Overrepresentation of African Americans as Lawbreakers

In a fascinating study of TV news, two media researchers, Travis Dixon and Daniel Linz, carried out a major content study designed to reveal information about how TV newscasts in a major U.S. city represented African Americans and Latinos in stories about crime.[43] Using random-sampling procedures, these authors sampled news programs from TV stations in the Los Angeles area over a period of 20 weeks. Their final sample contained 116 news broadcasts and included examples from virtually every news program broadcast in the Los Angeles area during the selected time period. A team of coders viewed these newscasts and coded all stories that reported crimes. The race of the people who were shown as perpetrators of each crime was coded, along with the race of the people who were shown as law defenders (police, judges, lawyers, etc.).

In reporting their results, Dixon and Linz relied on three types of comparisons. First, they used the **intergroup comparison**. This is a simple comparison of the percentage of one group to the percentage of another group. Intergroup comparisons have been used regularly in content analyses of racial representations. Dixon and Linz found that the news coverage across all the programs in their sample included 129 perpetrators of criminal offenses. Of those 129, 69 were Black perpetrators and 40 were White perpetrators. Stated in ratio form, for every White perpetrator shown on the news, there were 1.72 Black perpetrators. When the analysis was restricted to felony crimes, the ratio was even higher. For every White perpetrator, there were 2.46 Black perpetrators. The intergroup comparison is a convenient way to report and compare data for different groups. In this case, the data show that Blacks were more likely to be shown as perpetrators of crime than Whites. Dixon and Linz also reported similar data showing that Latinos were more likely to be shown as crime perpetrators than Whites—but not as likely as Blacks.

A second type of comparison used by Dixon and Linz was the **interrole comparison**. It is used to compare the distribution of the same group of people according to particular roles. For example, in their study, Dixon and Linz coded the race of the police officers depicted in the news stories as well as that of the perpetrators. There were 87 Blacks depicted in their sample of news stories. Of those 87, 69 appeared as perpetrators of crime, whereas only 18 appeared as officers. In ratio terms, for every Black officer, there were 3.83 crime perpetrators. When the same analysis was conducted for Whites, a different picture emerged. Of the 133 Whites who appeared in the crime stories, 93 appeared as officers and 40 appeared as perpetrators. In ratio terms, for every White officer, there were only .43 perpetrators. From this analysis, it seems clear that Blacks were more likely to be shown as perpetrators of crime than as officers; Whites were more likely to be shown as officers than as perpetrators.

Finally, Dixon and Linz used a comparison known as the **interreality comparison**. In this case, the authors were interested in comparing the percentages of Blacks, Whites, and Latinos who appeared in the TV crime stories with the percentages that showed up in actual crime statistics catalogued in the Los Angeles area. The interreality comparison is perhaps the most revealing of these three comparisons because it shows how media depictions may distort reality. When the authors went to the actual crime data, the records showed that Blacks accounted for 21% of all of the criminal arrests in Los Angeles. Whites accounted for 28%, Latinos for 47%. But when these percentages were compared to the percentages shown on TV newscasts, quite a difference emerged. Whereas Blacks actually accounted for the *lowest* percentage of arrests in the real crime statistics, they made up the *highest* percentage of perpetrators represented on TV news. Whereas their actual arrest rate was 21%, a full 37% of TV news perpetrators were Black. In contrast, compared to the actual arrest rate for Whites (28%), only 21% of the perpetrators shown on TV news were White. Just as Blacks were overrepresented as criminals on the news, Latinos appeared to be underrepresented. Compared to their actual arrest rate (47% of all arrests), only 29% of the criminal perpetrators on TV news were Latino.

In addition to providing a replication of some earlier studies on the depiction of Blacks and Whites as criminals on TV news, the study by Dixon and Linz is important because it is one of the first to report data on Latinos. It is also important in terms of the explanations that the authors advanced to explain their findings. Why might Blacks be overrepresented as criminals compared to Whites? The authors argued that TV news might be drawn to report blue-collar crime instead of white-collar crime. Blue-collar crimes such as assault and robbery are more visually dramatic and attractive to TV reporters. They may also be more likely to be committed by Blacks. Whites, who have access to more economic resources and positions of power, may be more likely to commit white-collar crime. In comparison with the highly visual drama of a violent arrest or car chase, white-collar crimes such as embezzlement don't offer exciting news footage. This may partially account for the representational distortions that Dixon and Linz uncovered.

What about the effects of these representations? You have already been reminded several times in this text that media content does not equal media effect. Dixon and Linz studied the media content—not the way that content had an impact on viewers. Nevertheless, they did underscore the need for some systematic research on the impact of these depictions. At the end of their research report, they stated the following:

> We suggest that immediate work must be undertaken with regard to how these portrayals might encourage or discourage stereotyping and increase fear of African Americans. Cultivation theory as well as the mechanisms explicated in the social cognition literature suggest that these representations may have a powerful impact on viewers (p. 151).[44]

You may want to review cultivation theory in Chapter 8, and see if you can determine what Dixon and Linz are concerned about. Recall that the theory basically states that heavy consumers of media will tend to be cultivated in terms of their attitudes and values toward the view of reality depicted by the media. One of the "mechanisms explicated in the social cognition literature" that the authors may have in mind could be **priming**, a concept discussed in Chapter 5. If the media continue to associate Blacks with the perpetration of crime and Whites with law enforcement, these associations may become so strong in a person's mind that merely thinking about one could prime thoughts of the other. Travis Dixon did more than just call for future research on the effects of these sorts of media depictions—he has explored the possible effects in a series of new studies. In one of his most recent studies, for example, he found that news viewers were more likely to perceive Blacks in general as violent individuals if they consumed heavy amounts of news in which Blacks were over-represented as criminal perpetrators.[45] In another experimental study, the results led him to conclude that "…the cognitive association between Blacks and criminality is so strong that exposure to one elicits images of the other" (p. 247).[46] These sorts of findings certainly seem to lend credence to the process of priming in this context. Dixon suggests that one main way to address this issue is to encourage media organizations to discontinue their practice of overrepresenting Blacks as criminals.

# THE IMBALANCE IN MEDIA RESEARCH ON STEREOTYPES

Countless content studies document representational distortions of various types. Such studies are so easy to conceive that if one of my graduate students seems lost in terms of a research idea for a seminar, as a last resort I will sometimes suggest a content analysis on the prevalence of some group or behavior that might be of interest in media messages. Often, specific behaviors, rather than groups of people, are the main focus of content studies. Content studies of media have examined cigarette smoking, alcohol use and abuse, seat belt use, a variety of aggressive behaviors, helping and prosocial behaviors, and so forth (see Study Box 10-4 for a focus on how some of these behaviors are depicted in movies). All of these studies have helped to contribute to our understanding of how the media may communicate subtle and not-so-subtle stereotypes.

One recent example that shows the concern about Black media stereotypes is not limited to criminal representations in the news comes from researchers at the Annenberg Public Policy Center at the University of Pennsylvania. In their article

---

## STUDY BOX 10-4 Substance Use in Teen-Centered Movies

Susannah Stern decided to study the depiction of smoking, drinking, and drug use in movies that featured teenaged characters. She was specifically interested in how these behaviors were depicted. How frequently did substance use occur? Which characters were most likely to use substances? What consequences were shown as a result of using substances? How frequently were teens shown turning down the use of substances? In order to investigate these questions, she examined the top 125 movies in terms of their box office revenues for the years 1999, 2000, and 2001. She narrowed the several hundred films on that list by focusing only on the 43 movies that featured at least one central character between the ages of 12 and 19. The films were about equally divided in terms of their MPAA rating, with most being either PG, PG-13, or R. What did she find? First, of the 143 teen characters in these movies, about 17% were shown smoking. Smoking behavior occurred equally for males and females, more attractive and less attractive characters, and for characters of different socio-economic status. Nearly 40% of the characters were shown drinking alcohol. Nearly 15% were shown drinking alcohol on multiple occasions. Of the characters who were shown drinking, over half of them were depicted as being drunk and nearly 9% of them were shown driving a vehicle while they were drunk. Only 25% of the characters who drank suffered any long-term negative consequences from their consumption. In general, most of those who drank did not experience any consequences at all from their behavior. Fewer teen characters (about 15%) were shown using drugs—but over half of those who did were not likely to experience any negative consequences from their drug use. Stern concluded that "... the world portrayed in recent teen-centered movies is one in which substance use is relatively common and mostly risk-free" (p. 340).

---

**SOURCE:** Stern, S. (2005). Messages from teens on the big screen: Smoking, drinking, and drug-use in teen-centered films. *Journal of Health Communication*, 10, 331–346.

"Burgers and Basketball," Joelle Sano Gilmore and Amy Jordan conducted a content analysis of 60 hours of children's programming over a six-week period. They focused on the advertising in those programs, analyzing over 1,000 commercials. Whites outnumbered Blacks by about 4:1 in the ads that contained at least one character. The two groups also differed with respect to the products that they were associated with. Blacks were heavily featured in ads for soft drinks and sandwiches while Whites tended to be featured in ads for breads, cereal, and dairy products. Blacks were also more likely than Whites to be featured eating meals in fast-food restaurants whereas Whites were more likely to be shown eating at home. Gilmore and Jordan concluded that ads in children's shows are modeling unhealthy eating behaviors for African American children—who are already at risk for heightened obesity. They suggested that children may be likely to imitate the behaviors that they see in the ads.[47] The "Burgers and Basketball" study is representative of the vast literature on media stereotypes in one important respect: It documents the *presence* of media stereotypes and only speculates about the possible *effects* of those stereotypes on media consumers.

The media literature reflects an imbalance between content studies and effects studies for good reason. First, although content studies are often more time consuming and tedious than studies of media impact, they also permit the researcher to avoid a number of obstacles that inevitably appear whenever people, instead of media messages, are the units of analysis in a study. Researchers who need human subjects must worry about securing approval from a human-subjects committee about the procedures that are planned. And once approval is granted, people don't always show up for the study. Sometimes they show up and then decide not to participate. Researchers must also be concerned about the ethics of exposing subjects to potentially harmful media messages. In short, research with human subjects poses many more significant hurdles than research with media messages. Often, beginning researchers will get their feet wet with a content study and never move on to research with human subjects, which is where we learn about media effects.

Another factor contributing to the imbalance may be the obligation to document the presence or absence of content *before* doing a study on media impact. For example, before I started to investigate how depictions of paranormal messages affected people's paranormal beliefs, I was concerned about the prevalence of paranormal messages in the media. It took a content study to determine that the messages were prevalent enough to warrant concern. Sometimes content studies are produced that don't end up leading to studies of media effects.

Another reason for the imbalance between studies of content and studies of effects is probably the main one: Documenting media effects is considerably more difficult than documenting the presence or absence of media content. Even in the most carefully designed sample survey, evidence for a clear causal effect remains elusive. And the most carefully designed laboratory experiment still has significant limitations in what it can reveal about media impact. Most lab experiments reveal short-term effects but tell us little about media impact over the long term. Added to these inherent design limitations, there are a host of thorny procedural details that can easily confound the best-laid plans of a would-be media effects researcher.

I don't want to be overly negative at this point. I have spent my career studying media effects, and I remain just as enthusiastic about doing effects research today as I was when I started over 30 years ago. But the point remains that solid conclusions about the content of the media are much easier to generate than solid conclusions about the impact of the media.

## AN INTRIGUING AND UNDER-STUDIED MEDIA DEPICTION: FACES

Before concluding our coverage of media stereotypes, there is one final phenomenon in which I became personally interested starting about 30 years ago. I hope you'll find this phenomenon interesting as well. In the fall of 1984, I was busy conducting research on people's emotional reactions to frightening mass media when I ran across an article that referred to a concept I hadn't heard of before. A researcher named Dane Archer, along with his colleagues, had published an article in the *Journal of Personality and Social Psychology* that was called "Face-ism: Five Studies of Sex Differences in Facial Prominence."[48] The title piqued my curiosity. What exactly was **"face-ism"**? The more I read in Archer's article, the more fascinated I became. As it turns out, face-ism refers to the tendency to represent people in terms of their face or head as opposed to their body. The face-ism index is a simple computation (see Figure 10-1) that Archer and his colleagues describe as

> ... the ratio of two linear measurements. The numerator of this index is the distance (in millimeters or any other unit) in a depiction from the top of the head to the lowest point of the chin. The denominator of the index is the distance from the top of the head to the lowest visible part of the subject's body.

Figure 10-1 shows the ratio visually and computes the face-ism index for two figures. Once I understood how the face-ism index was computed, the research findings uncovered by Archer and his colleagues seemed almost incredible.

For starters, the researchers examined more than 1,700 published photographs in the news and advertising sections of five major U.S. periodicals. They computed the average face-ism index for the males depicted in the photos and compared it to the average face-ism index computed for the females. The results were startling. For males, the average index was .65. But for females it was more than 30% less—about .45. Think about what these numbers mean. In photos of males, the head or face was depicted as about 65% of the entire male figure. But for females, the head or face was depicted as only about 45% of the entire female figure. Males were more likely to be represented in terms of their heads or faces, whereas females were more likely to be represented in terms of their bodies. It was unlikely that the difference in the face-ism ratio was due to chance. The probability of getting a difference by chance that was as large as the one documented in Archer's research was less than 1 in 1,000 ($p < .001$).

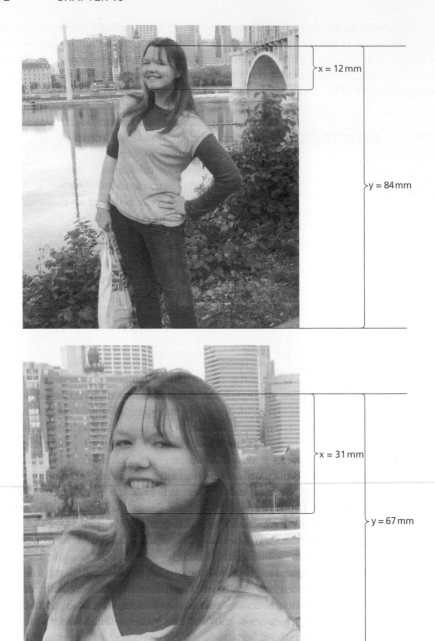

x = 12 mm

y = 84 mm

x = 31 mm

y = 67 mm

## Figure 10-1  Face-ism Ratios

The face-ism ratio is computed by taking the distance from the top of the head to the bottom of the chin and dividing it by the distance from the top of the head to the bottom of the body. In the top picture, the ratio is 12 mm / 84 mm, or 0.14. In the bottom picture, the ratio is 31 mm / 67 mm, or 0.46. In general, media depictions of males are more likely to resemble the bottom picture. Media depictions of females are more likely to be like the top picture.

As I started to think about what differences in face-ism might mean (the authors refer to these differences as the "face-ism effect"), Archer and his colleagues hit me with even more provocative findings. The face-ism effect is not limited to U.S. media. It was documented in publications from nearly a dozen countries across the globe. In addition to generalizing across countries, the effect apparently generalizes across centuries as well. The authors noted that in a study of nearly 1,000 portraits and self-portraits over a span of six centuries, the same face-ism effect emerged again and again. There was even some evidence that the size of the difference between male and female representations was increasing over time.

The authors also reported research that investigated the extent to which face-ism might be present in private representations as well as public ones. In drawings of college students that were requested from both males and females, the male images were repeatedly drawn with higher face-ism ratios than the images of females. I was intrigued by the factors that might lie behind this systematic difference in male and female representations. Of course, one obvious hypothesis is that the images simply reflect a real biological difference—that male heads are larger than those of females. However, this hypothesis turns out not to be true. As I searched for a less obvious explanation, Archer and his colleagues threw in the real kicker. In an experiment that manipulated face-ism ratios for photos of the same individual, naive judges rated the people who were high on facial prominence in the photos as more intelligent, more ambitious, and better looking.

Frankly, when I read about this research, I thought the potential effects of face-ism in the media were nothing short of staggering. If high facial prominence was associated with intelligence, ambition, and attractiveness, then what was the impact of media depictions of females (who were characteristically low in facial prominence) on the general way females were perceived in the culture at large: Were females perceived as less intelligent? Less ambitious? Less attractive? These were potential effects that, as far as I knew, had never been explored by media effects researchers.

My fascination with the face-ism effect might have taken a back seat to my other research had it not been for a graduate student, Christine Fehlner, who occupied an office nearby and happened to be working on a project that tracked news coverage of the presidential campaign of 1984. Just after I finished reading about face-ism, I came out of my office and saw a stack of newspapers that Fehlner had been collecting for stories of campaign coverage. There on the front page was a picture of Walter Mondale, the Democratic nominee for president, along with his vice presidential running mate, the first female ever to occupy this role, Geraldine Ferraro. At that instant, the idea to begin investigating the face-ism effect in the 1984 political campaign was born. Fehlner and I went on to conduct a study on this topic that was published two years later in the *Journal of Communication*.[49] We looked at the face-ism ratios of the two male Republican candidates, Ronald Reagan and George Bush, as well as those of Mondale and Ferraro. We looked at these ratios for all photos that appeared in *Time* and *Newsweek* during the months of the campaign. Our findings diverged a bit from Archer's. The face-ism ratios of the four candidates were essentially equivalent. But when we went back and looked at other males and females pictured in the same magazines, we found evidence of the same face-ism effect that had been reported in past research. Males were more likely to be depicted with higher levels of facial prominence than females.

We can't be certain exactly why we found no face-ism effect in how Geraldine Ferraro was represented compared to the male candidates. Perhaps the results of our study are best explained by a norm of equivalent representation for all candidates in a presidential campaign. We noted that in many of the pictorial layouts in magazines, the presidential candidates were presented in photos that were framed identically and appeared as offsetting, competing representations. It may be that in politics at the national level, the press is constrained to represent candidates in a photographically similar manner, regardless of gender.

In the end, the most interesting aspect of the face-ism effect is the fact that people's perceptions of those with higher facial prominence are more positive. Some scholars have suggested that this has to do with the fact that the head is where the brain is and that people think of the head or face as the center of an individual's intelligence. Whatever the reason, if the media represent males with higher facial prominence than females, the experimental data would suggest that this practice has negative implications for the evaluation of women. I would like to conduct a study in which people are asked to report their exposure to mass media and also asked to provide their own drawings of males and females. One hypothesis based on the current literature would be that heavy media consumers who spend more time processing faces that are systematically different according to the sex-biased face-ism effect might be more likely to show this effect in their own drawings. This is a study waiting to be done.

I am certainly not alone in expressing interest in the face-ism effect after reading the work of Archer and his colleagues. The face-ism effect has attracted some recent attention from other researchers. Miron Zuckerman and Suzanne Kieffer examined pictures of Whites and Blacks that have appeared in paintings, in periodicals, and on the face of postage stamps. Reasoning from the past literature that higher facial prominence was associated with impressions of power, they predicted that images of Blacks would have lower facial prominence than images of Whites. This is exactly what they found. Moreover, they also found concrete evidence that people represented in photos with higher facial prominence were perceived as being more dominant.[50] In examining the difference in facial prominence in the media between males and females, Sarah Konrath and Norbert Schwartz decided to make sure that these differences were not linked to actual anatomical differences between males and females. Relying on measurements collected from some 150,000 medical body scans, they found that the actual face-ism ratio from real bodies was larger for *females* (.1355) than for males (.1344). They went on to report that when they examined headshot portraits of politicians across several countries, males were shown with higher facial prominence than females.[51] In another study, Justin Matthews examined photographs that were embedded in articles in six different popular U.S. magazines. He found that for occupations that were focused on the intellect (politicians, lawyers, business, etc.), males had higher facial prominence than females. In contrast, for occupations that were focused on physical activity, females had higher facial prominence than males.[52] In a provocative exploration of the relationship between facial prominence and power, Rachel Calogero and Brian Mullen examined images of George W. Bush in political cartoons. They found that immediately after the onset of two different wars, Bush's facial prominence in cartoon images decreased—indicating, perhaps, that he was perceived as losing power as a consequence of his involvement in war.[53]

Finally, two communication researchers asked an interesting question recently about facial prominence: When people are given the choice to represent themselves online with a profile photograph, would males and females choose pictures that conform to the stereotyped research findings? In a content analysis of 1,400 photographs taken from social networking sites around the world (Facebook in the U.S. and analogous sites from six other nations), Lauren Reichart Smith and Skye Cooley documented that, indeed, the profile photos of men were significantly higher on facial prominence when compared to the photos of women. Just as in Archer's original work, Smith and Cooley's study shows that sex differences in facial prominence are not limited to a single culture but constitute a global phenomenon.[54]

So, where does all this leave us? The research reviewed in this chapter leaves little doubt that media stereotypes do affect people. Nevertheless, the challenge for the research community is to begin taking some of the well-documented stereotypical depictions (e.g., sex and race stereotypes) and showing precisely how they affect people's attitudes and behaviors. It is one thing to speculate on the importance of media stereotypes; it is quite another thing to actually document the importance with a carefully executed study that shows evidence of media impact. The only other study in the literature that I'm aware of—beyond the original work of Archer's research team—that shows how facial prominence is related to positive evaluations is an experiment that was reported over a decade ago in the journal *Sex Roles*.[55] Clearly, more research is needed.

# SUMMARY

This chapter reviewed research on various stereotypes in the mass media that have been documented by content analyses. Sexual stereotypes and racial stereotypes are two areas of research that have received the most attention. Although some studies on the effects of stereotypes have been undertaken, it was noted that content studies are far more prevalent than studies of impact. One area of effects is in the study of female body images and their possible impact on body dissatisfaction and eating disorders. Although there's evidence of an effect in this literature, the jury is still out regarding a strong consensus among social scientists. The reasons for the existence of fewer studies on effects and more on content were discussed, and the important distinction between content and effect was again emphasized. The chapter concluded with an examination of an intriguing phenomenon involving the depiction of male and female faces and bodies in the media. In comparison to males, females tend to be shown in terms of their bodies instead of their heads or faces. The implications of this phenomenon in terms of people's perceptions of males and females were highlighted.

## QUESTIONS TO FOCUS YOUR ATTENTION

1. Try to think about the ways you believe media depictions might stereotype certain groups of people. Which stereotypes do you think might be particularly harmful? Why?
2. Which media stereotypes, if any, do you believe may have influenced you while you were growing up? Was the influence positive or negative?
3. If some media stereotypes have negative effects, what's the most effective way to counteract these effects?

## KEY TERMS AND CONCEPTS

| | | |
|---|---|---|
| role schema | body image disturbance | interreality comparison |
| stereotyped | social comparison | priming |
| meta-analysis | critical media consumption | "face-ism" |
| construction of social reality | intergroup comparison | |
| body dissatisfaction | interrole comparison | |

## NOTES

1. Harrison, J. (2012). Huggies pulls ads after Dads insulted. *ABC News: Parenting*. [Online: Accessed 6-18-14]. Available: http://abcnews.go.com/blogs/lifestyle/2012/03/huggies-pulls-ads-after-dads-insulted/

2. Starpulse.com. (June 1, 2011). Naomi Campbell upset over Cadbury ad. [Online: Accessed 6-18-14]. Available: http://www.starpulse.com/news/Livia_Soong/2011/06/01/naomi_campbell_upset_over_cadbury_ad

3. Sweeney, M. (June 3, 2011). Cadbury apologises to Naomi Campbell over 'racist ad'. [Online: Accessed 6-18-14]. Available: http://www.guardian.co.uk/media/2011/jun/03/cadbury-naomi-campbell-ad

4. Kimberley, S. (2011). ASA rejects 'racist' Cadbury ad complaints. *Campaign*. [Online: Accessed 6-18-14]. Available: http://www.campaignlive.co.uk/news/1075981/

5. Clifford, S. (May 30, 2008). For Dunkin', a tempest in an iced-coffee cup. *New York Times*. [Online: Accessed 6-18-14]. Available: http://www.nytimes.com/2008/05/30/business/media/30adco.html?_r=0

6. Fiske, S. T, & Taylor, S. E. (1991). *Social cognition*. New York: McGraw-Hill.

7. Williams, T. M. (1986). *The impact of television: A natural experiment in three communities*. Orlando, FL: Academic Press.

8. Katzman, N. (1972). Television soap operas: What's been going on anyway? *Public Opinion Quarterly, 36,* 200–212.

9. Harris, R. J. (1999). *A cognitive psychology of mass communication*. Mahwah, NJ: Erlbaum.

10. Dobrow, J. R., & Gidney, C. L. (1998). The good, the bad, and the foreign: The use of dialect in children's animated television. *The Annals of the American Academy of Political and Social Science, 557,* 105–119.

11. Bred, D. J., & Cantor, J. (1988). The portrayal of men and women on U.S. television commercials: A recent content analysis and trends over 15 years. *Sex Roles, 18,* 595–609.

12. Jhally, S. (1994). *The killing screens: Media and the culture of violence* [Video]. Northampton, MA: Media Education Foundation.

13. Harris, R. J. (2004). *A cognitive psychology of mass communication*. Mahwah, NJ: Erlbaum.

14. Lauzen, M. M., Dozier, D. M., & Horan, N. (2008). Constructing gender stereotypes through social roles in prime-time television. *Journal of Broadcasting & Electronic Media, 52(2),* 200–214.

15. Herrett-Skjellum, J., & Allen, M. (1996). Television programming and sex stereotyping: A meta-analysis. In B. R. Burleson (Ed.), *Communication yearbook* (pp. 157–185). Thousand Oaks, CA: Sage.

16. Jhally, S. (1997). The electronic storyteller: Television and the cultivation of values. *Media Education Foundation.*

17. Bentley, A. (June 4, 2011). Simi Woman's Mission is to Get Girls into IT and Gaming Careers. [Online: Accessed 6-18-14]. Available: http://www.vcstar.com/news/2011/jun/04/simi-womans-mission-is-to-get-girls-into-it-and/

18. Hawkins, R. P., Pingree, S., & Adler, I. (1987). Searching for cognitive processes in the cultivation effect: Adult and adolescent samples in the United States and Australia. *Human Communication Research, 13*, 553–577.

19. Kimball, M. A. (1986). Television and sex-role attitudes. In T. M. Williams (Ed.), *The impact of television: A natural experiment in three communities* (pp. 265–301). Orlando, FL: Academic Press.

20. Oppliger, P. A. (2007). Effects of gender stereotyping on socialization. In R. W. Preiss, B. M. Gayle, N. Burrell, M. Allen, & J. Bryant (Eds.), *Mass media effects research: Advances through meta-analysis* (pp. 199–214). Mahwah, NJ: Erlbaum.

21. Fouts, G., & Burggraf, K. (2000). Television situation comedies: Female weight, male negative comments, and audience reactions. *Sex Roles, 42*, 925–932.

22. Malkin, A. R., Worman, K., & Chnsler, J. C. (1999). Women and weight: Gendered messages on magazine covers. *Sex Roles, 40*, 647–655.

23. Hefner, V., Woodward, K., Figge, L., Bevan, J. L., Santora, N., & Baloch, S. (2014). The influence of television and film viewing on midlife women's body image, disordered eating, and food choice. *Media Psychology, 17*, 185–207.

24. Stice, E., & Shaw, H. E. (1994). Adverse effects of the media portrayed thin-ideal on women and linkages to bulimic symptomatology. *Journal of Social & Clinical Psychology, 13*, 288–308.

25. Harrison, K., & Cantor, J. (1997). The relationship between media consumption and eating disorders. *Journal of Communication, 47*, 40–67.

26. Harrison, K. (2000). The body electric: Thin-ideal media and eating disorders in adolescents. *Journal of Communication, 50*, 119–143.

27. Tucci, S., & Peters, J. (2008). Media influences on body dissatisfaction in female students. *Psicothema, 20*(4), 521–524.

28. Hargreaves, D., & Tiggemann, M. (2003). Longer-term implications of responsiveness to "thin-ideal" television: Support for a cumulative hypothesis of body image disturbance? *European Eating Disorders Review, 11*(6), 465–477.

29. Aghata, D., & Tantleff-Dunn, S. (2004). The impact of media exposure on males' body image. *Journal of Social & Clinical Psychology, 23*(1), 7–22.

30. Harper, B., & Tiggemann, M. (2008). The effect of thin ideal media images on women's self-objectification, mood, and body image. *Sex Roles, 58*(9/10), 649–657.

31. Grabe, S., Ward, M. L., & Hyde, J. S. (2008). The role of the media in body image concerns among women: A meta-analysis of experimental and correlational studies. *Psychological Bulletin, 134*(3), 460–176.

32. López-Guimerà, G., Levine, M.P., Sánchez-Carrecedo, D., & Fauquet, J. (2010). Influence of mass media on body image and eating disordered attitudes and behaviors in females: A review of effects and processes. *Media Psychology, 13*, 387–416.

33. Hefner, V., Woodward, K., Figge, L., Bevan, J. L., Santora, N., & Baloch, S. (2014). The influence of television and film viewing on midlife women's body image, disordered eating, and food choice. *Media Psychology, 17*, 185–207.

34. Roberts, A., & Good, E. (2010). Media images and body dissatisfaction: The moderating effects of the Five-Factor traits. *Eating Behaviors, 11*(4), 211–216.

35. Jackson, T., & Chen, H. (2011). Risk factors for disordered eating during early and middle adolescence: Prospective evidence from mainline Chinese boys and girls. *Journal of Abnormal Psychology, 120*(2), 454–464.

36. Ferguson, C. J., Muñoz, M. E., Garza, A., & Galindo, M. (2014). Concurrent and prospective analyses of peer, television and social media influences on body dissatisfaction, eating disorder symptoms, and life satisfaction in adolescent girls. *Journal of Youth and Adolescence, 43*(1), 1–14.

37. Ferguson, C., Winegard, B., & Winegard, B. M. (2011). Who is the fairest one of all? How evolution guides peer and media influences on female body dissatisfaction. *Review of General Psychology, 15*(1), 11–28.

38. Irving, L. M., DuPen, J., & Berel, S. (1998). A media literacy program for high school females. *Eating Disorders: The Journal of Treatment & Prevention, 6*, 119–132.

39. Veldhuis, J., Konign, E. A., & Seidell, J. C. (2014). Counteracting media's thin-body ideal for adolescent girls. Informing is more effective than warning. *Media Psychology, 17*, 154–184.

40. Jhally, S. (1990). *Dreamworlds: Gender sex/power in rock video*. Northampton, MA: Media Education Foundation.

41. Jhally, S., & Kilbourne J. (2010). *Killing us softly 4: Advertising's image of women*. Northampton, MA: Media Education Foundation.

42. Harris, R. J. (2004). *A cognitive psychology of mass communication*. Mahwah, NJ: Erlbaum.

43. Dixon, T. L., & Linz, D. (2000). Over-representation and under-representation of African Americans and Latinos as lawbreakers on television news. *Journal of Communication,* 50(2), 131–154.

44. *Ibid.,* Dixon & Linz, 2000.

45. Dixon, T. (2008). Crime news and racialized beliefs: Understanding the relationship between local news viewing and perceptions of African Americans and crime. *Journal of Communication,* 58(1), 106–125.

46. Dixon, T. L., & Azocar, C. L. (2007). Priming crime and activating blackness: Understanding the psychological impact of the overrepresentation of blacks as lawbreakers on television news. *Journal of Communication*, 57, 229–253.

47. Gilmore, J. S., & Jordan, A. (2012). Burgers and basketball: Race and stereotypes in food and beverage advertising aimed at children in the US. *Journal of Children and Media,* 6(3), 317–332.

48. Archer, D., Intam, B., Kimes, D. D., & Barrios, M. (1983). Face-ism: Five studies of sex differences in facial prominence. *Journal of Personality and Social Psychology,* 45, 725–735.

49. Sparks, G. G., & Fehlner, C. L. (1986). Faces in the news: Gender comparisons of magazine photographs. *Journal of Communication,* 36, 70–79.

50. Zuckerman, M., & Kieffer, S. C. (1994). Race differences in face-ism: Does facial prominence imply dominance? *Journal of Personality & Social Psychology,* 66, 86–92.

51. Konrath, S. H., & Schwarz, N. (2007). Do male politicians have big heads? Face-ism in online self-representations of politicians. *Media Psychology,* 10(3), 436–448.

52. Matthews, J. L. (2007). Hidden sexism: Facial prominence and its connections to gender and occupational status in popular print media. *Sex Roles,* 57(7/8), 515–525.

53. Calogero, R. M., & Mullen, B. (2008). About face: Facial prominence of George W. Bush in political cartoons as a function of war. *Leadership Quarterly,* 19(1), 107–116.

54. Smith, L. R., & Cooley, S. C. (2012). International faces: An analysis of self-inflicted face-ism in online profile pictures. *Journal of Intercultural Communication Research*, 41(3), 279–296.

55. Leveque, M. J., & Lowe, C. A. (1999). Face-ism as a determinant of interpersonal perceptions: The influence of context on facial prominence effects. *Sex Roles,* 41(3–4), 241–259.

# 11

# The Impact of New Media Technologies

## THE REVOLUTION IN NEW MEDIA TECHNOLOGY

When I think about new media technology, I frequently recall the words to a song from my favorite musician, Paul Simon. A few of the lyrics from his song "The Boy in the Bubble" (*Graceland*, Warner Brothers) serve as a poignant reminder of the incredible age in which we live: "These are the days of lasers in the jungle/Lasers in the jungle somewhere/Staccato signals of constant information/a loose affiliation of millionaires/And billionaires, and baby/These are the days of miracle and wonder/This is the long-distance call/The way the camera follows us in slo-mo/The way we look to us all ..." For a scholar of media effects, the age in which we live today is truly spectacular. Nevertheless, over the past 75 years, media effects researchers have usually lagged behind in studying the impact of the latest media. As late as 1960, when TV had exploded on the scene, the prevailing wisdom among researchers was that electronic media had limited effects. You might recall from Chapter 3 that this "wisdom" was mainly the consequence of a single study—a large survey conducted during the 1940 presidential campaign, before the days of television. It wasn't until the mid-1960s, almost 25 years after the survey that ushered in the era of limited media effects, that researchers began systematically studying the effects of TV.

Of course, it makes some sense that research on a given medium would lag a bit behind. Any new technology has to be in place and in use by a reasonable proportion of the population before the research community deems it worthwhile to focus on the impact of that new technology. Consequently, when we ask questions about the effects of new technology, it makes sense that the number of studies at our disposal is not nearly as great as when we ask questions about the effects of a well-established medium such as TV or film. A complicating feature of research on new technology is that some technologies become old quickly or simply don't have the staying power that TV has proven to have. If a researcher is interested in doing a study that will endure in the literature, there's a greater risk of choosing to study the effects of the newest technology that's appeared on the scene. If that technology fades away, the relevance of the research may fade along with it.

Consider, for example, the platform known as Second Life. As a student in a university course on media, the chances are better for you than most people that you've heard about this virtual environment that was introduced back in 2003. On the Internet, you can visit the Second Life Web site, download the software, and then create an avatar (a visual representation of yourself) and do most anything in "second life" that you can do in your regular life. Maybe you even have an avatar in that environment and meet friends regularly in different places around the world. But when I mention Second Life to general audiences of older adults during some of the speeches I give around the country, I get furrowed brows and quizzical looks. I have to explain exactly what Second Life is all about. Increasingly, that's the same reaction I get from college students. Although somewhere around a million users still log on each month, the big buzz about Second Life has worn off and the explosive growth it saw a decade ago has essentially stopped.[1] If you're not familiar with Second Life, you can Google it and get up to speed quickly. Eight years ago, one executive told me that corporations are increasingly embracing this technology to hold important meetings as an alternative to having to travel thousands of miles to meet clients face to face. A number of colleges offer courses through Second Life, but the initial excitement about this new environment for learning has cooled considerably. If I had poured time and energy into research on Second Life, I might be feeling a bit irrelevant at this point.

Sometimes, it is only when we reflect on the past that we're able to realize just how quickly the new technology that surrounds us today is changing. The pace of change can seem staggering. When I wrote one of the previous editions of this text, only about 25% of my students reported that they had a personal Facebook page. That's all changed quickly. A few years ago, one student who sat in the back of the class and rarely spoke a word the entire semester, perked up when I asked who had a Facebook page. He bluntly pronounced, "If you don't have a Facebook page, you're a nobody." The rest of the class agreed. There wasn't a single student in the room who was willing to report that they weren't on Facebook. Two or three students reported that they had between 1,500 and 2,500 "friends" on their Facebook site. While the meaning of the term "friend" in this context may be different than the meaning we've been accustomed to in decades past, many of these online relationships are far from trivial. Dating sites specialize in helping people cultivate romantic relationships. In the last edition of the text, I noted that about one in every eight marriages in the United States started when the couple met online. That figure has now changed, as one study based on over 19,000 participants found that more than one in every three marriages in the United States begins online.[2] The incredible pace of technological change nearly guarantees that by the time you read these words, the situation will be different than it was when the words were written. My own students at Purdue seem to be shifting their interest to Twitter and away from Facebook in the last year or two. What about you?

When we talk about the impact or effects of new media technology, there are a host of effects that we might potentially contemplate. Computers and the World

Wide Web have certainly changed the way we behave in many domains. People shop online, trade stocks online, get their news online, initiate friendships online, and so forth. Children spend time online playing the latest computer games. The potential effects that we could discuss might easily turn into a separate, book-length volume. About all we can do in this short chapter is whet your appetite to explore the terrain on your own in greater depth.

What is all of this new technology doing to us? For one thing, it is encouraging traditional media effects scholars to ask new questions and design new research paradigms. One of the old labels used in media curricula at various universities is "mass communication." If you think about some of the new technologies that are emerging today, it seems clear that they challenge the traditional concept of mass communication (see the discussion of this at the beginning of Chapter 4). Scholars who were trained under the assumptions of the old environment are finding that they have to make some adjustments in their thinking about what counts as a legitimate phenomenon to examine. In the confusion, however, there is also much excitement about conducting research on media that are brand new and may be affecting us in different and undiscovered ways.

Nearly 15 years ago, two media scholars, Jane Brown and Joanne Cantor, outlined a series of crucial questions surrounding new technology that researchers need to continue to study in future years. They framed these questions in terms of the concept of **perpetual linkage**, the new tendency for youth to be constantly connected with each other through some type of technology. The authors asked the following questions:

> What is the impact of the connectedness that the newer media promote, i.e., the almost constant technological links that youth have with each other, using their cell phones, beepers, email, and other devices soon to be developed? What about the relationships young people have with others they have met only via technological links? Do youth, for example, have stronger social ties to their peers because they are in virtual contact for so much more of the time? Or are they more alienated because this technological contact comes at the expense of potentially richer face-to-face interaction?[3]

These questions have helped to define the new research literature, and we are beginning to get clues on some of the answers.

Another area of research that has caught the attention of researchers and public health officials in the past few years is the impact of video games on youth. You will recall from Chapter 5 that there has been a modest amount of research on games that involve graphic violence and permit the player to take the role of a "first-person shooter." In these games, the player handles a gun and fires directly at characters on the screen in an attempt to "kill" them. But violence in video games is not the only issue. Like the questions raised by Brown and Cantor, the questions that arise about the general impact of video games still demand more research before a consensus emerges among scholars. Even though there are still more questions about computer use and video games than there are clear answers in the research literature, studies have been published in the past few years that address some of the issues. This chapter introduces you to some of the studies that have been done in some of the key research areas and outlines some of the current controversies and issues that remain for future studies.

## COMPUTERS AND THE INTERNET: CONNECTION OR ALIENATION?

The latest statistics on Internet use suggest that nearly 87% of the U.S. population uses it regularly.[4] With a large share of American homes connected to broadband service (over 70%) and with the rising popularity of social networking, the late 1990s and first decade of the new millennium will go down in media history as the years when the Internet exploded onto the scene, much as TV did between 1950 and 1960 (see Chapter 3). The revolution is still unfolding. Although the Pew Research Internet and American Life Project reports that only about 14% of Americans use Twitter,[5] Twitter has fast become part of America's social networking fabric. A casual perusal of the research literature shows that scholars are actively involved in trying to understand how Twitter is functioning to enhance conversations about politics, as well as strengthen the sense of connection that people have with celebrities, companies, and discussion forums. In short, the "Twittersphere" is now a place where communication of all types thrives.

A good place to start gaining an appreciation for research on new technology is to examine what is now nearly a classic study on the Internet's impact on relationships—the HomeNet Study at Carnegie Mellon University. The study is important not so much for its particular findings, but for some of the theoretical concepts it introduced and for the groundwork it laid for future studies.

### The Carnegie Mellon Study

Over 15 years ago, a research team at Carnegie Mellon University, led by Robert Kraut of the Human Computer Interaction Institute, published one of the first major studies on the impact of Internet use. The researchers titled their study with a provocative question: "Internet Paradox: A Social Technology That Reduces Social Involvement and Psychological Well-Being?"[6]

The question gives a strong clue to the answer that their research provided. One thing that emerges quite quickly upon reading the original research report is that studying the impact of the Internet is not an easy proposition. The researchers had to put in a lot of effort to set up their study in a way that would yield meaningful results. As you will see, even after all of this effort, the study was severely criticized.

One of the positive features of the Carnegie Mellon study (sometimes referred to as the HomeNet study) was the fact that the researchers employed a longitudinal design. Recall from Chapter 2 that a longitudinal study is one in which data are collected at several points in time. In this case, the study involved 256 people in 93 different households during their first two years of being online. Each family received a computer, a free telephone line, and a free Internet connection. The families who participated had a high school student in the household or belonged to at least one community group in the Pittsburgh area. In return for the freebies, the families agreed that the researchers could track their Internet use with special software and periodically ask them survey questions during the time period of the study.

Despite the fact that the researchers found that the people in the study used the Internet to engage in communication with others, they also found evidence of a rather alarming state of affairs. Use of the Internet was associated with a general decline in communication with family members who lived in the household. In addition, those who used the Internet more frequently tended to report that the number of people in their social circle declined over the years of the study. Finally, Internet users tended to report greater levels of depression and feelings of loneliness than they did before the study began.

If using the Internet is really associated with these negative psychological effects, what specifically is it about using the Net that causes them to occur? According to Kraut and his associates, there were two main possibilities. First, the data might reveal an **activity displacement effect**. This sort of effect was discussed in Chapter 4 in connection with TV. People have a limited amount of time during any day to engage in their various activities. Once family members are hooked up to the Internet, perhaps they tend to spend more time in isolation from others, using the Internet for private entertainment and Web surfing. Second, perhaps the data reveal that the Internet **displaces strong social ties**. According to this explanation, when people go online, they often end up talking to people in chat rooms and even occasionally make new friends. But overall, the kinds of relationships that are formed online tend to be more superficial and are characterized by weaker ties than the relationships that people tend to have with family members and significant others who appear in one's life face to face on a daily basis. When people use the Internet, they may be depriving themselves of the richness of their deeper, strong ties with family and other significant friends in favor of relationships that are not nearly as deep or involving.

After considering these two alternatives, the authors clearly seemed to prefer the second option to the first. The main reason they rejected the activity displacement explanation is that their data showed that so many people in their sample used the Internet for social purposes. Clearly, if the reason for increasing isolation and loneliness was the fact that the Internet was displacing social contact, the data would have to show that people weren't using the Internet to connect socially—and that their overall social contact before Internet use was greater than it was after they started using the Web. But the data didn't show that at all. People used the Net for exchanging email, going to chat rooms, and so forth. Moreover, the authors claimed that some of their data actually showed that those who used the Internet for social purposes were more likely to suffer the negative social effects than those who used the Net for less social purposes. If the negative effects were due to the fact that Internet use displaced social activity, we probably wouldn't observe that particular pattern in the data.

The authors preferred to focus on the possibility that, rather than displacing social activity in general, Internet use tends to encourage a particular type of social relationship at the expense of another. They suggested that Internet users form more superficial relationships instead of connecting deeply to other human beings. If you take a moment to think about it, this view does make some sense. If the extent of your involvement with a person is through email, there is much about that other person that you don't know. Online relationships also don't tend to encourage the kind of mutual help and service that characterize most close friendships. When I think of the people in my own life who are closest to me, they all tend to be people who would feel comfortable calling me on the phone and asking me to run an errand for them. And I would feel equally comfortable calling them for the same. It may be that the deep intimacy that comes with relationships is built on a kind of involvement and mutual service that online connections simply don't tend to produce. And if people spend time online in these more superficial relationships, they are using up time that they would otherwise have for relationships of the deeper variety.

You may be skeptical of the "weak ties" idea. After all, if more than one out of every three marriages starts with an online meeting, perhaps there's more going on here than just the formation of weak friendships. Although there are *some* people who may have discovered deep intimate friendships while using the Internet, Robert Kraut and his colleagues pointed out that the best data seemed to refute this pattern as normative. They noted that their own data appear to converge with data collected by two other researchers, James Katz and Philip Aspden. In a national survey conducted by these authors, they found that only "22% of the respondents who had been using the Internet for two or more years had ever made a new friend on the Internet."[7] More recent research also seems consistent with this finding. A team of researchers who studied 251 adolescents concluded that their main use of online time was spent in making their off-line relationships stronger.[8]

The fact that most people may not be using the Internet to make new friends doesn't mean that they aren't using the Web to express their views to others. Some experimental work on Internet interaction suggests that even communicating with strangers can induce strong feelings. In one study, the amount of communication between participants in a chat room was positively correlated with the nature of the statements that people were making. The researchers examined both positive statements and negative statements made during chats. Positive statements were ones that complimented another person, expressed agreement with the other, expressed approval of some idea or behavior, expressed a positive emotion, and so forth. Negative statements were ones that criticized another person, expressed disagreement with the other, expressed disapproval, or expressed a negative emotion. Intuitively, you might think that the more positive the comments, the more communication took place. Actually, the correlation was in precisely the opposite direction. The more negative the comments, the more communication took place. At least in chat rooms, positive comments don't seem to get many takers. People seem more willing to argue and engage in various forms of hostility.[9] Why is this the case? Study Box 11-1 focuses on some experimental work on Internet communication that confirms that people experience intense feelings in Internet interactions. Study Box 11-2 highlights a more recent experiment that helps in understanding some of the dynamics at work when people express their hostility online. As it turns out, the lack of eye contact and what the authors call the "**online sense of unidentifiability**" appear to be key factors in hostile online interactions.

## STUDY BOX 11-1 Virtual Relationships Can Induce Strong Emotions

Researchers are now using the Internet to set up various kinds of experiments. Although there are some limitations to this type of research, psychologists and communication researchers will undoubtedly use the Internet to collect valuable data in future years. In one recent experiment, three researchers set up an Internet study that had nearly 1,500 participants from 62 countries. When the participants arrived at the Web site, they were told that the purpose of the experiment was to see if computers could be used as a tool in mental visualization. They were asked to engage in a relatively simple exercise in which they would virtually toss a flying disk to one of two other players who they thought were playing the game online at the same time. Actually, the other two players were generated by the computer software and were controlled by the program. During the task, the players were asked to visualize themselves throwing the disk and catching it. No disk actually appeared on the screen. The computer program informed the players when the disk was tossed, who caught it, and who should throw it next. Each player was represented on the screen with a color. The participants had to push a button when they were in possession of the disk to throw it to one of the other players. They also could select which of the other players (colors) to throw it at.

After two throws, the computer program assigned each participant to one of four experimental conditions. In two of the conditions, the participants were ostracized— they were almost never on the receiving end of a throw from the other two players. In one of these conditions, they were *never* thrown the disk. In the other condition, they were thrown the disk only 20% of the time. In the other two conditions, participants were either included in the game at a rate equal to the other two players, or they were over-included—receiving the throws 67% of the time.

Following the game, participants reported their feelings. As levels of ostracism increased, so too did the respondents' reports of bad feelings, perceptions of less control, and feelings of a loss of belonging. Even though the supposed players could not be seen, were complete strangers, were unlikely ever to be engaged in future interaction, and were throwing a virtual disk that was only imaginary, the participants in the experiment felt a dampening of their mood when they were excluded from the game. The authors concluded that "As our global society moves closer to worldwide use of the Internet, opportunities for exacerbating these feelings through real or perceived ostracism clearly exist and demand our attention" (p. 760).

Unfortunately, the authors' conclusion foreshadowed a recent tragedy when a 13-year-old girl, Megan Meier, took her own life after the young boy she thought she had been communicating with online for a month ("Josh") terminated the relationship and told her that he had heard that she was cruel. In the aftermath of the suicide, authorities discovered that Josh was actually a fictitious person that had been invented by Megan's former friend and family members as a prank. Not every victim of such a prank would decide to commit suicide, but this sad incident serves to illustrate the powerful emotional consequences that can result from online communication with an unseen and relatively unknown other.

SOURCE: Williams, K. D., Cheung, C. K. T., & Choi, W. (2000). Cyberostracism: Effects of being ignored over the Internet. *Journal of Personality & Social Psychology, 79,* 748–762; MSNBC: "Mom: Girl killed herself over online hoax" [Online]. Available: http://www.msnbc.msn.com/id/21844203/ns/technology_and_science-internet/t/mom-girl-killed-herself-over-online-hoax/

## STUDY BOX 11-2 Lack of Eye Contact Facilitates Hostility Online

Two researchers who wanted to study the factors that might contribute to online "flaming"—expressions of negative emotions that use swear words, insults, and threats during an interaction—decided to design an experiment. Using 142 participants who were enrolled at two academic institutions in Israel, each participant was paired with someone else and instructed to have an online conversation. Specifically, the participants were each told to imagine that a loved one or dear friend was dying and needed a life-saving drug—but that the drug could only be made available to one of them. Each participant was instructed to make the case to the other that they should be the recipient of the drug.

While the topic of the online interaction was the same for all of the participants, the conditions in which they interacted were different. First, the participants were assigned randomly to interact either anonymously (an assigned alias) or with their full identity known to the other (full name, gender, place of residence, academic major, and place of employment, if any). Second, participants in each of those conditions were assigned randomly to interact invisibly (no web cam) or visibly (with a web cam that provided a side-view of the person they were interacting with). Finally, half of the participants assigned to interact visibly had a second web cam that provided direct eye contact with their conversational partner, and they were instructed to maintain eye contact throughout the conversation. The researchers were able to give each participant an overall "flaming" score based on a combination of experts who judged the conversations. The flaming score also incorporated an objective textual analysis of the conversations as well as the self-reports of the participants.

The results of the study were revealing. Flaming behavior (threats and hostile comments) was more prevalent when the participants were anonymous and when they were invisible to each other. Of special importance, the number of threats and hostile comments were nearly double in the condition without eye contact. The authors concluded that the lack of eye contact "... caused more impact than either anonymity or invisibility in producing the toxic behaviors implied by online disinhibition." A new concept that the authors introduced to help explain the online environment is the "online sense of unidentifiability." In general, as one's sense of unidentifiability increases, so too does the probability of feeling free to hurl toxic comments and threats at a conversational partner.

SOURCE: Lapidot-Lefler, M., & Barak, A. (2012). Effects of anonymity, invisibility, and lack of eye-contact on toxic online disinhibition. *Computers in Human Behavior*, 28(2), 434–443.

## Applying the Lessons of History

You might recall from Chapter 5 on media violence that one of the earliest theorists who conducted research on the impact of televised violence was Seymour Feshbach. His theory of symbolic catharsis received some initial support from a few studies, and in the early 1960s many researchers thought that this idea would become a dominant one in the literature. Alas, as often happens in science, some ideas that receive initial support turn out to be wrong. In interpreting the results from the Carnegie Mellon study, we should be careful. The study is not without its critics. Donna Hoffman, editor of the journal *Marketing Science*, was quoted shortly after the study's release as saying, "Speaking as an editor, if this had crossed my desk, I would have rejected it.... The mistakes are so bad that they render the results fairly close to meaningless."[10] To what mistakes is Hoffman referring? After all, the study was published in a major journal, *American Psychologist*. In the final analysis, the Carnegie Mellon study suffers from three key limitations that should lead us at least to be cautious in interpreting the study's results.

First, the sample of people used in the study was not chosen randomly. This is certainly an important limitation: It means that we can't be confident that the results pertain to any general population of people other than the specific people who participated in the study. Kraut and his colleagues acknowledge the fact that the sample was not random, but they defend their technique. In choosing families who were involved in a community group or had a high school student living at home, they made sure that they included people in the study who already had some social connections with others in the community. Starting with a group who had connections meant that they had the possibility of observing some changes. Consequently, they had to control who participated to a much greater extent than a random sample would have permitted. True random samples permit no control at all of who gets into the study. The selection process is strictly by chance.

Second, there was no control group in the Carnegie Mellon study. Critics argue that the data would have been much more valuable if the results for those using the Internet could have been compared to those for a control group of people who did not use the Internet. Perhaps, the critics argue, there was some change across the entire society during the two years of the study such that even those without Internet connections would have reported more depression and loneliness. Again, Kraut and his colleagues counter that the use of a control group was simply not possible. There was no acceptable incentive to offer people in a control group for their continued cooperation in answering questions over a two-year period.

Finally, critics have complained that Kraut and his colleagues went too far in suggesting that their data supported a **causal claim**. Recall from the earlier chapters on research methods and the chapters on specific effects that surveys suffer from an important limitation. In principle, they simply cannot be used to argue unequivocally for causal relationships. The experiment is the only method that really solves that problem. Because Kraut's data are based on the survey method, it is always possible that the relationships observed are due to some other unmeasured variable. So what's the bottom line?

Since Kraut conducted his initial study, his research team and unrelated teams of other researchers have published more data on the impact of Internet use. The amount of data that we now have is increasing, and a complicated picture appears to be emerging that isn't well understood at present. Kraut's first study after the one described here "revisited" the negative effects of the original study by following up on the participants after three years. The results of this follow-up suggested that "the negative effects dissipated over the total period." Specifically, the authors stated the following:

> The original HomeNet sample began using the Internet in 1995 or 1996. Our follow-up of participants remaining in the sample in 1998 showed that, overall, the previously reported negative outcomes associated with more use of the Internet had all but disappeared, except for the association with increased stress.[11]

A visit to Kraut's Web site (kraut.hciresearch.org) shows that he has remained interested in this topic and has continued to produce new research. In a longitudinal study that he reported in June 2004, Kraut's conclusions again seemed to point toward negative social effects for Internet use. He and his coauthors concluded:

> Longitudinal analyses from a large panel of Internet use suggest that using the Internet may lead to declines in visiting with friends and family and perhaps phoning as well. In addition, the data suggest that while visiting a family member stimulates exchanging email with that person and phoning him or her stimulates visiting, emailing doesn't increase the likelihood of either visiting or phoning.[12]

In his most recent research, Kraut and his colleagues (led this time by Katherine Bessiere) return to one of the basic questions raised in the HomeNet study: Does use of the Internet cause increasing levels of depression among users?[13] The researchers began by noting a long-established empirical fact that people who live in close social networks with numerous friends and community ties tend to have a higher level of overall psychological well-being. They tend to be happier and less stressed.[14] One hypothesis the researchers wanted to test is the **social augmentation hypothesis**, which holds that people who use the Internet to communicate with others should expand their social networks, thus permitting them to derive many of the relational benefits that come with being more connected to other people. In contrast, the **social displacement hypothesis** is the notion that every minute spent on the Internet is a minute that one cannot use to engage in social relationships with family and friends. Consequently, heavy use of the Internet should cause people to communicate less with the people immediately around them and this should lead to the loss of the positive benefits that those social networks provide. According to this idea, heavy Internet users should become more depressed, less connected, and more isolated from others. Part of this hypothesis is the idea that time spent communicating online is not the same as time spent communicating face-to-face. Consistent with the notion outlined in conjunction with the HomeNet study, use of the Internet should displace strong social ties. A final hypothesis suggested in the literature[15] is the **social compensation hypothesis**. According to this view, the effects of the Internet on social and psychological well-being are positive—but only for certain individuals. For people who are impoverished socially and have few people in their social networks, use of the Internet may expand social horizons and lead to a greater sense of connection—thus increasing a person's emotional and psychological well-being. The idea here is that people who don't enjoy a rich set of social connections are able to compensate for their situations by going to the Internet. For those who are already well connected, this hypothesis doesn't really make any definite predictions about effects. One communication theorist who introduced ideas about computer-mediated communication that are consistent with both the social augmentation and the social compensation hypotheses is Joseph Walther. His **social information processing theory** emphasizes the notion that even though communication using computers lacks the rich set of non-verbal cues available in face-to-face interaction, people can still use the available verbal cues to establish intimate relationships that rival those formed in the face-to-face context. These relationships may form at a slower pace, but they can eventually arrive at a place of high intimacy.[16]

Given these various hypotheses about the effects of Internet communication, which ideas seem to be best supported? To find out, Bessiere, Kraut, and their colleagues used a random sample of households from the United States and surveyed more than 1,200 adults. They followed the first survey with a second survey six to eight months later. With respect to the key hypotheses, all three were supported in some measure. In support of social augmentation, those who used the Internet to communicate with family and friends reduced their levels of depression over time. The social displacement hypothesis was also supported—but only for those who used the Internet primarily to meet new people or talk in online groups. Perhaps the time these people invested in trying to find new relationships led to subsequent elevations in depression because the time spent on the Internet was time that couldn't be spent interacting with others face to face. The fact that the strongest evidence for the social displacement idea emerged mainly for people who had high levels of social resources to begin with (well connected with friends and family) supports the idea that existing relationships were actually displaced by Internet time. Finally, there was also some support for the social compensation hypothesis. Those with more limited social resources who used the Internet did not suffer increased depression over time. But they didn't show any real improvement in depression levels either. One of the main contributions of this study is to highlight the complexity of the effects of using the Internet to communicate with others. The role of **individual differences** needs to be taken seriously in sorting out the effects. Internet use may be beneficial for some and not so good for others when it comes to forming and maintaining social relationships. It appears as if the authors of this study plan to continue their research so that they can untangle these contingent effects of new technology in more detail.

With respect to social information processing theory, Joseph Walther's current position is that the empirical data so far seem to support some aspects of the theory but not others. For example, his initial view was that relationships developed more slowly when they took place through computer-mediated communication. The data don't seem to support that idea and Walther is in the process of making various modifications to some of the things that he first thought when he posed the theory years ago. You should note one striking feature about Walther's attitude toward his theory. Instead of trying to defend his theory in spite of evidence that points in a different direction, Walther is willing to go where the data take him. His attitude is truly commendable because it exemplifies the way science should always be conducted—as a genuine dispassionate search for the truth despite one's initial commitments. Consistent with some of the positive effects of Internet use anticipated by Walther, other researchers have found evidence that using the Internet leads to positive effects—including the formation of a new social circle,[17] the development of deep and significant new relationships,[18] and the provision of a new social space for existing communities to flourish.[19]

## Media Multiplexity Theory

One theoretical idea that seems to be enjoying some support from the most recent research on the Internet is Caroline Haythornthwaite's **media multiplexity theory**.[20] In addition to defining more precisely what is meant by "strong ties" and "weak ties" in terms of connection to others (see Study Box 11-3), the theory makes a prediction that runs counter to much of the very early literature on the Internet. Simply put, the theory predicts that relationships that are strong are those in which the people involved communicate with each other in multiple ways. In contrast, "weak tie" relationships are more likely to be those in which communication takes place over a limited number of media channels. I can illustrate with two people in my own life. My strongest tie is with my wife, Cheri. Consistent with the theory, I talk frequently with Cheri face to face because I see her every day. But I also talk with her on my cell phone frequently, and we exchange frequent text messages between the time we leave home in the morning and return in the evening. Over the course of a typical week, we also exchange email messages. And it isn't uncommon for us to leave each other messages on our respective Facebook pages. We also compete occasionally by playing against each other in various games on the Internet. Sometimes when we do this, we're sitting together in the same room—but sometimes we're not. In short, we use multiple means of communication to sustain our relationship. One of my weaker ties is with my nephew. It's been years since we've interacted face to face; I never talk with him on my cell phone, and I can't remember the last time we had a text message or email exchange. My contact with him is limited almost exclusively to checking out his Facebook status and making an occasional comment on his wall. When the Internet first appeared on the scene, many feared that spending time on email, texting, and social networking sites would take people away from face-to-face relationships. But the theory of media multiplexity predicts that the time I spend communicating on the Internet with a very close friend who I see frequently in person is not weakening my relationship. In fact, my use of multiple communication channels to exchange information with such a person is actually an indication of our closeness.

One communication researcher who has studied relationships and closeness on the Internet is Andrew Ledbetter at Texas Christian University. He recently led a research team who studied social connection and self-disclosure on Facebook. His findings are consistent with media multiplexity theory.[21] In their study of 325 participants, the team found that communication with a friend using an "off-line" channel (face to face, telephone, or text message) predicted the level of closeness reported

## STUDY BOX 11-3 The Difference between Strong Ties and Weak Ties in Our Connections with Others

When researchers studying the Internet began to distinguish between "strong ties" and "weak ties," it was apparent that more precision was needed in defining those terms. Recall from Chapter 1 that a good theory is one that clearly identifies key concepts. Caroline Haythornthwaite attempted to put some conceptual meat on the bare bones of the strong versus weak tie distinction in advancing her theory of media multiplexity. According to her, some of the key distinctions are:

Strong Ties: These are relationships between *close* friends who:

- Tend to be like each other
- Tend to travel in the same social circles
- Tend to draw their experiences, attitudes, information, and contacts from the same general pool
- Exchange all kinds of information frequently—including emotional messages
- Have a high level of intimacy and self-disclosure in their communication
- Have a high level of reciprocity in their communication
- Have a strong desire to share whatever resources they have

Weak Ties: These relationships are between *casual* friends who:

- Tend to be unlike each other
- Don't travel in the same social circles
- Tend to draw their experiences, attitudes, information, and contacts from different places
- Don't exchange information frequently—rarely exchange emotional messages
- Don't have much intimacy or self-disclosure in their communication
- Aren't as likely to reciprocate in their communication
- Aren't motivated to share their resources

SOURCE: Haythornthwaite, C. (2005). Social networks and Internet connectivity effects. *Information, Communication & Society*, 8, 125–147.

with that friend. More communication corresponded to greater closeness. But the researchers also found that communication with a friend on Facebook also predicted greater levels of closeness.

Consistent with media multiplexity theory and Ledbetter's findings is research released recently from the Pew Internet in American Life Project.[22] About 87% of American adults report that they use the Internet and almost 75% of adults report that they use a social networking site like Facebook and 42% use more than one social media platform. Some of the main findings in the most recent research on Facebook show that users actually have more close relationships than non-users. They also tend to trust others more than non-users. Perhaps most significantly, they get more social support than people who don't use the site. In addition, they tend to be more politically engaged and use Facebook to revive old relationships. In Study Box 11-4, I recount my own experience in reviving an old friendship from high school. Unlike

**STUDY BOX 11-4 Using Facebook to Pay Off Old Bets and Revive a Connection**

In October of 2012, my favorite baseball team, the Baltimore Orioles, was locked in a battle with the New York Yankees that they eventually lost. In the weeks prior to their faceoff for a chance at the World Series, I had been trolling around Facebook looking for people from my past. I discovered a long-lost friend (a die-hard Yankees fan) from my high school days in New Jersey who now lived in Florida. Shortly after connecting with him and taunting him about the coming defeat that the Yankees would suffer to the Orioles (I was wrong), he reminded me that back in high school, we had made many wagers on the outcomes of sporting events. He also reminded me that I had lost many of those wagers and had promised to pay my bets by giving him dozens of doughnuts. Why doughnuts? My parents owned a doughnut shop so paying off in doughnuts instead of money was an easy way to meet my obligation with no pain. By his count, I owed him 34 dozen doughnuts, and he had been waiting for payment for over 40 years.

I'm a man of my word. I decided to make this new Facebook friendship especially memorable. I contacted a sports journalist, Mike Berardino, whom I didn't know at all, but hoped would like my plan. I asked him if he might be interested in helping me deliver 34 dozen doughnuts to my old friend as a surprise. After I placed the order by phone from Indiana to a doughnut shop located near my friend's home, Berardino and his son, who lived in the area, picked up the doughnuts early on a Saturday morning and made the delivery. Fortunately, my friend was home. Berardino wrote up the story for his newspaper and if anyone Googles the phrase "34 dozen doughnuts" the first story that pops up is all about my crazy idea. In the two years since I paid off my bet, I've followed my friend on Facebook almost daily and we've exchanged several personal messages by email. Although my payoff cost me much more than it would have had I paid my debt in high school, I considered it all worthwhile. My experience resonates with what the research reveals: Social media is connecting people in ways that simply weren't possible just a few short years ago.

SOURCE: Berardino, M. (2012). Old friends settle a 42-year-old sports debt—with 34 dozen doughnuts. *Fort Lauderdale Sun Sentinel.* [Online: Accessed 6-17-14]. Available: http://articles.sun-sentinel.com/2012-10-08/sports/fl-mikeb-olddebt-yankees-mlb-1009-2-20121008_1_doughnuts-sparks-bullets-yankees-top-orioles

most experiences of this kind, mine was covered by the news media in several states. In summary, the latest data on Internet use should ease concerns about how spending time on social networking sites might be harmful to relational health.

Although it may be frustrating to encounter complexities in the data that defy easy summaries, it is probably a good lesson to learn that science can often be frustrating. But the flip side of that frustration is excitement. As we stand on the frontier of new research on the impact of the Internet and other new technologies, there is an excitement about doing more research and honing in on the ultimate answers to the important questions. Perhaps you or one of your fellow classmates will go on to do graduate work in communication and help us to answer these important questions with a greater sense of certainty.

## New Technology's Distinctive Attributes

When professors around the country who were using the first edition of this book were asked to provide an evaluation of its content, one reviewer commented that this chapter on new technologies ought to be eliminated. His point was that nearly all of the material in the chapter could be moved to other chapters in the text. He went on to suggest that the history of media effects shows that we tend to replay the same issues over and over again when any new technology is introduced—violence, sex, displacement effects, advertising, and so on. Why devote a separate chapter to new technology when the essential research that emerges can easily be placed under other, more traditional rubrics? As I pondered this reviewer's comment, I was nearly persuaded. In fact, I decided to move the material on violent video games, which formerly appeared in this chapter, to Chapter 5 on media violence. In the final analysis, many of the research issues that emerge with new technology do lead us back over familiar ground. The main reason that I decided to keep a chapter on new technology was that it seems to reflect more accurately the way most scholars are currently thinking about the area of media effects. A chapter dedicated to new technology also seems to offer a unique peg on which to hang some of the most recent research that might be difficult to place otherwise. For example, during the summer of 2008, new research was presented at the academic meeting of the American Psychological Association on some of the positive effects of playing video games. One finding reported that laparoscopic surgeons who played video games were 27% faster in learning advanced surgical techniques and made 37% fewer errors compared to a group that didn't play video games. A major conclusion at the academic meeting was that the effects of video games can be either positive or negative—depending on the content of the game and the particular skills being exercised.[23] More recent research on the potential positive impact of playing video games was published in 2013. Two psychologists from Canada studied nearly 1,500 adolescents and concluded that playing games that required role-play and strategy may contribute to an increased ability to solve problems—which in turn may be related to achieving higher grades in school.[24] As research on the impact of new communication technologies increases, our understanding of its effects promises to become more nuanced—just as it did with research on TV and other media (see Chapter 3 to review the history of media effects research).

In thinking about what's really *new* about new technology, William Eveland contributed a helpful conceptual scheme that encourages scholars to integrate their thinking about traditional media with their thinking about media that are newer. He refers to this scheme as the **mix of attributes approach** to the study of media effects.[25] Eveland contends that some researchers tend to react to a new technology with the attitude that it "changes everything." As he puts it:

> Virtual reality, these researchers might argue, requires new theories and new concepts, which then require all new research. Similarly, the Internet and its World Wide Web are somehow supposed to be fundamentally different from all that has come before, and thus research and theory must start from scratch. (p. 407)

In contrast to an approach that would emphasize that everything must change with a new technology, Eveland likes to think of all media in terms of a common set of attributes. Differences between media can then be discussed in terms of differences in these attributes. For example, he proposes that we might think of some of the common attributes as **interactivity**, **structure**, **channel**, **textuality**, and **content**. *Interactivity* refers to the extent to which a person is actually able to interact with the technology in a meaningful way. *Structure* might refer to the extent to which a medium is linear or non-linear. A newspaper article takes you from the beginning to the end in an uninterrupted, linear fashion. But an article on the Web might have various hyperlinks that divert you from the main text to explore other tangents. The Web article is more nonlinear. The *channel* might refer to whether information is presented visually, acoustically, or in both channels at once. *Textuality* refers to how much of the information in a medium is communicated in text form. Finally, *content* refers to the actual information conveyed by the medium, such as violence, sex, persuasive messages, or information.

To illustrate Eveland's point, let's take interactivity and textuality as examples. When the Internet exploded on the scene, some scholars hailed this new medium as a complete and total innovation, unrelated to anything that had come before. One of the qualitatively different things about the Internet was its interactivity. That is, on the Internet, people had nearly complete control over what information they were exposed to and what information they wanted to screen out. Unlike TV, which was thought of as a relatively one-way, non-interactive medium, the Internet was something completely different. But instead of thinking of these two media as qualitatively different, Eveland encourages us to simply think of them as occupying different places on the continua of common attributes. Although it may be true that the Internet typically has a higher level of interactivity than conventional TV, by thinking of interactivity as something that theoretically characterizes *all* media to some degree, we are better prepared to talk about TV as being more or less interactive. Depending on where you live, you may find that you now have the capacity to order a movie "on demand" and control it just as if you were watching a videotape. Consequently, your TV has become *more* interactive than it once was. The traditional label of the Internet as "interactive" and TV as "non-interactive" doesn't really apply any more. Each medium has a certain level of interactivity. The Internet may have more, but TV has changed over the past few years so that, at times, it has a higher level of interactivity than it did in the past.

Similarly, a traditional approach might refer to newspapers as a "print medium" and TV as a "visual medium." About 20 years ago however, the cable news channels introduced something new: They started to scroll text at the bottom of the screen that reported various stories that were not being discussed by the news commentator. By taking the position that *textuality* is one dimension of all media that can hold different values, scholars can talk about how certain programs have *increased* in textuality over what they were before. Likewise, if you pick up a magazine from the 1950s, you might be struck by the density of text on the page compared with today's typical news magazines. Magazines have undoubtedly decreased in textuality.

One consequence of the mix of attributes approach is that the advent of a new technology does not necessarily revolutionize the study of media effects. Instead of thinking about new technology as qualitatively different, we can think of it as simply having different values on the common set of attributes that all media share. This may result in a more sophisticated understanding of the differences between various media because we can precisely identify how media differ in terms of the core set of attributes.

In support of Eveland's contention that the so-called revolution of new technology seems to take us back over familiar ground, consider some of the various research topics that are being investigated as part of the revolution of new technology. As Chapter 5 points out, one of the hot topics is the effects of violent video games. Although the technology is newer, concern about media violence has produced hundreds of studies over several decades. Similarly, concern about the effects of sexual material on the Internet, particularly when seen by children, echoes the concerns reviewed in Chapter 6 about the impact of sexual content in the media. One review of the effects of new technology by Norbert Mundorf and Kenneth Laird reveals that with a few exceptions, the topics in the research are really not "new" at all. See Study Box 11-5. At least two communication researchers believe

---

## STUDY BOX 11-5 The Research Topics Associated with New Technology

The five areas mentioned in this box were summarized a decade ago as areas of "current" research on new technology. For each one, I illustrate the fact that although the technology is new, the area of research has been around for quite a while.

1. **Uses and Gratifications with the Internet**. Researchers study the ways people use the Internet and the gratifications they derive from such use. As discussed in Chapter 4, the uses and gratifications perspective has been around for a long time and has been applied to conventional media such as newspapers and TV for years.
2. **Effects on Social Interactions**. Chapter 4 discusses how one of the early concerns about TV had to do with the possibility that TV use displaced other important social activities. With the advent of the Internet, this concern is appearing again as a major theme in the media effects literature.
3. **Internet Addiction**. Chapter 4 discusses the notion of addiction to TV and reviews some research on TV addicts. The idea of addiction to media has been around for several decades. The only difference is that scholars are now discussing it as a possible effect of the Internet.
4. **Individual Differences**. Just as past studies on media effects show that the impact of media may depend on the individual, so studies on new technology are tending to show the same thing.
5. **Effects of Age and Gender**. Most media effects studies undertaken in past years have investigated the effects of age and gender. Today, these variables are also used to study video games and Internet use.

SOURCE: Mundorf, N., & Laird, K. R. (2002). Social and psychological effects of information technologies and other interactive media. In J. Bryant & D. Zillmann (Eds.), *Media effects Advances in theory and research* (pp. 583–602). Mahwah, NJ: Erlbaum.

that Eveland's mix of attributes approach will turn out to be particularly useful for studying digital media and they've attempted to demonstrate that usefulness in their study of user-generated content about politics.[26] Only time will tell how useful scholars find this new perspective.

## Screen Time and Face-to-Face Interaction

As you will see in the next chapter, some fairly provocative theoretical thinking is going on today about the impact of electronic media—thinking that doesn't have much to do with the actual content of the media itself. After studying the effects of media messages for over 35 years, I confess that I've been somewhat attracted to at least considering this line of thought myself. A few years ago, I teamed up with Dr. Will Miller, the former spokesperson for Nick at Nite. We wrote a book for the layperson called *Refrigerator Rights: Our Crucial Need for Close Connection.* The book has had a much longer life than I anticipated.[27] In that book, we engage in a kind of informed speculation about the effects of new technology. Consider how our social environments have changed today just in terms of the importance of looking at screens. If you're like me, your daily screens are important. I spend time looking at my TV screen at home, so I want that screen to be sufficiently large and as clear and vivid as possible. Today, many people want HDTV (I didn't have HD when I wrote the second edition of the text—now I have four HDTVs). At the office and at home, I also spend lots of time staring at my computer screen, as I'm doing right now. Sitting beside my computer monitor is a much smaller iPhone screen that I'll drop into my pocket and take with me tonight when I leave campus. A few years back, I added an iPad screen to my repertoire. The uses for this screen are expanding exponentially since it appeared on the market. The cable TV industry has transformed its products since I first wrote this section in order to deliver streaming TV to tablet devices as seamlessly as we get it on our TV screens. Researchers want to know how consumption of cable TV on a more portable basis might impact the audience. The newest automobiles feature built-in DVD and video screens, either for entertainment or for monitoring one's phone calls and global position while on the road. There is considerable concern that putting all of this technology on the dashboard may contribute to increased driver distraction and result in more traffic accidents.

What is the collective impact of all of this screen time? This is not an easy question to answer, but it is surely an important question to ask. As our society spends increasing amounts of time looking at virtual images on screens, are we spending less time looking at human faces in the context of face-to-face, in-person encounters? If so, what are the implications of this shift in how we spend our time? Are children who grow up in the electronic environment being socialized away from cultivating the social skills that we emphasized 50 or 60 years ago? At least one recent study does find some evidence that children who were viewing more than two hours of TV per day when they were 5.5 years old scored lower on measures of social skill than children who viewed less TV.[28] Does this mean that people growing up today may be more inclined to be rude to others or lack the civility that used to characterize polite social interactions? Are professors treated with less respect in the classroom today because students are so accustomed to being in the mode of processing "entertainment," where laughter, ridicule, and boredom are responses that need not be inhibited?

While I have my own suspicions, I don't know the answers to these questions. Perhaps your class can explore them in a discussion. A team of Australian researchers recently completed a systematic review of over 30 recent studies and concluded that screen time was negatively correlated with an overall sense of psychological well-being as well as the overall level of social support enjoyed by those adolescent girls who participated in the research.[29] So far, the literature on screen time deals most frequently with potential effects on physical health associated with sedentary behavior and obesity. Answering questions about the potential impact on interpersonal communication through the traditional methods of media effects research will probably be quite difficult. These questions do not lend themselves to carefully controlled experiments in laboratory settings. Nevertheless, the inability to study an effect doesn't mean the effect isn't taking place. Perhaps in future years the scholarly community will find some creative ways to begin to provide insights on these sorts of questions.

## Will Our Old Brains Catch Up to the New Technology?

Over 15 years ago, Byron Reeves and Clifford Nass published a provocative book that I believe was way ahead of its time. My hunch is that media scholars will be mining the insights in this book in future years and expanding them in all sorts of fruitful directions. The book is called *The Media Equation: How People Treat Computers, Television and New Media Like Real People and Places.*[30] You may remember that you read a little about this book back in Chapter 4 when the topic of discussion was the formation of parasocial relationships with media characters. In the opening pages of the book, Reeves and Nass explain "**the media equation**": "In short, we have found that individuals' interactions with computers, television, and new media are *fundamentally social and natural,* just like interactions in real life." They go on to explain that for a few hundred thousand years, Homo sapiens learned to react to the things in their environments without questioning their reality. Then, in the twentieth century, along comes an electronic revolution that essentially "tricks" our brains. In Chapter 7, you read personal accounts of people who became frightened of images that existed on pieces of celluloid and were projected onto a large screen. Why would someone actually become scared of these images? After all, they're not real. The answer from the media equation is that our new brains have not yet been able to overcome the deeply ingrained processing rules from our old brains that tell us to react to what we see as if it is real.

In an article published after his book, Clifford Nass and his colleague Youngme Moon reviewed a large body of evidence from experimental studies that show how extensive the media equation is across a broad range of different types of phenomena.[31] In one fascinating experiment, participants were randomly assigned to interact with a computer that asked them questions requiring some self-disclosure. For example, the computer might ask, "What have you done in your life that you feel most guilty about?" In one of the conditions, this question was presented only after the computer said, "There are times when this computer crashes for reasons that are not apparent to its user. It usually does this at the most inopportune time, causing great inconvenience to the user." The results of the experiment revealed that participants were much more likely to disclose to the computer details and feelings about something that they felt guilty about if they had first heard the computer disclose information about its tendency to crash! If you're like me, these results might strike you as strange. Everyone knows a computer isn't a real person. Why should your decision to disclose sensitive personal information depend on what a computer reveals about the tendency to crash? The point is that people tend to obey the same disclosure rules when interacting with computers that they do when they interact with people. If someone makes a personal disclosure, it invokes a rule of reciprocity. It is only appropriate to respond with a similar personal disclosure. The media equation asserts that people treat media (in this case, a computer) just as they treat other people. When I think of the conversations that my family has in the car with the global positioning system, the truth of the media equation begins to sink in. Some of us refer to the GPS unit as "the lady" (we usually have the system set on the female voice), and we often respond to her directions and comments with comments of our own. It is almost as if the GPS is another passenger in the car—and a knowledgeable passenger at that! Like any good theorists, Reeves and Nass have been about the business of trying to discover the limits of the media equation. In an interview with Em Griffin for Griffin's text on communication theory,[32] Nass remarked that there are obviously some limits to the phenomenon. For example, "people don't let computers marry their sister." Perhaps his remark was premature. In 2013, Joaquin Phoenix played the lead character in the movie *Her*, which featured a man who established a relationship with the female voice associated with a computer operating system. Far-fetched? Maybe not so much. In May 2014 a man from Florida sued the state for his right to marry his computer.[33] While requests to marry computers are surely the exception, scholars may still have underestimated just how true the media equation is for many of our encounters with media in everyday life.

## How New Technology Relates to Physical and Cognitive Health

In closing this chapter, I offer two more provocative areas of research on new technology for consideration: sleep and multitasking (sometimes called cyber-overload). A few years ago, a friend and colleague, Jan Van den Bulck, who works at a university in Belgium, surveyed more than 2,500 adolescents about their media habits. One of the things he discovered was how intrusive cell phone text messaging was for many of the adolescents in the study. Nearly 14% of the sample reported that they were woken up at night one to three times per month by an incoming text message on their cell phones.[34] Based on this study, Van den Bulck believes that text messages may constitute a serious source of sleep disturbance for young adolescents.

While research on media use and sleep is still relatively scarce, Van den Bulck is one of the few researchers who has done studies in this area. In addition to his study on cell phone texts, he also studied about 1,600 adolescents in Belgium and found a definite relationship between cell phone use at night and quality of sleep. Those adolescents who used their phone between the time their bedroom lights were turned off and 3:00 a.m. were nearly four times more likely to be "very tired" in their self-reports. Not even 40% of Van den Bulck's sample could report that they never used their mobile phone after their lights were turned out.[35] As we incorporate new technology into every facet of our lives, one of the key research questions will probably concern the extent to which we are overwhelming our brains with too much stimulation.

Related to the concern about media and sleep is the possible link between exposure to the light of a computer or TV set at night and the reduction of the body's natural production of a chemical called melatonin.[36] If the **light-at-night (LAN) hypothesis** has merit, then exposure to the light of a screen at nighttime may affect melatonin levels. Why is this of any concern? The answer to that question is simple: melatonin seems to be a natural weapon that the body uses to fight cancer. TV sets and computer screens could also be culprits in reducing melatonin if they are viewed at close distances. I find this possible relationship to be so important that I'm collaborating with Jan Van den Bulck with hope to study the issue.[37]

**Cyber-overload**  One of the themes to emerge in the last few years is that we're awash in so much information and new media that we literally can't function. Two common areas in which this theme shows up are in our driving behavior and our sleep behavior. The award-winning science journalist Matt Richtel has published extensively in *The New York Times* on the problems associated with cell phones and driving,[38] and research scholars are busy trying to understand **multitasking**—the behavior of media users who claim that they can simultaneously engage in more than one task at once.[39] If you have ever texted a message while driving, you may be under the illusion that you can successfully multitask. But it really is an illusion. Instead of doing two things at once, your brain has really switched its attention between the two activities very rapidly. This is known as **task switching**. When you're driving, task switching is particularly dangerous because while you may be under the illusion that you're actually paying attention to your driving, you really aren't during those seconds when your attention is on your cell phone screen. Joanne Cantor has written about this distinction in her book about cyber-overload. Her advice: Forget multitasking.[40] While Cantor's advice is wise, it isn't necessarily easy to implement. Zheng Wang and John Tchernev, two communication researchers who have studied multitasking, note that their research shows that people seem driven to multitask because the resulting environment yields emotional gratifications. In short, it feels good to surround oneself with multiple screen options.[41] Even as I write these words, I'm tempted to have the TV on in the background and my iPhone perched in plain sight just to the left of the keyboard. But Wang and Tchernev's research also shows that in setting up my digital environment to feel good, performance on my cognitive task suffers. I'll write better if I can avoid the distractions of my multi-screen environment (I've counted some 14 media screens throughout my house).

Before he passed away unexpectedly of a heart attack in 2013, Clifford Nass appeared in a documentary made for PBS TV in which he explained his research at Stanford University on how multitasking decreases cognitive performance. He summarized the results of his studies succinctly and persuasively when he said:

> Virtually all multitaskers think they are brilliant at multitasking. And one of the big discoveries is, you know what, you're really lousy at it. It turns out multi-taskers are terrible at every aspect of multitasking. They get distracted constantly; their memory is very disorganized. Recent work we've done suggests they're worse at analytic reasoning. We worry that it may be creating people who are unable to think well and clearly.[42]

If you think you're a good multitasker, you may be tempted to resist Nass' conclusions as ones that don't apply to your own situation. But the research shows that you'd almost certainly be wrong in coming to that judgment. The findings that Nass talked about were based on studies involving some of the highest aptitude college students in the world—and those who boasted that they were high-functioning multitaskers. They were stunned to discover that they were wrong. My guess is that over the next decade, scholars will produce even more data that show the limits of multitasking and will yield practical advice for how to deal effectively with the new technology that will continue to surround us.

## SUMMARY

This chapter has examined some of the newest research on the impact of the Internet. One of the central questions being explored concerning the Internet is whether this technology increases social alienation, depression, and loneliness. The Carnegie Mellon study suggested that this was the case. But the study has its critics. The research studies that followed have found evidence for the importance of individual differences in studying the effects of Internet use. In the coming years, we can expect to see more research that will help to provide insight and clarify the impact of the Internet on individual relationships. In considering the impact of new technology, it may be more helpful not to think in terms of qualitatively different media. Instead, it may be better to think of all media in terms of a mix of attributes. Regardless of how we think about it, there are still provocative questions for researchers to address in future research. One such question has to do with the media equation and is raised by Clifford Nass and Byron Reeves. What are the limits of our tendency to treat new media just as we treat people? Quite apart from this sort of theoretical question, there are other fundamental questions about the possible effects of electronic media (apart from their content) on our personal health and the amount of information that our brains can handle during any given day.

## QUESTIONS TO FOCUS YOUR ATTENTION

1.  Based on your own experience with the Internet, smartphones and social media, how do you think the new communication technology may be affecting relational health? What are some of the positive and negative effects that you believe you've experienced?

2.  Much has been written about the negative effects of video games and other new media. But some of the research suggests that there are positive benefits too. How should we think of the overall impact of these technologies? Have we gained more than we've lost or have we lost more than we've gained?

3.  How does your own personal experience with sleep and multitasking compare with the research on these topics that was cited in the chapter? Do you think people need to change their behavior in these areas? How difficult would that be to do?

## KEY TERMS AND CONCEPTS

| | | |
|---|---|---|
| perpetual linkage | social compensation hypothesis | channel |
| activity displacement effect | | textuality |
| displaces strong social ties | social information processing theory | content |
| online sense of unidentifiability | | the media equation |
| | individual differences | light-at-night (LAN) hypothesis |
| causal claim | media multiplexity theory | |
| social augmentation hypothesis | mix of attributes approach | multitasking |
| | interactivity | task switching |
| social displacement hypothesis | structure | |

## NOTES

1. Stokel-Walker, C. (2013). Second Life's strange second life. *The Verge*. [Online: Accessed 6-4-14]. Available: http://www.theverge.com/2013/9/24/4698382/second-lifes-strange-second-life

2. Cacioppo, J. T., Cacioppo, S., Gonzaga, G. C., Ogburn, E. L., & VanderWeele, T. J. (2013). Marital satisfaction and break-ups differ across on-line and off-line meeting venues. *PNAS Proceedings of the National Academy of Sciences of the United States of America*, 110(25), pp. 10135–10140.

3. Brown, J. D., & Cantor, J. (2000). An agenda for research on youth and the media. *Journal of Adolescent Health*, 27(2) (Supp.), 2–7.

4. Pew Research Internet Project. (2014). Health face sheet. [Online: Accessed 5-16-14]. Available: http://www.pewinternet.org/fact-sheets/health-fact-sheet/

5. Smith, M. A., Rainie, L., Schneiderman, B., & Himelboim, I. (2014). Mapping Twitter topic networks: From polarized crowds to community clusters. Pew Research Internet Project. [Online: Accessed 6-16-14]. Available: http://www.pewinternet.org/2014/02/20/mapping-twitter-topic-networks-from-polarized-crowds-to-community-clusters/

6. Kraut, R., Patterson, M., Lundmark, V., Kiesler, S., Mukhopadhyay, T., & Scherlis, W. (1998). Internet paradox: A social technology that reduces social involvement and psychological well-being? *American Psychologist*, 53, 1017–1031.

7. Katz, J. E., & Aspden, P. (1997). A nation of strangers? *Communications of the ACM*, 40, 81–86.

8. Reich, S. M., Subrahmanyam, K., & Espinoza, G. (2012). Friending, IMing, and hanging out face-to-face: Overlap in adolescents' on-line and off-line social networks. *Developmental Psychology*, 48(2), 356–368.

9. Rollman, J. B., Krug, K., & Parente, F. (2000). The chat room phenomenon: Reciprocal communication in cyberspace. *Cyberpsychology & Behavior,* 3, 161–166.

10. Caruso, D. (1998, September 14). Critics pick apart study on Internet and depression. *The New York Times,* p. C-5.

11. Kraut, R., Kiesler, S., Boneva, B., Cummings, J., Helgeson, V., & Crawford, A. (2002). Internet paradox revisited. *Journal of Social Issues,* 58(1), 49–74.

12. Shlovski, I., & Kraut, R. (2004). The Internet and social participation: Contrasting cross-sectional and longitudinal analyses [Online]. Available: http://www-2.cs.cmu.edu/-kraut/RKraut.site.files/articles/shklovski-pew-change-v4-4.pdf

13. Bessiere, K., Kiesler, S., Kraut, R., & Boneva, B. S. (2008). Effect of Internet use and social resources on changes in depression. *Information, Communication & Society,* 11(1), 47–70.

14. Baumeister, R. F., & Leary, M. R. (1995). The need to belong: Desire for interpersonal attachments as a fundamental human motivation. *Psychological Bulletin,* 117(3), 497–529.

15. McKenna, K. Y. A., & Bargh, J. (2000). Plan 9 from cyberspace: The implications of the Internet for personality and social psychology. *Personality and Social Psychology Review,* 4(1), 57–75.

16. For a good introductory overview of Walther's theory, see Chapter 10 of: Griffin, E., Ledbetter, A., & Sparks, G. (2015). *A first look at communication theory.* Boston: McGraw-Hill.

17. *Ibid.*, Kraut et al. (2002).

18. McKenna, K. Y. A., Green, A. S., & Gleason, M. E. J. (2002). Relationship formation on the Internet: What's the big attraction? *Journal of Social Issues,* 58(1), 9–31.

19. Wellman, B., Quan Haase, A., Witte, J., & Hampton, K. (2001). Does the Internet increase, decrease, or supplement social capital? Social networks, participation, and community commitment. *American Behavioral Scientist,* 45(3), 436–455.

20. Haythornthwaite, C. (2005). Social networks and internet connectivity effects. *Information, Communication & Society,* 8, 125–147.

21. Ledbetter, A. M., Mazer, J. P., DeGroot, J. M., Meyer, K. R., Mao, Y., & Swafford, B. (2011). Attitudes toward online social connection and self-disclosure as predictors of Facebook communication and relational closeness. *Communication Research,* 38(1), 27–53.

22. Duggan, M., & Smith, A. (2013). Social Media Update 2013. *Pew Research Internet Project.* [Online]. Available: http://www.pewinternet.org/2013/12/30/social-media-update-2013/

23. Science News: "Playing Video Games Offers Learning Across Life Span, Say Studies" [Online: Accessed 6-17-14]. Available: http://www.sciencedaily.com/releases/2008/08/080817223442.htm

24. Adachi, P. J. C., & Willoughby, T. (2013). More than just fun and games: The longitudinal relationships between strategic video games, self-reported problem solving skills, and academic grades. *Journal of Youth and Adolescence* (42)7, 1041–1052.

25. Eveland, W. P., Jr. (2003). A "mix of attributes" approach to the study of media effects and new communication technologies. *Journal of Communication,* 53(3), 395–410.

26. Dylko, I., & McCluskey, M. (2012). Media effects in an era of rapid technological transformation: A case of user-generated content and political participation. *Communication Theory,* 22(3), 250–278.

27. Miller, W., & Sparks, G. (2008). *Refrigerator rights: Our crucial need for close connection.* Barrington, IL: WillowCreek.

28. Mistry, K. B., Minkovitz, C. S., Strobino, D. M., & Borzekowski, D. L. G. (2011). Children's television exposure and behavioral and social outcomes at 5.5 years: Does timing of exposure matter? *Pediatrics,* 120(4), 762–769.

29. Costigan, S. A., Barnett, L., Plotnikoff, R. C., & Lubans, D. R. (2013). The health indicators associated with screen-based sedentary behavior among adolescent girls: A systematic review. *Journal of Adolescent Health*, 52(4), 382–392.

30. Reeves, B., & Nass, C. (1996). *The media equation: How people treat computers, television, and new media like real people and places.* Cambridge: Cambridge University Press.

31. Nass, C., & Moon, Y. (2000). Machines and mindlessness: Social responses to computers. *Journal of Social Issues,* 56(1), 81–103.

32. Griffin, E., Ledbetter, A., & Sparks, G. (2015). *A first look at communication theory.* New York: McGraw Hill. (Note: the interview containing the comment by Clifford Nass is available at the book's Web site: http://www.afirstlook.com/theory_resources/by_type/videos)

33. Millward, D. (2014). Florida man demands right to wed computer. *The Telegraph.* [Online: Accessed 6-17-14]. Available: http://www.telegraph.co.uk/news/worldnews/northamerica/usa/10814098/marriage-gay-marriage-mac-wedding-computer-Florida-Utah.html

34. Van den Bulck, J. (2003). Text messaging as a cause of sleep interruption in adolescents: Evidence from a cross-sectional study. *Journal of Sleep Research,* 12(3), 263.

35. Van den Bulck, J. (2007). Adolescent use of mobile phones for calling and for sending text messages after lights out: Results from a prospective cohort study with a one-year follow up. *Sleep,* 30, 1220–1223.

36. Kantermann, T., & Roenneberg, T. (2009). Is light-at-night a health risk or a health risk predictor? *Chronobiology International,* 26(6), 1069–1074.

37. Kotz, D. (2008, February 22). Light at night: How to counter the health effects. *U.S. News & World Report* [Online]. Available: http://health.usnews.com/health-news/family-health/cancer/articles/2008/02/22/light-at-night-how-to-counter-the-health-effects

38. Richtel, M. (2009). Driven to distraction: U.S. withheld data on risks of distracted driving. New York Times, July 20. [Online]. Available: http://www.nytimes.com/2009/07/21/technology/21distracted.html

39. Salvucci, D. D., & Taatgen, N. A. (2011). The multitasking mind. New York: Oxford.

40. Cantor, J. (2009). *Conquer Cyberoverload: Get more done, boost your creativity, and reduce stress.* Madison, WI: Cyberoutlook Press.

41. Wang, Z., & Tchernev, J. M. (2012). The "myth" of media multitasking: Reciprocal dynamics of media multitasking, personal needs, and gratifications. *Journal of Communication,* 62(3), 493–513.

42. Dretzin, R., & Rushkoff, D. (2010). Digital nation: Life on the virtual frontier. *Frontline*, WGBH, Boston. [Online: Accessed 6-17-14]. Available: http://www.pbs.org/wgbh/pages/frontline/digitalnation/view/

## 12

# Meet Marshall McLuhan

## A Less Scientific Approach
## to Media Impact

### IS THERE ANY VALUE TO CONSIDERING
### MARSHALL McLUHAN?

Some researchers who study media effects may raise an eyebrow of curiosity or feel some confusion about finding a chapter on Marshall McLuhan at the end of this text. From the very beginning, this book has taken great pains to introduce you to the scientific perspective of studying media impact. Each of the preceding chapters has emphasized empirical evidence collected in a systematic fashion as the most reliable way to learn about how media affect us. In contrast to the many other researchers mentioned in the earlier chapters, Marshall McLuhan didn't collect any research data. He never did content analyses, surveys, or experiments to test his ideas. Instead, he simply proclaimed what he thought about the effects of the mass media. To make matters worse, from the scientific perspective, most of his ideas seem to be unfalsifiable (see Chapter 1) and beyond scientific scrutiny. Why should his ideas be presented in a text of this sort?

I believe there are three good reasons for including a chapter on McLuhan's ideas about the media. First, whatever approach one might take to the study of media effects, McLuhan's ideas about media influence have stirred discussion and analysis by media scholars for more than 50 years. It seems clear that some of his ideas are also enjoying a reexamination as we enter the digital age of communication. A casual perusal of scholarly publication databases reveals that McLuhan's ideas are frequently discussed seriously in doctoral dissertations that focus on media. Students of media effects, regardless of their commitment to the scientific approach, should at least be familiar with McLuhan's analysis. Second, his ideas are so provocative and far-reaching in their implications that students of media effects ought to at least consider what he has to say. Finally, McLuhan's "theory" provides a great contrast to scientific thinking. In the end, although you may find his ideas fun to think about, you should also be able to see the frustration that comes with a body of theory that defies testing by recourse to empirical procedures. Ultimately, we simply can't test much of what McLuhan said. You may recall from Chapter 1 that when an idea can't be tested and potentially disconfirmed, it's difficult to offer compelling evidence in its favor, either. Such ideas have limited value to the scientific community. Rather than inventing such an idea for illustrative purposes, why not consider a provocative one that already exists?

## MEET MARSHALL McLUHAN

One way to begin to understand what Marshall McLuhan was referring to when he talked about the impact of electronic communication is to stop reading this book and pick up your pencil. Draw a horizontal line across the width of an 8½ × 11-inch piece of paper. Imagine that the line represents all of human history (roughly 40,000 years). The far left side of the line represents the beginning of that period of time, and the far right represents this present moment. If we wanted to locate the point in human history where electronic communication really started, we would have to move to the far right and go nearly to the end of the line. Electronic communication is new. One communication scholar, Don Pember, expressed the historical record of communication in this way:

> Imagine those 40,000 years of modern human history as a single calendar year. And right now it is midnight on December 31st, the last day of that year. Mechanical printing first occurred on December 27th, not quite five days ago. Newsbooks, the precursors of newspapers, first appeared in 1610, or about three-and-a-half days ago. Radio and motion pictures emerged as viable media in the early 1900s, about 9 o'clock this morning. And television first appeared in the United States at the end of the 1930s, or about 3:00 P.M. today. Despite its short existence, mass communications has come to truly dominate our lives today.[1]

It is difficult for people to comprehend a world without electronic media, and yet most of human history has been without it. Most people can't imagine what life would be like without newspapers, radio, or TV. Consequently, not many people would feel comfortable issuing proclamations about how the electronic media have changed the very fundamentals of the human experience. Proving such claims would be next to impossible. And how could anyone really be sure of these changes unless they had actually lived in the past?

Marshall McLuhan didn't seem to mind the fact that he couldn't *prove* any of his claims. He thought of himself as a **prober** or an explorer and found that there was a certain luxury in thinking about things that eluded clear-cut **proofs**. True, he might never be able to prove that his analysis was right, but others could never prove that he was wrong, either. McLuhan found this state of affairs to his liking. The genius of McLuhan (if any) was in his ability to stimulate thought about the exact nature of those changes that the move to electronic media had triggered. Even though he had never lived in the past, that didn't stop him from talking as if he knew exactly what the media were doing to us.

Marshall McLuhan was a Canadian scholar, born in Edmonton in 1911. After earning bachelor's and master's degrees at the University of Manitoba, he won a scholarship to Cambridge, where he earned a second bachelor's degree, a second master's degree, and a doctorate. He taught English literature at St. Michael's College of the University of Toronto. He died in 1980 after suffering a series of strokes. In the early 1960s, his reputation as a provocative new thinker about mass media started to grow (it was McLuhan who coined the term "the media"). Harold Innis and Walter Ong influenced him, but McLuhan was the one who wrote *The Gutenberg Galaxy* and *Understanding Media*, books that propelled him into the limelight.

It was not so much that his books prompted rave reviews. In fact, reviewers often complained that McLuhan's writings were dense, complex, and difficult to digest. Teachers, likewise, may be reluctant to suggest that their students begin their quest to understand Marshall McLuhan by reading his books. A popular anecdote about McLuhan illustrates this point well. Upon arriving at campus one morning, McLuhan expressed irritation when he discovered that a student had parked her car in his parking space. Before finding another space for his car, McLuhan dashed off a note and placed it on the student's windshield: "Please do not park in my space in the future." He signed the note "Professor McLuhan." At the end of the day, when McLuhan returned to his car to leave campus, he noticed that a note was attached to *his* windshield. It read, "Dear Professor McLuhan, the note that you left me on my windshield this morning was the first thing you've written that I've been able to understand." There is no doubt that some of McLuhan's ideas are difficult to understand. Nevertheless, many sensed something deeply provocative about much of what he had to say.

The best way to begin to grasp the importance of McLuhan's ideas is to consider his view of human history. In a way, his major thesis is historical in nature. If McLuhan was right about human history, then we are all currently living in one of the most amazing times to ever come upon the earth.

## THE ERAS OF COMMUNICATION HISTORY

### The Tribal Age

McLuhan saw the history of the human race in terms of **eras of communication**. When he looked at the dawn of human history, he saw people who lived in a **tribal state**. They communicated with each other orally, and they didn't have a well-developed alphabet or system of writing. In this period of history, there was a heavy reliance on acoustics, or sound. Because most communication took place through speech and other vocal sounds, the sense of hearing was important. McLuhan liked to point out that often the ear did not need to process information in any particular order to make sense out of it. That is, sounds from the environment come to one's ears in an "all-at-once" fashion, and frequently it doesn't matter which ones we process first. It is true that the order of spoken words does matter in most languages. But McLuhan believed that in the tribal age, the order of spoken words was only a small part of the meaning that people derived in the communication process.

If you are not in a totally quiet environment as you read these words, take a minute to close your eyes and see how many different sounds you can hear. How many were you able to identify? To appreciate McLuhan's point about the **all-at-onceness** of processing sound, ask yourself this question: What difference would it have made if the sounds you identified had occurred in a different order? The answer to this question is quite likely "not much difference at all." In fact, some of the sounds that you heard were probably happening simultaneously. As you will see in the rest of the chapter, McLuhan believed that this quality of acoustical information was important.

McLuhan also believed that processing information went beyond acoustics, with people relying heavily on the other senses as well. Sight, smell, touch, and even taste were all important sources of information to tribal peoples, who lived, as McLuhan pointed out, in a state of **sensory balance**; the five senses were all important sources of information.

## Moving from the Tribal Age to the Print Age

In terms of human history, the tribal age was the longest. Speech and the oral tradition persisted over thousands of years as the most important form of communication. Around 1500 B.C.E., however, the beginning of the end of the tribal age became evident when the phonetic alphabet emerged. This emergence, according to McLuhan, signaled the beginning of a major transition period to a new medium of communication and a new age of human history. Some versions of McLuhan's historical analysis note that the tribal age moved first to the age of literacy prior to its formal move to the print age. It was the invention of the printing press which allowed documents to be mass-produced that moved human history from literacy to the next major communication era. The printing press ushered in the formal **print age**.

McLuhan noted several things about the transition to the print age. First, he pointed out that the move to print was one that altered the sensory balance of the tribal age. McLuhan argued that, in the print age, the sense of *sight* became completely dominant in terms of processing important information. It was now possible to detach oneself from the tribe and still have access to the important information of human culture. One could read books in a private place. One could process important information without being in the physical presence of other people. The senses of hearing, touch, smell, and taste became less necessary in the age of print.

The print age disrupted the sensory balance of the tribal state as the eye became the central mechanism for processing information.

A second important consequence of the move to the print age, according to McLuhan, was that human beings started to think differently. Unlike the all-at-onceness of the old acoustical processing, the age of print forced people to process information in a *linear* fashion.

To see what McLuhan meant by the linear nature of print, try this simple exercise: Close your eyes and drop your finger at random onto this page. Write down the word that your finger lands on. Now do it again; then do it five more times. Look at the string of seven words that you have written. The chances are good that they don't form a coherent sentence. In the age of print, we must process our information in a particular order. If something scrambles that order, the message is lost. Even the essential ingredients of words, the letters, must appear in a particular order before we can make sense of them. The particular order of words or letters (left to right in English, top to bottom in some Asian languages) is not important. The important thing is that we have to assemble them in a linear order before we can derive meaning from them. You might be tempted to argue with McLuhan at this point by pointing out that the same is true for spoken words—they must be heard in a particular order to make sense of them. McLuhan's reply might have acknowledged this—but he may have also observed that speech is only one of many different sounds that one processes from the environment at any instant. The ears are open to hear everything in a way that the eyes are not open to seeing everything when they are reading a printed page. During reading, the brain must work in a linear fashion or nothing makes sense.

McLuhan thought that the shift to **linear information processing** altered people's basic thought patterns. Thought became more linear than it had been in the tribal state. This shift brought about an emphasis on deductive logic and on making sure that every thought connected well to the one that had come before. Messages that reflected the less linear pattern of the tribal age seemed increasingly strange and incoherent. Over time, they diminished in value.

## Moving On to the Current Electronic Age

According to McLuhan, the great technology of print completely transformed human culture. Then, in the late 1800s, Marconi's invention of the wireless telegraph gave rise to a new age in human history. The age of electronic communication had begun. Just as print transformed the old tribal age, so electronic media would transform the great culture of print. McLuhan pointed out that the transition from the print age to the **electronic age** would be similar to the earlier shift away from the tribal state. Both changes would occur over several hundred years. According to McLuhan, then, you and I are living at a most unprecedented time in human history. We are living on the cusp of two great communication technologies: print and electronics. If McLuhan is right, then a very provocative thesis presents itself for our consideration. McLuhan asks us to consider the possibility that much of the social upheaval and change that have occurred over the past 50 years are directly due to the shift toward electronic media.

It was in talking about the various consequences of the move to electronic media that McLuhan came into his own as a media guru. He enjoyed the attention he received from TV talk shows and movie celebrities (he made a brief appearance in Woody Allen's 1977 film *Annie Hall*). All of the media attention, combined with the obscurity of some of his ideas, caused him to lose favor in the eyes of the academic world. Still, McLuhan had some interesting things to say about what was happening to our culture with the steady rise of electronic communication forms.

First, McLuhan believed that in the electronic age, human culture was returning to a form of communication that was much more similar to that of the tribal age. He often talked about the **global village** produced by electronic media—a reference to the power of instantaneous communication to unify the world into a massive modern-day tribal community. Almost everyone who was alive at the time remembers exactly where they were on November 22, 1963. On this date, John Kennedy died at the hands of an assassin. McLuhan often explained that the media coverage that followed an event of this magnitude allowed people to experience "one big group emotion." Since 1963, we have often seen the power of the electronic media to unite large portions of the world by drawing their collective attention to the same event. Think about the space shuttle Challenger exploding in midair; the first night of fighting in Operation Desert Storm; the Berlin Wall tumbling to the ground; the death of Princess Diana; the O. J. Simpson car chase on the Los Angeles freeways; the tragic shootings at Columbine High School; the twin towers of the World Trade Center tumbling to the ground; or the moments following the announcement that Osama bin Laden had been killed. On occasions like these, it is not hard to appreciate what McLuhan meant when he said that electronic media bring about the experience of the global village. But the concept was not one that he reserved only for specific moments when a significant global event took place. He also had in mind the idea that when information flows back and forth across the globe at the speed of light, people who live in diverse geographical locations become psychologically and emotionally closer than anyone could have conceived possible years ago.

Because television was the dominant medium of the electronic age, McLuhan often used it to illustrate his basic points. Unlike the linear processing of print, television encourages a kind of information processing similar to the acoustical principle of the tribe. Processing a TV message is much more like the all-at-once processing of the ear than the linear processing of the eye reading a printed page. McLuhan was fond of pointing out that most people were in error in regarding television as a visual medium. On the contrary, he argued, television is fundamentally an acoustic medium. To make this point clear, he invited people to try a simple experiment. First, turn the sound down on the TV set for one minute during your favorite program. Now, for another minute, adjust the TV so that you can hear the sound but you can't see any picture. Which condition was more frustrating? Which condition gave you less information? McLuhan believed that people who tried this little exercise would invariably report more frustration in the condition where the picture was visible but the sound was inaudible. So, even though we think of television as a visual medium, McLuhan argued that it was primarily a medium of sound.

Second, McLuhan argued that the electronic communication forms were in direct opposition to the great technology of print. Linear thinking, deductive logic, and the private, information-packed experience of reading would gradually give way to the new electronic experience of radio and television. At the same time, the familiar way of thinking would gradually give way to a mode of thinking that was less linear, less logical, more spontaneous, and more like the thinking of our tribal ancestors. As far as McLuhan could tell, there was no way to stop these changes from occurring. The power of instantaneous electronic information would overwhelm the great culture of print in a matter of time. Although McLuhan claimed that he was almost always against the changes that he saw the electronic media instigating, he remained determined to understand exactly what was happening to us.

In his determination to communicate what he thought, McLuhan often relied on pithy sayings. His most famous of these, "**The medium is the message**," was really an attempt to summarize his view of human history just outlined. A closer look at this saying will reveal a key principle of McLuhan's analysis of the media age.

## THE MEDIUM IS THE MESSAGE

Part of McLuhan's popular appeal was his habit of coining slogans and phrases that he eventually referred to as "McLuhanisms." It was this habit that often got him into trouble with scholars, who typically wanted more depth and more explication of ideas than a simple slogan could provide. Nevertheless, McLuhan seemed to sense that these slogans were important tools of communication, and he churned them out with some regularity. As noted, perhaps his best-known saying was "The medium is the message." McLuhan seemed to realize that one of the advantages of a slogan like this one is that it could mean different things to different people at different times. He took full advantage of this feature and provided a number of different twists on the meaning of the phrase. It is no wonder that scholars often disagree strongly about exactly what McLuhan meant when he uttered these words. Some scholars have given up trying to understand what he meant and tend to dismiss all of McLuhan's ideas as little more than creations of an intellectual charlatan. Notice how the ambiguity that McLuhan seemed to cultivate around concepts such as this is diametrically opposed to the values of science. While not all scientific concepts are as clear as they might be, in science there is a constant push for clarity and precision that many scholars didn't sense in McLuhan's rhetoric.

But ambiguities aside, if we understand how McLuhan viewed human history, it is at least possible to get some insight from the idea that the medium is the message. The first thing to understand in considering this phrase is that it plays off the common notion that people change as a result of processing persuasive messages. When we think of television affecting a person's behavior, we usually think in terms of a particular program or particular message that provoked the change. Such thinking has good support from research studies. There are hundreds of research studies that lend credence to the fact that human behavior changes from processing messages. Almost every chapter in this book revolves around the idea that some particular type of media message has a specific effect on human attitudes, feelings, or actions.

McLuhan realized that most people tend to think of the messages in a given medium of communication as the agents of change. He didn't deny that messages have impact, but he wanted to get across what he believed was a much loftier and more far-reaching proposition. In claiming that the medium is the message, McLuhan was saying that what really changed people the most was not the message in any given medium of communication, but the medium itself. Hence, the medium *is* the message.

McLuhan believed that most people would find his concept to be a little strange and difficult to think about. His reason for this belief may seem stranger than the belief itself. McLuhan thought that all media were extensions of people: The wheel is an extension of the foot. The book is an extension of the eye. The electronic circuit is an extension of the central nervous system. McLuhan believed that these various extensions of ourselves intensified the particular organ or sense that found itself extended. In response to this intensification, he argued that the affected sense or organ would act to protect itself and engage in a numbing process that he equated with Freud's concept of repression. The result of this process in the case of electronic media would be to make people quite unaware of the media's effects. If we are unaware of the media's impact on our culture, the slogan declaring that the medium is the message is likely to sound a little strange.

But look back at McLuhan's view of human history. He claimed that the invention of print brought about cataclysmic change in human culture and that the invention of electronic media started a major revolution that we have yet to complete. McLuhan saw the important changes in human life arising from the changes in the dominant communication medium at given points in human history. This view stands in sharp contrast to the one that asserts that change arises from messages within a given medium. As he once said, "Societies have always been shaped more by the nature of the media with which people communicate than by the content of the communication."[2] This is probably the best way to understand "The medium is the message."

## THE EFFECTS OF ELECTRONIC MEDIA ON HUMAN BEINGS

McLuhan liked to emphasize that the dominant medium of communication changed human behavior more than the individual messages that the medium contained. He played with his own slogan a bit and changed it to "The medium is the *massage*." By this play on words, he meant to underscore the fact that communication media are not neutral. They affect people. He once commented that media "rough people up" and act "chiropractically." Comments like these prompted some to charge that McLuhan's mind could think only in metaphors—that he would create a metaphor even when there wasn't a need for one. But despite this criticism, McLuhan actually had quite a bit to say about the specific ways that electronic media were changing us. That is one reason this chapter is included in this text. Today, McLuhan's theory if often studied under the general rubric of something called **media ecology**. The term "ecology" reflects a concern for the environment. *Media* ecologists study changes in the media environment. If "the medium is the message" is to be taken seriously, some of the most significant changes in our environment are being driven by changes in the media that increasingly dominate our daily living environment.

The remaining portion of this chapter presents some of McLuhan's thoughts on the effects of electronic media. Keep in mind that he couldn't really prove that any of these effects were actually taking place. He did try, however, to point out the things that were consistent with his claims. And although many scholars scowled at McLuhan's inability to offer hard evidence for the effects he talked about, there was always that nagging doubt that maybe, just maybe, he was onto something. As author Tom Wolfe put it, "Suppose he is what he sounds like, the most important thinker since Newton, Darwin, Freud, Einstein and Pavlov? What if he is right?"[3] Because little hard evidence one way or the other presents itself, most scientists throw up their hands when it comes to a serious consideration of McLuhan's ideas. As noted earlier in the chapter, they hark back to the notion of falsifiability of theory (see Chapter 2) and point out that since the ideas can't be falsified, their validity cannot be established. In the next section, I present McLuhan's ideas on several topics that he talked about frequently. To what extent do you find McLuhan's thinking about the media effects outlined here to have the ring of truth? Can you think of ways that they could be subjected to scientific test?

## Education in the Electronic Age

During the 1960s, it became clear that television had completely changed the typical household in the United States. Almost every home had a TV set, and viewing time was increasing daily. Interestingly, something else was also starting to happen at around this same time. The scores that students earned on standardized educational tests started to drop slightly. That decline remained almost steady until the 1980s. Since the 1960s, scores on the verbal portion of the SAT have dropped 50 to 60 points. Educators often bemoan the fact that many of today's college students demonstrate reading and writing skills that are far below the levels of their predecessors.[4] After a period of fairly steady SAT scores, there's been a small but steady drop since 2005 on both the critical reading and the mathematics portions of the test.[5] And since 2006 when the critical writing test was introduced, scores have dropped about 5 points. In early 2014, the folks who design the SAT test announced that the essay portion was being dropped from the test. This announcement came in the wake of news that data from the class of 2012 revealed that reading and writing test scores had dropped to their lowest levels yet.[6] The crucial question that demands an answer is "Why?" Without a carefully controlled study (which is practically impossible in this case), a definitive answer seems to be beyond our grasp.

Many things have changed in society since the dawn of TV. There are more single-parent homes, there is more drug abuse, political instability has increased, and the quality of schools in the inner cities has declined. The most recent declines could be a function of the fact that the method of test taking has also changed (longer tests and a new writing section) or the fact that fewer students are taking the test multiple times (scores on a re-take tend to improve by an average of 30 points). Any one of these things might be responsible in part for a decline in standardized test scores. But according to McLuhan, declines in test scores were predictable long before they happened—because of television. He argued that such declines have to do with the fact that the traditional educational system thrives on the great print technology. Since television took over as the dominant medium of communication, the print-based educational system is a system under siege. By the time today's children arrive in the classroom, they have spent thousands of hours processing electronic information in a non-linear, acoustic fashion. When they encounter the print-based educational system of the typical classroom, there is a huge incompatibility. Print-based education finds it difficult to win out over the instantaneous acoustic form of television.

McLuhan had an interesting way of articulating one of the dilemmas of traditional, print-based education in the electronic age. Prior to the mid-1900s, he argued, a person knew that when he or she entered the classroom, the information level inside that room was always going to be *higher* than the information level outside the room. Think about that for a minute. Before electronic media, people couldn't find out about the workings of government or foreign affairs or almost anything else of importance unless they went to school and spent time *reading*. Books were the only window on the world. But today, this is no longer true. In fact, McLuhan said that when today's children enter the classroom, they soon realize that, because of electronic media, the information level outside the room is *higher* than the information level inside. In a sense, McLuhan said, today's children know that going to school is an interruption of their education.

McLuhan was fond of pointing out all of the various signs of the failing educational system. Elementary school teachers who had taught for 20 years before the rise of television frequently reported that the children raised on a steady diet of TV were harder to teach. They were more impatient, less well behaved, and more eager for entertainment than for learning through books. McLuhan argued that we should come to expect such reports. It made perfect sense to him that the rise of electronic media would throw the old print-based educational system into crisis.

McLuhan once noted that we are "playing the old story backwards." In ancient Greece, he pointed out, a well-educated person was someone who had memorized the great epic poems like Homer and could sing them to his harp. This style of learning was consistent with the old acoustic form of the tribal age. The rise of literacy completely wiped out this definition of an educated person. As McLuhan put it, literacy wiped out Homer. And, he argued, if literacy could wipe out Homer, then rock 'n' roll music could wipe out literacy. He believed rock 'n' roll was a new acoustic form of education that threatened the entire print establishment. He predicted that rock music would thrive, while the traditional educational establishment would falter and grope for a way to survive. McLuhan empathized with frustrated parents raised in the old print culture, who thought that something profoundly disturbing was taking place when rock music captured the imagination of their children. But these parents probably took little comfort in McLuhan's explanation of what was happening. He made one famous remark that combined his belief about rock 'n' roll with his notion that the electronic media ushered in a communication environment similar to that of the tribal age. Parents of the Western world, McLuhan said, were in the process of watching their children become "third-world" kids.

If he were alive today, McLuhan would not be surprised to learn that many people describe our educational system as being in disarray—while simultaneously, the music industry is thriving. I remember thinking about McLuhan's analysis years ago as I watched the first feature-length film on an Omnimax projection system as it enjoyed its second holdover for a longer run at Chicago's Museum of Science and Industry. The Omnimax system used more than 70 speakers for the sound track and projected the film's images onto a domelike screen. The entire projection system, complete with sound equipment, had a price tag of more than $2 million. McLuhan would have probably smiled confidently upon learning that the film that people were flocking to see at $15 per person was a documentary about the infamous rock group, the Rolling Stones.

McLuhan believed that education would be successful in the electronic age only to the extent that it adapted to the new electronic forms. This process of adaptation would not be easy, because the ways of print die slowly. As in almost every other area of human life, McLuhan predicted turmoil and struggle as the two great communication technologies clashed in the twentieth century. Although he believed that successful adaptation was possible, he wasn't sure how it would emerge or if it would emerge at all. For evidence of the predicted turmoil and struggle in the education context, McLuhan's devotees would probably want to point to an article that appeared in the June 16, 2008 issue of *The Chronicle of Higher Education*.[7] The article reports on the growing controversy in some law schools about permitting students to have open laptops on their desks during class sessions. While many students use laptops to take notes, the article explains that "Students with laptops, [professors] argue, surf the Web instead of engaging in class, and play games, shop online, or email friends, distracting themselves and those who sit near them." The conflict over laptops in the classroom shows that adaptation to the new electronic forms may not be so easy. It also illustrates McLuhan's claim that the information level outside the classroom is increasingly higher relative to the information inside the classroom—and that students craving that outside information find it difficult to give it up.

## War in the Electronic Age: Not So "Hot"

For most of the latter part of the 1960s, Americans witnessed a real war on television for the first time in history. World War II, in contrast to the Vietnam War, was a radio war. Yes, there were newsreels that people could see in local movie theaters before the weekly feature film began. But these didn't have the same impact on our emotions as watching and hearing our favorite news anchor (in most cases, Walter Cronkite of CBS) narrating the details of the latest battle each night. And the war went on and on … and on … and on. Each Thursday evening in the New York area, one of the local news stations would play the Vietnam "honor roll," a list of all of the soldiers from the New York/New Jersey area whom officials had pronounced dead during the week as a result of the Vietnam conflict. The list of white names on a blue background scrolled slowly up the TV screens of hundreds of thousands of viewers. On some evenings, the list would continue scrolling for many minutes before all the names had been displayed. On a daily basis, as well, news reporters sent back film footage of live conflict from the battlefields of Vietnam, filled with images that were often deeply disturbing.

As Americans experienced this steady diet of images of war, they grew increasingly uncomfortable. More and more people came to believe that the United States had involved itself in a conflict that was hopeless. The war became a political hot potato. In 1968, President Lyndon Johnson refused to run for a second term, and many speculated that he would not have won anyway because of his unpopular Vietnam policy. Richard Nixon won the White House by promising an honorable end to the war in Vietnam.

Why was the Vietnam War so unpopular? Marshall McLuhan thought he knew the answer to that question. He argued that people experiencing the war through television found the brutal images to be extremely unpleasant and ultimately unbearable. Television, McLuhan argued, was a cool medium. **Cool media** were those that allowed high levels of participation and involvement. **Hot media** were those that had higher information definition, and consequently did not involve the recipient of the message as intensely. Newspapers and radio were relatively hot media. Film was also a hot medium. According to McLuhan, hot media could tolerate higher levels of violence because people could not become actively involved in the processing of messages delivered over hot media. Newspapers and film thrive on violence, but television must be more careful in its portrayal of violent events because it is so involving.

If the distinction between hot and cool media seems a little vague to you, you are not alone. McLuhan never really explained the difference between hot and cool media in a way that made it easy to grasp. On some occasions, he would simply say, "Cool is involving—hot is not." At other times, he would launch into a much more technical explanation. For example, he argued that the reason television was highly involving was that there was never really a complete picture on the screen at any given instant. This is because the TV picture consists of hundreds of lines that the screen fills in over fractions of a second. At any given instant, the screen contains only a partial picture. Consequently, McLuhan argued that the viewer had to work to fill in or complete the screen's image. This process of filling in the picture with one's mind was highly involving and helped to make television an intense experience. Film, in contrast, consists of individual frames. Each frame is a total picture when it flashes by the projection bulb and appears on the movie screen. It does not require the viewer to fill in anything. Thus, the level of participation in processing film images is much lower than for television. Film is a hot medium relative to TV.

It is difficult to appreciate how this technical difference between the television image and the film image could have such a huge impact on the psychological experience that viewers have with TV and film. McLuhan's critics questioned him about this: "What happens when you take films and put them on television? Is the result a hot medium or a cool one?" McLuhan might answer, perhaps in frustration, that the result was lukewarm. These sorts of answers were not very satisfying.

McLuhan's distinction between hot and cool media may confuse as much as it enlightens. But it is difficult to argue with McLuhan's general thesis that Americans found a television war to be most unpleasant. Consider the nature of war on television since Vietnam. The crisis in Kuwait was over in a matter of weeks. The recent war in Iraq dominated the 2004 presidential campaign and was a key issue again in the 2008 presidential race. In both Kuwait and Iraq, the nature of the news coverage was controversial. During the Kuwait crisis, the U.S. government argued that strict control of the press was necessary to protect strategy and tactics. But critics argued that these controls went too far and were unnecessary. In any case, there were few TV shots of real human suffering. Some observers compared the typical news footage to a video game. We saw exploding buildings—but little more. More of the same type of coverage followed when NATO bombed Serbia over the crisis in Kosovo. And this sort of coverage continued in 2011 as NATO bombed Libya. While the war in Afghanistan has continued for over a decade, Americans have seen precious little raw TV footage of that conflict. McLuhan would probably say that the networks learned to adjust to the electronic age. They learned their lesson from Vietnam: raw war footage does not play well on TV. When this type of footage is aired now, it is often sanitized and only brief images are shown. The last edition of the text, which I wrote prior to the 2008 presidential election, contained the following statement: "[The] good student of McLuhan might warn Senator John McCain that to the extent that his candidacy becomes associated with continuing reports of war casualties in Iraq and Afghanistan, his chances to defeat Senator Barack Obama might be diminished." Of course, Obama eventually defeated McCain. As I write these words, the Republicans are beginning to jockey for position in preparation for the 2016 election. At the moment, while the economy and Obamacare loom as the biggest issues, Obama is carefully avoiding any direct conflict with Russia even after their takeover of Crimea. A good student of McLuhan's might advise Democrats to stay out of any military conflicts in the days preceding the election or else face the prospect of seriously jeopardizing their chances.

If McLuhan were alive today, he might take some solace in the published experimental research of Michael Pfau and his colleagues. Pfau's research team assigned participants to watch news reports of the Iraq war in one of two conditions. The first condition featured only descriptions of the war operations by a news anchor with no visual footage. The second condition featured news commentary that was accompanied by two minutes of visual footage that featured casualties of the war. The results of the experiment showed that while the two groups didn't differ in terms of their negative emotional reactions to the news reports, they *did* differ in terms of the extent to which they felt involved in the issues surrounding the war and in terms of their attitude toward supporting continued involvement in the Iraq conflict. The group that saw the images of war casualties reported greater involvement in the war issue and were more likely to have a negative attitude about the United States continuing to be involved militarily in Iraq. While it would be a stretch to argue that this experiment serves as any sort of strong test of McLuhan's notion of hot versus cool media, the results certainly seem to be consistent with McLuhan's analysis of how television images of war involve viewers so deeply in an uncomfortable situation that profound political consequences are ultimately experienced on a large scale.[8]

## Politics in the Electronic Age: Was Barack Obama "Cooler" than Mitt Romney?

In the 1960s, when McLuhan was at his peak of media popularity, he offered his own political analysis of the presidential campaigns. John Kennedy, McLuhan explained, was the first television president. In an insightful interview that McLuhan granted to *Playboy* magazine (the entire interview is available online at: www.mcluhanmedia.com), he remarked:

> TV is an inherently cool medium, and Kennedy had a compatible coolness and indifference to power. ... Any political candidate who doesn't have such cool, low-definition qualities, which allow the viewer to fill in the gaps with his own personal identification, simply electrocutes himself on television— as Richard Nixon did in his disastrous debates with Kennedy in the 1960 campaign. Nixon was essentially hot; he presented a high-definition, sharply defined image and action on the TV screen that contributed to his reputation as a phony. (p. 61)[9]

If McLuhan had been observing the 2012 political campaign, he would undoubtedly have seen Barack Obama as the cooler of the two presidential candidates. Obama continued to use the Internet to organize his campaign in a way that was even more impressive than in his first presidential run in 2008. He presented an image that was progressive, relaxed, casual and, in McLuhan's vocabulary, cooler than that projected by Mitt Romney. McLuhan, who was a fierce critic of the standard debating format, would have applauded the move to a more casual debating style that Obama and Romney staged at Hofstra University for their second "town hall" debate. McLuhan argued that the usual debating format had the candidates standing behind elaborate podiums in some of the "hottest" stuff that television was capable of producing. This style of debating was, in McLuhan's view, totally incompatible with the cool medium of television. Although it is easy to say now that McLuhan is long gone, I'm confident that he would have found Obama to be cooler than Romney.

Many political scientists would probably consider it naive to predict the outcome of a complicated presidential election by appealing to one or two fuzzy concepts in McLuhan's theory. The fact that McLuhan comes across as a startling prophet on some issues and yet seems hopelessly foggy on others makes it difficult for many people to arrive at a final conclusion about the merit of his ideas. You will definitely want to read the material in Study Box 12-1 before you make your final decision about how to evaluate McLuhan's ultimate contribution.

---

### STUDY BOX 12-1 McLuhan's Failed Experiment: The Wonders (?) of Prohtex

If you are on the fence about how to evaluate the ideas of Marshall McLuhan, perhaps this little tidbit will push you over. One of the themes in the "theory" of Marshall McLuhan is that when the print age supplanted the tribal age, the sensory balance of communication was disrupted. According to McLuhan, tribal communication involved all the senses—including the olfactory. The sense of smell was an important and valued commodity in the tribal state. If, as McLuhan argued, the electronic age was a return to the acoustic communication environment of the tribal era, then it was also a return to an environment where more of the senses would once again become involved in communication. Consequently, McLuhan thought that the electronic age would be an age in which the sense of smell would become increasingly important.

McLuhan was a person who was not afraid to invest in his own theoretical ideas. According to Gary Wolf, who wrote in *Wired* magazine, McLuhan announced a new product in 1971. In collaboration with his nephew, Ross Hall, who was a chemist, McLuhan actually patented a unique chemical solution that was designed to be applied to people's underpants. That's right, there was no misprint in that last sentence. It was designed to be applied to people's underpants. It gets even better. The secret formula, registered under the trademark Prohtex, worked marvels. It removed the smell of urine from one's underpants while leaving the more interesting body aromas associated with perspiration. McLuhan was convinced that natural body aroma was an important part of communication in the tribal state. According to Wolf, McLuhan really believed that "when electronic technology turned the world into a global village, tribal odors would make a comeback too." Needless to say, Prohtex didn't make McLuhan rich. Perhaps it was ahead of its time. Maybe the coming revolution that will usher us into the electronic age will pave the way for this odd formula to become an everyday best seller. Then again, maybe not.

---

SOURCE: Wolf, G. (1996). The wisdom of Saint Marshall, the Holy Fool [Online: Accessed 4-19-14]. Available: http://www.wired.com/wired/archive/4.01/saint.marshal_pr.html

## Drugs in the Electronic Age

When George H. W. Bush became president in 1989, he launched a war on drugs. Four years later, although his administration would claim some success, the drug problem that plagued the United States was worse than ever.[10] The last year has shown what appears to be a growing trend toward legalization of marijuana in the United States. What seemed unthinkable in 1989 has come to pass in a short 15 years. I don't think McLuhan would be at all surprised. In the same *Playboy* interview in which McLuhan discussed John Kennedy's advantage over Richard Nixon, he commented on the drug problem:

> The upsurge in drug taking is intimately related to the impact of the electric media. Look at the metaphor for getting high: turning on. One turns on his consciousness through drugs just as he opens up all his senses to a total depth involvement by turning on the TV dial. Drug taking is stimulated by today's pervasive environment of instant information, with its feedback mechanism of the inner trip. The inner trip is not the sole prerogative of the LSD traveler; it's the universal experience of TV watchers. The attraction to hallucinogenic drugs is a means of achieving empathy with our penetrating electric environment, an environment that in itself is a drugless inner trip. (p. 68)[11]

McLuhan was among the very first scholars to talk about "television addiction" (recall Chapter 4's discussion on TV addiction and review Study Box 4-2). Although the evidence for a true physical addiction to TV is still debatable, some believe that there are individuals who have a literal addiction to the tube. In support of their claim, they point to people who seem to suffer the familiar symptoms of withdrawal—anxiety, physical nervousness, and depression—when deprived of TV viewing.[12]

## Privacy in the Electronic Age: Fading Fast

One area of McLuhan's thought that got little attention for decades but now seems increasingly relevant is the area of privacy. McLuhan noted that privacy was a value that was cultivated in the age of print. The print age permitted people to retreat to private spaces to read. Privacy became expected and valued as a result. But in the electronic age, McLuhan observed that privacy would be a value to come under constant attack. First, he claimed that just by watching TV, young people became disinterested in a sense of "private identity." Instead, they became much more interested in fitting into their peer group and conforming to the customs and habits of others like themselves. Second, with instantaneous information flow, privacy is something that is increasingly difficult to maintain.

If McLuhan were alive today, he would undoubtedly be smiling to see his ideas about privacy receiving vindication. In virtually every sphere of society it seems, we're struggling with maintaining our private identity. Many people feel bewildered when they log into a Web site and find ads that are seemingly tailored directly for them. How much information about your electronic habits is being collected? Who is able to read your email? Do you run the risk of losing a job because of what someone posts on Facebook? How comfortable would you feel if a police officer stopped you for a traffic violation and demanded your cell phone to inspect for recent texting? These are just a few of the questions that people are struggling with today as privacy seems to come under assault from every quarter. Since writing the last edition of this text, one of the major news stories to dominate worldwide attention was the one that featured Edward Snowden's leaks about the surveillance operations of the CIA and the NSA. Suddenly, American citizens were wondering about the extent to which their personal privacy was being systematically invaded with sophisticated and relatively invisible technology. Actually, McLuhan thought that the stakes involved with the assault on our privacy were much higher than just individual private identity. In the following comment he made in his famous interview in *Playboy*, he insists that entire societies are at risk:

> All our alienation and atomization are reflected in the crumbling of such time-honored social values as the right of privacy and the sanctity of the individual; as they yield to the intensities of the new technology's electric circus, it seems to the average citizen that the sky is falling in. As man is tribally metamorphosed by the electric media, we all become Chicken Littles, scurrying around frantically in search of our former identities, and in the process unleash tremendous violence. As the preliterate confronts the literate in the postliterate arena, as new information patterns inundate and uproot the old, mental breakdowns of varying degrees—including the collective nervous breakdowns of whole societies unable to resolve their crises of identity—will become very common.[13]

In August of 2010, I had the opportunity to visit Cairo, Egypt for two weeks as part of a work assignment. Shortly after I returned, Cairo erupted in massive demonstrations that eventually brought down the country's leader and spread to other Middle Eastern countries. As I write this paragraph today, the world has witnessed great upheavals in Tunisia, Yemen, Egypt, Iraq, Iran, the Crimean peninsula, Ukraine, and Syria—just some of the major points of unrest. I have to admit that in the face of what appears to be taking place across the globe at the present time, McLuhan's words above—written over 40 years ago—seem to echo like the words of a prophet. Was he on to something profound or was his prediction just a nebulous guess that anyone could fit to certain circumstances if they looked hard enough?

## WHY DOES McLUHAN'S "THEORY" FAIL AS A SCIENTIFIC APPROACH?

At the outset of the chapter, I noted that one reason to include a chapter on Marshall McLuhan was to be able to contrast his approach with the scientific approach to media effects. Exactly why does McLuhan's approach fail to fit the approach of science? To answer this question, you might want to go all the way back to Chapter 1 to review the essential characteristics of a scientific approach. As it turns out, McLuhan's work appears to fall short on a number of the key criteria.

First, you might recall that one of the hallmarks of the scientific method is systematic observation. While it is certainly true that McLuhan made lots of observations, his method could hardly be called systematic. Instead, after reading McLuhan, one senses that his observations were very carefully selected to fit his ideas. His critics complained that if they selected an observation that seemed to run counter to his views, they were either ignored or chastised. That doesn't conform to the scientific goal of systematic observation that allows one to observe all sorts of possible lines of evidence—even ones that might conflict with key theoretical ideas.

Second, recall that scientific hypotheses are falsifiable. That is, the theorist ought to be able to specify exactly what sort of evidence should count as evidence that disconfirms the theory. In my own reading of McLuhan, I never remember him specifying what sort of evidence would disconfirm his ideas. Moreover, in order to have falsifiable hypotheses, one has to have a practical way of being able to observe confirmations and disconfirmations. In science, empirical techniques like surveys and experiments form the backbone of general observational strategy. McLuhan never pursued such techniques during his career. It was sometimes observed that the only experiments he did took place inside his own head.

Finally, recall that the goals of science are achieved by advancing logical theories. Also recall that McLuhan was never willing to call his body of work a theory—even if others sometimes gave him the benefit of the doubt. McLuhan was more comfortable talking about his "probes" of exploration. So, with no formal theory to work with, no falsifiable hypotheses, and no systematic observational techniques, we'd hardly be willing to place McLuhan in the halls of science. On the other hand, also recall from Chapter 1 that science can't answer certain kinds of questions. Some of the questions that McLuhan tried to address probably don't fit well with the hallmarks of the scientific method.

## McLUHAN'S INFLUENCE

Because McLuhan's ideas seem to defy direct empirical testing, they have been of little value from a scientific perspective. But scientists often give high marks to theoretical thinking that instigates new discussion and controversy—even though that thinking itself may not enjoy much direct support. If we use this standard to evaluate McLuhan's contribution, perhaps there is some shred of scientific value.

McLuhan started writing about the media more than 50 years ago. Communication scholars still use his ideas and extend them to new areas. McLuhan's basic perspective of "**technological determinism**" (the medium, not the message, determines changes in human behavior) is particularly evident in two books that have received wide acclaim. In his book *Amusing Ourselves to Death: Public Discourse in the*

*Age of Show Business*, Neil Postman argues that television has trivialized public discourse. He states:

> There is no more disturbing consequence of the electronic and graphic revolution than this: that the world as given to us through television seems natural, not bizarre. For the loss of the sense of the strange is a sign of adjustment, and the extent to which we have adjusted is a measure of the extent to which we have been changed. (p. 80)[14]

Another scholar, Joshua Meyrowitz, has written a provocative book, *No Sense of Place: The Impact of Electronic Media on Social Behavior*. The following excerpt from the book's introduction sounds like McLuhan himself:

> [T]his book suggests that the widespread use of electronic media has played an important part in many recent social developments, including the social explosions of the 1960s, the many "integration" movements (blacks, women, elderly, children, disabled, etc.), the rise of malpractice suits, the development of "halfway" houses for prisoners and the mentally ill, the decline of the nuclear family. The theory suggests that a broad, seemingly chaotic spectrum of social change may be, in part, an orderly and comprehensible adjustment in behavior patterns to match the new social situations created by electronic media. (p. 9)[15]

To be sure, both Postman and Meyrowitz go well beyond McLuhan's notions in advancing their own thoughts on electronic media. But McLuhan's influence on these widely read scholars and others writing about media impact is quite evident and openly acknowledged. There is no escaping the fact that McLuhan's basic ideas about media impact are at least worthy of some attention.

## FINAL REFLECTIONS

You should recognize McLuhan's perspective on media effects as qualitatively different from those represented in the other chapters in this book. In the case of Marshall McLuhan, there is little if any scientific evidence to support his ideas. And yet, no book on the effects of mass media should ignore McLuhan. The media effects that he talked about were not trivial. If his assertions are right, the effects documented in the preceding chapters should take second seat to the kind of sweeping cultural effects that he claimed the electronic media initiated. If you are like most people, you found some of McLuhan's thinking to be provocative and full of insight. But you may have reacted with skepticism to other parts of his analysis. In the end, media effects scholars don't really know what to do with McLuhan, because his ideas fall short of the testability criterion that scientists embrace. Nevertheless, we must credit McLuhan with stimulating the entire scholarly community to think about the power of the electronic media. He left several provocative ideas for scholars to contemplate (see Study Box 12-2). If he was right, we may be only at the dawn of the full realization of the electronic age.

## STUDY BOX 12-2 Some of Marshall McLuhan's Provocative Ideas about Electronic Media

1. "The Medium is the Message": This phrase attempts to transform the way we think about media impact. Instead of the messages or the content of the media having the main impact on people, McLuhan asserted that it was the media themselves that changed human beings far more than the content of those media.

2. Hot versus Cool Media: McLuhan categorized different media on a continuum anchored at the endpoints as "hot" or "cool." Cool media (e.g., television), he asserted, were involving while hot media (e.g., newspapers), with its relatively higher definition, were not. This concept is probably the one that most casual readers have the greatest difficulty comprehending. One source of the difficulty is that McLuhan often offered very different explications of what he meant by the distinction.

3. The Global Village: Instantaneous electronic communication connects people around the globe in a way that was never possible before electricity. As we become connected, we start to become involved emotionally in the affairs of people who are geographically very far away. That is to say, the world begins to resemble a much smaller village in which everyone is busy being concerned about everybody else's business. As I write these words, my wife Cheri is visibly and emotionally upset at the images and details coming to us from South Korea. A large ferry carrying hundreds of high school students capsized and sank. Many are dead. Before electronic media, stories like this had no potential to affect the emotional lives of people living thousands of miles away.

4. Erosion of Private Identity: Television, McLuhan argued, turned adolescents into people seeking identity in a group. Group membership would become more important in the electronic age than being an individual, private person. As we move into the electronic era, we ought to expect that the definition of privacy will change. We will be forced to give up to the public sphere things that were once regarded as private. Laws protecting privacy will be challenged by new electronic forms. Increasing turmoil will result because people will discover that things they regarded as part of their private identity are now public.

5. Media Are Extensions of Ourselves: McLuhan argued that the wheel was an extension of our feet. It intensified the function of the feet such that we could move around at a much higher rate of speed. Print is an extension of the eye. The eye put us into contact with our immediate physical environment. Print puts us into contact with worlds far away and with places limited only by our imagination. Electronic media extend our central nervous systems—which are, after all, an elaborate system of electrical signals. Electronic media are actually an extended part of our most intricate and sensitive selves. Consistent with this idea, it isn't uncommon to witness people who can hardly function if they are separated from their smartphone. McLuhan might argue that their entire system of internal electric circuitry seems to malfunction when this important extension of the body goes missing. A missing phone actually feels like a missing body part.

# SUMMARY

Some media effects scholars may question the extent to which a chapter on Marshall McLuhan belongs in a book of this type. Three arguments for including such a chapter were presented. McLuhan saw the field of communication historically. He described at least three major eras in communication history: the tribal age, the print age, and the electronic age. His observations about the fundamental nature of communication in each era formed the core of his "theory." He achieved fame in applying his insights to all sorts of modern-day phenomena, including drugs, education, politics, war, and privacy. Many of his ideas were difficult to grasp, and he disliked scholarly criticism. His perspective is nearly impossible to test scientifically. Although this did not ultimately endear him to the scholarly community, it did permit him to roam freely with his speculations. No one could really prove him wrong. In the final analysis, McLuhan's perspective on the impact of the electronic media is worth thinking about—even while recognizing that gathering empirical evidence in favor of it seems unlikely.

## QUESTIONS TO FOCUS YOUR ATTENTION

1. Should students studying the scientific perspective on media effects be encouraged to read about Marshall McLuhan? Why or why not?
2. Do you think, as McLuhan did, that education in the electronic age is in a state of crisis? What evidence would you bring to support your opinion?
3. Can you think of any scientific studies that might be designed to test any of McLuhan's ideas—or is his body of theory completely beyond scientific scrutiny?

## KEY TERMS AND CONCEPTS

| | | |
|---|---|---|
| prober | print age | media ecology |
| proofs | linear information processing | cool media |
| eras of communication | electronic age | hot media |
| tribal state | global village | technological determinism |
| sensory balance | the medium is the message | |

## NOTES

1. Pember, D. R. (1992). *Mass media in America*. New York: Macmillan.
2. *Playboy* interview: Marshall McLuhan. (1969, March). *Playboy,* 53–54, 56, 59–62, 64–66, 68, 70, 72, 74, 158.
3. [Video] (1984). Marshall McLuhan: The man and his message. McLuhan Productions, Canadian Broadcasting Corporation. Produced and Directed by Stephanie McLuhan.
4. Shanker, A. (1992, January 6). The higher education crisis. *New Republic,* 200, 2.
5. 2010 SAT Trends. (2010). *College Board Inspiring Minds*. [Online: Accessed 4-19-14]. Available: http://research.collegeboard.org/programs/sat/data/archived/cb-seniors-2010/tables
6. Lorin, J. (September 4, 2012). SAT reading, writing test scores drop to lowest levels. *Bloomberg News*. [Online: Accessed 4-19-14]. Available: http://www.bloomberg.com/news/2012-09-24/sat-reading-writing-test-scores-drop-to-lowest-levels.html

7. Foster, A. L. (2008). Law professors rule laptops out of order in class. *The Chronicle of Higher Education,* 54(40), A1.
8. Pfau, M., Haigh, M. M., Shannon, T., Tones, T., Mercurio, D., Williams, R., Binstock, B., Diaz, C., Dillard, C., Browne, M., Elder, C., Reed, S., Eggers, A., & Melendez, J. (2008). The influence of television news depictions of the images of war on viewers. *Journal of Broadcasting & Electronic Media,* 52(2), 303–322.
9. *Playboy* interview: Marshall McLuhan.
10. McKernan, V. (1992, September 21). The real war on drugs. *Newsweek,* 120, 14.
11. *Playboy* interview: Marshall McLuhan.
12. Smith, R. (1986). Television addiction. In J. Bryant & D. Zillmann (Eds.), *Perspectives on media effects* (pp. 109–128). Hillsdale, NJ: Erlbaum.
13. *Playboy* interview: Marshall McLuhan.
14. Postman, N. (1985). *Amusing ourselves to death: Public discourse in the age of show business.* New York: Penguin.
15. Meyrowitz, J. (1985). *No sense of place: The impact of electronic media on social behavior.* New York: Oxford University Press.

# IMPORTANT SOURCES ON MARSHALL McLUHAN

Canadian Broadcasting Corporation. (1984). *McLuhan: The man and his message* [Video].
Innis, H. A. (1972). *Empire and Communication,* rev. ed. Toronto: University of Toronto Press.
McLuhan, M. (1951). *The mechanical bride: Folklore of industrial man.* New York: Vanguard Press.
McLuhan, M. (1962). *The Gutenberg galaxy: The making of typographic man.* Toronto: University of Toronto Press.
McLuhan, M. (1964). *Understanding media: The extensions of man.* New York: McGraw- Hill.
Ong, W. J. (1982). *Orality and literacy: The technologizing of the word.* New York: Methuen.
*Playboy* interview: Marshall McLuhan. (1969, March). *Playboy,* 53–54, 56, 59–62, 64–66, 68, 70, 72, 74, 158.

# Glossary

# Theories and Theoretical Concepts Discussed in the Text (by Chapter)

**Accessibility Principle** An idea used to explain media cultivation effects. The notion is that when people are asked to make judgments about the social world, they will rely upon ideas that are most accessible in their minds. Heavy media consumers are likely to draw upon media messages in making these judgments since media messages are highly accessible. (8)

**Addiction to Media** A concept first introduced by Marshall McLuhan to describe the extreme attachments that people form with media. The concept is used frequently in connection with new media technologies and is related to "perpetual connection" discussed in Chapter 11. (4)

**Additive Effect** Used in connection with the possibility that media news reports of suicides cause more suicides. If they do, are these suicides simply "rescheduled" from when they would ordinarily occur—resulting in no overall increase in suicides? Or is the effect additive, which *would* lead to an overall increase? Research suggests the latter. (9)

**Agenda-Setting Theory** The idea that the news media don't tell people what to think but they do tell people what to think about. (9)

**Attitude Change** One of the possible outcomes of exposure to a persuasive media message. Attitudes refer to the feelings that people have toward ideas, people, objects,

and so forth. Attitudes may change as a function of processing media messages. (3, 8)

**AVIDS (Acquired Violence Immune Deficiency Syndrome)** A concept introduced by David Grossman to describe desensitization to media violence. People are not naturally immune to the emotional effects of media violence but can acquire such immunity through repeated exposure. Grossman views such immunity as a deficiency resulting in undesirable consequences. (5)

**Behavior Change** One of the possible outcomes of exposure to a persuasive media message. Behavior refers to the things that people regularly do, and behavioral intent refers to the things that people intend to do. Behaviors and behavioral intentions may change as a function of processing media messages. (3, 8)

**Binge Viewing** A type of TV viewing in which viewers watch TV for many consecutive hours without stopping. Such viewing tends to be associated with services like Netflix or cable TV systems that offer multiple episodes of a dramatic series that viewers can continue to watch in sequence. (4)

**Ceiling Effect** The situation in which it is difficult to observe any change in a given variable as a result of media influence (or, more generally, as a result of any independent variable) because the values on that variable are already extremely high and have no room to move higher. (3)

**Content-Specific Effects** Media effects that arise because of exposure to a specific kind of content. For example, theories that discuss effects due to media violence predict effects that are content-specific. (3)

**Conversion** A case of persuasion in which a person "converts" from one perspective, position, or viewpoint to a new one, usually as the result of attending to and processing a persuasive message. (3)

**Cool Media** A term coined by Marshall McLuhan to describe media that, in his view, were highly involving. The term created a certain level of confusion in the way McLuhan applied it and in the various explanations he gave to clarify it. TV is a cool medium; newspapers and books are hot media. In general, media that are more highly defined are hotter and don't invite the deep participation and involvement that McLuhan thought characterized cool media. (12)

**Copycat Phenomenon** The idea that a person might see a behavior depicted in the media and become inspired to copy or imitate that behavior him- or herself. (5)

**Cultivation Analysis** Part of George Gerbner's Cultural Indicators Paradigm that is concerned with the long-term, cumulative impact of media messages that shape the media consumer's view of the social world. Heavy consumers of media messages are more likely to become cultivated than light consumers. They are more likely to adopt a view of the social world that conforms to the world depicted in media. This type of analysis tends to produce surveys of viewers that document relationships between media consumption and views about the social world. (5, 8)

**Cultural Indicators Paradigm** George Gerbner's theoretical paradigm for studying media. The paradigm includes three main types of analysis: institutional process analysis, message system analysis, and cultivation analysis. (5)

**Desensitization** The idea that emotional responses to a given stimulus will decrease in intensity with repeated exposure to that stimulus. The idea is often applied in the context of discussions of media violence to explain how certain individuals who have consumed large quantities of media violence might become relatively immune to the usual intense negative reactions that unexposed consumers typically have to the same violent depictions. (5)

**Developmental Theory** A general theoretical perspective that seeks to describe, predict, and explain reactions to media content by emphasizing consumers' place on the continuum or sequence of stages of human development. The perspective is often employed to understand differences in children's preferences, interpretations, and reactions to the same media content depending on their age or level of cognitive development. (7)

**Diffuse Effects** Media effects that are not strongly associated with any particular kind of content but occur more as a function of the existence of media themselves. One example may be the presumed link between TV viewing and obesity, where obesity is thought to be caused not so much as a result of exposure to any particular media content, but by a general increase in physical inactivity associated with the act of media consumption. (3)

**Displacement Hypothesis** The general idea that media may bring about effects as a result of its capacity to displace other activities. TV viewing may lead to obesity because it displaces physical activity; Internet use may lead to a decrease in conversational skill because it tends to displace face-to-face interaction. (4, 11)

**Drench Hypothesis** Media effects that occur as a result of processing a particularly powerful or critical message that is unusual, intense, or highly involving. Effects that occur through the drench process are relatively immediate and easy to document because of the power of the critical image. (8)

**Drip Hypothesis** Media effects that occur as a result of long-term cumulative exposure to similar content. In contrast to effects that might conform to the drench hypothesis, effects that conform to the drip hypothesis take time and are relatively difficult to document since any change is slow and requires observations through time in order to capture the change dynamic. (8)

**Dual-Coding Theory** A theory about how information is processed that maintains a distinct difference between verbal and visual processing. Verbal and visual types of information may compete for central processing capacity and the brain may handle the two types of information differently. Some research suggests that verbal information is recalled better when it is processed in the absence of vivid visual images. (9)

**Elaboration Likelihood Model** A theory of persuasion by Richard Petty and John Cacioppo that conceptualizes the persuasion process in terms of two major routes or pathways: the central route and the peripheral route. Central route persuasion occurs with close scrutiny to the message and careful deliberation. Peripheral route persuasion occurs with less attention to the message and is a function of exposure to peripheral cues such as ones designed to entertain consumers in the context of media advertising messages. (8)

**Empathic Responses to Media** The tendency for media consumers to empathize with a media character's situation or emotional state such that they become highly involved in a character's ultimate fate or general situation. Individuals may differ in the extent to which they empathize with media characters. (7)

**Entertainment-Education** Attempts to affect viewers' attitudes or behavior in positive ways by building deliberate persuasive messages into entertainment programming. (8)

**EORM (Entertainment Overcoming Resistance Model to persuasion)** A type of entertainment-education designed to overcome viewer resistance to a particular attitude or behavior. By drawing the viewer into a highly involving plotline, initial resistance to particular attitudes or behaviors is overcome and the viewer is more likely to change. (8)

**Excitation Transfer Theory** Dolf Zillmann's theory that provides an explanation for why people feel certain emotions with particular intensity. The theory holds that arousal from a prior source (e.g., an emotion or physical exercise) can transfer to intensify a subsequent emotion, making it more intense than it would have been without the source of prior arousal. (6, 7)

**Experimental Validity** The extent to which the findings of any experiment are valid. There are four different types of experimental validity that need to be assessed: **statistical** (was there really a reliable difference between experimental conditions?), **internal** (did the treatment cause the effect or was it due to some other unwanted factor internal to the experiment?), **external** (does any effect generalize to other people, places, times, and situations?), and **construct** (do the treatment and dependent variables reflect the theoretical variables of interest?). (2)

**Face-ism** The tendency for males to be depicted in the media with higher levels of facial prominence than females. Face-ism is computed in any media depiction of a person by measuring the distance from the top of the head to the bottom of the chin and dividing it by the distance from the top of the head to the bottom of the body. Higher facial prominence leads to perceptions of a number of positive attributes (e.g., intelligence and competence). (10)

**Facilitation Effect** A media effect in which some specific behavior is made more likely as a result of exposure to a media message (e.g., exposure to media violence facilitates aggressive behavior). (5)

**First-Order Cultivation Effect** The process in which heavy viewers come to believe that the real world is like the TV world. (8)

**Forbidden Fruit Effect** The effect predicted by the theory of psychological reactance, which holds that free behavior that is eliminated or threatened with elimination will become more desirable. Researchers entertained the possibility that the MPAA movie rating system that restricts certain content from some viewers might cause those viewers to increase their desire to consume that content. (1)

**Framing** In the context of news reports, framing refers to how the media might do more than just tell viewers what to think about (agenda-setting); it might help to tell viewers what to actually think. Through the process of selecting certain details, excluding others, and emphasizing and elaborating upon others, news reports can suggest exactly what media consumers ought to think about a news event. (9)

**Gender Role Socialization** The process of socialization that differs according to the appropriate roles that are presented as normative or expected for males and females. Media may be a powerful socializing force with respect to setting gender-appropriate expectations—not only for acceptable roles in society but also for acceptable ways of responding to particular media messages. Males may be socialized to show mastery at a frightening film while females may be socialized to show fear. (7)

**General Aggression Model (GAM)** A model for understanding aggressive behavior

that integrates a number of different concepts and variables in order to predict and explain aggressive responses to media. Craig Anderson used the model in the context of studying the impact of playing violent video games on subsequent aggressive behavior by the players. (5)

**Global Village** The concept introduced by Marshall McLuhan that describes one of the consequences of moving into the electronic age. As information flows at the speed of light, people who live in different locations geographically will be connected in ways that make them feel like they are living in close proximity. The entire world begins to feel like a small village because everyone has access to the same information. (12)

**Hot Media** A term coined by Marshall McLuhan to describe media that, in his view, were highly defined and not very involving. The term created a certain level of confusion in the way McLuhan applied it and in the various explanations he gave to clarify it. TV is a cool medium; newspapers and books are hot media. Film is hot; TV is not. In general, media that are more highly defined are hotter and don't invite the deep participation and involvement that McLuhan thought characterized cool media. (12)

**Illusion of Personal Invulnerability** A concept usually used in the persuasion context to describe the self-perception that one is not susceptible or vulnerable to the persuasive effects of messages. The concept can also refer more generally to the perception that one is not susceptible to media effects of any sort. (8)

**Illusory Placebo Effect** A specific type of effect in an experiment, discussed here in the context of experimental work on the effects of subliminal messages. In that context, participants who are told that a subliminal tape contains a particular message show evidence of a placebo effect in that they express the belief that the message affected them in ways consistent with what they were told. However, the effect is illusory because no actual effect is evident—it is only perceived by the participants. (8)

**Individual Differences** The view that not all individuals are affected in the same way to the same stimulus. Individuals may differ in numerous ways that may predispose them to respond to media messages in predictable ways. For example, sensation seekers may tend to seek out messages that increase arousal—a tendency not generally characteristic of all media consumers. (5, 11)

**Institutional Process Analysis** Part of George Gerbner's Cultural Indicators Paradigm that is concerned with the inner workings of media institutions—particularly the ones that are involved in producing media messages. This type of analysis seeks to understand why media institutions produce the messages that they do. (5)

**Law of Apparent Reality** One of the "laws of emotion" summarized by Nico Frijda. In the media context, the law states that the intensity of one's emotional experience will increase as the level of perceived reality of a media depiction increases. Media images that are perceived as "fake" or far removed from reality should not generate intense emotions; images that are perceived as realistic should generate more intense emotions. (7)

**Limited Effects Model** The model of media effects that gained influence as the dominant model in the 1950s following the publication of *The People's Choice*. This book detailed the results of a large survey study of the 1940 presidential campaign and revealed very little impact from exposure to media messages. The model shifted the prevailing view that media messages determined effects and that audiences were weak to one which emphasized that media messages had minimal influence and that audiences were powerful; they determined what messages to process and had a large role in determining how those messages would affect them. (3)

**Magic Bullet or Hypodermic Needle Model** The model of media effects that characterized scholarly thought from roughly the 1920s through the early 1950s. Built upon the Payne Fund study's "legacy of fear," the model held that media messages were powerful forces that could easily sway audiences, influence attitudes, and change behavior. The model gave way to the "limited effects model" in the mid-1950s after the publication of *The People's Choice*. (3)

**Mainstreaming** One of the major hypotheses of the theory of media cultivation. The hypothesis states that TV viewing "mainstreams" viewers such that they become more similar in their views about the social world. Expected differences between people who belong to very different groups (e.g., political parties or ethnic groups) are diminished as TV viewing increases. (8)

**Media Ecology** The general theoretical perspective typified by Marshall McLuhan's approach to understanding media impact. Ecology is the study of the environment. Media ecology is the study of how media change the human environment. (12)

**Media Equation** The concept elucidated by Byron Reeves and Clifford Nass that argues that people treat media in the same ways that they treat other people. In particular, the concept of the media equation is that we carry on interactions with media that are fundamentally natural and social. (11)

**Media Multiplexity Theory** The theory introduced by Caroline Haythornthwaite which predicts that strong relationships between people are ones in which the individuals involved communicate through multiple media modalities. "Weak tie" relationships are ones in which people communicate through a limited number of media modalities. (11)

**Medium Is the Message** One of the most popular, important, and misunderstood concepts introduced by Marshall McLuhan. The phrase plays off of the idea that people are changed as a result of attending to and processing messages. In declaring that the "medium" is the message, McLuhan was claiming that instead of focusing on messages as the source of change in the way people live, the focus ought to be on the media that surround us. In his view, the dominant media that we use have changed the human condition far more than any of the messages disseminated through those media. (12)

**Message System Analysis** Part of George Gerbner's Cultural Indicators Paradigm that is concerned with the nature of media messages. This type of analysis tends to produce systematic content analyses of media content in an attempt to arrive at comprehensive descriptions of that content. (5)

**Micro- and Macro-Level Effects** Different types of media effects according to the level of analysis being used by a researcher. Micro-level effects refer to effects on individuals (e.g., a person might become scared after watching a frightening film), and macro-level effects refer to effects on groups, cities, countries, or larger entities (e.g., cities without a local newspaper may not be as politically active on election days). (3)

**Mix of Attributes Approach** The perspective on media introduced by William Eveland that seeks to characterize any particular medium in terms of its values on a set of common attributes that can be used to discuss all media. Those common attributes are interactivity, structure, channel, textuality, and content. (11)

**Mood-Management Theory** The theory introduced by Dolf Zillmann that predicts that people will select their media exposure to manage their moods. One of the main predictions is that people who feel low in spirit will tend to select media that will elevate their mood. (2, 7)

**Need for Cognition** An individual difference variable that is often used to understand different preferences for media exposure. People who are high on need for cognition enjoy thinking deeply about issues and considering nuances of information. As such, they may seek out heavy amounts of news in different media outlets. Those low on need for cognition don't prefer to engage in deep analytical thinking and would have less need to seek out different types of news surrounding a given issue. (9)

**Online Sense of Unidentifiability** The concept that when people enter the online environment, they are aware that they may be unidentifiable to others. Consequently, they may feel more free to engage in hostile or insulting behavior since these behaviors will not be associated directly with them. (11)

**Optimal Level of Arousal** The idea that individuals have different "set points" in their arousal levels that are wired in and resistant to change. Individuals with low set points may need to seek out stimulating experiences (e.g., arousing media) in order to raise their arousal levels to an optimal level, and individuals with high set points may need to seek out quiet or relaxing experiences (e.g., slow-paced and relaxing media) in order to lower their arousal levels to an optimal level. (4)

**Parasocial Relationships** The strong connections media consumers sometimes form with people or characters depicted in the media. These connections resemble conventional interpersonal relationships in many respects. They often trigger strong emotions about things that happen to a media personality. They are associated with feelings of loss when the media personality dies or leaves a TV show to take on a different acting role. Parasocial relationships are also associated with thoughts that the media personality actually cares personally about the media consumer's attention and involvement. These relationships are often studied under the rubric of the Uses and Gratifications theoretical framework. (4)

**Perpetual Linkage** The phenomenon of people being connected to the virtual world without interruption as a result of the new technologies that surround us—smartphones, computers, tablets, and so forth. (11)

**Persuasion** To change someone's attitude or behavior as a result of exposure to a message or series of messages. Significant persuasion includes the notion that both attitudes and behaviors are affected as well as the idea that any change must persist over time. (8)

**Political Sophistication** An individual difference variable that researchers often use to make predictions about media exposure to political news and political messages. Included in the concept is knowledge about politics and a well-developed political ideology. Those who are both highly knowledgeable and possess a clear ideology are considered to be high on political sophistication. Low political sophistication is characterized by low knowledge and no commitment to a particular ideology. (9)

**Priming** A process in which thinking about one thing triggers thoughts of other things associated with the initial thought. The concept is used in theories of media violence to study how consuming violence can trigger thoughts about aggressive behavior. (5, 10)

**Protection Motivation Theory** A theory used to predict the conditions under which persuasive messages containing a fear appeal will be effective. The theory holds that if a fear appeal convinces an audience of the severity of the threat, their vulnerability to the threat, and their ability to respond effectively to the threat, the message will be persuasive. (8)

**Psychological Reactance Theory** A theory developed by Jack Brehm, sometimes summarized as the "forbidden fruit effect." The theory holds that when one's freedom to engage in a behavior is eliminated or threatened with elimination, psychological reactance is triggered and results in an attempt to reestablish the free behavior. (1)

**Reinforcement** An effect of persuasive messages characterized not by conversion or attitude change on the part of the audience but by solidification of an existing attitude or behavioral tendency. In the *The People's Choice* study in the 1940s, researchers found that exposure to political ads failed to convert people from their initial voting inclinations—but it *did* reinforce their commitment to their initial inclinations. (3)

**Repositioning or Rescheduling Effect** An effect that could occur when media depictions of murders or suicides trigger subsequent increases in actual murders or suicides. If such an effect is a repositioning or rescheduling effect, the media depiction only changes the time at which murders or suicides might happen—increasing them immediately after the media depiction but not increasing them over the long run due to a compensating drop that follows the temporary increase. In contrast, an *additive* effect would produce an absolute increase in murders and suicides after the media depiction. The repositioning or rescheduling effect does not result in any absolute increase. (9)

**Resonance** A hypothesis from the theory of media cultivation in which TV content that depicts a world highly similar to the world of the viewer will resonate with the viewer's experience and exert a powerful cultivating effect. (8)

**Role Schema** A part of a person's thought process that helps to organize thoughts and expectations about appropriate roles for particular people or groups of people. Such schema can result in stereotyped expectations if they guide one's thought in ways that lead to different role expectations for one group compared to another. (10)

**Safety Valve Theory** The idea that the use of sexually explicit materials might provide a "safety valve" for people who are inclined to act on their sexual impulses—particularly impulses that might lead to criminal behavior. The idea is similar to symbolic catharsis theory that predicts that angry people exposed to media violence will be less likely to engage in aggression behavior. (6)

**Second-Order Cultivation Effect** Heavy media viewers adopting a particular attitude as a result of their media exposure. (8)

**Selective Exposure** The idea that people attend to some messages and ignore others according to a deliberate decision process. The assumed motivational force guiding the decision process is to pay attention to messages that are agreeable and tune out messages that are disagreeable. (3, 9)

**Sensation Seeking** An individual difference variable that describes the tendency to seek out experiences that are exciting or highly arousing. In the media context, high sensation seekers may be more likely to express a desire for violent or frightening entertainment. Low sensation seekers may prefer relaxing, calm media content. (4)

**Sexual Uncertainty Hypothesis** The idea that adolescents who are exposed to sexually explicit materials (particularly on the Internet) may confront depictions of sexuality that are inconsistent with the values they have been taught and subsequently become less certain about those values. (6)

**Social Augmentation Hypothesis** The theory that people who use the Internet to communicate with others should expand their social networks, thus permitting them to derive many of the relational benefits that come with being more connected to other people. (11)

**Social Comparison** The tendency for media consumers to compare themselves with others who are depicted in the media. Depending upon the dimension that is being compared and the conclusions reached after the comparative appraisal, consumers may be affected in various ways—either positive or negative. (10)

**Social Compensation Hypothesis** In the context of Internet use, this hypothesis holds that the effects of the Internet on social and psychological well-being are positive only for certain individuals. For people who have limited social networks, Internet use may expand social horizons and lead to a greater sense of connection and general well-being. (11)

**Social Construction of Reality** The notion that people "construct" their views about the social world based on various sources— including exposure to media messages. In research testing the media cultivation hypothesis, heavy TV viewers are often found to have different sets of beliefs about their social world—ones that are consistent with the TV messages that they consume. (10)

**Social Desirability** A response tendency in research participants characterized by a desire to answer questions in a way that makes them look good in the eyes of the researchers. (4)

**Social Information Processing Theory** Joe Walther's theory that even though communication using computers lacks the rich set of nonverbal cues available in face-to-face interaction, people can still use the available verbal cues to establish intimate relationships that rival those formed in the face-to-face context. (11)

**Social Learning Theory** Albert Bandura's theory of learning that he applied to the study of media violence, which emphasizes that attending to a media model who is rewarded for aggressive behavior will make aggression more likely on the part of a viewer. When the model is punished for aggressive behavior, aggression is less likely on the part of a viewer. (3, 5)

**Spiral of Silence** The theory introduced by Elisabeth Noelle-Neumann that predicts that minority views can die out over time even though they are held by substantial numbers of people because people who feel their views represent a minority position fear social isolation and don't express their opinions. The absence of those opinions seems to constitute more evidence that those opinions are not popular and leads to even more reluctance to express the opinion, and so on. The result is a spiral of silence with respect to certain views even though they may be held by many people. (9)

**Stereotypes** According to Susan Fiske and Shelly Taylor, stereotypes are a "particular kind of role schema that organizes people's expectations about other people who fall into certain social categories." Thus, people may have certain expectations about men or women, people of different ethnicities, political parties, occupations, and so forth. Such stereotypes may be accurate or inaccurate. (10)

**Strong Ties versus Weak Ties** A concept explicated in media multiplexity theory. Strong ties refer to relationships in which people tend to be like each other, exchange information frequently across different media, and exhibit high levels of intimacy and a strong desire to share their resources. Weak ties refer to relationships that exhibit the opposite tendency on all those dimensions. (11)

**Subliminal Persuasion** The idea that people are influenced by message features they cannot consciously perceive because they are presented in such a way that they are below the minimum threshold of awareness. The classic example is a subliminal cut in a film or video that appears on the screen for a matter of milliseconds—a duration so short that people cannot consciously perceive it. While sensational claims about the persuasive effects of subliminal messages are easy to find, scholarly research shows no evidence for these claims. (8)

**Subliminal Priming** The idea that people are influenced to respond in certain ways immediately after processing a word or signal that is presented subliminally—below the conscious level of awareness. The idea is potentially related to subliminal persuasion, although the influence of subliminal primes

decays very rapidly and is not strong enough to motivate significant attitude or behavior change. (8)

**Symbolic Catharsis Theory** The theory presented by Seymour Feshbach that predicted that angry people exposed to media violence would have an opportunity to purge their feelings of pent-up anger and would be less likely to behave aggressively after their viewing. While this idea still enjoys wide appeal, empirical research (especially in connection with research by Leonard Berkowitz) consistently revealed evidence that disconfirmed the major hypothesis of symbolic catharsis. (5)

**Technological Determinism** The general perspective on media that underlies the theory of Marshall McLuhan. While much of media effects research focuses on the impact of media messages, the perspective of technological determinism emphasizes the media technology themselves as the main agents of change in human behavior. (12)

**Third-Person Effect** The tendency to think that media influence is stronger for other people than it is for oneself. (8)

**Threshold Effect** An effect that doesn't emerge until some threshold is met or exceeded on a particular variable. One example of a threshold effect occurs with the relationship between TV viewing and academic achievement. There is a negative association between the variables, but not until weekly TV viewing reaches 10 hours per week. (4)

**Trigger Hypothesis** Claims that exposure to sexually explicit materials will cause a response in some individuals that will provoke them in such a way that it may lead them to commit a sex crime. (6)

**Two-Step Flow** The idea that media impact is limited to a few key people—opinion leaders—who in turn influence others through face-to-face interpersonal communication. (3)

**Uses and Gratifications Perspective**
A general theoretical framework introduced
by Elihu Katz and Jay Blumler that was
designed to lend insight into the ways people
use media to meet their needs. (4)

**Voter Volatility** A general political climate
in which significant numbers of people fail
to identify strongly with a single political
party or ideology, are more likely to call
themselves political independents, may or
may not vote in a given election, and are
more likely to split their tickets by voting
for candidates of different parties. This
climate increases the general importance
of political messages because more people
are open to changing their political
preferences. (3)

**Werther Effect** Named after the book
*The Sorrows of Young Werther* by Johann
Wolfgang von Goethe, published in 1774.
The lead character in the book commits
suicide, and the book was blamed for
subsequent suicides among the citizens
of Europe. Modern-day research has
documented that suicide rates increase
after suicide stories are widely publicized in
the press—an effect now named after the
fictitious character in this book. (9)

# Name Index

# Subject Index